A HOPE
in the
UNSEEN

RON SUSKIND

A HOPE
in the
UNSEEN

An American Odyssey from
the Inner City to the Ivy League

BROADWAY BOOKS
New York

BROADWAY

ISBN 0-7679-0125-8 (hardcover)
Designed by Jennifer Ann Daddio

TO CORNELIA,

FOR HER FAITH IN POSSIBILITY

I am a part of all that I have met.

Yet all experience is an arch where-thro'

Gleams that untravell'd world, whose margin fades

Forever and forever when I move.

—FROM *ULYSSES*, ALFRED, LORD TENNYSON

CONTENTS

I

SOMETHING to
PUSH AGAINST

A hip-hop tune bursts forth from the six-foot-high amplifiers, prompting the shoulder-snug slopes of black teenagers to sway and pivot in their bleacher seats. It takes only a second or two for some eight hundred students to lock onto the backbeat, and the gymnasium starts to thump with a jaunty enthusiasm.

Principal Richard Washington, an aggressive little gamecock of a man, struts across the free throw line to a stand-up microphone at the top of the key as the tune (just a check for the speaker system) cuts off. He dramatically clears his throat and sweeps his gaze across the students who happen to be present today—a chilly February morning in 1994—at Frank W. Ballou Senior High, the most troubled and violent school in the blighted southeast corner of Washington, D.C. Usually, he uses assemblies as a forum to admonish students for their stupidity or disrespect. Today, though, he smiles brightly.

"Ballou students," he says after a moment, "let's give a warm welcome to Mayor Marion Barry."

The mayor steps forward from a too-small cafeteria chair in his dark suit, an intricately embroidered kufi covering his bald spot. He grabs the throat of the mike stand. "Yes," he says, his voice full of pride, "I like what I see," a comment that draws a roar of appreciation. The mayor's criminal past—his much publicized conviction for cocaine possession and subsequent time served—binds him to this audience, where almost everyone can claim a friend, relative, or parent who is currently in "the system."

The mayor delivers his standard speech about self-esteem, about "being all you believe you can be" and "please, everyone, stay in school." As he speaks, Barry surveys an all-black world: a fully formed, parallel universe to white America. Providing today's music are disc jockeys from WPGC, a hip-hop station from just across the D.C. line in Maryland's black suburbs. A nationally famous black rhythm and blues singer—Tevin Campbell—up next, stands under a glass basketball backboard. Watercolors of George Washington Carver and Frederick Douglass glare from display cases. All the administrators are black, as are the ten members of the muscular security force and the two full-time, uniformed cops, one of whom momentarily leaves his hallway beat to duck in and hear the mayor.

Along the top rows of both sets of bleachers, leaning against the white-painted cinder blocks, are male "crews" from nearby housing projects and neighborhoods in expensive Fila or Hilfiger or Nautica garments and $100-plus shoes, mostly Nikes. Down a few rows from the crews on both sides of the gym is a ridge of wanna-bes, both boys and girls, who feel a rush of excitement sitting so close to their grander neighbors. All during the assembly, they crane their necks to glimpse the crews, to gauge proximity. Next in the hierarchy are the athletes. Local heroes at most high schools but paler characters at Ballou, they are clustered here and there, often identifiable by extreme height or girth. They are relatively few in number, since the school district's mandatory 2.0 grade point average for athletic participation is too high a bar for many kids here to cross.

The silent majority at Ballou—spreading along the middle and lower seats of the bleachers—are duck-and-run adolescents: baggy-panted boys and delicately coifed girls in the best outfits they can manage on a shoestring budget. They mug and smile shyly, play cards in class, tend to avoid eye contact, and whisper gossip about all the most interesting stuff going on at school. Hot topics of late include a boy shot recently during lunch period, another hacked with an ax, the girl gang member wounded in a knife fight with a female rival, the weekly fires set in lockers and bathrooms, and that unidentified body dumped a few weeks ago behind the parking lot. Their daily lesson: distinctiveness can be dangerous, so it's best to develop an aptitude for not being noticed. This, more than any other, is the catechism taught at Ballou and countless other high schools like it across the country.

As with any dogma, however, there are bound to be heretics. At Ballou, their names are found on a bulletin board outside the principal's office. The list is pinned up like the manifest from a plane crash, the names of survivors. It's the honor roll, a mere 79 students—67 girls, 12 boys—out of 1,389 enrolled here who have managed a B average or better.

With the school's dropout/transfer rate at nearly 50 percent, it's understandable that kids at Ballou act as though they're just passing through. Academics are a low priority, so few stop to read the names of the honor students as they jostle by the bulletin board. Such inattentiveness drives frustrated teachers to keep making the board's heading bolder and more commanding. Giant, blocky blue letters now shout "WALL OF HONOR."

The wall is a paltry play by administrators to boost the top students' self-esteem—a tired mantra here and at urban schools everywhere. The more practical effect is that the kids listed here become possible targets of violence, which is why some students slated for the Wall of Honor speed off to the principal's office to plead that their names not be listed, that they not be singled out. To replace their fear with pride, Principal Washington has settled on a new tactic: bribery. Give straight-A students cash and maybe they'll get respect, too. Any student with perfect grades in any of the year's four marking periods receives a $100 check. For a year-long straight-A performance, that's $400. Real money. The catch? Winners have to personally receive their checks at awards assemblies.

At the start, the assemblies were a success. The gymnasium was full, and honor students seemed happy to attend, flushed out by the cash. But after a few such gatherings, the jeering started. It was thunderous. "Nerd!" "Geek!" "Egghead!" And the harshest, "Whitey!" Crew members, sensing a hearts-and-minds struggle, stomped on the bleachers and howled. No longer simply names on the Wall of Honor, the "whiteys" now had faces. The honor students were hazed for months afterward. With each assembly, fewer show up.

Today's gathering of the mayor, the singer, and the guest DJs carries an added twist: surprise. There was no mention of academic awards, just news about the mayor's visit, the music, and the general topic of "Stay in School."

As the R&B singer takes his bows, Washington steps forward, his trap in place. "I'll be reading names of students who got straight A's in the second marking period. I'd like each one to come forward to collect his $100 prize and a special shirt from WPGC. We're all," he pauses, glaring across the crowd, "very, *very* proud of them." A murmur rumbles through the bleachers.

Washington takes a list from his breast pocket and begins reading names. He calls four sophomore girls who quietly slip, one by one, onto the gym floor. Then he calls a sophomore boy. Trying his best to vanish, the boy sits stone still in the bleachers, until a teacher spots him, yells, "You can't hide from me!" and drags him front and center. A chorus of "NEEERD!" rains down from every corner of the room.

Time for the juniors. Washington looks at his list, knowing this next name will bring an eruption. "Okay then," he says, mustering his composure. "The next award winner is . . . Cedric Jennings."

Snickers race through the crowd like an electrical current. Necks are craning, everyone trying to get the first glimpse.

"Oh Cedric? Heeere Cedric," a crew member calls out from the top row as his buddies dissolve in hysterics.

Washington starts to sweat. The strategy is backfiring. He scans the crowd. No sign. There's no way the boy could have known about the surprise awards; most teachers didn't even know. And Jennings, of all people. Jennings is the only male honor student who bears the cross with pride, the one who stands up to the blows. The only goddamn one left!

The principal clutches the mike stand, veins bulging from a too-tight collar, and gives it all he's got, "Cedric Jenningsssss . . ."

Across a labyrinth of empty corridors, an angular, almond-eyed boy is holed up in a deserted chemistry classroom. Cedric Jennings often retreats here. It's his private sanctuary, the one place at Ballou where he feels completely safe, where he can get some peace.

He looks out the window at a gentle hill of overgrown grass, now patched with snow, and lets his mind wander down two floors and due south to the gymnasium, where he imagines his name being called. Not attending was a calculated bet. He'd heard rumors of possible academic awards. Catcalls from the assemblies of last spring and fall still burn in his memory.

Off in the distance are skeletons of trees and, behind them, a low-slung, low-rent apartment complex. His eyes glaze as he takes in the lifeless scene, clenching his jaw—a little habit that seems to center him—before turning back to the computer screen.

"Scholastic Aptitude Practice Test, English, Part III" floats at eye level, atop a long column of words—"cacophony," "metaphor," "alliteration"—and choices of definitions.

He presses through the list—words from another country, words for which you'd get punched if you used them here—and wonders, scrolling with the cursor, if these are words that white people in the suburbs use. A few screens down, a familiar-sounding noun appears: "epistle." Sort of like "apostle," he figures, passing by choice "A) a letter" and clicking his mouse on "B) a person sent on a mission."

He looks quizzically at his selection. Probably wrong, but he likes the sound of that phrase—"a person sent on a mission." Sort of like me, he thinks, on a mission to get out of here, to be the one who makes it.

Cedric Jennings is not, by nature, a loner, but he finds himself ever more isolated, walking a gauntlet through the halls, sitting unaccompanied in class, and spending hours in this room. He is comforted by its orderliness, by the beach-blanket-sized periodic table above his head against the back wall and the gentle glow of the bluish screen.

He scrolls back to the top of the vocabulary list and reaches for a dictionary on the computer table. The classroom's occupant, chemistry teacher Clarence Taylor, wanders into the room and registers surprise. "Didn't go down there, today, huh?" asks Taylor, a bearlike man in his mid-thirties, short but wide all over. "I'm disappointed in you."

Cedric doesn't look up. "They give out the awards?" he asks nonchalantly.

"Yep," says Mr. Taylor.

"Glad I didn't go, then. I just couldn't take that abuse again," he says evenly, this time glancing over at the teacher. "I'll just pick up the check later. They have to give it to me, you know?"

Mr. Taylor offers a mock frown, now standing over the boy, eyes wide, brows arched. "That's not much of an attitude."

Cedric flips off the power switch with a long, dexterous finger. "I know," he murmurs. "I worked hard. Why should I be ashamed? Ashamed to claim credit for something I earned? I hate myself for not going."

He sits and stares at the darkened screen. He can hear Mr. Taylor ease away behind him and unload an armful of books on the slate-topped lab table near the blackboard. He knows the teacher is just fussing, walking through a few meaningless maneuvers while he tries to conjure a worthwhile response to what Cedric just said.

Mr. Taylor's moves are familiar by now. The teacher has personally invested in Cedric's future since the student appeared in his tenth grade chemistry class—back then, Cedric was a sullen ninth grader who had just been thrown out of biology for talking back to the teacher and needed somewhere to go. Taylor let him sit in, gave him a few assignments that the older kids were doing, and was soon marveling at flawless A papers. Taylor took Cedric for an after-school dinner at Western Sizzlin', and they were suddenly a team.

In the last two years, Taylor has offered his charge a steady stream of extra-credit projects and trips, like a visit last month with scientists at the National Aeronautics and Space Administration. He challenges Cedric with elaborate intellectual riddles, withholding praise and daring the pupil to vanquish his theatrical doubting with a real display of intellectual muscle. It's call and response, combative but productive. Mr. Taylor even sets up competitions among the top students, like a recent after-school contest to see who could most swiftly write every element in the periodic table from memory. As usual, Cedric rose to crush the competition, reeling off all 109 elements in three minutes, thirty-nine seconds.

Cedric is still staring at the dead screen when he finally hears Mr. Taylor's squeaky wing tips coming back around the lab table.

"You see, Cedric, you're in a race, a long race," the teacher says as

Cedric swivels toward him, his arms crossed. "You can't worry about what people say from the sidelines. They're already out of it. You, however, are still on the track. You have to just keep on running so . . ."

"All right, I know," says Cedric, smirking impatiently. With Mr. Taylor, it's either a marathon metaphor or a citation from Scripture, and Cedric has heard the race routine many times before. "I'm doing my best, Mr. Taylor. I do more than ten people sometimes."

Mr. Taylor clams up. So much for *that* race *metaphor,* Cedric thinks to himself, delighted to employ an SAT word. He jumps up from the chair and paces around the classroom, picking up things and putting them down, looking caged.

"So, did you mail the application yet?" Taylor asks, trying to keep the conversation alive.

"Yeeeess, I maaaiiiled it," Cedric says, rolling his eyes.

This is not just any application. It's a bid for acceptance into a special summer program for top minority high school students at the Massachusetts Institute of Technology. It's highly competitive, drawing from a nationwide pool and taking kids for an intensive six-week program between their junior and senior years. It offers academic enrichment but also sizes up whether the students could cut it at MIT. About 60 percent are eventually offered a blessed spot in the university's freshman class for the following year.

Cedric does not dare speak about it to anyone except Mr. Taylor, who helped him with the application. He feels too vulnerable. His yearning is white hot. It's his first real competition against invisible opponents—minority kids from far better schools—in what Cedric rightly knows is a dry run for the college applications that must be mailed in the coming school year. It could even mean a slot, eventually, at MIT.

It will be nearly two months before he hears whether he's accepted, but the program is quickly consuming Cedric's thoughts. His notebooks in math, physics, and English have MIT doodles—the three magic letters Gothic here, three-dimensional there, then crossing over one page and written fifty times on the next. Being accepted there would be the reward for years of sacrifice.

"You think I'll get in?" he asks, awkward and momentarily exposed, but catches himself. "I mean, you know, whaaaatever. What does it matter?"

"Will you get in?" begins Mr. Taylor, launching another discursive riff. "Well, let me note . . ." The class bell rings, interrupting him, and Cedric prepares to go, having lost his taste for an answer.

The hallways fill as a wave of students from the gymnasium washes through the school. Leaving the chemistry classroom, Cedric keeps his eyes fixed forward on a shifting spot of linoleum about a yard ahead of his front foot. He hears someone from behind, a boy's voice, yell, "Where was you Cedric—hiding in the bathroom?" followed by a burst of nearby giggles, but he won't look up. Just don't get into it, he says over and over in his head, trying to drown out the noise.

Today, though, it's no use. He wheels around to see a contingent behind him, two hard-looking boys he barely knows and an accompaniment of girls.

"Why don't you just shut up," he barks, facing them while backpedaling. "Just leave me alone." Fortunately, his math class is the next doorway and he slips into the almost empty classroom, relieved to have avoided an altercation.

"Ready for the test today, Cedric?" asks Joanne Nelson from her desk across the room. She's a round, soft-spoken, dark-skinned black woman who also had Cedric in tenth grade.

"Uh-huh," he nods, regaining some composure. "Yeah, I mean, I think I'm in real good shape."

The test is in Unified Math, his favorite subject. Each day, Cedric looks forward to this class, composed of eighteen kids from Ballou's special math and science program.

With the program, Ballou is attempting a sort of academic triage that is in vogue at tough urban schools across the country. The idea: save as many kids as you can by separating out top students early and putting the lion's share of resources into boosting as many of them as possible to college. Forget about the rest. The few kids who can manage to learn, to the right; the overwhelming majority who are going nowhere, flow left.

Cedric, like some other math/science students, applied to the program and arrived a year early to Ballou, which allows a handful of ninth graders to arrive with the eight-hundred-student tenth grade class. While at Ballou, the math/science students mix with the general student body for subjects like English and history but stay separated for math and science classes, which are called "advanced" but are more at a middle level of classes taught at most of the area's suburban high schools.

Slipping into a favorite desk, Cedric watches as the rest of the class arrives, mostly girls, many of them part of a tiny middle-class enclave from nearby Bolling Air Force base. He is friendly with a few of the girls, but today the room is tense and hushed, so he just nods a quick hello or two. Soon, everyone is lost in the sheaves of test papers.

It takes only a few moments for a calm to come over him. Knowing the material cold is Cedric's best antidote to the uncertainty that sometimes wells up inside him, the doubts about whether any amount of work will be enough to propel him to a new life. He takes out his ruler and confidently draws two vertical lines, noting points for asymptotes, limits, and intercepts. He moves easily through the algebraic functions on the next few questions, hunched close to his paper, writing quickly and neatly, the pencil's eraser end wiggling near his ear. For half an hour, he is steady and deliberate, like someone savoring a fine meal.

When he arrives at the last question—which asks students to write about the topic they have found most interesting thus far in the semester—he starts tapping his pencil on the desk. So much to choose from.

Finally, he begins to write: "The part that most interested me was finding the identity of the trigonometric functions. I had a little bit of trouble with them at first, but they became easy!" He reels off ten lines of tangent, sine, and cosine functions, an intricate equation springing effortlessly from his memory, and arrives at a proof. Cedric sits back to admire his work. It's so neat and final, so orderly. So much confusion, all around, such a long way to travel to get out of this hole, but here, at least, he can arrive at modest answers—small steps—that give him the sensation of motion.

He's done and puts down his pencil. Still ten minutes to the period bell. Then, suddenly, he smiles for the first time in days and again grabs the dull No. 2. Across the bottom, he scribbles "I LOVE THIS STUFF!"

Each afternoon, there is a choice of bus stops. The stop right in front of the school is usually quiet and empty late in the afternoon, while another one, a few hundred yards away on bustling Martin Luther King Avenue, is always hopping.

At 5:02 P.M. on this day, a week after the awards assembly, Cedric Jennings emerges from Ballou's side entrance, having already finished his homework and another SAT practice test in Clarence Taylor's room. He slings his bookbag over his shoulder, freeing his hands to pull closed his three-year-old black parka with the broken zipper. Day by day, he's hearing fewer barbs in the hallways about the awards assembly, and his spirits lift a bit as he sees a fading late afternoon sun shining across the teachers' parking lot. He pauses to look at it a moment—there hasn't been much sun lately—and decides today to opt for Martin Luther King.

In a moment, he's strolling on the boulevard—Southeast's main street of commerce, legal and otherwise—and taking in the sights. There's a furious bustle at this time of day. Darkness, after all, comes earlier here than in those parts of Washington where the streetlights work, where national chains have stores with big neon marquees, and where everything stays open late. In those places, the churn of commerce isn't halted, as it is here, by a thoroughly rational fear that seems to freeze the streets at nightfall.

Cedric huddles against the cloudy plastic window of the bus stop hut and watches the drug dealers near the intersection at 8th Street. He wonders what draws him out to the avenue bus stop, where—God knows—he could get killed. People do, all the time; he muses today, as he often does when he stands at this stop, about whether coming out here means he's going a little crazy.

Two crack dealers are chatting about twenty feet away. Both guys are in their early twenties, with hair mottled from being outside all day—one in a fine-looking long-sleeve Redskins football jersey and the other in a soft leather jacket. Cedric cranes his head around the hut's aluminum edge to pick up the conversation. He's sure they're armed, and he spots telltale bulges on each with his trained eye.

"So, you see, this bitch, she sucked my dick just to get her a little rock," says the Redskins jersey.

"Hey, next time you send her to me," says the soft leather, throwing his head back in a toothless laugh. "I'll give her what she needs real bad."

Cedric listens, not breathing, and then pulls back behind the plastic wall just as the one in leather turns toward him.

Hidden behind the bus shelter, he replays the dialogue in his head, where he will continue to chew on it for days afterward. He smells the rich greasy aroma of Popeye's Fried Chicken wafting from across the street, hears a saxophonist just up the boulevard, playing for quarters. A few guys he recognizes from Ballou, including some crew members, wander into view and he watches them flirt—or "kick some game"—with some cute girls who are rolling their eyes but definitely not walking away.

Spending so much time alone, he finds it hard to resist observing the fiery action all around. No diving in, not for him, not ever, but what's the harm in watching a little, picking up bits of this or that? He spots the bus a few blocks down. Clenching his molars to flex muscle at the bend of his still smooth, boyish jaw, he steps out into the wind.

Apartment 307 on the third floor of the blond brick High View apartments at 1635 V Street, Southeast, is empty, dark, and warm at 6:04 P.M., when Cedric unlocks the door. There hasn't always been heat, with overdue bills and whatnot, and he always appreciates the warmth, especially after the long walk from the Anacostia bus and subway station in the icy dusk wind.

He slips out of his coat and backpack and goes from room to room turning on lights, something he's done since he was a small kid, coming home alone to apartments and tiptoeing, with a lump in his throat, to check if intruders were lurking inside closets and under beds.

It's not a very big place—two bedrooms, a small bathroom, a kitchenette, and an attached living and dining room—but it's one of the better apartments that he and his mother, Barbara, have lived in. He's even got his own bedroom in the far back corner.

He flips on the switch. It's like a bear's winter cave of strewn matter—a thick padding of clothes, magazines, rubber-soled shoes, books, loose papers, and more clothes.

Cedric turns on his beloved Sharp Trinitron, a 19-inch color TV that his mother rented for him in ninth grade from a nearby Rent-a-Center (just paid off a month ago at an astonishing total price of nearly $1,500) and flops onto the bed. Like his proclivity for spying on street hustlers, the TV is a vital element of Cedric's secondhand life. He loves the tube, especially the racy, exhibitionist afternoon talk shows, which he watches for a few minutes tonight before turning to the local news—the lead story about a shooting not far from here—and then flipping to *The Flintstones,* a favorite.

He hears the thump of a door slamming.

"Lavar, you home?" comes the voice—calling him, as his mother always has, by his middle name—but he doesn't get up, figuring she'll wander back. In a moment, Barbara Jennings, hands on hips, is standing in the doorway.

In the sixteen and a half years since Cedric's birth, Barbara Jennings has been on a path of sacrifice and piety that has taken her far from the light-hearted haughtiness of her earlier self—the woman with a blonde wig, leather miniskirt, white knee-high boots, and a taste for malt liquor. Cedric has seen pictures of that skinny young thing, a striking girl with a quick smile who, as he has discerned from his mother's infrequent recollections, searched for love and found mostly trouble.

She stopped searching long ago. Barbara is a churchwoman now. On weekdays she works in a data input job at the Department of Agriculture, where she has been for almost eleven years, and splits the rest of her time between a church in a rough section of Washington north of the Capitol dome and this small, messy apartment.

Cedric looks her up and down and smiles thinly. Today, like most days, she has opted for a black dress and sensible shoes, an outfit most appropriate to her general mood, needs, and heavier frame. But her features—her smallish nose and pretty, wide-set eyes—have held up well, even at forty-seven and without makeup.

"I thought you would have made dinner by now," she says, slipping a thin chain with her dangling Department of Agriculture photo ID from around her neck. "How long you been home?"

"Only a couple of minutes," Cedric says, turning back to the tube. "What we got to eat?"

"I don't know, whatever's in there," she says curtly before disappearing into her room to change out of her work clothes. Taking his cue, Cedric moves into the kitchen and begins breaking up ground beef into a frying pan. He pours in a can of navy beans, some oil, chopped onions, some pepper, salt, a little paprika, and other condiments. He does this without complaint or enthusiasm—it's what he does most nights—and soon there are two heaping plates of steaming hash.

"Hey, it's ready and all," he calls around a short breakwall behind the stove to Barbara, who's sitting in a bathrobe on the white living room couch watching TV.

Usually, he takes his plate to his room and she eats on the low, wide living room coffee table—each sitting in front of their own TV. Tonight, though, she clears away newspapers and unopened bills from the dining room table.

"I haven't talked to you in ages, it seems," she says softly as they sit down to eat.

"I've been around," he says, grateful for her attentions. "Just been a lot going on—at school and whatever."

So it ends up being a night that they talk. It happens every couple of weeks. It's not needed more than that, Cedric figures. He knows that his mom wants to give him his space, now that he's sixteen and, by his reckoning, almost grown up, so she doesn't bother him in his room, where he spends most of his time. Maybe too much time, she tells him sometimes, but it's the only place he feels he has any privacy. After all, it's not as if he goes out late on weekend nights with friends, like most kids at school. Inside his room is the only place he can really relax.

He describes last week's assembly, about his not going, and she shakes her head dismissively. "What did I tell you? Before you know it, you'll be leaving them all behind. Just pay them no mind."

"Okay, okay," he says, "but what if I get rejected by MIT? That'd kill me." Barbara heeds this more carefully. It was she, after all, who found a description of the program in a scholarship book that someone gave to her at the office.

"You can't be worrying about MIT, Lavar. Just pray about it. If God has meant it to happen, it will." She looks up between bites and sees he's not convinced. "Look, your grades are perfect, your recommendations are good. What can they not like?"

"Yeah, I guess," he concedes.

"What's the point of getting down on yourself?" she says. "People will see that you're special."

He nods, letting her words sink in, and they eat for a while in silence—just the two of them, the way it has been for years. Barbara's two older girls, Cedric's half-sisters, are twenty-six and thirty-one and long gone, leaving mother and son to rely on each other in more ways than they can count.

Through years of ups and downs—times when he was certain that he was unworthy of success or love or any reasonable hope of getting something better—her faith in him has been his savior. It always amazes him. Having finished dinner quickly, he watches her clean her plate contentedly, and he shakes his head. She's just rock solid certain that he's going to MIT. Who knows, he wonders as he busses their plates and begins washing the dishes. Maybe she's right.

Both return to their customary evening routines—Barbara back to the couch and her sitcoms while Cedric dries and puts away the dishes and silverware. Quieter now, with the sink water not running, he hears what sound like pops from outside, almost certainly gunshots. He looks over at his mother sitting by the window but she doesn't react, so he begins wiping down the kitchen counters.

Gunshots are part of the background score here. Listen on most nights and a few pops are audible. The corner nearest the house—16th and V—is among the worst half-dozen or so spots in the city for crack cocaine dealing. The corner a block north—16th and U—is, of late,

the very worst. There has been lots of shooting on both corners recently, but still they're open all night, and the traffic of buyers on 16th
remains strong and steady in all weather.

Cedric knows that the surrounding mayhem is not something he
and his mother need to talk much about. Still, it's always there, ionizing
the air in the apartment, lending it some extra gravity, which, Cedric
told his mother a couple of weeks ago, gives him "a little something to
push against."

Cedric hangs up the wet dish towel on a drawer handle and strides
toward the short hallway leading to his room. He glances quickly at
Barbara as he passes and realizes that the TV is on but she's no longer
watching it. Her eyes are on him.

He stops. "What you looking at?"

She pauses as though she's trying to remember something. "What
did I once tell you?" she asks finally, in a tentative voice.

"Ma, what are you talking about, talking crazy?"

"What did I once tell you, Lavar?"

"I don't know. You tell me lots of things."

She stands, tying her robe closed, and slowly points a finger at him,
buying an extra moment to get the words from Scripture just so: "The
race," she says with a satisfied smile, "goes not to the swift nor the
strong, but he who endureth until the end."

Oh yes, that's a good one, Cedric agrees, and nods. Hasn't heard
that one in a while. "Thank you, Jesus," he says to her with a wry smile
as he makes his way toward the back bedroom. Stopping at the threshold, he turns and calls back: "But it wouldn't be so terrible to be all
swift and strong—just once in a while—and let some other people do
all the enduring."

Barbara, sunk back into the couch, can't help but laugh.

A TTENTION, STUDENTS. WE ARE IN CODE BLUE."
Cedric Jennings gazes at the silvery mesh intercom speaker
above the blackboard in Advanced Physics. Images of tumult form in
his head.

"REPEAT. IT'S A CODE BLUE!" barks the scratchy voice of the assistant principal, Reggie Ballard. "EVERYONE SHOULD BE WHERE THEY'RE SUPPOSED TO BE . . . OR ELSE."

Through the open door to the physics classroom, the sounds of frenzy become audible for Cedric and fifteen other math/science students. The rules of this game are simple: anyone in the halls during a "code blue"—called from time to time when students are supposed to be settled into class after a period change—is hauled to the cafeteria and cataloged for after-school detention. With the warning duly issued, ten security guards with walkie-talkies—large black men in plain clothes—fan out through the halls, grabbing students by the collars and sleeves.

Everyone in physics sits still, ears perked up, as light footsteps tap down the hallway of the school's science wing, followed by heavy slaps on linoleum and then a shout from the nearby stairwell: "DAMN YOU, LET GO OF MY CLOTHES!"

It's an unseasonably warm day in early March, a day to make one think that spring is already here. It's also one of those bad days at Ballou, when anarchy is loosed and it suddenly becomes clear to kids, teachers, and administrators—all at once—that no one is even remotely in charge. Some random event tends to trigger it. Early this morning, for instance, a teacher got punched by a student and bled. The news traveled, and other kids, looking for any excuse to blow, were emboldened.

At a few minutes after 10 A.M., there was a fire in the downstairs bathroom, forcing everyone out into the parking lot as four fire trucks arrived to drench a flaming bathroom trash can. Afterward, kids milled about the halls, and two separate scuffles ignited on different corners of the first floor. Security crews moved to one but neglected the other, and a social studies teacher—a large, heavily built man—jumped in to break it up. He avoided injury, other than getting his glasses knocked across the hall.

Like other students, Cedric kept himself apprised of the morning's commotion, but he had other business to occupy him. Before physics— as Ballard was consulting with Washington about preparations for calling the code blue—Cedric sauntered into the administration office and leaned against the chest-high Formica counter. He spotted the assistant principal and started right in. "Hey, Mr. Ballard. Look, Mr. Dorosti gave me a B+ on the midterm in computer science and I deserved an A, and I've got all my weekly quizzes to back it up," Cedric said, trying to give a little bass to his voice. "He can't mark something I did as correct on a quiz and then mark the same thing wrong on a test— right?"

"I guess not," Ballard replied. "Bring me what you've got and I'll take it under advisement."

"You better, and Mr. Dorosti better, 'cause I'm fighting this one."

As Cedric turned to stalk out, Ballard whispered to Washington, "That Cedric . . . nothing but trouble. Quick tongue and too proud."

Pride. Cedric's 4.02 grade point average virtually ties him for first in the junior class with a quiet, studious girl named LaCountiss Spinner. Pride in such accomplishment is acceptable behavior for sterling students at high schools across the land, but at Ballou and other urban schools like it, something else is at work. Educators have even coined a phrase for it. They call it the crab/bucket syndrome: when one crab tries to climb from the bucket, the others pull it back down. The forces dragging students toward failure—especially those who have crawled farthest up the side—flow through every corner of the school. Inside the bucket, there is little chance of escape.

The code blue excitement subsides, and Mr. Momen, an Iranian immigrant with a thick accent, closes the classroom door. "All right, every one of you, listen," he says. "We have today, for you, some exercises that have to be done by the end of class. No exceptions." He passes out the core teaching tool at Ballou: the worksheet. Attendance is too irregular and books too scarce, even in the advanced sections, to actually teach many lessons during class. Often, worksheets are just the previous day's homework, and Cedric can finish them quickly.

Today, though, he runs into trouble. A few minutes in, he looks up and realizes that a girl in the next row is copying his work.

"Hey, what're you doing?" he snaps. She begins to giggle and then parlays his attention into a sexual jibe.

"Listen, Cedric, if you looking for something hot and wet, I'll give it to you."

Guffaws all around.

"Yeah, and I'll give you something hard and dry right back," he counters as the class erupts in catcalls. Cedric is removed from the room. "I put in a lot of hours, a lot of time, to get everything just right," he says to Mr. Momen from a forest of beakers and microscopes in the adjoining lab area. "I shouldn't just give answers away."

"Cedric," Mr. Momen says as he turns back to the others, "you have to figure out a way to get along better with people. Other students try hard, too. They're not all trying to get you."

Cedric sits for a moment, alone again, and quietly pushes through the worksheet, calculating, at the very least, what's being asked of him in physics. He leads the class—including his rival, LaCountiss—in grade points for the semester.

After class, he makes his way across the width of the building toward the cafeteria, thinking about what Mr. Momen said and what it's supposed to mean. How can he possibly get along with kids who hate him, he asks himself as he walks, lifting his gaze from the floor and searching the faces of kids flowing in the opposite direction in the hallway. Hate? Well, maybe not hate exactly, he decides. It's more that they hate what he represents, or something.

As he watches them pass, Cedric struggles with something that he would rather not know and that he manages, day in and day out, to keep safely submerged: that these kids are not all that different from him, that what mostly differentiates him are transferable qualities like will and faith. Just like him, they are almost all low-income black kids from a shadowy corner of America. His exile is, in large measure, self-induced and enforced. If he changed, soon enough he'd be accepted.

He knows all this but pushes the thoughts out of his head. Reaching out to any fellow ghetto kids is an act he puts in the same category as doing drugs: the initial rush of warmth and euphoria puts you on a path to ruin. His face, uncharacteristically open and searching a moment ago, slips into its customary pursed-lipped armor. Don't give up, don't give in. Other kids, passing him in the hall, pick it up. No one's a fool here. They recognize Cedric's face—pinched, dismissive, looking right past them. They've seen this look before, on the faces of white people, and they respond accordingly.

"Can you believe that sorry ass Cedric," whispers a pudgy boy, leaning against a locker as Cedric passes.

A boy on his left—a tall drink of water in a Nike shirt—nods. "Right, just look at him, would you? Kind of pants are those?"

"He needs a good beating," murmurs a third, just loud enough for Cedric to hear.

Cedric cuts forward like a torpedo. Around the next bend comes Phillip Atkins, a tough, popular fellow junior sporting a C− average who is, lately, in Cedric's face.

"Oh, look, it's the amazing nerdboy," Phillip chides as he approaches. Cedric tries to slip by, but there's a crowd up ahead watching a craps game in the hall, causing a backup. There's nowhere to go.

"Come on nerdboy, you and me, let's do it, right now," says Phillip, feigning a punch as a girl holds him back and two boys, standing nearby, giggle. Phillip is known for his sense of humor.

"Why don't you leave me be, Phillip?" says Cedric after a moment. "What'd I ever do to you?"

Phillip, satisfied at getting a rise, just smiles. The two stand for a minute, eye to eye: Cedric in a white shirt, khakis, and black felt shoes, math book in one hand, the other hand clenched in a fist, shaking nervously; Phillip, a bit shorter and wiry, dressed in a brown T-shirt with jeans pulled low. The latter offers a menacing deadeye stare, copied immaculately from the gang leaders he admires, and Cedric breaks it off, looking away, flustered.

The craps game is over, and his exit has cleared. Throwing a sidelong scowl at Phillip, Cedric slips forward through the dispersing mob, in the midst of which Delante Coleman collects his dice and rises from a crouch. Delante, known to all as "Head" because he helps run one of the school's largest gangs, the Trenton Park Crew, is short and stocky, with caramel-light skin, hazel eyes, and the temerity of a killer. He helps manage a significant drug dealing and protection ring, directs a dozen or so underlings, drives a Lexus, and, in his way, is every bit as driven as Cedric. It's what each does with his fury and talents that separates these two into a sort of urban black yin and yang.

Cedric passes tight against the lockers, and Head, flirting with some girls, doesn't see him—which is just as well. Head and some of his crew enjoy toying with honor students, or "goodies," as he calls them, messing with their hair, taking their books (if they're foolish enough to carry any), scuffing them up a bit.

By now, Cedric has cut hard to the left into a different hallway, one that leads toward the cafeteria, which is a few feet ahead. He often tries to eat in empty classrooms—the cafeteria being the type of free-fire zone that someone of his lowly social status is wise to avoid—but today a friend of his, a girl, convinced him to meet her at the cafeteria. Just inside the side entrance, she is waiting for him.

" 'Bout time you got here, Cedric. I'm starving," says LaTisha Williams, arms folded but smiling radiantly. "It's wrong to keep your boo waiting."

Cedric says nothing, just smirks at her and rolls his eyes. LaTisha is not his "boo," slang for girl- or boyfriend. She's bubbly and has a pretty face, but she's huge—five-foot-two and maybe 250 pounds. She's an outcast, just like he is. But, he concedes, handing her a pinkish tray, she usually manages to cheer him up.

Mostly, she talks and he laughs, offering modest rejoinders, and now off she goes again. Today she's doing a riff—mostly for the benefit of another girl with them in line—about Cedric's long-ago flirtation with Connie Mitchell, a gorgeous, light-skinned ingénue from the Bolling Air Force base area, who arrived here midway through tenth grade.

"You see, Cedric goes up to her and says, 'Hi. Hi, you new here? Can I do anything for you. Can I, can I?' " says LaTisha. "He was on her like a dog, sniffing her up and down." Cedric chuckles at this, appreciating any story showing that, sexually speaking, his clock ticks in the traditional fashion. He's made passes at other girls, though it never amounts to much, and he's begun to see himself through other people's eyes, wondering if he's just not manly enough to have any success with women. Though his voice has yet to change, he has no feminine affectations. He's pleasant looking and tallish, his dress unflamboyant but neat and usually color coordinated. He suspects that it is this terrain that's atypical and upside down—but he's not sure. All he knows is that, here, no one wants to be with an honor student—a pariah—except maybe LaTisha, who has few alternatives. Cedric Jennings simply has no social currency at Ballou.

"Cedric, you just ain't a woman's man," LaTisha says a few minutes later, once they're seated, certain she'll get a rise out of him. But Cedric, increasingly glum about the subject and anxious to leave the cafeteria, bears down on his grilled cheese and doesn't get into it. LaTisha quietly eats her undressed salad and leaves to get a second one.

Looking across the raucous cafeteria crowd, Cedric is reminded of the assembly—probably most of these kids were there—and what he said that day to Mr. Taylor, about how not going made him feel ashamed.

Ashamed. The word has been smoldering inside him for weeks. What he said, it didn't track somehow. Was he ashamed of getting all A's? No, he was proud of that. So why wouldn't he show his face? Is it maybe that he's ashamed of being alone all the time, of being so lame? No girlfriend. No close guy friends. He tears at an empty carton of milk with his long, agile fingers. No, that doesn't seem right either. That's all part of his solitary mission to get out of here and off to a famous college.

LaTisha comes back. "You okay, Cedric? You look kind of bad."

"Yeah," he says. "I'm all right. Just been thinking about why I feel the way I do."

With the afternoon temperature reaching seventy, students start slipping out early from one of Ballou's ten exits. Cedric sits through his afternoon classes and finds himself absently watching the clock. After the dismissal bell, he runs into LaTisha in the hallway and tells her he's not going to stay his usual two hours or so after school. He thinks he'll just "go home, watch TV, and crash."

She says she's going home, too, and they walk outside to the bus stop just in front of the school. In the very late afternoons, when Cedric often leaves the building, this stop is empty. At 3:30, though, it's jammed and rowdy with kids who've been cooped up for the winter in nearby public housing projects, small apartments, or modest homes, all now feeling the free sunshine on their faces.

He and LaTisha take different buses home, so she's talking fast to fill the few moments they'll have before parting. He's nodding and half listening. Then something happens.

A boy a few feet away from them grabs another boy around the neck, pulls out a pistol, and holds it to the other kid's head. People are screaming and trying to get away, bumping into each other, not sure which direction to run. Cedric, backing onto the grass, turns to see the gun again and feels himself flinching. He sees that LaTisha has fallen down, her great girth slumped onto the concrete.

And then it's over. The kid with the gun runs across the street and disappears. No shots were fired, and some kids murmur about whether the gun, which was an odd greenish color, was real.

Cedric's bus comes and, after helping LaTisha up, he gets on, shaken, and finds a seat. He pushes himself tight into the seat's corner, leaning his shoulder against the bumpy tin siding as the bus rolls up to the avenue stop. The dealers are out in force today, and, looking at them, he realizes that he's been fooling himself, that there is no safe distance, no safe place to go, not in school, not on the street, not anywhere.

His breath feels short. He closes his eyes, presses his fingers against them, and feels that his hands are trembling. In the dark field behind his closed lids, he sees clearly the gun, the terrified face of the kid with the barrel pressed against his temple, and LaTisha falling. He jerks his eyes open, tries to push the images away, and finds himself recalling something that happened in school a year ago. It was just a day or two after last spring's awards ceremony. A kid came up to him in the hall, a smallish kid in a green army jacket. The kid said something about not liking Cedric's face and how he saw him get his $100 award check and it made him sick—and there was a bulge in the army jacket's pocket. The heavy green fabric was tented into a triangle pointing out from the kid's hip. Cedric looked down and could see the back of a rat-gray steel handle.

Cedric can't remember much else—just that he couldn't speak, that he ran through a cluster of kids into the bathroom, terrified, and decided not to tell Mr. Washington or anyone about it, afraid that there'd be retaliation if he squealed. He never saw the kid again.

He hasn't thought about any of that for almost a year. He just pushed it out of his mind. But now, as the bus rumbles through the gritty circus on Martin Luther King Avenue, it suddenly dawns on him. Maybe that's why he didn't go to the awards assembly. It wasn't that he was ashamed of his achievements or too weak to face the razzing. He was scared. Maybe that kid's still out there. That's why he hid. He's scared right now. Nothing wrong with that.

He lets out a little high-pitched laugh, drawing an anxious stare from an old woman sitting next to him. He smiles at her and she looks away. Yes sir, he muses, feeling a weight lift. His absence didn't mean they'd won and he'd lost. He was simply scared to death. That's something he can live with.

2

DON'T LET THEM
HURT YOUR CHILDREN

Barbara Jennings sits in her cubicle on the third floor of a sprawling Department of Agriculture building in downtown D.C. She looks at the check lying like a mackerel in the middle of her calendar mat: $445.22, made out to her landlord.

Rent. There's a knot in her gut, like a squeezing fist. She feels it on the first day of almost every month—and today is March 1. In a few minutes she'll begin her involved ritual, taking two buses to the offices of the real estate firm that operates scores of buildings in Southeast so she can personally deliver this payment.

She hates having to do it, but she has no grounds to quarrel. Yes, payments, in the past, have been late. Yes, her credit report is like a train wreck on computer paper. Not that it's uncommon for folks in her neighborhood. What galls her is how her landlord profits enthusiastically from understanding the vulnerability of his customers. If you're one day late, it's an additional charge of $32.50. If it goes two weeks, eviction proceedings commence and legal fees swiftly pile up.

She leaves the office building, popping open her umbrella against a light rain, and decides to take a roundabout path to the subway to stop by the bank machine. She slips in her card as an act of faith. Maybe she calculated wrong, or there's been some sort of credit, or one of her prayers has been answered.

Not today. Available balance: $478. She withdraws $30 and slips the folded $20 and $10 bills into her skirt pocket.

"Lord," she mumbles, "the bad week is here again."

The ride is long, arching around half the city to the landlord's office. From there, she catches another bus for the winding journey to church. Tonight is the Tuesday night prayer meeting. Last year, Cedric said he didn't want to go on Tuesdays, that he had too much home-work, and she assented. He goes on Thursdays and Sundays, and she decided, reluctantly, that that is enough.

As she slides into a good seat by the window, she recalls something she didn't do today: call her brother Butch. The house where she and her nine siblings were raised on 15th Street, Southeast, has been in abeyance during the two years since their father died, leaving no will, and Butch moved in. He's been living there almost for free, and Bar-bara and her four sisters think they really should settle it—either have him buy out their shares or sell it outright. It could mean almost $7,000 apiece for them, money Barbara sure could use, money that could finally get her ahead for once.

The bus inches along in the rush hour traffic of Washington, and she fingers the cash in her pocket. As a church missionary, she's sup-posed to give $20 tonight, and she desperately wants to. The pastor says that every dollar given will return tenfold. She puts the $10 in her purse and leaves the big bill in her pocket, where she can reach for it quickly.

Thinking of Butch brings her mind to the clapboard two-story on 15th Street where so much of her old life unfolded. The porch is the first thing she always thinks of, because that was always her refuge, the place to which she fled. Inside, the house was often an angry place. Her parents had moved to Washington from Plumbranch, South Carolina, when Barbara—the third oldest—was three. Seven more children fol-lowed. Her father, Maurice, was a construction worker by day and a janitor by night. Her mother, Janey Bell, worked an evening shift as a cook. Starting at nine years old, Barbara, a quiet, shy girl, mostly took care of the younger children. Other daughters were favorites of one parent or the other, and all the boys got off easy. Barbara worked, trying to win affection that never came, and then worked some more. Along the way, there were beatings. Both parents, overwrought with too little money and too many children, fiercely swung the belt—or anything they could grab. It would be decades before she got some distance from the violence. "They didn't call it child abuse then," she said years later to a friend.

By sixteen, she was searching for someone to take her away from it all, often dreaming of what might be as she stood on that porch, her back turned to the house. Plenty of someones came by, but none helped her escape. A decade later, she had two girls—Nanette, or Neddy, and Leslie—from brief relationships with two different men.

Those years took their toll, and she was a weary, pencil-thin bleached-blonde at twenty-eight when she rounded the corner of 15th Street one day in August 1975, after a long day of data input in her low-rung federal job. Though she'd recently found an apartment for the girls and herself, Barbara couldn't shuck off the weight of her past. Still the dutiful daughter, she was stopping by to cook her father's dinner and noticed a man on the porch chatting with her sister Chris. A moment later, when introductions were made, she learned his name was Cedric Gilliam. Barbara said she'd seen him around. With a wide, quick smile, he took the hands of Chris's two-year-old son, Maurice, and walked him across the floorboards. "You staggering, just like your daddy. You didn't know I know your daddy," he said, as Chris giggled. When he passed the baby to Barbara, she noticed he was gentle with him.

"Any kids?" she asked.

"You kidding? I'm a free man," he said. "Maybe someday, you know, I'll settle down. But not yet."

She found out a few things about him—just enough, she didn't push. He had served time for bank robbery, was paroled last year, and had just finished his bachelor's degree in business from D.C.'s Federal City College, part of a program for former convicts.

College? She tried not to show that she was impressed, but it was easy to see. He pointed down the street to a hunter green Chrysler Cordoba. "All that fine Corinthian leather," he said, mimicking Ricardo Montalban in the famous ad, and Barbara chuckled. "That's right," he told her. "That car's brand spanking new."

"Okay, I might need a ride later," Barbara said coyly, before slipping inside.

She in fact did need a ride that night to her new apartment, and soon Cedric Gilliam was a regular visitor. Over the coming year as they ran and partied together, she found out some things that should have made her cautious. There was more to his criminal past than she had at first thought, including a long string of bank robberies—serious, gun-in-the-face crimes—and the fact that he both dealt and used drugs. Most troubling, though, were some things he told her late one night about his father, Freddie. A truck driver, he mercilessly beat everyone in the Gilliam household, especially Cedric's mother, before deserting the family when Cedric was seven. Lying next to him, watching him as he slept, Barbara thought about how that desertion might have left the type of wounds that never heal.

But she had become a woman with few choices. She was busy and so was he, and when they were together everything was easy.

Until one morning in the fall of 1976. She called him from work and said that he should come by that night, that there was something they had to discuss.

"Well, I'm pregnant," she started as he settled into a kitchen chair across from her later that night. "And, the thing is, I really want to have this baby. I've wanted a boy, you see, and I think this could be it."

"Could be a girl," he replied evenly.

"I have this strong feeling, though, that it's not," she ventured, not sure if her hunch about the baby's gender was just a desperate wish. Growing up, she'd envied her brothers' easier lives and hoped to some-day have a boy, too.

"You see," Cedric said, "I don't want no kids right now. Getting my degree and all, I'm getting my life on track." Barbara knew there were other women, and she wondered if he'd already decided to have kids with one of them, but she wouldn't press the point.

So around they swirled for hours—she, searching for emotions in him that she had long feared were absent, looking for something, any-thing, that might have bonded them together around the idea of a child; he, blunting her initiatives, seemingly telling her everything but the truth.

As dawn approached, after a lot of crying and screaming, she de-cided to drop her last card. She couldn't go any lower.

"You know, I've had some abortions before we met and all," she said, feeling her stomach tighten. "They say it ain't good to have too many. I mean, if I have another, it could ruin me."

He flinched, but he recovered quickly. "You already got two kids. Why you need more?" The words sounded godawful, and in a moment he was up, pounding around the living room, shaking his fists, ranting about how they "had it so good, everything going great, now this."

"Look, it's simple!" he hollered finally, his voice going shrill. "Either the baby or me. You have this baby, you won't be seeing me again. Ever!"

A few hours later in the mid-morning, she went to an abortion clinic near Capitol Hill, trying her best to stick with her plan to focus on how she was doing this for him, for their relationship. But she left, unable to go through with it, and called Cedric, hoping for some sympathy. She got only fury, as he told her flat out: "Keep the child and *we* are over."

After a few weeks of meandering reappraisals, she was back at the clinic. As a nurse with a clipboard asked if she'd had any abortions before, Barbara nodded and then said nothing for a moment. She began recalling all the broken promises, the years of betrayals from grinning, sweet-talking boys pretending to be men who had all by now run away.

"I've had enough," she said firmly, coming to. "I'll be going now." She nodded a thank you to the nurse, got up, and walked out into the crisp, brilliant November day, feeling an unfamiliar sense of purpose.

At 6 A.M. on July 24 of the following year, 1977, she caught a ride to Columbia Women's Hospital. After so much having gone wrong in her life, finally she was right about one thing. "Missus Jennings," the obstetrician said. "It's a boy."

Shifting on the bus to make room for an old man in the seat beside her, Barbara smiles as she recalls the words: "It's a boy," her boy. As the bus picks up speed again, she notices the passing landscape for the first time in half an hour, entering the Shaw neighborhood of D.C. Just a dozen blocks east of the lawyers and lobbyists on Connecticut Avenue and K Street, Shaw is a rutted, forgotten area of vacant lots, wandering prostitutes, and small, struggling shops tucked in the shadows of grimy row houses. She's been coming here a few times a week for over sixteen years.

With little effort, she could calculate it to the day, she muses. Her son was three months old and she was depressed when a concerned friend dragged her to the Baltimore Armory to hear some middle-weight preachers. They were Apostolic Pentecostals, fiery men who leapt and yelped and danced, whipping the crowd to a frenzy of faith. People were running down the aisles, speaking in tongues, and she got swept up in it. A hole in her heart seemed to fill, if not heal, and she wept and wailed along with the rest of them.

The star that night was a skinny, boyish preacher named C. L. Long, and a few days after first hearing his booming voice Barbara was standing in his church, ready to be baptized by the water and to receive the Word.

Just shy of thirty years old, she finally seemed to find some bear-ings—enough, at least, to make a few decisions to stick by. First, she'd always call her son by his middle name, Lavar; second, they would spend every minute they could in the sanctuary of Scripture Church, the refuge of Pastor Long.

After the bus takes its usual last turn and stops, Barbara rises and slips out the back door onto the street. Towering before her is Scripture Cathedral, a soaring, drywall barn built a few years ago where the dour, brick Scripture Church once stood. Pastor Long is now called Bishop Long, a leader in the fast-growing order of black Pentecostalists who've been steadily siphoning parishioners from mainstream urban churches.

The rain has stopped, and Barbara checks her watch. The service will be starting in ten minutes, so she walks briskly into the main entrance, passing under a hundred-foot wall of stained glass. She sits in the back for a moment. When she filters through memories as she did on today's bus ride it reminds her how she's invested everything in Lavar—all her hopes—giving their relationship a ferocious intensity, almost as volatile in some ways as the house she grew up in. She's so bound to his success, it sometimes scares her.

People are already filing down the mauve aisles and into the pews. Barbara walks slowly toward her regular pew near the pulpit where the other missionary ladies are standing. It's faith, all about faith, she decides. If she can just keep Lavar's faith in God and in righteousness living intact for a little longer, blessings will come. Rewards will come. She knows they will.

The service crests forward in swells of fervor, then contemplation and then more fervor—all mixed in with traditional gospel standards. The rhythm is familiar and relaxes her. People come forward for blessings, and the crowd—about four hundred on this damp night—cheers for them and for themselves. She knows that Bishop Long will make a strong appeal for contributions (the church, as always, has pressing needs) and she settles back for the close of the service as he makes his plea.

"Let's talk about when you give your last dollar to God," shouts Long, now a heavyset man in his early fifties, with a wide, leonine head atop a cinder block body and the delicate ankles of a dancer. Smiling broadly, he eggs them on. "Then, and only then, will you know what faith is all about. Faith is taking the last $10 from your checking account and saying, 'God, I give this to you, because I have *nothing* but faith, I live on faith, and I know in my heart that you'll bring it back to me in ways too grand and too many for me to even imagine.' "

The missionary men, holding out wicker baskets on long wicker poles, begin their walk down the aisles. Barbara fingers the $20 in the pocket of her dark blue skirt. Numbers start running through her head: she'll need money for the week's commute; and whatever's left they'll need for food—a little, at least, for the four days until this Sunday's chicken dinner at church. The baskets are moving, filling up sure and steady, only three rows away. She shakes her head in frustration and stamps a heel on the carpet. Can't do it. She pulls her hand from her pocket, grabs her purse from the seat, hurriedly snatches out the $10, and drops it gently on the soft nest of bills.

A boy, if he's lucky, discovers his limitations across a leisurely passage of years, with self-awareness arriving slowly. That way, at least he has plenty of time to heroically imagine himself first. Most boys unfold in this natural, measured way, growing up with at least one adult on the scene who can convincingly fake being all-powerful, omniscient, and unfailingly protective for a kid's first decade or so, providing that invaluable canopy of reachable stars and monsters that are comfortably make-believe.

By this reckoning, Cedric Lavar Jennings wasn't so lucky. Despite Barbara's best efforts, he was confronted at an early age with adult-strength realizations about powerlessness, desperation, and distrust, taking his dose right alongside the overwhelmed adults. This steady stream of shocks and reactions leaves so many boys raised in poor, urban areas stumbling toward manhood with a hardened exterior masking deep insecurities.

From the start, Cedric received a steady diet of uncertainty and upheaval. He and Barbara moved around a lot. There were too many stops to remember as they bounced from tiny, short-term rentals to pullout couches or bedrolls at one of Barbara's sisters' apartments. But at least they were together. Barbara's third big decision (after vowing to call him Lavar and to frequent the church) was to quit her secretary's job and go on welfare. Her son had just turned two. She had been made a junior missionary at the church, and being with her Lavar in these crucial years ("when," as she'd often say, "a child either gets the love he needs or he doesn't") was part of a reordering of her priorities. They lived frugally. The girls were in school, and Barbara and Lavar took buses to thrift shops in low-rent strip malls. She'd buy him books there and sometimes clothing. She'd prowl through the racks while he played with the secondhand toys. She bought cards with colors and numbers and they'd sit while she flashed the cards and drilled him. They visited museums and the Anacostia library. Countless hours were spent at the church. There were plenty of women around—between Barbara's sisters and Scripture's missionary ladies—and young Lavar was the pride of a matriarchy.

This sheltered, early period, though, was bound to be short lived. Just after Cedric's fifth birthday, Barbara knew she'd have to start building his defenses. He would start a full day of kindergarten in the fall, and she would go back to work. But before that, there were things Barbara wanted him to know.

They were living in Northeast on a busy python of traffic and noise, Benning Road, just over a dry cleaners. It was 1982, and cocaine dealers were discovering the potency of a new concoction they called rock (later, crack), and dealers were beginning to use small children to make deliveries.

One day in late August, after Cedric and Barbara trolled a few thrift stores, they began walking the streets on all sides of the apartment. Barbara spoke to Cedric in careful, measured words. "You're gonna be a big kindergartner next week. And I got to be going back to get a job, when you're at school. Now, walking back from school, I don't want you to be talking to anyone, understand?"

He nodded, picking up on her seriousness. Then she squatted next to him, so their faces were side by side, and she pointed across the street. "See that man over there?" she said firmly. "He's a drug dealer. He sometimes asks kids to do things. Don't ever talk to him. He's a friend of the devil." Block by block, corner by corner they went, until she'd pointed out every drug dealer for five blocks in either direction. Later that night, she slowly explained the daily drill. After school, he would walk by himself to the apartment, double lock the door, and immediately call her—the number would be taped by the phone. And, along the way, he would talk to no one.

The first day of school arrived. She'd bought him an outfit specially for the day: blue slacks and a white shirt. She walked him over to Henry T. Blow Elementary, which was just behind their apartment.

"Here, I got something for you." She took from her purse a fake gold chain with a key on the end and put it around his neck.

"This, so you won't lose it."

"Ma," he said, already conscious of his appearance, "can I wear it underneath?"

She nodded, and he slipped it inside the crew neck of his white shirt. Years later, he would recall that dangling key—the metal cold against his smooth chest—and think ruefully about how exhilarating it felt: a first, cool breeze of freedom.

By that afternoon, he was a little man, walking purposefully across the playground and around the block to the apartment, unlocking and then locking the door, calling his mother to say he was all right. She started a new job as a data input clerk at the Department of Agriculture, and soon Cedric knew the phone number by heart. It was a ritual he'd repeat almost every day—double locking the door of this apartment or that—for nearly a decade.

And one other thing changed. The birth certificate that was required to enroll him in school listed his full name. He might be Lavar at home and at church, but now he was Cedric Jennings at school. "Saydric . . . Seeeedric . . . Cedric," he'd say over and over, sitting alone in the apartment after school, watching afternoon reruns of *I Love Lucy* or *The Brady Bunch* or *All in the Family*. The name felt odd, like a bad fit, and he'd often wonder why his mother chose it.

He was Barbara's little partner, sticking close to the trinity of school, church, and the locked apartment, trying—with sterling behavior and glowing notes from his teachers—to keep her from worrying all the time. Once, when his half-sister Leslie was baby-sitting, she had taken Cedric with her to visit her boyfriend down the street. As Leslie dragged him home later, having lost track of time, she whined, "God, hurry up Lavar. Ma'll be back soon." Suddenly, they were caught by a frightening specter: a nearly maniacal Barbara, wild-eyed, switch in hand, who snatched Leslie in midstride and snapped the switch across her face. Terrified, Cedric began to scream. His mother's continuous apprehension—and attacks, like that night, of genuine panic—left Cedric certain there was danger everywhere.

When Leslie and Nanette had gone off to live with relatives, Barbara and Cedric left the apartment on Benning Road to live with her sister Rose "Tiny" Jennings. One Friday night in the early spring of 1985, the phone rang at their apartment.

"For you, Barbara," Tiny called to her sister, "It's some guy." The two-bedroom apartment—shared by Barbara, her sister, Cedric, and his two cousins—was small, and Barbara got quickly to the phone.

"Ummmm. Barbara? This is Cedric. Cedric Gilliam. I was wondering if I can see the boy."

"What's the occasion?" she asked coolly, not skipping a beat. He explained that word of his fatherhood had gotten out—the one girlfriend of his who knew told another one who didn't. "So what's the point of hiding it? And, you know, I'd like to know him."

The next morning, Barbara sat Cedric down, turned off his cartoons, and explained that his father was coming. The child, just seven years old, was beside himself with joy.

That day, Cedric Sr. took his son to the beautiful two-bedroom apartment he shared with a woman named Joyce, who seemed like a wife. There was the closet full of suits, the giant TV, the stereo, and the still plush green Cordoba. They had lunch and went to K-mart, where he bought his son a Bugs Bunny costume, with Halloween coming soon. The child wore it to bed that night and under his Sunday best the next day to church.

There were a few other visits. Barbara would always be there when Cedric got home, seeming more anxious than ever. To calm her, Cedric told her of everything he and his father talked about and of all those silky possessions.

Walking amid the plenty in his father's apartment one Saturday, Cedric saw a pewter mug full of coins. He poured them into his pocket and later told his mother they were a gift. In fact, they were rare coins that a desperate customer had bartered in exchange for heroin. At the next week's visit, Cedric Jr. walked into an ambush when his father, a lifelong thief, determined he would teach his newfound son a lesson about stealing. The boy was made to strip, and the whipping with a thick leather belt was ferocious, halted only when Joyce finally grabbed Gilliam's arm and screamed for him to stop.

Cedric had now learned about betrayal and misplaced trust. And, a few weeks later, about abandonment. Cedric Gilliam was picked up for heroin dealing and armed robbery. He disappeared for a term of twelve to thirty-six years into Lorton Correctional Institution, the D.C. Federal prison in northern Virginia.

The shocks kept coming to his son, fast and steady. Barbara, concerned about both the risks Cedric faced in their treacherous neighborhood and the effects of his father's beating, mustered a furious run at a better life for them both. She used all of her money to rent a four-bedroom apartment in grassy, suburban Landover, Maryland, a working-class area just across the District line. Neddy and Leslie, now teenagers, returned home. Cedric had his own bedroom, played in the complex's landscaped courtyard with other children, and attended a mostly white elementary school, where his studiousness and good manners quickly ingratiated him to his teachers. The furniture was from Rent-a-Center.

The apartment was far beyond Barbara's minimum-wage means, and six months later the eviction crew arrived. All of it ended up on the street, picked over and hauled off by neighbors. Everything vanished, except maybe the psychological scar left on Cedric while he sat on the stoop and cried, watching as kids divvied up his beloved He-Man action figure collection.

More apartments and more evictions followed for mother and son before a move back to the dreaded house on 15th Street. They made another move to a tiny apartment in a building that caught on fire while Cedric was home alone. Then finally they landed on V Street, Southeast, in a tiny, dank, one-bedroom near some of the city's worst drug dealing. Always careful not to part the curtains more than a crack, Cedric would watch the dealers, guns sometimes visible, stash drugs in the alley beneath his window.

Any parent surveying this wreckage would have been dispirited, and Barbara no doubt was. Everyone of every age in this neighborhood ingested gut-churning dread regularly. Gunshots. Arrests. Sirens all night. The chances of a boy emerging from here intact were almost nil. In desperation, Barbara tried to keep a tight grip on just the basics: strong physical discipline and tight scheduling. She made sure her son was either in school, in the locked apartment, or at church, visiting Scripture Cathedral four times a week.

One Sunday, Barbara was, as usual, down in the church basement, cooking the congregation's dinner, to be served after the midday service. It allowed her to get a meal for nothing, rather than paying $3, and to slip a free one to Cedric.

One of the missionary ladies ran down to the kitchen. "Your baby is singing—front of everyone."

"What?" Barbara screamed, dropping the fried chicken tin and running upstairs.

The children's choir, about fifty strong, had been singing, with

Cedric in his usual role anchoring a clutch of boy tenors, when something seemed to well up inside him and he suddenly stepped forward.

"He will never leave me or forsake me," Cedric sang, his voice rising above the others. "Please don't let them hurt your children. Oh, God, please don't let them hurt your children."

Watching this drama of the spirit, the crowd yelped with joy. "Do it! Sing it!" someone cried out.

Barbara heard the cheers as she bounded up the stairs toward the sanctuary, wiping her hands on her skirt as she ran.

"Please don't let them hurt your children," he sang out, growing, with each verse, more comfortable in front of the crowd. "Please, ooooh please, Jesus, don't let them hurt your children." His mother, bursting through the rear doors a moment too late, heard only the applause.

After this breakthrough, Cedric seemed to nudge himself along. He learned to talk about Cedric Gilliam without getting upset, and, with Cedric Sr. safely in jail, Barbara felt freer to be candid about all that had gone sour in his father's life. Soon enough, she became convinced that such knowledge actually motivated her son, only a fourth grader, to live in reaction to his father, using Cedric Gilliam's rutted path to find coordinates for an opposing course he would carve.

For both mother and son, one thing was certain: at the darkest moments, there was always the sanctuary of Scripture Cathedral. Like for so many inner-city blacks who left mainstream churches for Pentecostal congregations in the 1970s and 1980s (making it the fastest-growing denomination in the country), Scripture Cathedral offered Cedric and Barbara neat designations of good and evil and strict rules forbidding even common activities, like watching movies or dressing provocatively. For Barbara, who, like so many, came to fervent Pentecostalism from a life broken by poverty and neglect, the church provided both moral orderliness and an absolution for past failures that finally allowed her peace about all that had gone wrong over the years. Here, success was not an honor, nor privation a dishonor; the Lord assiduously threw up tests and kept score based solely on faith. Bishop Long, in his sermons, railed against the sins of pride and ambition.

Yet one meritocracy was permitted: music. That was the path Cedric stumbled onto. Those who could sanctify God with their sweet or strong voices—a dozen adults and half that many children—were permitted a special place, front and center. Cedric became a youthful star of the children's choir, a soloist. Where so much about life at Scripture Cathedral, indeed, meant a withdrawal from this world, the confidence infused in a young boy, standing before six hundred or so parishioners on a Sunday, was a single, buoying item an eleven-year-old Cedric, as a fifth grader, could carry beyond the church's walls.

At this age, Cedric aimed to please. He did his chores, which were many, with Barbara often telling him that she'd done her share when she was a kid and he would do his share. And he was obedient. Having felt Barbara's wrath, he took seriously when she'd warn, "I tell you once. I don't tell you twice." By sixth grade, he was a skinny, earnest, straight arrow, a little taller than the other kids and mostly quiet— waiting to be noticed.

Then came a victory: acceptance into Jefferson Junior High School, a magnet junior high, an anointed place. Jefferson was the type of school that had sprouted from the urban landscape in the past few decades like a flower, nourished by the rich decay and detritus all around. One out of every twenty or so sixth-grade applicants made it in. Three years later, most of those students managed to be accepted into one of the District's few top magnet high schools, which in turn sent almost all their graduates to college.

Safely inside the gates of Jefferson, Cedric found for the first time something resembling a traditional American school. There were other smart, mostly well-behaved kids, sort of like him. Soon he was part of a group of boys—LaKeith Ellis, Torrence Parks, and Eric Welcher—from working-class, mostly two-parent black families. Barbara would some- times overhear Cedric on the phone with one of them and pick up just the right mix of friendly jostling and competitiveness. At night, Cedric studied ardently. The expectations here were much higher than he'd been used to—the kids were motivated. The seventh-grade curriculum stressed memorization of basic concepts in math, English, and history. Cedric's ardor and ability to focus helped him accumulate a loose-leaf notebook full of A papers.

In the evenings, after he was asleep, Barbara would flip through the notebook, gently fingering the papers, memorizing the comments from teachers. Sitting there, she'd often think that she also had to do her part. She was thankful to the church for Cedric's success, and she showed her gratitude with money in the Sunday basket. He needed better clothes and school supplies and maybe a little money to spend with his new friends. She needed to look presentable when she met with teachers or Vera White, the principal. One afternoon, she left work and strolled through fashionable shops in downtown D.C. She knew what she wanted, it would just take a while to find it. That night she brought home a crimson sweatshirt for Cedric, with "HAR-VARD" stamped across the chest.

But, just like in Landover, when she pushed too hard or wanted too much or became too hopeful, a few small stumbles would upset her balance.

Her finances on $5 an hour were, as always, precarious. Again, some of the furniture was rented. Tiny indulgences were enough to push some must-pay bills past thirty days. Old creditors, some collecting on bills dating back years, kept calling. Leslie was still sleeping at the apartment but running with a racier crowd. One of her boyfriends wound up at Lorton and called her collect from the prison pay phone to talk for hours on some evenings. The bill blossomed, and the phone got cut off.

When the first cool days of autumn came in 1990, both mother and son felt it. The gas had been turned off, which meant hot plates for cooking and no heat. Barbara and Cedric taped plastic over the windows. Living without heat was harder than either of them could have expected. When winter arrived, Cedric slept in thermal underwear and thrift-store down jackets. Sometimes there was no food in the house. The electricity was cut off, restored, then cut off again. Cedric started showing up late for school, often hungry and wearing mismatched clothes.

Barbara watched what was happening, helplessly, just like in the last days at Landover. Meanwhile, Cedric's workload increased, as the eighth-grade curriculum stressed more analysis than memorization, and he began to resent having to study at night in the cold, sometimes dark apartment. One night in frustration, he yelled at her, "How can I compete? It's like I'm living in a refrigerator!" She moved to hit him, to punish him for disrespecting her, but guilt held her back.

Each Tuesday, Thursday, Saturday, and Sunday they went to church. Barbara still tithed her 10 percent, prayed for strength and faith, and usually dropped a $20 into the Sunday basket. One night, thinking about how Cedric would someday go to college, she prayed that men from the congregation would come forward to pay for it, and she dropped her last dollar in the basket.

Like Barbara's dammed-up debts that eventually broke in a flood of dunning calls and legal threats, Cedric, too, had built up a debt of sorts. His voice had won him an indulgence—years of dispensation—in the type of prideful individual achievement that the church otherwise frowned upon. In the tough winter of eighth grade, much of what kept him going was being on the bishop's special TV choir, which sang on a local UHF station, and, most important, standing front and center on Sunday, reaffirmed by the congregation's shouts of "Amen" and "Praise Jesus" as he sang out his faith.

Quietly at first, the complaints were whispered to Bishop Long and other church leaders. Why him? He's been up there so long, why not give some other kids a chance? Barbara heard the grumbles and tried to ferret out the sources. She knew how important the singing was to Cedric.

But it was no use. On an early spring Saturday during choir practice, Steve Lawrence, Scripture's young choir director, took Cedric aside. "Some people are complaining about you singing all the solos," he told him. "It's time for other people to have a try singing solo."

And so, on Sunday, Cedric stepped back. When people asked why, he wasn't sure what to say, and it boiled inside him.

Barbara tried to offer counsel. They talked often late into the night about it, as she tried to find passages from Scripture that would help ease his feelings of rejection and censure. "It's like I've done something wrong for being proud to sing God's praises," he moaned one night. He said he was tired, too tired to do homework, and went to bed early.

A month later, a call came from Maggie Brisbane, Cedric Gilliam's mother, who was organizing a family visit to Lorton prison. She would take Cedric to visit his father, while another grandson would visit Cedric Gilliam's brother, Darren, who was also serving time. Barbara, thinking it might be just the thing to restore her son's drive, to remind him of why he must work hard and trust in God, agreed to allow it. But the visit went badly. Cedric Gilliam talked mostly to his nephew, a tough, self-possessed high school football star, and ignored his skinny, studious son. Cedric returned home dumbstruck and livid, with nowhere to turn.

Near the end of the long winter, Barbara got a note about a minor altercation at school—just a push fight, but not something she'd expect from Cedric. After that, she heard complaints from teachers that Cedric was talking back, that his fuse was short and his tone disrespectful. He started to be kept after school to clean lockers or mop the cafeteria, the self-styled discipline program of the school's tough principal. Because Barbara understood his resentment and frustration, she had trouble blaming him. And her reliable ally, the church, suddenly seemed to lack enough answers—or solace—to challenge all that beset her son.

Come spring, a call came from Vera White's office summoning Barbara to a meeting at school. On the way, she kept reminding herself that Ms. White called Cedric "one of our brightest students" at the previous fall's PTA meeting. This time the message was different: it was no longer worthwhile to bus Cedric all the way to Jefferson. He wouldn't be invited back for ninth grade. It was decided that he could go to Ballou, arguably the most troubled school in the District, despite its middling math/science program.

For Cedric and Barbara Jennings, there was nothing left to say. After all their struggles, they both were certain they had been left behind.

Barbara walks out the church's double doors and onto the street, which is busy with nightlife now that the rain has stopped. On her way across the street to catch a ride home from a friend, she passes a clutch of female hookers hovering near the church. She sees the woman in a spangly blue dress who came up to Cedric last year after one Sunday worship and said, "You're a cute one, you're gonna drive them wild."

Barbara, who is alternately concerned and thankful that Cedric doesn't have a girlfriend, tells this story often, always adding, "She's a pro, she ought to know." Cedric concurs, hopeful of this expert testimony about his impending sex appeal.

Feeling charitable, like a Christian woman should, Barbara nods a greeting toward the prostitute, though the woman doesn't notice.

She gets home from church near midnight. Cedric is asleep, and when she wakes up at 7:15 the next morning he has already gone. On her way to work, she carefully breaks the remaining $20, buying five days' worth of bus tokens—$2.20 for a round trip—which costs $11. Today, she'll eat no breakfast or lunch.

At 6:10 P.M., Barbara walks heavily into the apartment, feeling tired and anxious.

"How's school today, Lavar?"

"Fine," he says, his voice high and solicitous, not looking up from the TV.

"Choir practice Saturday, don't forget. You know, I'll be going all day too for missionary meeting."

He nods from the couch.

"I hope you knew to eat a big lunch today?" she says as she moves to the bedroom to change. "You know, it's the first week, with rent and all."

"Yeah," he says softly. "I knew. Got seconds on salad. Ate all I could."

By the time she emerges in her white pullover house dress, he's already in his room, having ceded her the couch. She slumps onto it, weak and bone-tired from a long day and no food.

She begins to flip channels and figure out a five-day budget in her head. In the morning she'll get some packs of Oodles of Noodles, a cheap, add-water noodle dish, for tomorrow night and maybe some macaroni and cheese for Saturday. That'll about use up the $9 she's got left but get them to Sunday dinner at church. She can write a check on Monday, which won't arrive at the bank until Tuesday, when her weekly check will have been deposited.

Relieved to have some sort of plan, she puts her head back and drifts off. At 10:15, she awakens with a jerk in the glow of the TV. She walks around the apartment to clear her head and grabs a glass of some flat Coke from the nearly empty refrigerator. She looks over at the overflowing sink.

"Lavar?!" she calls out, loud and testy, as she makes for the couch. "What about these dishes?"

Cedric stomps out of his room, takes off his gray wool polo shirt, torn at the elbow, and bellies up to the sink in his white undershirt.

He thrusts his arms into the wet dishes and muck. Barbara sees him from the corner of her eye. She knows there's nothing worse than doing dishes when you're hungry.

"This is completely disgusting," he mumbles, and looks toward the couch. She heard him but looks straight ahead at the TV, deciding she's not going to respond.

She feels herself start to simmer. She would have gotten a beating for saying that to her father, much less her mother. A bad beating. A switch seems to flip in her gut, starting a familiar internal monologue: she's been working like a slave her whole damn life and *she* never complains. . . . She's been killing herself, her lifeblood channeled through scriptural pieties and long-shot hopes for Cedric's future, leaving her own urges untended and volatile.

"I hate doing these damn dishes," he says, this time too loud to ignore.

She jumps up, thumping across the room, fast, right up into his face. "I pay the rent here. I support you. I give everything to you. You don't want to do your part? You don't like it? When you complain it makes me want to kill you. You hear me?"

He's stunned and begins to cry. His hands, full of grease and congealed fat, stay plunged in the water.

The switch now flips back, the fury gone, and she looks away, ashamed. An apology rises toward her lips, but she bites it off. No, no. Can't apologize. She goes back to the couch.

Cedric gathers himself, silently finishes the dishes, and then gets the bucket and Ajax under the sink to scrub the bathroom.

Barbara Jennings will lie out here tonight, like every night (her double bed long ago buried under a mountain of clothes), hating that she erupted, wondering how Jesus might help her with her anger, wondering where it springs from. For now, though, she flips the channels fast, barely able to make sense of the flashing pictures.

3

RISE and SHINE

The sun rises at 6:12 A.M. on a March morning a few days before the start of spring. In the dewy dawn mist, a shadowy figure descends the crumbling concrete stairs outside 1635 V Street, two steps at a time.

Cedric Jennings has been sleeping fitfully for the past few weeks, waking up briefly to check his digital clock at 4 A.M., then 5 A.M., and finally at 5:30. That's when he bounds into the shower. By 6, he's dressed.

A few nights ago, Barbara told him that she thought he was losing his mind getting up at such crazy hours, and he just laughed. There's nothing he needs to talk to her about. It just feels better to get up, head to school, and start working. At least then he's not just sitting around worrying about MIT, or his all-important junior year grades, or the upcoming SATs, or some fuzzy notion of his future. He's actually doing something about it.

Yesterday after school he tried to explain this swelling anxiety and his desire to meet it head on. "It's like I'm at this crossroads," he told Mr. Taylor once he was convinced that a few other kids milling around the chemistry class weren't listening. "Like it's going to happen now or it's not, like I'm gonna either make it or crash."

Mr. Taylor looked at him nervously.

"It's not like I'm planning to do anything—it's just a feeling," Cedric said, exasperated. "Oh, whatever."

This morning, as he cuts across the apartment building's moist front lawn and skips onto the street, he thinks about that conversation with Taylor. He decides it's better not to talk about this sense of urgency with anyone. No one understands that this is *the* crucial moment for a show of academic force, a display of pure will. He feels himself getting riled up. Now is the time!

When he first started waking in the darkness at the beginning of March, he discovered that sunrise is the best time to pump himself up like this. Marching through the eerie silence of V Street, cutting through the long shadows and wedges of morning sunlight, he feels heroic.

He hits the corner of 16th and V—as always, open for business.

"What's up?" Cedric barks. The drug dealers—one guy in his late teens, the other in his thirties—shake their heads and kind of chuckle. They see him every morning. He usually just hurries by.

"He sure is 'all that' today," one of them says to the other, plenty loud, so that Cedric nods an acknowledgment as he passes.

At 7:15, the only sounds echoing down the first-floor hallway of Ballou are those of the tapping keys from the computer lab, where Cedric is already at work.

Later this morning, he will work on his school science fair project, an assessment of the growth rates of hydroponic plants. He plans to research another science experiment—a chemical analysis of acid rain on monuments—after school, to be entered in a citywide science fair competition sponsored in part by the U.S. Environmental Protection Agency. Last year, he won third prize for a project on asbestos hazards.

With his whole day mapped out, Cedric leans into the computer like it's a bobsled.

"You sure are making me get here early these days," says Mr. Govan from across the room. He runs the computer lab and opens it up before classes begin, mostly for Cedric.

"It's the only way I'll be able to compete with kids from other, harder schools," says Cedric, defining a block of text from one screen and moving it to another. "I mean, what choice do I really have?"

This is Cedric's standard line—he's been saying it as a sort of half-apology since he arrived in ninth grade and realized that with so little work being done during class time, extra-credit projects would be crucial to learning anything. Today, though, he enunciates the words with a measured clarity, like he's addressing an audience. For now, the convenient aphorism "kids from other, harder schools" is metamorphosing into real flesh and bone. He'll be hearing from MIT any week now. As he sees it, it will be those kids or him. Lately, he's managed to conjure them up and hate them. He doesn't analyze what he's doing, but he knows it's working.

Among other things, it crowds out a vision that drove him all but crazy: the look on some MIT professor's face when he sees Cedric's abysmal score of 75 out of a possible 160 on the Preliminary Scholastic Aptitude Test, or PSAT. He tortured himself for a week with this one—various Ivy League faces staring in horror at his application. One was an old, venerable white-haired guy with bifocals, another was some young brilliant Jewish guy, like one of the teachers he had at Jefferson. Cedric panicked on the PSAT last fall. So much was riding on it. He pumped himself up too much, and, racing through, not considering the questions carefully, he had lost track of how much time he had. Then he went back to recheck answers and started erasing some ovals right before time ran out. It was a nightmare. His PSAT score is equivalent to a 750 on the SATs out of a possible 1600, which would put him in the bottom third percentage of test takers.

That was then. He's past all that now, no longer dwelling on his fear. He gets up from the computer and moves like a missile through the crowded hallway to first period. His mother's right—what's the point of getting down on himself and his prospects?

As he considers what his hated competitors—those smart black and Hispanic applicants from much better schools—are up to each day, the daily curriculum at Ballou looks increasingly like a thin academic soup. Cedric's response is to eat every lesson plan in sight. He's wrecking the curve in Unified Math II, piling on answers to problems he knows cold, making sure he always gets the A+. In physics, he's extended his lead over LaCountiss in accumulated points, though she probably has the greater gift for science.

By offering some competition to keep Cedric's edge, the morning's regimen of math and science can funnel his up-at-dawn enthusiasm. But come midday when math/science kids must start to mix with the rest of the student body for other subjects, there's simply nothing to push against. Passing grades are granted for just showing up.

Cedric settles into a chair for history class. Tired and graying, Mrs. Mildred "Midge" McBriarity is one of about 40 percent of the teachers at Ballou who are white. There are twenty desks; the class roster lists as many kids who should be here. The starting bell rang more than ten minutes ago, but only Cedric and one other boy are present.

"All right," she says finally. "Our reading for today was about Calvin Coolidge and the coming Depression." She continues, "Were the 1920s a period of true intellectualism, or was it just a facade of intellectualism?"

Cedric raises his hand. She looks up and hesitates, as though there are many to choose from.

"Ummm. Let's see . . . Cedric?"

"What's a facade?"

"It's a fake front, a veneer of some kind, maybe of, for example, sophistication. Do you understand?"

"Yeah, facade, okay. . . . It was, you know, also a time of materialism," he says, ducking the trickier subject of intellectualism.

"That's right. And how, Cedric, did that materialism manifest itself?"

"With get-rich-quick ideas."

"Right," she adds. "In the stock market, they bought stocks on margin. Do you know what that is?

"Buying something?"

"Well, sort of," she says, skipping past that.

As the class discussion limps forward, Cedric finds it hard to remember what he felt like at dawn. In his afternoon classes—Government, SAT prep, and Spanish—he is often the only student to have completed homework. The classes are often nearly empty, especially as the days grow warmer, and he is left to learn in this awkward question-and-response style across a sea of unoccupied desks. Most of the time, he's simply reciting, calling out a subject heading from the text or a worksheet. He knows he's not developing the analytical skills that come from complex class discussions and thoughtful reasoning.

A few hours later, after the day's dismissal bell rings, he files into Mr. Taylor's empty room behind Tanya Parker, a skinny, shy math/

science classmate, and the ever present LaTisha. They chat about some great Timberland boots Cedric saw in a magazine, a kid who punched a teacher, and a math/science classmate of theirs—a C student—who is now living at a homeless shelter.

While Cedric remains guarded about discussing his application to MIT (fearing, already, the ridicule if he's rejected) he begins to talk around it, near it, mentioning how, someday, he'd like to go to "some Ivy League or whatever."

LaTisha and Tanya both balk. LaTisha says she's planning to go to the University of the District of Columbia, or UDC, a middling, financially troubled school that accepts almost any graduate of a D.C. public high school. Tanya is not certain. She adjusts her eyeglasses and says, "I'll probably go local."

Cedric tries to explain. "It's just that I've sacrificed so much. You know, giving over my whole life to schoolwork and then just going to UDC. I mean, come on now. I'd get laughed at."

LaTisha smirks. "You don't even know where some of those Ivy schools are at," she says. "All those Yales and things. You ain't been there."

"I know where they are," Cedric counters, tentatively. From the corner of his eye, he sees Mr. Taylor move from the adjacent lab area into the connecting doorway, eavesdropping.

"Yeah, where Harvard at . . . huh?" LaTisha probes.

"It's, you know, in Boston," says Cedric.

"Ivy League?" she says with a flourish. "Why do you want to go so far away from here, somewhere you ain't even seen?" LaTisha keeps on him, talking faster now. "See, what kind of fool spends his life trying to go somewhere he ain't even seen or has no idea about. Damn, you may not even like it. Then what? Your life be ruined."

Mr. Taylor's shoe taps the linoleum, and LaTisha turns. "Oh, hi, Mr. Taylor," she says, all effervescence. As the afternoon wanes, she and the silent Tanya take off for a 4:30 city bus. Cedric, brow furrowed, stays behind.

Mr. Taylor shuffles some papers on the lab table at the front of the room, waiting for the boy to speak.

"I saw you listening," Cedric says.

Mr. Taylor saunters around the desk, his dusty black wing tips squeaking.

"You didn't have much to say to LaTisha," he says. "What about all that?"

"I could never dream about, like going to UDC or Howard, or Maryland or wherever," Cedric says. "It just wouldn't be worth what I've been through."

Mr. Taylor nods and oomphs his body into the desk chair next to Cedric, like he's squeezing into a tuba. "I know there are people you want to prove things to," he tells the boy in a confidential whisper.

"NO, NO," Cedric's shakes his head. "Don't go there. It's not that." But Mr. Taylor presses forward. "It's all right to feel like you want to show people, so long as that's not all you want, so long as you don't think that will really change anything. Proving things to the other kids or, let's say, to your father, won't make them like you or apologize to you. It won't make them cheer you on."

Mr. Taylor rises with a groan, cleans a few worksheets off the wide black-slate windowsill, and folds shut his grade book, glancing over once as Cedric mulls over his last offering.

Cedric looks at the teacher for a moment. The mention of Cedric Gilliam, always a lurking presence in his son's life but rarely spoken of, pricks at Cedric's rage, as well as his furious drive for acceptance. He knows it but backs away from it. He's not going to get into a long discussion about his father, not today. "Yeah, whatever," he says, rising from the desk, gathering his things. "You know about all that already, me wanting my father to love me or whatever. I hear you. But I want to make it to MIT or wherever for me, too. I know it's crazy, but I believe that's where I belong, even if they're places I haven't really seen."

Mr. Taylor smiles, all Cheshire cat now, rocking back on his heels. And Cedric immediately guesses where the teacher's mind is racing. Incoming Scripture.

"Oh God, what now?" Cedric says, grabbing his bookbag, shaking his head with a there-you-go-again grin.

"Hebrews 11:1," says Mr. Taylor. "The substance of faith is a hope in the unseen."

"NO. Wrong—you messed it!" Cedric laughs. "It goes: 'Faith is the substance of things hoped for, the evidence of things not seen.' Man, Mr. Taylor, you always getting 'em wrong."

Mr. Taylor howls. "All right, extra point for you," but, as usual, he wrestles the boy back to middle ground, thwarting an outright victory. "The Word, of course, is the Word my young friend. But make it into what's right for you. That's the lesson for today. Take from the Holy Scripture only what you need, nothing more."

Cedric looks quizzically at Mr. Taylor. "You always be talking in riddles," he says with a chuckle and waves farewell as he strolls by. What, he wonders, did all that mean—take from Scripture only what you need? Maybe, he wonders, passing through the doorway, it means deciding on a few lessons from Scripture you can really use, day to day, and holding tight to them. Everyone's life is different, after all, and everyone hears the Word a little differently.

Then he turns the botched line over in his head and hears his giggle echo through the empty hallway. A hope in the unseen. Sort of a pocket-sized version of the original, and not really a religious phrase, he decides, but one you can definitely take with you.

The Bluebird, a squat diesel bus custom-painted the cobalt blue and eggshell white of the U.S. Marshall's service, idles just inside the barbed-wire gates of Lorton Correctional Institution, waiting for the morning's cargo.

A hundred yards away, inside a long, low mess hall, Cedric Gilliam looks disdainfully at the steam trays of corned beef hash before sliding forward his Styrofoam tray for a ladleful. At 4:45 A.M., on the edge of northern Virginia's suburbs, the minimum security section of Lorton's sprawling, 10,100-prisoner complex in the grassy Blue Ridge foothills is in a half-conscious state. Literally. About half this facility's 930 inmates are here for breakfast in their pale-blue cotton two-piecers, most of them planning to return to bed once their bellies are full.

Like every morning these days, Cedric Gilliam sits quietly at a four-man table, picking at his food and savoring a faint scent of privilege. Everyone knows the score: he's one of about three dozen guys dressed in jeans and casual shirts who will soon be transported by the Bluebird through the curling thicket of barbed wire to work/release jobs in Washington. But now that Cedric is entering the eighth month of his gig cutting hair at a barbershop in Northeast D.C., most of the "first time in a long time" moments are long past—like his first big-screen movie (sixth day out), his first lay (that same afternoon), and his first reunion with his mom's home cooking.

Not that each dawn to dusk of freedom—following eight long years of captivity—isn't vivid and invigorating. It is. Each moment. Full of temptations, too, which are steadily eroding his initial resolution to follow the rules. No surprises there. He has recently convinced himself that it's natural for any man to partake of some things he's so long been denied and that it's the smart man who can be careful about it.

He slides the barely touched plate of hash into the dishwashing window, nodding a perfunctory greeting to a rubber-gloved inmate pulling early duty. Then he snakes through a few hallways and stops to check out at a guard booth near the doorway to the parking lot.

It's a forty-five-minute ride due east to a drop-off point near Union Station, a quick ten minutes on the subway, and a two-block walk that lands him at an apartment just across the Maryland line as morning breaks.

"You're nothing if not punctual," says Leona, opening the door. She's an attractive, high-cheekboned woman of forty-six, two years his senior, who he's dated on and off since the mid-1970s when he was juggling her, Barbara Jennings, and another woman while living with a fourth. In the past few months of work/release, he's seen Leona just about every morning. She always gives him a quick kiss and spins away to gather her purse and briefcase. They both have jobs—a busy day ahead with people to see, just like a couple of young professionals, Cedric muses. A moment later, he's holding her Starbucks travel cup as she threads her blue Toyota Corolla through D.C. traffic, talking fast about how he is, how she is, how they are, and what he might feel like doing this coming Saturday. The car slides up near Hooks Barber Shop.

"Late, hun," she says, ushering him out with another kiss and begins to nose her car back into the flow of traffic, bound for her computer programming job at the Department of Justice.

"I'll phone you a little later today," Cedric calls after her. He pats the Toyota's trunk as he skirts around it, then heads into the barbershop to officially begin his day.

It took a little while to set up—to get the system down—but now things are running pretty smoothly. "Like a Rolex watch," he says out loud, and then thinks to add, "sold off the street." He nods a hello to R.J., the shop's owner, who's half asleep, sunk in a barber's chair.

Cedric slips on his black rayon barber's smock, pulls a small, black dayminder book from his jeans pocket, and surveys today's appointments. It's going to be mighty busy, about thirty customers coming. He walks to the pay phone at the rear of the narrow, four-chair shop and calls a man he talks to almost every morning to order his heroin.

Cedric does cut hair as well, averaging between five and eight heads a day. He's quite good at it and takes pride in his work, whether it's taking payment and a tip from a customer here or an unauthorized pack of cigarettes from a cleanly shorn prison guard down at Lorton. But over the months he has waded into easy money through his greater talent. Not simply selling drugs, which he's been doing since he was fourteen, but precisely managing needs (of his heroin customers, just like his women) and not giving a morsel more than is required. Cedric's particular prowess is at always making sure his margins are good.

With an hour to kill before his supplier arrives, he sits on the barbershop's concrete front stoop, sipping a carton of orange juice from the convenience mart next door. He tilts his face upward to get the most from the warmth of a pale morning sun and feels a sense of well-being wash over him.

The last eight years inside Lorton may have blunted parts of him— some of his cockiness, for sure, and the rage that led him into so many fights during his first long prison stay, six hard years for a bank robbery he flubbed at age eighteen. If it counts for anything, what he's really learned during his present term is how to *do time* shrewdly. Mostly, that means thinking things through, five or six steps ahead, before edging in any direction. It means sizing people up, carefully, though at a distance, before deciding how—or whether—to deal with them. It means keeping one's own counsel and staying clear of messy situations. Cedric thinks, as he crushes the empty Tropicana container, that he's always had a natural acumen for these sorts of calculations.

He looks down at his watch, almost 9 A.M., and thinks about what they're all doing right now at Lorton, the sorry-ass bastards. But the place is fading further behind him with each day, and the thought quickly passes.

Soon, a middle-aged black man in a polo shirt and alligator boots arrives with thirty palm-sized plastic bags. An hour after that, a middle-aged black man in a dark-blue business suit with a Department of Corrections badge arrives to make sure Cedric is at work. Both men are on their daily rounds, with lots of people to check on and little time to dawdle. Cedric greets each of them with a sort of arm's length charm. He understands what they're after and artfully fills the bill, allowing his day—and theirs—to waft forward uneventfully. By late afternoon, six heads have been cut and twenty-nine heroin customers have been in and out. The accounting is straightforward—haircuts and dime bags each cost $10. His cash from the barbering, $60, is folded into a money clip for deposit late tonight in his Lorton escrow account. It's a rule: everything an inmate earns goes into the prison account, so their work/release doesn't leave them flush with cash that could juice up Lorton's black market for almost any good or service. Cedric Gilliam, the barber, sticks by that rule faithfully. He puts the money clip in his hip pocket.

As the afternoon fades, the man in alligator boots strolls by for his cut. Sixty percent of the thirty bags, $180, is handed over, and Cedric pockets the remaining cash, tying it in a tight bundle with a rubber band. Business concluded, he slips into the phone-booth-sized bathroom next to the pay phone with a bag he bought for himself. Breaking out a stub of plastic straw, he snorts down the powder.

He leans his hands on the toilet tank, eyes squeezed tight, and feels warmth flowing toward his extremities, like a river washing into cavities he didn't know were there until the instant they fill. After some time, he's not sure how long, he finds himself squinting at the harsh lightbulb, and he bumps out through the half-hinged door, uncertain, suddenly, of his footing. He leans against the phone to recover his balance. The hit of heroin is plenty to smooth him out, to compel his whole being into an exhale but—he hopes—not more than enough. Anyone who wrestles with compulsion knows that though self-control is an unwelcome friend, it may be the only friend. And soon Cedric welcomes it, happy to feel centered and potent again, ready to manage things anew. He picks up the receiver to dial up Leona but pauses momentarily to consider calling Sherene, a woman he met late last year and has seen a few times. He decides Sherene can wait (he needs to set up some romance with her more thoughtfully) and that he and Leona should catch an early dinner and then have some precious private time at her apartment. After that, she has to drive him to the pickup point near Union Station. He needs to be there by 7:30 for the return migration of the Bluebird.

All goes neatly, tidily, the way he likes it. On the bus back, he leans across the aisle in the rear to huddle with two other prisoners. They are also working as barbers, so their receipts should all match. Barbershops in certain sections of D.C. are well-known fronts for drug dealing, so they all have to be careful. With Cedric's guidance, they are. Inside the trailer near the prison parking lot, the strip search goes fine—he spent his heroin profits on Leona, as usual, dinner and a little gift, so he doesn't have try to smuggle cash with his ass cylinder. While he's slipping clumsily back into his jeans, he has a momentary concern about appearing high. But he reminds himself that he foiled urine tests by the prisoner intake unit plenty of times, and his worry passes quickly. He could gulp down eight glasses of water (that did the trick once) or finagle a switch of urine with another inmate. If they want to test, let the bastards go ahead.

But they don't. Cedric—who knows some of the guards from junior high and one even from his days thirty years ago in youth detention—is certain that they're no geniuses. Lorton has its own peculiar hierarchy, where everyone knows everyone and everyone knows that pulling off a successful hustle is what the best people do.

As he strolls across the wide concrete courtyard on the way to cell block three, taking his sweet time and taking in the moonlight, Cedric Gilliam feels complete—muscles and limbs exercised, wits challenged, every part of him pressed into service. The heroin high is pretty much gone, but he doesn't feel depressed, inasmuch as he has a lot going down and he's got to be keeping it all together.

After breakfast the next morning, refreshed from a sound sleep, he notices that the guard at the parking lot checkpoint is looking at him cockeyed.

"What?" Cedric ventures, feeling a hint of discomfort.

"You're not going anywhere today, Gilliam," says the wide-bodied guard, a black guy about his age. He's all smug, arms folded, Cedric thinks, in his dollhouse booth and folding chair.

"Hell you talking about?" Gilliam says, his voice wavering as he glances out toward the Bluebird's headlights.

"They pulled your work card. Something about you earning more money than you turn in every day. You're supposed to check with the program officer this afternoon. He'll lay it all out."

So, after lunch, Cedric checks it out. "There's been a lot more traffic in and out of the barbershop than just six or seven customers a day," the program officer explains, eventually looking up from a file on his desk. Their eyes lock, and then Cedric's break away first, looking down. There's no need to say any more. Work/release canceled, indefinitely.

Cedric leaves the covey of administrative offices, wanders absently back to the cell block, flops onto his cot, and falls in and out of sleep for several hours. Lying awake in the late afternoon, eyes closed so people will think he's asleep and leave him the hell alone, he feels an awful, familiar restlessness clouding over him. He thinks about what he'd be doing right now on the outside—working out his day's receipts, joking with R.J., and getting ready to see Leona or maybe that Sherene. It's excruciating to think about all that, and his mind searches frantically for replacements, for decisions to make, issues to parse. Maybe now would be a good time to sign up for that class he was thinking of taking early last year, an environmental science thing at the prison library. He's already got two bachelor's degrees: one in business from the 1970s and another one, in urban affairs, he picked up in 1992. It gave him something to do during the early stretch of the long, dull years. Maybe he'll get a third degree, in environmental science. But the notion dissolves swiftly. It might have been an okay idea last year, but it seems impossibly bland now that he's been outside, living full tilt, for all these months. And what's the point anyway, he broods. No one's going to hire a drug dealer and armed robber who has spent nearly half his life locked up. Get real. He could have a hundred degrees.

He sits up and checks his watch. It's dinnertime, but he has no appetite, and besides, everyone at the mess will want to know what happened. He gazes across the quiet cell block, at the forty-four beds spaced evenly between green metal stand-up lockers along cinder block walls. No one's around, thank goodness. He considers strategies to persuade a guard he knows to give him access to a phone. He should call Leona, who'll be worried about what happened, or R.J., who'll be curious but won't give a damn. He fusses over what to do, back and forth—call Leona or not call—until inertia catches up with him and his mind turns in on itself.

Thinking about phone calls is what starts it. That phone in the prison library, the best phone around. A guard whose hair he cuts can get him in there sometimes so he doesn't have to wait in line at the outside pay phone with a pocket full of quarters. It's a free phone for local calls, and D.C. is local, so you can talk as long as you want. Which is why he planned it all so carefully one night last year—just a month before he heard the good news about work/release—meticulously arranging matters to get to that library phone to call Lavar.

He starts to chew on it, nice and slow, so the important details each present themselves in sequence, like they've been tagged and numbered. Oh yes, he went into the library with hopes for a good call, the kind of conversation a father ought to have with his son. And why not? Things back then weren't going so bad, he reflects. He and Lavar had exchanged a few calls and two letters over the spring.

He pauses from the recollection for a moment, sits up, pillow propped against the cinder blocks, and gathers himself. Replaying moments from the "outside," Cedric knows, is what inmates do; they prep and dissect them endlessly, for fresh, hidden meanings. It can drive you mad. He keeps on anyway, though, feeling pathetic but unable to stop, sort of, he thinks, like those poor strung-out bastards who mess with their needle tracks, trying to recapture the sensations from each tiny pinprick.

And then he's back at it, remembering how that evening's phone call started just like he had hoped. Barbara didn't pick up, that was the first break. That woman paralyzes him, and he held his breath as it rang once, then twice. Lavar picked it up and they just started chatting, real casual, like ol' poppa was just checking in, calling home from some extended business trip or whatever. So, how you doing? How's school? Any girlfriends yet? God, it felt good, easy and good. And it feels good thinking about it now, which is part of the point, he thinks, as he canopies his eyes with a heavy hand. You can almost go back.

He's inside it now, easing the memory forward toward a cliff he's been over before, and he feels his stomach tighten. The problems started when he found himself running out of things to say after half an hour and ended up rooting through a bare cupboard of shared references, anything to keep the connection going. He recalls the regrettable words and how he didn't want to say them even as he did. "Hey, Lavar, remember how you talked back to my mother over the Kings Dominion amusement park thing? You shouldn't have been disrespecting your grandmother like that. Telling her to shut up." It was an ancient matter. Lavar couldn't have been more than ten when he told Maggie to shut up and get off the phone because he was anxious for her to take him to the amusement park and she was gabbing away. It was an old nothing.

But it had been eating at Cedric Sr. for a long time. And once it spilled out, it seeped down into everything, all the explosive matter under the surface.

Oh, but that Lavar was ready. He shot right back, didn't lose a second, starting out with, "What are you saying?! You've been disrespecting your mother every day of your life by being in jail. You've been disrespecting her since you started getting into trouble when you was fourteen. Don't tell me about disrespect."

Absolutely, that boy's got a quick tongue, Cedric Sr. stews as he rolls the lines over in his head a few times. Disrespect, that's at the heart of it. That's why the boy had to be told not to "fuckin' talk that way" to his father, or he'd get his "mouth smacked."

But the thing is, he didn't back down. Cedric Sr. thought he would. If they were face-to-face, he would have. No doubt there. He'd be hiding. But maybe because it was over the phone, Lavar just kept coming back at him, shouting about not telling "me what to do or not to do, like you've been around for me. I'm not some child anymore for you to raise. Those days are over and you missed 'em!"

That boy knows how to hit and hit low, Cedric ruminates, and he thinks over some things he might have responded with, clever things, instead of just blowing up, shouting like a madman, right there in the library, for Lavar to "just shut the fuck up!" Yelling, "I'm still your father. You talk to your grandmother that way again, I'll beat the shit out of you. I'll blow your fucking brains out!"

Then the dial tone. That's the way the memory always ends, with the dial tone after Lavar slammed down the receiver. That was the last time they talked. Cedric has thought of calling his son a hundred times since then, though not so very much in the last couple of busy, en-grossing months.

But now he's back to it, sitting here on the bed with nothing left to distract him from mulling it over, again and again: the phone call, the screaming. His son had blown up at him before but never that bad, and the thought of it has left his whole body rigid, like he's in a vise. Here he is, a master at playing people, at managing their needs *his* way and on *his* behalf, and yet there's no appeasing this boy, nothing works. Nothing, Cedric Sr. thinks, as he feels the bitterness coming on. Just look at the boy, he says to himself. Could he be more different than me? All nerdy and faggy, a straight-A momma's boy who gets no respect from any of the kids at school, least of all the tough kids.

He shakes his head, unable to quiet his agitation. Is Lavar that way in spite of me, Cedric mulls, or to spite me, or both, or neither . . . or do I not really register at all in who he's become?

The questions are unbearable, maybe unanswerable, and Cedric tries to pull away from them, searching now for a quick way to lance it, to reach out to Lavar but not compromise himself. He unearths some-thing he'd thought up last year, in the weeks after the phone call. Figuring that he'd be paroled by the time Lavar graduated from high school, he planned to find out the time and place of the graduation ceremony. He'd enter through the back of the auditorium, quiet and unnoticed, once it started. He'd see Lavar graduate and then slip out, not letting anyone know, not wanting to disrupt his son's big day. But maybe he'd let him know about it later, that he'd made it. That way, Lavar might see that his father cared about him and all.

It might still work, Cedric speculates, feeling a welcome sense of closure. But then it dawns on him that any prospect of parole might be changed by this work/release cancellation. With only nine years gone on a twelve-to-thirty-six-year term, there's a chance he won't be out in time for Lavar's graduation from college, much less high school. He puts his head back and lets out a deep breath.

With the sun starting to set, people are coming in from their evening constitutionals in the cement courtyard. Cedric jerks back to the present. He looks at his legs stretched out on the bed, at his best Lee jeans, argyle socks, and stylish brown Clark loafers.

What's the point of wearing this nice stuff now? He should store it away in his footlocker like everyone else, folded and safe for when someone might visit. But he can't bear to slip back into his pale-blue two-piecer, with its drawstring waist. He simply can't. And he sits for the longest time, trying to decide what the hell to do.

Look everyone, Cedric handed in all his vocabulary cards. Isn't it amazing!" says Janet Johns-Gibson, the teacher in SAT-PREP, a required course for juniors at Ballou, as she holds high a pack of ninety-six index cards bound by a thick rubber band.

Cedric slumps at his desk in the back as a roomful of teenage eyes turn toward him, several of them clearly scornful. He stares forward, expressionless, fighting the urge to shake his head, disgusted that the teacher would make such a fuss. The vocabulary card homework—a simple exercise of looking up ninety-six words from a handout and writing their definitions—was assigned nearly two weeks ago. "Amazing." Her word echoes in his head. Why should it be amazing, he wonders, that someone actually did their homework? Isn't the whole idea that you're *supposed* to do it?

He looks out the window and takes a deep breath. It's raining hard, which accounts for today's strong showing in SAT-PREP, one of the afternoon classes that on sunny days is half empty. He watches the drops of water run down the long pane, snaking into canals before disappearing onto the slate sill outside. It's the end of March, with still no word from MIT, and when he looks at the raindrops—at anything these days—he always sees the same huge question mark.

Cedric has finally rationalized that his chances of being accepted there for the upcoming summer are slim—about as slim as his chances of ultimately ending anywhere other than some no-name college.

Looking out the window, he thinks back to his last days at Jefferson, how different it was, with him and his three friends, LaKeith Ellis, Torrence Parks, and Eric Welcher, all jockeying for the best grade. He sometimes came up short—those guys were demons—and pressed to catch up. It was sort of fun. And he learned more in a year there than in two, maybe three, here.

Eric Welcher lives just across from Ballou in a little cluster of tidy single-family homes. His dad is a computer programmer. A few days ago after school Cedric went over there to try out Eric's new Supernintendo. It had been a long time since Cedric had seen Eric, who now goes to Banneker, the District's magnet math/science high school. Each year, Banneker sends a few kids to the Ivies and plenty to other top schools. They talked a little bit about school, enough to give Cedric a glimpse of Eric's classroom life: coursework more advanced than Cedric's, lots of tough competitors, kids scoring in the 1500s on their SATs. Cedric felt anxiety creeping up on him. "So, are we going to play Supernintendo or what?" he groaned after a bit.

Ms. Gibson passes out the *SAT Vocabulary* workbooks to the class, delighted to have so many kids present.

"Cedric. . . . CEDRIC?"

"Oh, yes, Ms. Gibson," he says, coming to.

"I'm dividing the class into teams—into two groups—would you lead one of them?"

"Yeah, sure," he says quietly.

To lead the other group, she chooses Phillip Atkins.

"I'd like to thank a lot of people—so many of them such little tiny people—for this honor," Phillip says, with the perfect pitch and rhythm of a stand-up comic. "And, of course, the academy." This draws hoots from everyone, even Cedric.

The day's exercise is to match vocabulary words with definitions, and Cedric begins swiftly completing matches as his seven partners mostly recline, one of them spreading cards on his desktop for a game of solitaire. "He's not letting us do any, he knows all the answers," one of his teammates, a boy on the football team, complains a few minutes later.

"Thing is, Ms. Gibson, Cedric's getting them all right because of me, I worked with him just before class, using my amazing grasp of the language. So can I leave early?" cracks Phillip from across the room, and the class breaks up again.

This time Cedric looks up from his book. "Don't you have anything better to do, Phillip?" he says as his light-footed nemesis, clearly on a roll, frowns like he's in pain.

"Ms. Gibson, Cedric hurt my feelings." More laughter.

"That's enough, Phillip," snaps Ms. Gibson before she turns to chat with a colleague who's just wandered in from a neighboring classroom. Time passes slowly as Cedric presses through the pages. Some of these words he already wrote out on his ninety-six cards. He hears a giggle and looks up. It's from a pretty girl in Phillip's group. She seems to be looking at someone in the hallway. Cedric cranes his neck. It's Head. He's standing back a few feet, so Ms. Gibson doesn't see him as he makes hand signals and mouths words to the girl. Cedric tries to make out what he's saying—seems to be something about her going out with him after school. Or God knows what. All Cedric knows is that she's very cute. And so is this other girl sitting in that group who's leaning forward across her desk, whispering something to Phillip. She's so close to him, her lips right against his ear, then she pulls back and they both laugh under their breath. She seems to like him. A lot of girls like Phillip.

Ms. Gibson spots Head and shoos him away, chasing him into the hallway. She returns to the class, checking gingerly on the groups, which should be almost finished with the assigned pages from the workbook. Phillip, losing track of where she's standing, flips to the answers in the back of the workbook. Ms. Gibson, who gives daily grades for in-class performance, is incensed. She gives his group an F.

Phillip is undaunted. "Help me, I'm taking the fall," he yelps, clutching his chest and slipping from his chair. The class howls, and Ms. Gibson can't resist a smile.

And then something dawns on her. She excitedly tells the class the name of a Ballou junior, one of those rare middle-class kids from Bolling Air Force base, who took the SAT in January and got a 1050—an unspectacular score out of a possible 1600 but noteworthy around here.

"Cedric'll do better than that," says Phillip, now back in his seat, in a tone that actually sounds a little awed. "He's such a brain. If he don't do even better than that, people'll be shocked."

In the back of the room, Cedric flips shut his workbook and again looks out the window, this time to avoid Phillip's gaze.

The bell rings and Cedric leaves the class feeling tired. He lopes into the math class of Mr. Dorosti, an Iranian immigrant like Mr. Momen, who teaches Cedric computer science in an independent study program.

"Looks like you just lost your best friend," says Mr. Dorosti, a youthful, effusive man, folding his arms across his linebacker-wide chest. "Want to talk about it?"

"Be nice if I had a best friend," says Cedric, who slumps before a computer at the room's rear and starts working the keyboard, showing the teacher he'd rather just stew.

The last thing Phillip said really hit home, but Cedric, curiously, doesn't feel his usual swell of anger. He knows that Phillip is smart. You can tell, if you really get to know him. He's made his choices, Cedric mulls, as he thinks a little about Phillip's life—the girls, the friends he has from lots of different cliques at school, always making people laugh and have a good time.

When the school day finally ends, Cedric decides he's not going to work on the acid rain project for the citywide competition today. He just doesn't feel like it. He decides this in the stairwell and considers whether he should go tell Mr. Taylor. He's sure the teacher is expecting him, but if he goes, Mr. Taylor will have him in there an hour, asking all sorts of questions about whether he's feeling confident and if his faith is intact. He'll be quoting Scripture; he probably has some passages already earmarked.

No way, Cedric decides. He sits down on a step, figuring he'll wait for fifteen minutes until most of the kids are gone and the bus stop isn't so crowded. He puts his calculus book on his lap, making like he's reading it so he doesn't have to look at the other kids as they pass on the graffiti-filled stairwell.

Ten minutes later, one of those kids happens to be LaTisha, on her way upstairs to visit a teacher. "Hey, what're you doing here, Cedric?"

"Nothin', ummm, just nothin'," Cedric says, jumping up. The book thuds down two steps.

The stairwell is quiet. Most of the kids have already fled in the rush following the final bell. She leans on the railing next to him, as always picking up on his mood. "Look at the face on you," she says. "You sick or something?"

He pauses a moment. "It's time I got a life, you know?" he says quietly. "I mean, what kind of life is this? Me killing myself, getting ridiculed, and for what? I'm not gonna make it anywhere special."

He tells LaTisha that a few days ago he asked his mother for a pair of extra-baggy, khaki-colored pants, a style made popular by Snoop Doggy Dogg. "But my ma said no way, that it symbolizes things, bad things, bad people, and murder," he says. "It's just a pair of pants. I mean, I've gotta live."

"You *are* livin'," she says in feigned exasperation. "You just don't see what I see. You *got* something special. Something you got from your ma. It's a thing. I mean, I wish I had it. It's this thing where you know what it's going to take, and then you get it done. You push yourself and you get there. For whatever reason, I didn't get it, that thing. Maybe, you know, my home life didn't give it to me, with my folks splitting and me always fighting against my mom rather than hearing what she has to say. I don't know. . . ."

LaTisha looks down the stairwell, distantly. Cedric doesn't say anything, mindful that LaTisha is confessing things, opening herself up to try to help him.

"It's really simple," she says, looking up and right at him. "You've worked too long, too hard, to give up now." She puts a pudgy hand on his forearm. "You're a special person, Cedric. It's not like you're so much smarter than everyone else, necessarily. It's just that you know in your heart that you're gonna make it—and that's the key."

He looks back at her for a long moment and, suddenly, they hug. He feels the warmth of her face against his chest but keeps his chin up so—good God—they don't start kissing or something.

They separate, and Cedric, flushed, tries to nod her a smile to let her know he appreciates her being around for him. But he just feels quiet and kind of sad, like some fire has gone out of him. There's nothing more to say. He lifts his bookbag, heavy with homework, and walks slowly down the steps, not bothering to look up at the message scribbled with thick black Magic Marker high on the plaster wall, a proclamation he's walked by a thousand times—"HEAD LIVES!!!"

It works! Phillip Atkins marvels as he turns up the volume on a tiny transistor radio. He bought it for a buck out on Martin Luther King. All it needed was a new battery.

He finds an oldies station he likes, puts the radio to his ear, and drops his jaw in astonishment: "Elvis, my man. . . . Oh yes, it's a sign!"

The hallway is crowded between periods, and Phillip, always mindful of his audience, begins to twirl and sway to "Love Me Tender." A passing girl, tall with braided and beaded hair, asks who he's listening to. "Elvis—the King," says Phil, all charm, looking her up and down. "You know, he met me for lunch just yesterday—and he ate like a damn hound dog."

Teachers here, looking for ways to praise and motivate poor achievers, will pick any characteristic and try to inflate it into a career path. So the school is full of kids who are told they'll be the next Carl Lewis or Bill Cosby or Michael Jackson. That Phillip is tagged as the next Richard Pryor and rarely as a student who could excel academically is testimony to how effectively he hides so many parts of himself.

He gets a laugh out of the girl, and he turns as she passes to watch her walk away. He has at least five minutes before he needs to be in his next class—which he may or may not go to—so he scans the crowd. What next?

At the far end of the hall, he spots his favorite foil opening his locker. Cedric!

Phillip dodges through the crowd currents, shoving the radio in the pocket of his low-riding jeans, and flies by in a twirling leap, snatching a small book off the locker's top shelf above Cedric's head.

Cedric spins and slams the locker as Phillip slaloms around clusters of passing students. Cedric tries to follow him. At the end of the hall, Phillip stops, panting, not wanting to navigate the staircase, as Cedric, laughing a little, closes in and grabs him by the shoulder of his black T-shirt.

Leaning against the lockers, they both catch their breath, Cedric holding tight to Phillip's shirt.

"Hey, give me the book," Cedric says.

"Why should I?" says Phillip, putting it behind his back. "Say *please*—real nice."

Cedric tries to reach around but can't get it, and Phil grabs the front of Cedric's shirt.

With the two of them only a few inches apart—each holding a handful of shirt—their eyes lock.

"Wouldn't mind pounding me, would you Cedric?" Phillip says, trying to keep his rising bitterness under control.

"Just give me the book—I'm not playin'," Cedric says, his voice flat, even, and all business.

It was just a game, thinks Phillip, who was feeling so buoyant a minute ago and doesn't want this to end with the two of them rolling on the hard linoleum.

Why does Cedric have to make everything so hard, Phillip wonders in frustration as he lets go of Cedric's shirt and looks down at the bony fist still stretching his T-shirt.

"Hey, chill." Phillip spits, dropping the book on the floor from behind with one hand and punching Cedric, hard, in the chest with the other.

Cedric winces, letting go of the T-shirt, and Phillip slips away into the crowd, looking back once to see the angular boy in hush puppies quietly pick up his book from the floor.

As the day passes, Phillip's act sags a bit. His timing is just a little off, and he blames it on his feeling bad about punching Cedric—about letting that whole thing get out of control. In his late afternoon classes he finds himself slipping into a pensiveness that, these days, makes him uncomfortable.

After school, with nowhere special to go, Phil wanders out a side door and settles on the stone steps that overlook the track, where the team is running wind sprints.

Being the class clown allows him to be in control, energized, making them all laugh, setting the tone. But some days—like today—it seems like battery acid leaks out of him, soiling his charming, hip-hop veneer. Punching Cedric like that? It has not been a good day.

Sitting there, grabbing handfuls of pebbles and powdered concrete from a crumbling corner of the steps—no audience in sight—he slips into reflection about what he calls his "double life."

He does this every couple of weeks. It always means thinking back, if only briefly, to a time three or four years ago when there was a certain coherence to his life at home and at school, a consistency between the goals he publicly embraced and his inner desires, between the outward and the inward.

Back then, he didn't feel like two people but one: a nerd. Phillip carefully guards his memory of that kid and his life. He wore straight-legged pants and an ironed white shirt, with a bow tie on Sundays. He was a top student who read a lot and would spend hours spinning the globe with his father, thinking about all the places he'd someday go to. Every Saturday, there'd be a morning prayer meeting at the Atkins house in the Highland Dwellings public housing project that would adjourn to the streets, and Phillip and his father would go door to door proselytizing and passing out *The Watch Tower*, hallmark of the Jehovah's Witnesses. The Atkinses were a leading family at a local Kingdom Hall, where Phillip's father, Israel, was a church leader.

All of that is easy to remember, because most of it remains intact.

At home, at least, Phil is still like that, but everywhere else the other Phillip has emerged.

Whenever Phillip thinks about how he's changed—a gradual process and not all for the worst—he always thinks of how it started one afternoon in the spring of eighth grade. He saw an older boy in the projects—a boy he knew and admired—gunned down right before him. He watched it all from his bedroom window. He thought the shooters saw him. He said nothing but feared retaliation. He didn't sleep. Police came to the house and interviewed him. That made it even worse, the idea that people in the project, including the shooters, might think he'd been cooperating with the cops.

After that, something was extinguished in Phillip. He began a slow but steady shift in outlook and appearance to creating an identity that he considers a completely sane response. He is now a popular member of Ballou's mainstream, sporting his tough guy/clown demeanor and a new nickname he recently came up with, "Blunt," slang for a marijuana cigar. Phillip parties with his buddies on weekends, and his friends lately chide him for having red eyes in school. No matter—he's rough, he's fun, and he can walk among almost any group at Ballou. He's earned himself some comfort and security.

He looks down at the track, at the select group of kids—one of the city's top track teams—running sprints on the grassy oval. He remembers the look on Cedric's face after he punched him. Being like Cedric is crazy at a place like Ballou, Phillip thinks. It makes you a target. The kid is asking for it. And, what's more, Phillip mulls, Cedric is damn lucky it was just me and he *just* got a little punch. Imagine if he'd mixed it up with Head or one of the school's genuinely tough kids. That'd be that.

He stands up, brushes the grit off his jeans, and looks around. Not much to do. He was talking to a friend not too long ago, and the friend asked what Phillip was thinking about doing, in the future and all. The question kind of stumped him. Of course, there won't be any college or anything like that. Lately he's been wondering privately about how he might develop his creative, humorous side, on the way, someday, to trying stand-up comedy; as a fallback, though, he might end up owning a nightclub or, better yet, a comedy club. But it was hard to explain all that stuff, so Phil went for the easy line, which ended up being truer than he wanted it to be: "All I know is what I do now. I act stupid," he said. At least he got a laugh.

An hour later, Phillip arrives home—a sparsely furnished four-bedroom ground-floor apartment in Highland Dwellings, a housing project with D.C.'s usual accompaniment of gangs and drugs. He retreats to the room he shares with his older brother, Israel Jr., a brilliant saxophone player who graduated from Ballou last year and is now a cafeteria cook.

This is the site of Phillip's other life: going to church, passing out *The Watch Tower* in his white starched shirt, and living according to God's Word. He looks around the room, takes a deep breath—relieved that another confusing day is coming to an end—and flops on the bed, his head next to the open window, feeling the breeze.

Just outside, reclining in a kitchen chair on the apartment's concrete back patio, Israel Atkins Sr. is talking to an adult friend about the problem of shooting too high. A lyrically articulate man who conducts prayer sessions at his home on weekends, he gives this advice to his eight children: hoping for too much in this world can be dangerous.

"I see so many kids around here who are told they can be anything, who then run into almost inevitable disappointment, and all that hope turns into anger," he says, catching a few last minutes of sunshine before he goes off to work the night shift cleaning Budget rental cars in downtown D.C. "Next thing, they're saying, 'See, I got it anyway—got it my way, by hustling—the fancy car, the cash.' And then they're lost."

Phillip, lying on his bed, half listens. He's heard this line of preaching before, his father's "shoot low" philosophy. Life at the Atkins household, like that at the Jennings place, is dominated by faith, and their denomination is also growing wide and strong by pulling converts from more traditional mainstream urban churches. The denominations differ in tiny calibrations of literalism. Jehovah's Witnesses, using the threat of excommunication, have long stood in opposition to a much longer list of worldly endeavors than the Pentecostals. Jehovah's, the thinking goes, should have jobs, not careers. Following God's will is the career, so attending college, in the view of many witnesses, is a selection of the temporal over the divine. "Set goals so they're attainable, so you can get some security, I tell my kids," Israel says to his friend as he rises and prepares to get into his red uniform for work. "Then keep focused on what success is all about: being close to God and appreciating life's simpler virtues." He pauses. "Like, take Phillip doing this tap dancing, for instance . . ."

Phillip snaps up to lean against the cool plaster wall, his ear a few inches from the window frame. While Israel knows almost nothing of his son's hip-hop life on weekend nights and in Ballou's hallways, he recently found out about Phillip's latest—and maybe last—stab at some form of achievement: tap dancing. For the past couple of months he has been sneaking off to a few after-school practices a week but not telling many of his friends, uncertain whether it fits with his carefully crafted demeanor. Sooner or later, though, his father was bound to find out. Phillip hears the conversation crest forward, with tap dancing mentioned in the same breath as a similar controversy—now ended—over his brother Israel's sax playing. Israel was called one of the best sax players to ever come out of Ballou when he graduated last year. It seems like a long time ago; Israel barely touches his horn nowadays.

The very idea of a creative career rubs against their father's sensible "shoot low, simple virtue" philosophy. "Tap dancing, like sax playing, won't get anyone a steady job," he says, lingering for a last moment in the sun as he rises from his chair. "Being an entertainer? God almighty. That's getting on a path to being poor, desperate, and losing your soul!"

The friend laughs, and so does Israel—like it's some kind of joke—and, inside, Phillip lies back again, pushing his face into the pillow.

One Friday afternoon at the beginning of April, Phillip slips into Ballou's empty auditorium, where a small group of kids is waiting on the stage. Over the next hour, Phil reviews and rereviews a complex choreography, a dress rehearsal for the next day's long-awaited show. He moves masterfully through a sequence of fifty-three different steps, slides, and spins. The dance teacher applauds zestily as he finishes, and Phil, a blush appearing on his light skin, indulges a bow.

The next day, a sunny Washington Saturday, the Kennedy Center auditorium comes alive with a wailing jazz number. Phillip and four other dancers spin and tap their way flawlessly through a complicated routine. The audience—about two hundred parents, brothers, and sisters of performers—applauds wildly.

After the show, in which three other ensembles also performed tap routines, all the kids slip through a stage door to an adjacent dressing area. Phil is practically airborne, laughing and strutting in his yellow "Ballou Soul Tappers" T-shirt. A few teachers from the school came, and one is carrying a video camera, taping the kids as they whoop and embrace in the afterglow.

"Hey, over here," Phil yells, and the camera wheels around. "I'd like to thank a lot of people . . . this honor really belongs to them. . . ." He's off into high gear, jumping voices—first an aw-shucks Elvis, then Eddie Murphy's white guy accent, then a dead-on Richard Pryor nasal-speak, his body all twisting at the waist, hips out, a Pryor move. "And remember, all you kids out there," he riffs in a voice now closing in on his own, "you are our future, you can be anything you want, you can go anywhere your heart leads you."

The camera goes off. He hugs a girl from the troupe, and then a guy, and then isn't sure where to go. He stands in the middle of the chaos of kids, all grabbing gym bags, changing shirts, flashing Polaroids and hugging some more. He just watches, not wanting it to end.

During the show he was craning to catch a glimpse of his parents. All that was visible on the other side of the footlights, though, were rows of silhouettes. His dad, always punctual, probably got his family here early, so they probably got something near the front. He wondered what the old man's reaction would be. The songs included a few old jazz and blues numbers that his dad might recognize from what Israel calls his "confused, younger days," when even he "had some trouble dealing with what was expected of me by God."

The kids spill from the dressing area into one of the Kennedy Center's Oz-like foyers—lit up by incredibly high, arched windows—where the parents patiently wait to rejoice.

Phil casually scans the thick, regal red carpeting.

"You seen my people?" he asks one of his fellow tappers.

"No, haven't," she says.

"Your people here?" he asks, tentatively.

"Sure, my mom's over there," the girl says, pointing.

His throat seems to catch. He shakes his head. He looks again across the crowd, now clustering into families and beginning to drift toward the elevators. "Yeah," he says, "I'll find out where they are, why they couldn't come." He tries to force a smile, but, for the first time, he can't seem to manage it. "I'll find out later."

Cedric Jennings, at sixteen and three-quarters, has decided that he's been unnaturally focused and narrowly driven in the last couple of years, and definitely in the last couple of months.

And what better time to explore what's natural and innate and waiting to emerge than in springtime, the season so suited to adolescence. Most kids his age have an impulse to try on new poses and voices to see what feels right, but for Cedric it comes as a modest awakening.

Not much about him has changed, outwardly. At the start of April, with no word still from MIT, he's just spending a lot of time walking around with a glower, feeling particularly edgy and thinking a lot about how to alter people's reaction to him—looking to "get to them" before they get to him.

He still stops by Mr. Taylor's room after school but manages to keep the conversation away from heavy fare, mostly by talking about clothes or hip-hop music, stuff Mr. Taylor doesn't know much about. Since the stairwell hug of two weeks ago, LaTisha has been a touch more amorous than usual, so he finds himself steering clear of her.

Cedric is on his way to the computer science classroom one morning in the first week of April. He's not carrying any books. Left them in his locker. As he flows along with the between-periods crowd, he sizes himself up, his arms splayed a little out from his hips and not swinging much. He's got a few inches on Phillip, whom he now feels ready for. If he really cut loose on Phillip, Cedric concludes, he could hurt him.

The period bell rings, and Cedric ducks into the bathroom. He doesn't have to worry so much about the time. He has math this period, but he already did all the problems they're working on, so Ms. Nelson said he could work on his independent study project in computer science. After finishing his business in the boys' room, he lingers for a moment, looking in a long mirror over the sinks, narrowing his eyes to make his face look hard. He has put on a little weight lately. If his face fills out some more, he posits, he won't be so bad looking, really.

A few minutes later, he saunters into the computer science classroom of Mr. Dorosti.

A class is under way, and Cedric strides purposefully between the row of desks closest to the door and the wall. He sits at a computer table in the back and flips on the Apple Macintosh. Near his head is a bulletin board with several sterling papers (one by Cedric, marked "100%, Excellent") and an ancient, curling, three-by-five-inch photo of a Ballou student who went to Cornell nine years ago.

His independent study course with Mr. Dorosti allows Cedric free access to the teacher's upgraded desktop computer, even while classes are under way. Cedric views this as one of his few tangible perks. He's conspicuous, yes, as he enters a class in progress, but at least he has a special status, he lives by different rules than the others.

Today, though, Dorosti happens to have other plans. "Cedric, listen, someone in this class needs to use the computer," he says in broken English lacking sufficient nuance for Cedric's tripwire sensitivities. "You'll have to go."

Cedric swiftly hits his boiling point. He doesn't budge but stares a hole in the glowing screen. He hears a few sniggers in the room.

"Come on, let's go now, Cedric," Mr. Dorosti reiterates. "Not tomorrow."

Cedric smacks off the power button and storms out. Crossing through the doorway, he blurts out, "Damn immigrant."

Mr. Dorosti's eyes widen, and the chase is on. Cedric, half running to keep a thirty-foot lead, ducks into an adjacent hall, then takes the stairs two at a time as a panting Mr. Dorosti shouts: "YOU'RE IN BIG TROUBLE NOW CEDRIC! YOU HEAR ME?!!"

Cedric spends the rest of the day feeling like a fugitive—not just from Mr. Dorosti but also from his own vaulted expectations for success that suddenly seem to be pursuing him as well.

He strides across hallways and into Mr. Taylor's room. He tells the teacher that he isn't going to enter the citywide science fair with his project. It would have been the centerpiece of a mentoring program with a black executive organized through the EPA. "That guy, the mentor, I'm not seeing him anymore, either," he says to Mr. Taylor. "It's over."

Mr. Taylor is speechless as his star student practically runs for the door.

"I'm tired, I'm just getting out of here," Cedric says as he disappears into the hallway, not bothering to look back or stop at his locker for his bookbag.

There's an April shower outside, steady but not too heavy, and he passes by the bus stop nearest the school, bound for Martin Luther King Avenue. The rain actually feels kind of good—so what if he gets wet?—and he decides to walk a while, maybe all the way home, about two miles, or maybe somewhere else.

A few hours later, as dusk approaches, Scripture Cathedral stands like a giant glowing ark above the ruins. It is oddly shaped, with its front—a long, sloping wall of windows—jutting out like the prow of a ship.

It's a towering presence. As Pentecostalism has grown in urban America, so has this church. After four years of ongoing renovations and expansions—just completed—it is truly a cathedral for Washington's down and out, a cavernous place with a sixty-foot ceiling in the airplane hangar sanctuary, big enough to sit 1,500. A forty-foot-tall illuminated cross rises behind the wide, multileveled altar to watch over them.

With the Thursday night prayer meeting about to begin, Barbara searches nervously for Cedric, scanning the crowd of three hundred or so women in hats, men in bow ties, and a few polite, casually dressed children. Cedric's lack of spirit has, in the last week or so, begun to worry her, so she made him promise that he'd come tonight. Her mind wanders as she slides into the pew, craning around every few seconds to glimpse toward the room's entrance doorways in the rear. It seems like the whole month of March, since the bad incident over the dishes, Cedric has been something less than his prickly, headstrong self. He didn't call her at work today like she thought he would. He's never late. Should have been here by now.

The music swells to signal the start of evening services, and the choir comes in through a door in the back wall of the altar—a string of about twenty singers moving in a practiced, smooth procession to a rousing swirl of the gospel favorite "Jesus Is Everything to Me."

The clapping and swaying is infectious. So many here have arrived from a bruising Thursday—staring at a computer screen or cleaning some school's messy halls or hanging off the sidebar of a garbage truck. As they throw their heads back, shouting lyrics toward the far-off, recessed lighting, their release is palpable. It is deafening.

And then the room is hushed. Bishop Long rises from a cushioned chair at the center of the altar and moves to his pulpit.

"Tonight," he announces, "I have a heavy heart."

He pauses, waiting for the joyous faces to turn somber, matching his, and in a moment they do.

"There is evil in this world, a darkness of the unholy, that is taking our children," he says, whispery, masterfully quiet. "I presided over a funeral today. A boy, only fifteen years old, cut down like so many of our young ones."

Faces sag and heads nod as the crowd moves up and down on the arch of his words.

Cedric slips into a back row, unnoticed, looking haggard. He has on the same black jeans and knitted sweater with a rip under the arm that he wore to school. He walked a long time in the rain, ducking into a few shops, but mostly just walking. Eventually, he arrived at the subway on Martin Luther King Avenue, took the train to a stop in downtown D.C., and then had to wait for the bus to get here. His sweatered shoulders and short hair glisten with moisture.

All around, a cacophony is rising. Bishop Long has launched into a rousing sermon, and as he speaks, his rolling cadences echo through the sanctuary, bringing the three hundred parishioners—a fine turnout on a rainy night—to their feet.

"If you don't have a dime in your pocket, if you don't have food on your table, if you got troubles, you're in the right place tonight," he shouts, as people yell out hallelujahs, raise their arms high, and run through the aisles. Cedric sits passively tonight, keeping his distance.

His mind is still back on the streets of Southeast, and he tries to keep it there. Today he walked close by the crowds of men who stood in doorways and under awnings, watching him pass. He looked some of them in the eye, and nothing happened to him. He even stood a while under the letterless marquee of an abandoned movie theater a few blocks from the subway station on Martin Luther King. A bunch of wayward men about his father's age were there. Cedric just stood with them and nodded, like he understood everything about them. It felt warm under there, comfortable and dry.

The congregation is clapping now, singing another song. Cedric looks around. A few ladies down the row look over at him, friends of his mother. He doesn't want to clap, but one of them might tell his mother later—like there's something wrong—and then he'll have to deal with her. So he starts clapping a few times and then skips half a beat to get in time with everyone else.

The rhythm and sway of the room slowly begins to seep in. Another song starts up, one he used to sing up front that he hasn't heard in what seems like forever, and, feeling some of the old juices flow, he ends up singing out and singing loud.

A lady in the row in front of him whom he's known forever turns halfway around after the song and makes a motion—a silent, puckered-lipped "whooaaa"—that's clearly about Cedric's robust singing. A smile breaks across his face.

Bishop Long takes his spot back at the podium. He speaks haltingly, starting out slow. "I know all about it. . . . I know all about what you're up against. I've been there. Trust me, I have. Do you trust me? Do you?" Long looks across each row of the room, at each face, with his one good eye. Cedric's brow furrows. It's like Bishop's talking right to him. "Teeerrible things are happening!"—his voice begins to rise, gathering force. "You're low, you're tired, you're fighting, you're waiting for your vision to become reality—you feel you can't wait any-more!"—he's thundering—"Say 'I'll be fine tonight 'cause Jesus is with me.' SAY IT! SAY IT!"

Cedric feels a wave crashing over him. He jumps to his feet, the spark back in his eyes. "Yes," he shouts. "Yes!"

It's a long service, and by the time mother and son pass the drug dealers and walk up the crumbling stairs to their apartment, it's approaching midnight.

Barbara gets the mail. On top of the *TV Guide* is an orange envelope from the U.S. Treasury: a stub noting the direct deposit of her check and the automatic 10 percent deduction into a savings account for her church tithing.

Under the *TV Guide* is a creamy-white envelope.

Cedric grabs it from her. His hands begin to shake. "My heart is in my throat," he says.

It's from MIT.

Fumbling, he rips it open.

"Wait. Wait. 'We are pleased to inform you . . .' Oh my God. Oh my God!" he begins jumping around the tiny kitchen. Barbara reaches out to touch him, to share it—her moment, too—but he spins out of reach.

"I can't believe it. I got in," he cries out, holding the letter against his chest, his eyes shut tight. "This is it. My life is about to begin."

4

SKIN DEEP

Fifty-two pride and joys mill about in a wide, wood-paneled dormi-tory lobby, a small, select colony of minority achievers in cut-off jeans and faded college T-shirts, many of them laughing with the breezy, can-hardly-believe-it giddiness of someone collecting on a wa-ger.

Standing among them, breathing in the cool, electric air of New England and MIT, Cedric feels reconstituted—bigger, somehow, than who he was before.

He's in. He's here. Two months ago he may have hated them without knowing them, he thinks, looking from one smiling brown face to the next, but that was just to gird himself against the possibility of rejection. All of it, at this instant, is meaningless prologue. Now, he's one of them.

Looking out a tall foyer window at the dorm's brick courtyard, tinted reddish gold by the late afternoon sun, Cedric is suffused with a sense of belonging, even though he is impossibly far from home. It has already been a long, adrenaline-filled day of breathless travel, from a plane boarded in humid Washington, to a special MIT van at Boston's Logan Airport, to the top floors of a high-rise dorm overlooking the fabled Charles River, and, finally, into a genuine college dorm room, with clean sheets stacked neatly on a striped mattress.

He meticulously made up the bed, unpacked his bags, checked the detailed schedule in his program packet to make sure the next hour was free, and then collapsed in delicious relief onto the tightly tucked green wool blanket, drifting into sleep.

——————

"Okay, everyone! Let's move as a group over to the dining hall," shouts one of the undergraduate chaperones, a tall black guy in a navy blue MIT shirt. "And please try not to get lost."

Cedric feels the push of the crowd and edges forward across the sprawling lobby of MacGregor House—his nineteen-story home for the next six weeks. He listens to a conversation over his left shoulder between a Hispanic boy and a black girl who have just realized they're wearing identical T-shirts from a high school national leadership conference for minorities. "This is great," chirps the boy, as the girl laughs in assent. "Kind of like we're all on our way up, all together."

Cedric nods. He likes that—all together. He's got company. The solitary journey, at least for now, is over.

They all jostle across the campus's trimmed lawns, still light green in the early summer. They are acutely conscious of themselves and everything they pass, busily affecting gaits and postures and instant smiles that suit this collegial moment. Cedric modulates the speed of his step to stay tucked in the middle of the crowd as it winds a quarter-mile to MIT's newish glass-and-steel dining hall, following a spicy aroma into a banquet room where a tower of pizza boxes is waiting, closed and still steaming.

Following a ruckus of flopping slices, overflowing two-liter bottles of soda, and bumping chairs, everyone settles in, munching away, for the first official meeting of MIT's Minority Introduction to Engineering and Science, acronyficiently called MIT MITES—as in embryonic MITers, soon to be born.

Bill Ramsey, a sixty-eight-year-old black engineer from MIT's class of '51 who arrived to run this program seven years ago to "give something back," speaks first, welcoming the students and offering a gruff but lovable "call me Bill, but no other names, please" salutation. He encourages everyone to work hard, have fun, follow the rules, and, dropping an octave, "not end up in my office for the wrong reasons." Then his leathery features break into an alligator smile: ". . . not that I'd ever be less than delighted to see any of you." He's a charmer.

And, in his role as the program's administrative director, he's a skilled orchestra leader. While there's nothing extravagant about a pizza dinner, everything tonight—like so many events over the coming weeks—has been extravagantly planned to give this precious group of budding minority achievers the *proper* messages.

Ramsey, a successful, retired corporate executive and black father figure, ticks off the summer semester's schedule of study periods, midterms, and finals. Looking on are the program's eleven student counselors, mostly college undergrads from MIT and nearby Harvard. MITES alumni themselves, five are black, four Hispanic, one of Middle Eastern descent, and one Asian.

That the ethnic mix of the counselors roughly mirrors the composition of the fifty-two wide-eyed initiates is not lost on Cedric as he gnaws the crust of his second slice of pepperoni and counts heads—about half black, half Hispanic, a few assorted others, and one boy who's definitely white. How did *he* get here, Cedric wonders, and realizes that he forgot to count himself: he makes fifty-three.

Cedric watches Ramsey wrap it up. He likes the way the guy looks: his wide torso draped in a stylish blazer, his crow's-feet and gray-flecked hair making him look sort of wise, but underneath he's got a fist-to-the-chops toughness. He's blunt, Cedric thinks, but he must have earned the right to be.

"And now," concludes Ramsey, "let me throw the evening's presentation to our faculty director, Professor Leon Trilling."

A bald white man with thick-rimmed glasses rises slowly and nods a silent hello. He is the distinguished professor of aeronautics and astronautics at MIT—the lead capsule bio in the welcome packet. He stumbles forward over a slight Polish accent, residue of his childhood in Eastern Europe, as he tells them that they'll meet with him at the end of the program to "see how you've done and how you've all enjoyed your visit." All the kids are silent. Almost no one is eating. They're just staring at this thin-lipped lab goat who exudes pure, arrhythmic, white power.

Almost every novitiate now has his or her visceral confirmation of the order of things—this dour man will carry forward the hard business hinted at in their welcome packets. He's the one who will review their six weeks of classwork and size up each little MITE's hopefulness before telling him or her whether the summer has a been a sprint to victory, toward the next starting gate as an MIT undergrad, or a fool's errand.

Cedric looks quizzically at Trilling as the professor begins speaking, but, unlike most of his neighbors, his attention drifts. For him, whites remain largely theoretical. His meaningful interaction with them has been limited, mostly to a few teachers at Jefferson and a couple at Ballou. In any event, after so much exhausting worry about whether he'd ever make it to this esteemed place, he suddenly feels immune from doubt. He looks around at everyone staring at Trilling and notices that the pizza has been neglected. No point in letting it go to waste. What's wrong with these kids, he wonders. Isn't anyone still hungry?

Three days later, early on a Wednesday morning, Cedric rises, dresses, and watches the sky sift from azure to pink to orange outside his ninth-floor window. He moves purposefully about the room, organizing his desk, sorting through his fresh notebooks, and slipping the ones for Physics, Design Workshop, and Chemistry—his three morning classes—into a large red plastic folder with a zipper along the top and "MITES" stamped on the front. He carefully selects two pens and two pencils, drops them in, and examines the battered spines of a long row of textbooks lining his desk. These books, lent to him from Ballou's storehouse of used texts, will be all he needs to succeed, he hopes. They're all he's ever needed.

It's only midway through the first week of the program, and the intensity is already palpable. All the MITES were given diagnostic tests on Monday to divide the group into advanced and basic-level classes for math and science. Yesterday Cedric found out that the only advanced group he's in is calculus.

After breakfast on Wednesday, he heads across campus to a mostly empty academic hall and quietly settles into a desk. He rotates his neck once and bounces his white Nikes on the speckled linoleum, like an athlete preparing for a trial heat. Handouts are passed out. He looks his over. What is this? Kinematics and vectors. In physics? Thought that was calculus. He looks up as class commences. After a quick good morning, Thomas Washington, a handsome, young black grad student who's a Ph.D. candidate at MIT, starts ripping across the blackboard. Cedric, hunched forward, begins jotting madly.

After a bit, he looks around. He sees that not all the kids are scribbling. Some are just nodding. Is he missing something, he wonders. He looks back at the digit-jammed chalkboard. Better get it down now and try to figure it out later.

The same thing occurs throughout the day—each class leaves him sweaty, his hand cramped from nervous note taking. Only in calculus is he following the line of the lecture, and just barely. That night, he retreats inside his cinder block walls, working over the handouts, trying to make sense of them by double checking each one against his notes. Press, dig in, concentrate, he tells himself, and it will come. After hours of work, feeling like he has a slim foothold on some of the material, he manages to fall off to sleep.

The next morning in chemistry class, third period, he's poised and ready. Three black girls who seem to know each other move into the desks in front of him. He hasn't said much to anyone since arriving, but the proximity and atmospherics seem right, so he strikes it up.

"This stuff is like pretty hard, ain't it?" he says to a tall, light-skinned girl with gold sickle-shaped earrings and expensive clothes. "I mean, I'm like afraid my hand is gonna fall off taking notes."

"Yeah . . . well . . . some of it looks a little different from what I've done in school, but I guess that's why we're here," she says, shrugging, before moving on to choicer, getting-to-know-you topics. Her name is Jenica Dover, she tells Cedric, and she lives in Newton, Massachusetts, where her parents are both high school teachers. The two other girls—Isa Williams, the daughter of two Atlanta college professors, and Micah Mitchell from Baltimore, whose mom is an insurance claims adjuster and dad is a lawyer—join in, crowding close.

"You sure talk funny, southern, sort of, and you know, slangy," says Jenica, lightly.

"For reeeal? What, like I'm slurring my words or something?" Cedric replies haltingly. "You mean, I guess, that I talk sort of 'ghetto.'"

"I guess—if that's the word for it," she says, and the other girls laugh, but warmly, which surprises Cedric, and he tries to turn it all into banter: "Don't you girls be teasing my accent." Just then the teacher arrives, calls for quiet, and soon Cedric is, again, panting to keep pace.

On Saturday night, he saunters into his neighbor's room and chats the guy up. His name is Mark McIntosh. He's soft-spoken but in a firm, laid-back, cool way. Cedric already met his twin sister, Belinda, in his physics class. They live in a modest house south of Miami, the children of a toll taker and an accounting clerk. Cedric, in a half-hour of nods and "yeah, uh-huhs," is certain they're sort of lower middle class, like the kids he met the year that he, his mom, and his half-sisters lived in Landover. They sit around drinking Cokes from a hallway machine and crank Salt-N-Pepa on Mark's tape player. Eventually, Cedric feels relaxed and emboldened enough to venture a dangerous, direct question.

"So, how d'jou do, on the SATs and all?" he asks.

"You know, I mean, it went pretty good," says Mark, setting up the number under cover of bad grammar. "Like, you know, a 1380."

Cedric tries to control his reaction but can't, and he finds his mouth hanging open. "I don't want to get into it," he mutters, shaking his head, "but that's a lot better than me."

In the last few months of his junior year, Cedric did something he hasn't thought much about lately—he took the SAT. His score was a 910, composed of a 380 in verbal (ranking in the thirty-fifth percentile of college-bound seniors) and a 530 in math (placing him in the sixty-fifth percentile). When he got his scores in May, he immediately decided to take it again in the fall. He decided he had been nervous and overwrought that first time. He stuck the test envelope in a drawer and refused to think about it.

But having pried Mark's score from him, Cedric is anxious to round out a random sampling—to get some numerical comparisons to correlate with what he sees exhibited all around him in language, dress, and general worldliness.

By the middle of the following week, there's no need for more data. Belinda, Mark's sister, hit 1350. There are assorted others in the 1300s, lots of 1200s, and a few 1100s. One morning after chemistry, a black girl he just met bashfully demurs, "It's embarrassing, but I sort of froze up and I only got 1090." Cedric is so happy he spontaneously hugs her, effusing, "At least I'm not the only one." But such an outburst is an anomaly. On balance, he's learned to be reserved, for fear of slipping into a mispronunciation or some embarrassing parochialism. Better to listen than to risk speaking.

Two days later at dusk, a clutch of kids rushes to the eastern side of the ninth floor and squeezes into the room of Kelly Armendariz, a tall, sensitive piano prodigy and math whiz from Carlsbad, New Mexico.

It's the end of the program's second week, a time by which cliques have formed as kids cluster in packs of five or six, mostly along the lines of race, similar background, or shared interests. Cedric is bouncing among clusters, unable to find a single match.

But there's still some free-form mixing, especially on a night like this, when it's possible for even striving, insecure adolescents to look at the sky and forget about themselves for a bit.

Kelly turns off the lights and everyone stands close as Boston's exuberant fireworks explode over the Charles River, lighting their astonished faces.

"Amazing, huh Cedric?" effuses Kelly.

"Yeah," whispers Cedric, mostly to himself. "It's like a dream."

Hi, Ma."

"Lavar! Hey baby. How is it?"

"Fine."

"Everybody being nice and all?"

Barbara, so excited to hear Cedric's voice, begins jumping fast across subjects that are tangible to her—the room, the food, his clothes. "You have enough to wear?"

"Uh-huh."

"You studying hard?"

"Uh-huh. Up until two every night almost. But, you know, I think it's coming along, getting easier," he tells her, lying, which he hates to do. "Thing is, though, I think I'm like the only ghetto kid. I've sort of been checking."

"Oh come on. I'm sure that's not the case—it's a minority program and all," Barbara says.

"I guess," he demurs, and changes the subject. They talk for a while until some kids come by on a social visit and Cedric tells her he has "to get going, 'cause me and my friends are having a study session."

"Well, okay. In any case, Lavar, don't start losing faith. Nothing you can't do if you set your mind to it. Always remember that."

And he tries to.

Midterms are fast approaching, and Cedric is slipping below the water line. Physics has become a recurring nightmare. In chemistry, he's constantly confused. Not that the MITES program is easy for anyone. It demands work even from the top students. Shock therapy is part of the point. Using the rote skills learned at Ballou, he finds himself writing and rewriting class notes, figuring that there are clues to be found in there, somewhere.

English provides no break. In the heavily Afrocentric curriculum of the D.C. public schools, he can always apply some personal experience to a passage from Toni Morrison or Maya Angelou. Here, the first major text in his English class is Aldous Huxley's *Brave New World,* tied to a goal of familiarizing the minority students with mainstream texts. In class, he carefully transcribes the outline from the blackboard:

Population divided into castes (social class, rank)
   1. Alphas and Betas
       a. More intelligent and manage society
   2. Deltas and Gammas
       a. Less intelligent and do menial tasks
   3. Epsilons
       a. Unhappy, though conditioned to be content

He looks down at it admiringly, neat and perfect. But he can't relate it to anything; he sees only strange terms in a foreign context.

Only in calculus, his forte, has he managed to stay afloat through relentless effort. At least there he's more confident and feels comfortable asking questions. And he gets a close look at the top students in the program, especially Andrew Parker, a student from Hawaii who seems to be part Asian, part black, and partly something else. All anyone knows for sure is that he's brilliant. Every day in calculus, Cedric finds himself studying Andrew, the way he cocks his head or handles his pen, as though attitude and demeanor might hold clues to his success. It's as if the instructor, Joseph Leverich, is talking only to Andrew in some secret language.

Sitting at his desk with the door closed as midnight approaches, Cedric mulls whether he can bring himself to do it: to ask Andrew for help. The kid drives half the MITES crazy. He's so damn cocky, always holding forth. His favorite aphorism is some Asian saying about how "the hungriest lion is not the one at the top of the hill, but the lion just beneath him, who wants to get to the top." Why is he always saying that, Cedric wonders, if it's clear to everyone that Andrew's at the top of the hill?

But it has been a long night of toil, and Cedric feels he's finally closing in on a real understanding of some new ways to calculate acceleration and velocity. He just needs a nudge forward.

A few minutes later, he spots Andrew walking in the hallway and makes his request. "I really don't want to be tutoring people, okay Cedric? That's what the counselors are for," Andrew says, polite but unyielding. And, maybe thinking of his beloved lions, he adds, "I have to be looking up, not down, beneath me," and he strolls into the men's room.

Cedric, alone in the hallway holding his drooping notebook, is ready to explode. He races back to his room and slams the door, his brain burning with the words "beneath me." "What a thing to say," he rants, talking to the wall, "like I'm some kind of inferior human being!"

A few nights later, a crowd of students jostles into MacGregor's lounge for Chinese food, soda, and a rare moment of release from the weekend's study marathon for midterms. While whispers of romances have been circulating and study groups have more or less crystallized along black or Hispanic lines, this long day of wearying study has left most of the kids hard pressed to remember who's supposed to hang with whom. Kelly Armendariz busily tries to teach the opening bars of Beethoven's *Moonlight Sonata* to Mark McIntosh on an old piano in the lounge. Two Hispanic girls are singing a Selena song with a black guy, and, a few feet to their left, on the lounge's industrial green carpeting, Isa Williams is teaching Micah Mitchell how to click her heels.

The counselors, having once gone through this program already, look on with tight smiles, always watchful. The academic pressure, they know, is intensifying. Midterm exams start tomorrow—along with all-nighters and panic. Some students will grow depressed; others will get sick from exhaustion. The counselors watch closely to see if anyone seems glum, confused, or bent on straying from the group.

Tonight, all the students seem happy and accounted for.

Except one.

Upstairs, Cedric is lying on his bed with the door closed and lights off, waiting for a miracle that will allow him to keep up with the others. He simply can't work any harder. It's only 10:30, but exhaustion from weeks of toil has overtaken him. Lying on his back, looking at the ceiling, his forward motion halted, he realizes that there's only so much he can do. It's not his fault that he started miles behind where most of the other kids did and he'll have to run twice their speed to catch them.

Not that this provides him much comfort. He has been cutting back on calls to his mother, not wanting to tell her that things aren't going so well. Still, he thinks of her often and what she would say: "Don't get down on yourself, Lavar, you can do anything you set your mind to."

If she told him that right this second, he thinks he'd definitely respond, "Listen, Ma, it's not that simple." He takes the phone card his mother gave him from his wallet, dials a number, and waits a moment.

"Hey, Torrence," Cedric says, sitting up on the bed. "It's me, calling from Massachusetts."

Torrence Parks is one of the Jefferson gang that Cedric checks in with from time to time. He's now at Woodrow Wilson High School, one of the better D.C. high schools. Since they parted after junior high, Torrence and Cedric have kept in touch by phone. In their last call a few months ago, Torrence said he had recently become an enthusiast of Islam and was spending a lot of time at a local mosque.

Cedric lets on that things aren't going so well, and Torrence is at the ready with sweeping explanations from Islamic dogma for Cedric's unhappiness.

"It's simple, Cedric. You should stick to your own," he says. "You're feeling bad, deep down, because you're betraying your people, leaving them all behind, by going up to a big white university. Even if you manage to be successful, you'll never be accepted by whites. You're just being used by the white power structure to make them feel good, like they're doing their part and giving a few select Africans a chance."

Cedric, who usually argues these points, mumbles something unintelligible to let Torrence know he's listening.

His friend is emboldened. "Look, you may not agree with me, but you have to admit that those kids know how to play the game of white academic success better than you do. And that's why they'll get ahead and you won't. Am I right? I bet there are not a lot of real brothers up there."

"Yeah, I guess not . . . I don't know, Torrence. Look, I'm kinda tired. I think I fried my brain or something. I'll talk to you later."

He hangs up the phone, wondering if he has trouble arguing with Torrence because some of what he says may be right.

A few grueling days later—each day starting with a blistering exam and capped by an anxious late night of study—Cedric wakes up in a haze and goes to physics class. There's a buzz in the room as midterms are handed back. Cedric forces himself to look down at the cover page: 4 points out of 26. Clean misses on three of the four word problems. He stands at his desk, walks out into the hallway, and lets out a scream.

Mr. Washington runs after him into the hall. "What's wrong? Good God!"

Cedric, unable to speak, just waves the test paper at him.

"Come on, now," says Washington. "Don't be so hard on yourself. A lot of the material is new to lots of the kids. Just keep at it. It will get easier." He looks carefully at Cedric, then tells him to take the morning off and go get some sleep.

In the afternoon, the calculus midterm comes back: 68 out of 104 possible points. God knows what Andrew Parker got, Cedric thinks, wandering out of the classroom, trying his best to look away from everybody and everything.

He avoids the MITES for the rest of the day. Walking across far reaches of the riverside campus until long after nightfall, he slips silently back into the room to turn in. Tossing and turning, too troubled to sleep, he sits up on his bed and looks out at the lights of MIT, trying on the hair shirt of failure, of his never making it to an undergraduate class at MIT or anywhere like it. The campus seems more beautiful than ever, with the white and yellow lights flickering at midnight over the football stadium. "I'll never make it to this place," he says to himself, seeing if he can say it. "I'm just fooling myself."

As the hours pass, he falls in and out of sleep. When he wakes with a jolt, Cornelia Cunningham, an elder at Scripture Cathedral, is on his mind. A surrogate grandmother who had challenged and prodded Cedric since he was a small boy, "Mother Cunningham" died two weeks before he left for Cambridge. He packed the special pamphlet with her picture, biography, and her favorite prayers from her funeral in his suitcase for MIT.

At some unknown hour of the early morning darkness, Cedric feels like her spirit is with him in the room. He presses his eyes closed, not breathing, certain he can hear her saying, "Cedric, you haven't yet begun to fight."

A few hours later, he sits up, awake and befuddled, not sure if it was a dream, but then not caring, either. A message came through. He leaps out of bed and over to the desk, hunched forward in his pajamas, diving into calculus as never before.

The auditorium rings with raucous cheering as teams prepare their robots for battle. This is the culmination of a semester-long exercise in ingenuity and teamwork that the MITES do every year. In the program's first week, each three-student team is given a small, remote-controlled engine and a box of levers, wheels, hooks, and plates to build a robot. Today, the robots will fight over a small soccer ball in an elimination tournament.

This year, something has gone awry. The trios, which in past years were carefully chosen and mixed by instructors with an eye toward racial diversity, were self-selected this year by the students. The kids did what came naturally: segregated themselves based on race. As the elimination rounds begin, "Puerto Rico, Puerto Rico!" is chanted from the Hispanic side.

Black students whoop as Cedric's team fights into the quarterfinals. When they lose in a tough struggle, Cedric—momentarily unself-conscious—stumbles in mock anguish toward the black section, into the arms of Jenica and Isa, who are anxious to come to his aid.

Tutors look on nervously as the auditorium divides into an edgy call and response. "Latinos Live!" shouts a row of Hispanic boys. "Africa Forever!" comes the return cry from the other side.

The winner, oddly enough, is a team led by the MITES lone Caucasian—a boy from Oklahoma who qualified for the program because he is $1/128$ Potawatomi Indian. Both camps are muted.

Bill Ramsey looks on sourly at the fractious scene. Now is the time, with just over two weeks left in the program, that natural divisions between the program's blacks and Hispanics should be easing after a month of socializing and competition.

Not to worry, he thinks, leaving the auditorium and walking across campus. The racial dynamic of this group will soon evolve along the same grid as in classes of previous years: the kids eventually move past the initial division of black versus Hispanic to a solidarity along the deeper fault line—minority versus Caucasian—as they realize that they'll all face similar challenges assimilating into the white professional class. They'll get plenty of messages about this in the next two weeks, from counselor chats about future careers to class discussions in English about being successful while retaining one's ethnic identity.

He strolls into his modest office on the second floor of Building #1 (here, most buildings have numbers rather than names) and hangs his blazer over the back of the chair. He begins rooting across his desk and through the drawers.

"Susie, where's that damn file on the acceptance rates?" he yells through the open office door to his assistant, a West African woman who rolls her eyes. "I'm sure it's around somewhere," he murmurs, pawing through a few more desk drawers. "If people wouldn't always borrow it."

Requests for the numbers come steadily, from MIT's admissions office, from journalists, from writers of academic newsletters, and from a slew of other programs that have modeled themselves on MITES. This is the Cadillac of university-based minority enrichment courses, and the numbers, at first glance, are stunning.

Susie finally finds the file in the outer office, peeks in the doorway with a smile, and drops it on Bill's desk.

"Have I told you that you're brilliant yet today?" he flatters her and then asks her for the file of a student who will be visiting in a few minutes.

He flips through the thick folder of data, though he knows these numbers by heart. On average, 82 percent of the MITES who apply to MIT get accepted. His tracking of the kids is obsessive, prideful. Almost all the MITES who matriculate to MIT's freshmen class end up graduating: sixteen graduates out of seventeen one year; another crop went eighteen for eighteen.

He puts the file in his out box to have some copies made as his assistant drops off the student file. It's a black kid. There was a complaint from one of the girls from Puerto Rico about this kid being too touchy-feely with her a few days ago, making her uncomfortable. No big deal, happens around here a lot. Boys and girls, far from home, trying to figure things out.

He quickly reviews the file. Bad midterm grades, some comments from teachers and student tutors about him being volatile and depressed. Then a note from one of the student counselors about him seeming to emerge socially in just the last week or so. Fine, he thinks, so he's feeling his way along.

He closes the file and leans back in his chair. Still a few moments until the kid arrives, so he looks out the window, something he's doing an awful lot of these days, letting his mind drift elsewhere. He's in good shape for a man of sixty-eight, still strong as bull, though seven years running this program has taken a toll. When he first arrived, taking over a program that had been up and running for two decades, he had grand plans to find poor black and Hispanic kids from urban America—kids who had somehow learned math and science in what are all but war zones—and give them the boost. Within his first year, he saw he'd been dreaming. A few kids he'd chosen from those bleak spots were much further behind academically than he'd ever imagined. And they're further behind now than they were then. It would take two years of tutoring, not six weeks, to bring some of the inner cities' brightest up to a level where they might be accepted to MIT. Their similarity to the polished, suburb-bred minority kids goes little more than skin deep. Is it fair to set them up for a fall, or maybe worse? He's had a few of them over the years, ghetto kids, and he's seen it play out: they come up here filled with hope, people back home banking everything on them as the one who will make it out, proving that people *can* make it out. And what happens? They get a taste of the big time and at the same time they learn that a taste is all they'll *ever* get. A whole program of those kids, he'd be raising suicide rates at MIT, something they already have enough trouble with.

He's run through this train of logic before, countless times. He strokes his brow, something he does when he feels stress coming on, and settles into his fallback position. It's simple, he concludes. MIT wants minority undergraduates, and the program's corporate sponsors eventually want minority employees. That's why he's ended up running a program filled with self-assured middle- or upper-middle-class black and Hispanic kids—leaders of tomorrow, all—many of whom are here for little more than résumé padding.

Still, every year he'll find room for a few poor kids from bad schools. And they're the ones that drive him crazy with yearning, the ones who dream in Technicolor but can't integrate fractions to save their lives.

He chuckles—that last line's not bad. Susie tells him the student has arrived, and he rises from his chair.

"Have a seat, Cedric," Ramsey says gruffly. He runs through the complaint from the girl as Cedric sits still on the edge of the chair, wide-eyed, a "Please don't throw me out" look on his face.

"Look, it's no big deal. You're not being sent home or anything," says Ramsey, finally. "Just be careful when you flirt with the girls. Some of them can be a little sensitive."

"Okay," Cedric says. "I will. Or, I won't, you know, whatever."

"Fine," says Ramsey, unable to suppress a smile. Then he pauses for a moment, not sure if he should take it any further. "Hasn't been such an easy summer for you, has it?" he finally says.

"Naw," says Cedric, looking down. "A lot this stuff, I just didn't expect. I guess I thought there'd be more kids like me here."

Ramsey nods, feeling his gut tighten. Just once, he'd like to rant a bit, to let a ghetto kid like this know that the affirmative action deck has been stacked, that the best of intentions, these days, mostly mean embracing upwardly mobile blacks and Hispanics who are likely to succeed, and that he shouldn't blame himself for not being able to keep up with the others. But where to begin, what to say? Instead, after a moment, he stands, letting Cedric know the meeting's over. "Look, just keep at it. There's still two weeks left—a lot can happen in that time," he says, as Cedric nods, thankful, it seems, for the encouragement, and quietly leaves.

Sitting alone in his small office, Ramsey shakes his head. It just seems like there's no way to give kids like that credit for the distance they've already traveled. This Cedric had to run three more laps than the other kids, but he's still two laps behind, so he loses. Beautiful. He starts to think about how long his own journey has been—how isolated he was as one of the only black undergraduates here in the early 1950s, the tensions in his family because some of them thought he was on his high horse, off to the big university. But, even now, he remembers that he knew with great clarity what he needed to do, how he needed to turn away from slights and confrontation and let his grades speak loudly for him. He felt like some sort of black pioneer whom others would follow.

He thought that by now there'd be a lot more black professors and students around here. He catches himself. He knows he shouldn't go down this path—it always ends with him cursing and riled up, and he's been feeling this way too many days of late. Because what the hell *is* this program doing with a white faculty director? Nice guy, Leon Trilling, done a lot for minorities, but come on. "Enough," he says to himself. He can't be getting all worked up, not at his age.

He rises and begins gathering his things to go home, looking out the window again, thinking of his lovely wife, his successful grown kids, and his retirement place in Saint Kitts, which more and more is beckoning to him.

The TV reception is lousy. Cedric flips the knob, adjusts the contrast, and fools with a mysterious red button, but all he can get are shadow images of the soulful Sisters With Voices, or SWV, mugging on MTV.

Someone's behind him. He spins. The whole gang is standing in the doorway of the small TV room on MacGregor's first floor: Mark and Belinda, another boy named Arryn, along with Jenica, Isa, and Micah. "Happy Birthday, Cedric," Mark says in his raspy tough voice. "Here's your present. It's a ghetto bag, 'cause you're soooo ghetto."

Cedric hoots. He can't believe this. His birthday is in a couple days, and the paper bag has condoms, M&Ms, Nivea skin creme, batteries for a boom box, a two-play rap CD—little stuff, nothing expensive. But it's the idea that's great, and everyone's in on it. Ghetto! It has been Cedric's favorite word in the past two weeks—his imprimatur of coolness. Someone can be ghetto in what they say or do or own—like cassettes or shirts or shoes—if they suggest the edgy urban version of blackness.

The whole thing, Cedric marveled a few days ago, is simply amazing. In this crowd of assimilated, careerist black and Hispanic kids, it is he, Cedric—king of the Ballou nerds, bottom of the Southeast D.C. pecking order—who can claim a particular brand of racial authenticity. Here, by default, he's actually an arbiter of the fashions, tastes, and habits of inner-city life that exert some sway over young blacks of any stripe. Just amazing.

What's happening, though, goes a bit deeper. Cedric is slowly letting his true self emerge. Midterms triggered it, forcing him to accept that he's way behind the others and might as well reveal his background rather than hide it. What's the point of putting up a false front, he finally decided, of affecting a posture like he's some suburban doctor's son hitting triples in every class? Yes, he's way behind, academically. How could he not be, coming from Ballou?

So he's opening himself up the only way anyone ever can: bit by bit. After presenting the birthday bag, some of the girls start talking about the activity-jammed weekend, which will start with a bus trip to Cape Cod the next morning.

Everyone is going. "I can't wait to see you swimming, Cedric," flirts Isa.

"I can swim and all," Cedric says, just in case anyone thinks he can't. "But, I'm not going. Lots of work and stuff." This prompts a pile-on. No one's letting him slip away. It's six on one. They all agree there must be some other reason, and then they bore in for the truth. Finally, he gives in: no bathing suit.

A moment later, he's being dragged by a posse, amid much laughter, across a walking bridge over the Charles River to the posh stores on Boston's Newbury Street. The girls fuss over which one looks best. Cedric says that it needs to be big in the crotch, and there's some wrestling among the racks, giggling and arm punching.

On the bus to the Cape, he's at his buoyant best, leading the group in song, bouncing with ease through an array of hip-hop hits. Singing in front of the other kids feels fine, with people clapping and humming, affirming his specialness, sort of like he used to feel in church. He has replaced gospel classics with rhythm-and-blueser Warren G, hip-hopper R. Kelly, and rapper Da Brat. He knows every lyric and vocal inflection of countless tunes—about violence or romance, about fearless men and sex-hungry women—songs that are a fixture of his proscribed, secondhand life back home.

The next night, July 24, his seventeenth birthday, he brings a plastic bag of cassettes onto the Boston Line ferry for a dance-party cruise around Boston Harbor. "Wow. You really know music," the black DJ says as Cedric runs through a playlist from his collection.

"Well, it's sort of all I got," Cedric says, shrugging. He spends much of the evening happily watching a bunch of very smart kids dance to his tunes.

By the middle of the following week, even Cedric realizes that something has happened. Something unexpected. Perseverance finally seems to be paying off. In the last two weeks, he has risen to the solid middle of the advanced calculus class. While not quite to the heights of

Andrew Parker, a tireless Cedric is clearly the hungrier lion. He is improving in chemistry, adequate in robotics, and showing some good comments on his writings for English. Physics remains the sole sore spot. And even here, blackboard scribbles are actually starting to make sense. His exhausting panic is steadily dissolving. He's getting some answers right in chemistry, and almost all of them right in calculus. It feels good after five long weeks of confusion.

Good enough, in fact, that he's able to keep his mind off what he has to do after classes end today, Wednesday, July 26. When English class is dismissed at 2:05, he examines a campus map from the MITES welcome packet. He searches for the building near Guggenheim Laboratory, home of the aeronautics and astronautics department. No trouble finding it on the map, but his bearings are a little off. He goes to one wrong building, then another, and eventually finds himself running through long corridors—mostly empty for the summer—of what he thinks must be the right building.

He finally sees an office door half open and light coming from within.

"Professor Trilling," he says, catching his breath. "Sorry I'm late."

Though Cedric has managed not to think too much about this meeting—his mind and spirit wrestling, each day, with so much else—now that he's in the office he finds himself paralyzed. He stands just inside the doorway, awkward and frozen.

The professor, in a casual, checked, short-sleeved shirt, steps around his wide desk so the two are standing face-to-face, and he ushers Cedric to a chair with a sweep of his hand.

Cedric, trying desperately to get his voice to work, looks down at Trilling's shoes. Brown bucks. His mind races. "Those are nice, umm, they Timberland?" he says haltingly. Trilling looks down, as though unaware he was even wearing shoes, and says nothing. He returns to his desk and gets down to business.

He opens a manila file and, after a moment, asks if Cedric is "thinking about applying and coming to MIT."

"Oh, yeah," Cedric says, squeezing out a tight laugh. "I've been wanting to come for years. Like my whole life."

There's an interminable silence, five seconds maybe, as Trilling looks down at the file again and then lifts his gaze to meet Cedric's eye. "Well, I don't think you're MIT material," the professor says flatly. "Your academic record isn't strong enough."

Cedric is stunned. Wondering, momentarily, if he's now supposed to get up and leave, he tries to extend the meeting by asking the professor to elaborate. "What do you mean by 'academic record'?" Cedric says, surprised he got the sentence out. "I mean, my high school grades couldn't be much better."

Trilling looks back down at the file to retrieve a key number. "I see your SATs are only a 910," he says, "and right there, that's at least 200 points below what they need to be to be accepted at MIT."

"And also," the professor adds, trying to close it out before Cedric can respond, "your work here this summer has not been up to that of many of the other students."

Cedric looks down at the carpeting, searching for something, anything, that might save it, that might make this white guy understand what it's been like for him, how hard it has been, what it took to get this far. "The thing is," he says, speaking with a slow, word-by-word cadence, like a recitation, "I can work harder than other people. When I really set my mind on something, anything, I can get there. It's about wanting it more in your heart." His throat catches on the last word.

Trilling leans forward in his chair. He's been at this juncture with many students before, but this boy is putting up a fierce fight. He takes a deep breath. "That perspective, that belief, Cedric, is admirable, but it also can set you up for disappointment. And, at the present time, it just doesn't seem to be enough."

On that last word, he quickly reaches for a pen on his desk and tears a sheet from his memo pad. "Here, let me give you the name of a professor I know at Howard University in Washington," he says, looking down and scribbling, "and another one I know at University of Maryland. You should call them. If you do well at either of those colleges in your first year or two, maybe you can apply for transfer to MIT."

Trilling holds the paper out across the desk.

Cedric, his eyes wide, can barely hear what is being said. His teeth are grinding, pressing together with such force it feels like his bulging temples will explode. He watches his fingers reach out for the small square of memo paper. But it feels like someone else's hand, and then someone else's body that rises from the chair and turns to silently leave.

When he gets to his dorm room, he slams the heavy wood door shut and leans his back against it. He looks down and sees the slip of paper still in his hand, held gingerly between the thumb and forefinger just the way he plucked it from Trilling's hand. He crumples it, throws it at the garbage can haphazardly, and watches it hit the wall.

He recovers his bearings enough to walk stiffly to the bed and lie down, closing his eyes and beginning a first replay of the scene: of him in the office, of Trilling's words—"not MIT material." Remembering how small he felt sitting there, how he tried to heave up some explanation of all he'd been through, a word starts crowding into the passing images and he tries to press it down—it's not right—but he can't.

With his eyes still closed, Cedric yells, "RACIST!"

The door stays locked as the hours pass and night falls. Isa comes by and knocks on the door. And later, Jenica. They call out, wondering if he's inside, and he holds his breath until he eventually hears their footsteps fade away in the hall.

The next morning, he walks into physics class just as it starts, slips into a front-row desk by the door, and looks forward at the blackboard, not following any of what's being scribbled. A moment later, he feels a tap on his arm. It's Isa, a row behind him, passing him a note at hip level, her eyes fixed on the teacher.

He opens it: "What happened?"

He writes a note back describing the meeting and saying he's thinking of leaving, of just going home. Washington hands out a worksheet, and Cedric gazes at it, unable to concentrate. Twenty minutes later, the note comes back. He opens it and looks down at the bottom. It's also signed by Jenica, who's sitting to Isa's left. "You can't just run away," the note says. "You have to stay and prove to them you have what it takes. . . . We all care about you and love you." Cedric reads the note twice. He's afraid he's going to start bawling, right here in class, and swallows hard a few times. He folds the note gently and puts it in his hip pocket.

The hour's about to end. The worksheet lies on the desk, barely touched. Cedric takes his pencil and, pressing hard, scrawls "I AM LOST" across the sheet as class is dismissed. He drops it on the teacher's desk and rushes quickly toward the door and through the crowd.

Jenica runs to catch up with him, to commiserate. But it would be difficult for her, or most of the kids here, to know what to say. She had a meeting with Professor Trilling a few appointment slots after Cedric. He encouraged her to apply to MIT. She shrugged off the invitation. "Actually," she told him, "I was planning to go to Stanford."

On a sweltering day in late August, all three air conditioners are blasting in the apartment on V Street. Cedric sits on his bed, piled high with clothes. The suitcase on the floor has yet to be unpacked, even though he returned home from Cambridge three weeks ago.

He thinks a lot about MIT, grouping scenes in clusters, running through them from different angles. The last days of the program were fitful. He didn't go to the final banquet, where awards were presented, because he didn't want to see Professor Trilling again. But, on the last morning, as vans were loaded for trips to the airport, his whole gang got up at 6:30 to see him off. Ramsey, standing alongside the van, handed him an envelope with the certificate saying he'd completed the program and warmly wished him luck.

It felt funny coming home—like he'd been away for a year—and he was surprised that he actually felt sort of happy, or maybe just relieved, to get back to this rutted street, with its abandoned cars and people making noise all night.

Since returning from New England, he has spent almost every day either at church or just knocking around the apartment while his mom is at work. There's stuff to do. Barbara brought him a scholarship book from her office. It's full of application request forms and addresses. She's been on him, so he's been sending off some letters, half-heartedly.

Then there's Torrence, who has been joined in his passion for Islam by Cedric's first cousin, Aisha. Mostly, Cedric just listens and doesn't argue with him, figuring that Torrence will think that silence means agreement and just lay off a little.

It's near the end of the month—a while before next month's rent has to be paid—and last night he and Barbara had a nice chicken dinner. Thinking about it, Cedric gets up from his bed and goes to the refrigerator. He pulls out the carcass—plenty of meat still left—and sits down with it at the dining room table. He thinks back on what his mom was saying over dinner—sounded like she'd rehearsed it—telling him he has to stop sleeping so much and start thinking about what he's going to do next about school.

There have been some scholarship offers from private schools, including Phillips Exeter in Exeter, New Hampshire, and St. Albans, the exclusive Episcopal boys school in Northwest D.C. Barbara, having done some research, told him that "it's something a lot of kids from not such great high schools sometimes do. They go to a place like that for their senior year, and maybe even another year after that, then they end up doing real well at the best colleges."

Cedric just shrugged. They are both schools with lots of rich kids, almost all of them white, and you have to wear a coat and tie. As he got up to bus their plates, he told her he'd think about it but she looked at him like she knew he'd already made up his mind.

Sitting there, picking at the chicken, he remembers that he had the bad dream again last night. He's actually had it a couple of times in the past few weeks. It's always the same: he's thrown himself into a deep gulch. All alone at the bottom, he shouts for help. The bluff up ahead is too steep to climb, the safe, grassy ledge impossibly high. He turns around, toward the cliff behind him, his jump-off point, and yells for someone to save him. There is never an answer by the time he awakens.

He rises, puts the carcass back in the refrigerator, washes the grease from his hands in the kitchen sink, and returns to his bedroom. Face down on the floor, half covered by a large white sock, is a ten-page letter from MIT that came about a week ago. It is his final evaluation for each subject: evaluations that turned out better than he—and perhaps even Professor Trilling—had figured. He showed improvement up until the very last day.

Cedric steps over the letter on his way to lie down, not bothering to pick it up. He can't chew over the whole MIT thing again. The summer left him feeling battered. It was weird up in Cambridge, meeting black kids who were so much different from him left him confused about what being black means. He struggled to keep up and didn't quite make it. Still, after a while, he sort of felt like he belonged with them, that strange crowd of smart, secure, casually confident blacks. Sort of, but not really. Maybe just not yet. Maybe not ever. Before he went, it seemed like he was infused with hopefulness, that he had a plan: he'd go to MIT for the summer program, then, in the fall, he'd apply to some top colleges—MIT included—and it might all work out. But it's a lot harder to imagine all that now. He's not even sure, at this point, if he even belongs at some top college. For what? To have this summer replicated for four years? He rubs his eyes and sits up, quickly, shaking his head. Every time he goes down that path, trying to figure out where he belongs, it feels like he's coming apart. He just can't stress about it.

He hears a police siren approaching and, by reflex, rushes over to the window. He parts the venetian blinds and watches it pass, the blare muffled by the whir of the air-conditioning. He thinks again about his mom's look last night—a look of resignation, like she knew he'd already made up his mind about what to do next.

Then, suddenly, he smiles, a funny grim smile with his lips tight together. Of course he's decided. He's going back to Ballou. All he has to do is to talk himself through it. The scenes instantly take shape in his mind—the graffiti in the hallways, Mr. Taylor's classroom, the bus stop on Martin Luther King. At least at Ballou, he knows where he stands. Not much of a place, but at least it's his. And maybe being back there will help him get his bearings back, give him something to push against. People are comfortable with what they know, and, in an odd way, he feels sort of comfortable there, at his miserable old school.

"Comfortable," Cedric Jennings whispers in disbelief through the dusty white blinds. "Comfortable in this place that I hate."

5

TO HIM
WHO ENDURETH

On a crisp autumn morning in late September, Cedric rises with a secret purpose in mind and gingerly opens the bedroom door to poke out his head. All quiet. His mother said she'd be leaving early for work this morning, and she's already gone.

After a quick shower, he's back in his room, prowling through the closet. A new uniform is swiftly assembled, and he appraises himself in the full-length mirror behind his closet door: a plain white polo shirt and black Dockers pants—if not exactly baggy ghetto chic, at least comfortably loose. Rather than his usual black, felt-covered bucks, to-day he opts for a pair of white Nikes.

Then he plunges his long arm through clinking wire hangers and suits that no longer fit, until his hand touches leather. He jerks out a double-breasted black leather jacket with a longish cut. Cedric pressured his mom into buying it for him last Christmas, and she immediately regretted it. It wasn't just that she couldn't afford it. She worried that on V Street and at Ballou, kids are sometimes killed over leather jackets. She knew of mothers who had lost their sons over clothing of lesser quality. Almost every time Cedric has donned the jacket, she has managed to block his path out the door. He strokes the leather, which still smells fresh, and slips it on, turning up the collar, disapproving, and turning it back down. Finally, the coup de grâce: a jaunty "apple cap," a pinwheel of black leather with a tiny stem in the center. He pulls it down, cocks it a little to one side, and looks at himself approvingly, pushing out his hairless chin.

Forty minutes later, he saunters into Ballou's cafeteria, doing a sort of hitch-stepped "pimp roll." Kids are hanging out at the long tables, killing time before homeroom, a few doing homework, some drinking juice from a free federal breakfast program. Cedric slides to a small table, his face squeezed into a glower.

The new principal, Dr. Kenneth Jones, approaches. When Mr. Washington retired as principal in the spring, exhausted and frustrated, he was replaced by the more diplomatic Dr. Jones, formerly head of an adult education program at another D.C. high school. A tall, light-skinned man with generic good looks, Jones was quick to learn that Cedric is a star student.

"Cedric, what are you doing? Take off that hat," he says. "You know hats aren't allowed indoors."

It's a well-known rule. Hats, sometimes used to identify crew membership, are piled in a corner of the principal's office, even though most kids can identify who belongs to what crew without sartorial cues.

Cedric stares back at Dr. Jones, wondering what a person in a fine leather jacket and jaunty cap—clearly a player—might respond to such a command. He auditions a new rap. "No way, Dr. Jones, this hat is phat."

Dr. Jones arches a brow, perplexed. He plucks off the leather lid and drops it in Cedric's lap. What's a player to do, Cedric thinks, looking down at his fine lid? The only response, in this context, is to escalate—to not give in, not ever. So, as Dr. Jones turns and walks away, Cedric quickly puts the cap back on. He knows it's the sort of in-your-face behavior that will merit serious punishment—detention, certainly, and maybe suspension—if Dr. Jones, now just a few feet away, happens to turn. A brazen act of defiance? A black-leather hip-hop get-up? From Cedric Jennings?

On this sunny morning, what saves Cedric is a fight that breaks out on the far side of the cafeteria. Dr. Jones, just as he begins to look back in Cedric's direction, must sprint across the wide room to break it up.

Cedric, sitting like a mannequin, breathes a small sigh of relief. This rebellious posture, he thinks, feels all right, but thank God he didn't get caught.

Across from him at the narrow table, James Davis lifts his nose from calculus homework to watch, visibly bemused, the spectacle of Cedric trying to look "baaaad." James is a familiar high school type: the popular scholar-athlete who steadily goes about the business of getting good grades, playing football, and avoiding trouble. His brand of modest well-roundedness is plentiful in most high schools but in short supply at Ballou, where most boys face Phillip Atkin's choice: *either* social acceptance *or* academic achievement.

If, to some degree, James is allowed to have it both ways, it may be because he's 220 pounds of muscle, and crew members, who tend to enforce the school's social order, are friendly with his equally imposing twin, Jack, who sometimes runs with them. Basically, the tough kids have given James a bye.

Up to a point. A few weeks ago in physics, James told Cedric that he's hoping for a college football scholarship rather than notice of his academics. He and James have discussed this before. James understands that to get an academic scholarship from a barren school like Ballou you have to be as blazing and conspicuous as Cedric—all A's, dense extracurriculars, special programs, behavior that makes even James a target. He and Cedric understand each other's choices. Which is why Cedric, trying to look tough, can't maintain his composure in a stare fight with James for more than a few seconds. Both of them descend into big, howling laughs. James reaches out his python arm, takes the hat gently off Cedric's head, and lays it on the table.

"Boy, keep that hat off," he says, sounding almost rueful. "You don't need to be doing all that. You're supposed to be a role model. You're fine, just the way you are."

A smile crosses Cedric's face—the first real smile in a month. Didn't know it until now, he thinks, but that's something he's wanted to hear since ninth grade.

"All right . . . forget the hat, but I'm keeping the jacket on," Cedric says with a self-deprecating chuckle before sliding around to help James with calculus.

After morning homeroom, Cedric stops by his locker. The river of kids flowing through the halls crowds close to him, but he doesn't pay any mind. He puts the books he's carrying on the floor, opens the locker, and slips off the jacket, with the apple cap now tucked in the pocket. He strokes the leather collar once, intently, before hanging it on the hook. And, a moment later, he's surprised to feel relieved as the metal door slams shut.

At the start of this afternoon's college prep class, a kid whom Cedric thought was pretty tough sort of blushes as he hands in a rough-hewn personal essay. Near the back wall, a few boisterous and obnoxious kids grow quiet, flipping through the glossy applications book. Every time this class meets, Cedric is surprised by this silence, like a spell has come over everybody.

In some ways, this class—the senior year's complement to junior year's SAT-PREP—is the cruelest offered at Ballou. Many kids take it, spending a casual hour each day leafing through books listing colleges and scholarships and filling out applications, even though few are actually college bound. Many of them won't even graduate from Ballou, but it's hard, still, not to be curious about what might have been.

For Cedric, application books are both irresistible and excruciating. In this first, confusing month back at Ballou, he's been experimenting with resignation. It's been a week since he put away the leather jacket. Now, though, he's assessing a fallback position: at best, he'll end up going to a middle-rung college.

He can manage to retain that idea as he goes through the motions in most of his classes. Then he comes into this room. He gets up and retrieves the phone-book-sized *Barron's College Guide* from the resource table and flips pages, starting from the back. What happens every day he's in here happens again: he stops at Yale, then Stanford, Princeton, and MIT. He has read each description many times already, but he reads them again, trying to find some opening—some avenue for entry—that he might have missed. Invariably, he ends up staring at the nose-bleed average SAT scores of applicants. He looks up from the book and thinks of Rev. Keels, a science teacher who offers informal tutoring to athletes trying to raise their SAT scores and is lately in Cedric's face about his dismal 910. In a hallway encounter earlier today, Keels told Cedric his score "won't rate," that "top schools, Ivy League schools, don't care about your grades if your test scores are sub par."

Keels offered to give Cedric some pointers before he takes the SATs again in early October, but Cedric refused.

He hates Keels, who's always talking about how many great students there were at Ballou in the early 1980s, and he imagines himself beating the man to a pulp—right there in the hall. After indulging this idea for a bit, he recalls, vaguely, that last year Keels mentioned a Ballou student from way back—some athlete he tutored at least a decade ago—who got into Brown University.

He's heard a bit about Brown over the years. He flips past Cornell, Columbia, and Carleton College to the B's. There it is: Brown University, Providence, Rhode Island. He reads the synopsis. It's top drawer all right—strong on math and science. With a 22 percent acceptance rate, it's less competitive than Harvard and slightly more competitive than Yale. But the curriculum looks uniquely loose and fluid. Taking classes pass/fail is encouraged. It's still tops, still Ivy League, but it seems like you can go at your own speed.

He checks the numbers. Average SAT score of 1290. His 910 puts him nearly 400 points shy, but maybe a last try on the test in a few weeks will bring the score up. He fills out a request letter for materials for Brown, and—on a whim—decides to send requests to Duke University and Dartmouth College as well and drops the envelopes on the teacher's desk at the end of class.

A few weeks later, sitting in the same classroom, he stares at a pile of application forms, trying to muster the optimism he'll need to fill out each one convincingly. He took the SATs again on October 8 and is waiting for the new scores. Who knows? It felt a little better this time, but not much. He flips open one application, then another. Each asks of him the same untenable thing: to distill himself into neat categories like GPA, SAT score, extracurricular activities, and favorite subjects.

He looks at the Duke application. Then at Dartmouth. Each asks for a personal essay. Here's one area where he can explain why he's different. He poises his pen over a blank sheet of notebook paper and searches for inspiration, running over old sayings and homilies, memories of awards he's won and names of memorable teachers.

He can't seem to find much in those old memories for an essay, and he puts down his pen. He wonders how hard it must be for most kids here to flip through the glossy books. Looking across the desks, now mostly vacated by classmates who don't bother coming to this class anymore, he feels a funny chill, though the room is toasty warm. He turns his gaze out the window, and the applications lie untouched.

When the SAT scores finally arrive in early November, they're nothing to cheer about. His math score went up to 580, an improvement of 50 points over the spring, probably due to his summertime rigors at MIT. The verbal scores, however, dropped to a bleak 330. Thankfully, the Educational Testing Service lets you combine your best math and verbal scores, mixing Cedric's 580 math from this time and the 380 verbal from last time to total 960. He's up a bit from 910, but still way short of what he thinks he'll need for almost any of the top schools.

All the applications are put in a drawer except one: Brown. Cedric has read more about the college, picking through every college guide he can find. Brown's math department is particularly strong for a school so widely known for liberal arts. And there seems to be a lot of minorities there. And he read in one of the guides that nearly one-third of Brown students are nonwhite.

Sitting one cloudy afternoon near mid-November in Mr. Taylor's room, a word takes shape: *accepting,* a close relative to the unspeakable *acceptance.* He tries it out: "Mr. Taylor, Brown is Ivy league, real esteemed, but seems more *accepting* of different types of people."

Mr. Taylor, looking over his shoulder as he wipes down the blackboard, seems to genuinely agree. "Yes, Cedric, they seem to be more, well, accepting of diversity," he says absently.

A few nights later, Cedric enters the apartment, eats a quick dinner of Oodles of Noodles, and goes to his room. Though his mother is at Tuesday night prayer meeting, he still closes his door, committing himself to the room for as long as it takes.

He changes into gym shorts and a T-shirt and sits at the desk. Most of the Brown application is filled out, and it looks fine: plenty of awards and extracurricular activities—student tutoring, class treasurer (no one else ran)—and all of his special mentoring programs. His grades are perfect, his recommendations from Mr. Taylor and Ms. Nelson must be good. Of course, almost everyone applying to Brown has that stuff, along with stratospheric SATs.

He looks down at the application's blank personal essay page for a few minutes before grabbing his pen and pulling out two pieces of notebook paper to try a draft.

"When people come in contact with me," he begins writing, "I want them to see that Godly love. I am very religious, and I know that the only reason I have achieved so much is because I continued to put God first in everything that I do.

"It is He who brought me through many situations in my life that could have been my downfall. I could have dropped out of school or gotten into all kinds of trouble. But with the Lord in my life, I realize He has a greater work for me to do."

He pauses and then writes about how "being a black male in a single parent home is sometimes tough without that male figure to help in the growing process. But I thank God for my loving mother. I even see some of my peers that have a mother and father, but are heading in the wrong direction. Some of them are into drug-dealing and others try to be 'cool' by not doing good in school and not going to classes. But my mother has instilled so many positive values in me it would be hard to even try to get on the wrong track.

"The most important thing that she's taught is that being a man comes from the heart and mind, and a real man can accept responsibility and can take care of himself.

"I realize that I used to be into grades and test scores and awards, but if I strip myself of all of these things and look at myself in the mirror, can I honestly say that I know who I am and where I am going. Getting straight A's, having 1400 on the SATs, and getting a lot of awards is great. But if these things are the only things that can say good things about me, as a person, then there's a problem. I would need to reevaluate myself. Because if I can't interact with people and be able to deal with different personalities, all of these things are futile.

"Yes, success depends on how hard one works. But individual advancement and continuous progression depend on one's ability to deal with different people."

He surveys the essay and rereads it a few times. He decides he needs to make them understand just how much he wants this to happen, to be accepted, and he writes, "I am a very focused and determined person. I yearn for knowledge and I am not afraid to say 'I don't understand.' These character traits have served me well. Thinking positively and holding my head 'up to the heavens,' is something I take great pride in doing."

He fusses over some words and then it's just fine. It's taken an hour. He copies it onto the blank page of the Brown application form.

Then he signs it, paper-clips on the $50 check that his mother gave him a few days ago, along with a picture he took in September at a mall photo booth, and slides it all into the large envelope.

It has been a long, confusing fall, with his senior year already nearing the midway point. Last summer, when he arrived at MIT, he felt he could almost taste how sweet it would be to make it to a renowned college—like he was practically there!—but what remains is an aftertaste of how far he still has to journey, how improbable it is that he'll ever get there.

While that dose of sobering sophistication has slowed his step, the last few months walking the halls of Ballou have slowly restored some of his old balance. That strange morning with James Davis; the sour words of Rev. Keels about how he was unworthy of acceptance; the faces of kids in College Prep, which turn grim right before they disappear from class.

He leans back in his chair—the apartment now so quiet he can hear the clicks of the electric radiators—and peers through a slit in the plastic miniblinds. After the unsettling summer, he thought the familiar terrain of school would offer some respite and maybe solace to his bruised ego. Now he realizes he's not comfortable at Ballou either. Or anywhere, really, he thinks, looking down on the flat, tar paper roofs of V Street.

He turns back to the desk and looks down for a while at the light brown envelope. He can't imagine being comfortable up ahead either, not at one of the truly competitive colleges. He knows now that getting accepted at one of those places is a pipe dream, though they still glitter with possibility and promise.

He licks the envelope and seals it. So this will be his gamble—an early application to Brown. It has to be postmarked by tomorrow, November 15, and he'll hear back in a couple of weeks. If he's rejected, that will be that. He'll have time to figure out what's next, maybe apply to some no-name school or something. The thought makes him gag. If he hadn't worked so hard and endured so much to push himself ahead—little by little, year after year—it might be easier to swallow a compromise. But he can't. He just can't. Dreaming of great universities was the only thing that could get him through the halls of that miserable school.

He studies the maroon Brown University seal in the envelope's corner and loses track of time. He thinks of people at church, old men and thick-hipped single moms who get up on the pulpit, give their last $100 to Bishop Long, and then pray that they'll get a house of their own. That if they're pure in faith, God will give it to them. No reason to believe they'll get a house, but sometimes they do. Yeah, sometimes they do.

He puts his hands on the envelope, stretching his fingers to cover its edges. "God, this is where I want to be," he whispers, self-conscious about speaking too loudly all alone in his room. But as he continues, his voice grows stronger. "I worked so hard. I deserve it. Yes, I believe this is it. This is the place I want to be. Bless me, Lord. Let your will be done. If this is where I'm supposed to be, let your will be done."

It's already midmorning when Barbara Jennings lifts her head from a propped couch cushion and checks her wristwatch on the magazine table.

She doesn't often take a day off—not as often as some of the ladies in her office—but after twenty-three years in office support jobs with the federal government, she figures doing it once in a while won't kill anyone.

She walks into Cedric's room and thinks back to a Tuesday night about a month ago when he bounded out of the room to greet her from church—something he hadn't done, it seems, in a long while—

exclaiming that he'd just completed his essay for Brown. He didn't give it to her to read, and she, feeling self-conscious about her lack of schooling, didn't ask.

The next morning, though, he told her he had prayed over the envelope and that he was certain he'd get in. She recalls how she laughed, nodding her encouragement about the power of "God's will" but warning him to "keep your dreams to yourself—no need to be telling everyone."

So what does he do that very day?! Tells half the school that he's "just about certain"—those were the very words he used recounting it for her at dinner that night—"just about certain I got into Brown." Eyebrows rose all over Ballou.

She hasn't thought much about Brown since then, but being in the room brings it all to mind. Though it's a long shot, he might just get into one of those fancy schools, she supposes, and this room will be empty for good.

Barbara sits down on the squeaky bed and looks around, thinking that it's odd that she and Cedric are already at this point in their journey, that all of a sudden it seems to have gone by quickly. Maybe, she figures, it's because the feeling she has today—of staying behind while the bustling world squeezes into buses and subways and crowded offices—is the same sensation she recalls from a time fifteen years ago when she suddenly quit her GAO job to go on welfare and stay home with her little boy. Like today, she remembers, it was so quiet at home, just the two of them with the whole day to themselves, and she was so sure of what she had to do: teach him everything, make him laugh, make him feel that he was safe and watched over.

This instant, it feels like all of it was just so he could leave her now. She shakes her head, thinking how things were so clear and simple back then. Resting her hands on her thighs, she pushes herself up from sitting and crunches over papers as she leaves Cedric's room.

In the evening Cedric meets her at church and, as he's been doing for the last year or two of his adolescence, sits in a distant pew. Bishop Long is angry tonight, angry at people "who profess to love God and speak the Word but don't live the deed." He challenges parishioners who "don't want to be here and don't want to live according to the word of God" to "just leave—go on, leave!" No one budges. He does this every few months, firing up his fury at his flock's godless ways. They have indulged in activities he forbids—like smoking, drinking, and having premarital sex, along with a host of less potent pursuits, like going to movies. Confident that she ranks high on the pyramid of righteous living, Barbara lets herself look across the packed rows for guilty faces as Long runs through his litany of don'ts.

She stands on tiptoes, trying to catch a glimpse of Cedric far across the cavernous sanctuary. She finally spots his face and sees he is placid, showing no sign of rejoice or remorse. She knows that Bishop's message is no longer sinking in as deeply as it once did. But it's already in Cedric—the Holy Spirit, the Word—and it will guide him wherever he goes. At least that's what she hopes.

She and Cedric get a ride home with a church member who lives nearby in Southeast and end up arriving at their apartment building near midnight, both of them bone tired.

Barbara opens the lobby mailbox with her thumbnail key and pulls out a fistful of envelopes and catalogues.

Suddenly, she spins. "I'm not giving it to you," she teases, holding the creamy-white envelope up high and away from him. "I'm just going to throw it away."

"Hey, give it to me—I'm not playing," Cedric cries, lunging around her for it.

He takes it in his hands. "It's thick. I think that means I got in," he says, having at least learned that trick from some friends at MIT.

He neatly tears it open and unfolds a multicolored packet with a white letter on top. He reads it aloud: "I hope you are as pleased to get this letter as I am to send it to you. You have been admitted to the 232nd class to enter The College of Brown University."

Cedric shakes his head. "I told you I'd get in," he says, but looking dreamy, like he's witnessed a miracle.

"Still and all, it sure is nice to see," she says, beaming. They walk up the stairs in silence, Barbara unable to find words that are adequate to the moment.

"Gaawwd, am I glad that's over with," Cedric says finally as he enters the apartment.

Barbara goes to the kitchen to see if there's any ginger ale left, and maybe some crackers, while Cedric slumps over on the couch and reads the letter again. Next thing, she feels him peck her on the cheek.

"Whatchyou doing, Lavar?" she says, spinning around, startled.

"Ma . . . ummm . . . thanks," he whispers.

She gently cups his cheek in the palm of her hand, knowing there's nothing she needs to say.

"You know," he says after a moment, "I'm kind of tired. I think I'll turn in," and he shoots her a smile as he turns for the hallway.

"Yeah, me too," she says, though she feels like she could stay up half the night. And she does, sitting on the couch in the TV's glow as her mind wanders far forward on a freshly cut path that now seems to pass through Providence, Rhode Island.

Even though Cedric has finally received the golden acceptance, Barbara and he—almost by reflex—keep to their rituals as though nothing has occurred. Barbara, for one, has been going to PTA meetings for a dozen years. Never missed one, even during the worst times, and she isn't about to miss one now.

So, one night in mid-January, she dresses carefully—as always, mindful of making a good impression at school—and leaves for a meeting of Ballou's PTSA (the S added a few years ago to make students feel welcome). Tonight's meeting is a sparsely attended affair. About twenty-five parents gather in the auditorium's first three rows as PTSA president James Bunn, who operates a tax preparation storefront in Southeast, speaks to the group about "the crisis of parental involvement . . . we're talking about the lives of our children."

Barbara, resplendent in a flowing maroon-and-gold sleeveless dress with African designs on top of a white double-knit T-shirt, looks over her shoulder at the rising slope of empty seats behind her. She has been stirred by such speeches in countless half-filled auditoriums and cafeterias through the years, and it feels strange to her to be able to tune it out. On the way into school tonight, she bumped into one of Cedric's former teachers—sophomore class, she thinks—who congratulated her on his getting into Brown, and then an administrator who did the same. Everyone knows that Cedric has received the coveted acceptance letter. Cedric said he wasn't surprised but acted like it was a letter straight from God. Made twenty copies to pass out the day after he got it.

Twenty copies!? That boy, she thinks, is so outgoing sometimes, so *out there*—not quiet, like her. She looks at him in the seat next to her, admiringly, and then motions for him to stop tapping his foot, that it's driving her crazy. Cedric told her yesterday that he wanted to come tonight to see his grades for the advisory, that he must see them "the moment they're available, or I'll just die." Grade sheets are passed to parents on PTSA night as a prop to build attendance and because, otherwise, many report cards wouldn't make it into the hands of any parent—with shrewd kids knowing when and how to intercept a key piece of unopened mail.

After the PTSA president finishes, everyone wanders from the auditorium to designated homerooms. Barbara follows Cedric upstairs to the second-floor classroom of Ms. Wingfield, a quiet black woman who has been Cedric's homeroom teacher since ninth grade. She lights up when she sees Barbara, clasping both her hands in congratulations. "You've won a great victory, Ms. Jennings," she says.

A moment later, Ms. Wingfield passes out the grade sheets. Cedric grabs it from Barbara's hand and gasps. "I got a B in physics! I can't believe it."

He begins ranting about the cheating in his class, about how he thinks a lot of other kids cheated on the main exam for this advisory. Barbara remembers that he mentioned something about this a week ago—but she dismissed the whole matter.

Squeezed into a school desk next to him, she wants to tell Cedric that it doesn't matter. None of it. Some small hubbub about cheating and grades is meaningless now that he's been admitted to Brown, the top college acceptance of any Ballou student in years.

But, of course, he knows all that, too. And the more dismissive her look, the more rabid he becomes. Then she gets it: it's about her watching over him, defending him, always being there. ". . . I mean, what are *we* going to do?!" he shouts at the end of his furious soliloquy about what's right and fair and just.

She's up. "Well, Lavar, we'll just have to go have a word with that teacher." A second later, they're stomping together through the halls, headed for the physics classroom of an unsuspecting Mr. Momen. They find that he is alone. He turns and offers greetings as they enter, but Cedric launches right in—the whole diatribe, offered with added verve from his rehearsal with his mom.

Mr. Momen, a wry, sometimes sarcastic man in his mid-forties, mournfully shakes his head, a helmet of gray-flecked hair. "Cedric, you got a B for the marking period," he says in precise, accented English. "The test for you is irrefutable. The curve says yours is a B, and that, for you, is a B for the marking period. So, okay. That's it, yes?"

"But kids are cheating! You leave the room and they open the book. Lots of them. You don't know what goes on. You shouldn't leave the room, that's when it starts. It ends up that I get penalized 'cause I won't cheat."

"Cedric, stop. I can't, myself, just accuse all of them of cheating," says Mr. Momen, shrugging.

Barbara watches the give-and-take, realizing that the teacher has artfully shoved Cedric into a rhetorical corner by placing her son's single voice against the silent majority—his word against theirs.

Years of practice at this have taught her much: choose your words meticulously and then let them rumble up from some deep furnace of conviction. "My son doesn't lie," she says, like an oracle, "not about something like this."

The silent majority vanishes. She stands, straight and motionless, a block of granite. Momen looks back at her, eye to eye. Soon, the silence becomes unbearable. He's forced to move. "I guess he could take a retest I make for him," he says haltingly. "It will be a hard test, though, that I will make for you, Cedric."

"Fine," says Barbara, closing the deal. "Thank you, Mr. Momen. We can go now," she says. Once they're in the hallway, she whispers to Cedric, "You *will* be getting an A on that test, Lavar. You understand?" She doesn't expect an answer.

After a week of ferocious study, Cedric does get his A on the special test—scoring 100—and an A for the marking period. He brings home the paper and lays it on the dining room table, like a prize, a trophy.

Barbara looks at it for a moment. "On the next stop, you know you'll be on your own. I won't be there to come to the rescue," she says, feeling as though a clause of their partnership has expired.

"Well, then," he says a little tersely, tapping the paper once with his index finger, "I guess this paper is sort of your diploma."

By the end of February, she can already feel him moving ahead, his eyes now locked on Brown. Sure, he asks her about this and that, but she finds she hasn't much to say. She's learning, day by day, just how little guidance she can offer for that journey. When he comes home one night in early March and asks if LaTisha is right in worrying that Cedric may lose his identity at Brown, Barbara shakes her head non-committally. She roots through some well-worn references—a little New Testament, a little self-help. She has no idea what a large, distant, mostly white university looks like, what sort of challenges Cedric may face "up there."

"As long as you're a whole person," she says finally, paraphrasing something Bishop Long once said, "you have nothing to worry about. You'll always be sure of who you are."

He looks at her, clearly unconvinced, rises from his chair with an exasperated "Whateveeeeer," and retreats toward his room.

Barbara Jennings sits in the straight-backed dining room chair, completely still—wondering if she just got her first glimpse of the future—and listens for his door to click shut.

Cedric steps onto a courtyard of white marble and looks way up. He reads the phrase "Equal Justice Under Law" and tries to make out the characters carved just above it, a row of squatting, deliberating white men from some period of antiquity or other—Greek, maybe, he thinks—but muscular, like black men.

He clutches his spiral notebook and looks around, suddenly self-conscious. He heads for the entrance, feeling smaller with each step up the vast marble staircase of the U.S. Supreme Court.

Near the top step, he has to veer around a cluster of high-school-age kids who are listening to a tour guide. Cedric, living just two miles away, has never been here. No class trips. No family visits. No reason to come. Until now.

He walks inside the court's six-ton bronze doors to the metal detector. "I'm here to see Clarence Thomas," he says tentatively.

"Do you have an appointment?" a black security guard asks, firm but curious.

"Yes, yessir, I do," Cedric says, standing to his full five-foot-ten, having picked up a few inches this year. "I mean," he shrugs, "I think he's expecting me."

Now, three years after his blistering confirmation battle in 1991, the justice is firmly established as Washington's most famous recluse. The hearings left Thomas dazed and stumbling into an afterlife of bizarre duality: as both the most powerful black man in America and a walking, grimacing Rorschach on wrenching issues of race and gender. His uniform response, for years now, has been to withdraw, to shun media inquiries and most invitations for social events and speaking engagements.

There is, though, one quiet act of outreach: he meets periodically with promising black students from the area—generally, poor kids with good grades—to mentor and guide them. In a profile in the *Washington Post* around the time of Cedric's visit, a longtime Thomas aide said that visiting with young people "helps him heal."

Last year, Cedric was featured in a story in the *Wall Street Journal* about kids at Ballou High School that was read by Justice Thomas, who put him on his visitation list. Though months of phone messages and rescheduled appointments pushed this meeting to mid-March, it is occurring at a time when Cedric—by virtue of the natural rhythms of his final springtime of high school—feels a particular need for advice, counsel from someone, anyone, who can offer insight about where he is bound.

Standing on the other side of the metal detector, Cedric is directed to the Supreme Court marshall's office, where one of Thomas's assistants is called to escort him to the justice's chambers.

"Are you Cedric Jennings?" comes a voice from the doorway a few minutes later. Cedric spins. A smallish black man in his mid-twenties is smiling at him. "Hi, I'm Justice Thomas's assistant. I'll be escorting you. My name's Wayne Graham, like the cracker."

Cedric nods and off they go, as Wayne explains that the justice is finishing some work and he'll be delayed a few minutes.

As they walk, everything Cedric sees looks outsized and incredibly white. He has rarely felt so conspicuously black. Maybe it's something about the marble, he thinks, as they move through the Great Hall, a sort of grand corridor leading to the court's majestic courtroom. They walk past shimmering marble busts of dead chief justices—a grumpy Charles Evans Hughes, a stately John Marshall, a sweetly dopey William Howard Taft—under a marble ceiling that's got to be eighty feet up. The only shades, here, seem to be shades of white, Cedric muses, like it must be in heaven.

Wayne makes small talk as they tour and buys Cedric a ham sandwich in the first-floor cafeteria before delivering him to the second-floor offices marked simply "Justice Thomas."

In here, everything changes. It feels cozy and warm. The walls are oak. The two Thomas assistants who smile at him as he enters are black women, both sitting at desks in the reception area under large, colorful paintings of black workers in the rural south. A few handsome young white guys in their middle or late twenties walk through the reception area and smile at him.

Cedric's eyes are drawn straight ahead to a large painting of slaves—or maybe just poor blacks—in a field picking cotton and loading bales onto a horse-drawn wagon.

At the secretary's behest, he sits at a small mahogany desk and chair ensemble near the door, a desk crammed with potted plants and odd Lucite signs on mini-easels. He notices they're all over the office—little inspirational billboards: "There is no limit to what you can do or where you can go, if you don't mind who gets the credit" says one; "To avoid criticism do nothing, say nothing, be nothing," says another. He squints to read what's across the room on the credenza: "He who will not listen to reason is a bigot, he who cannot is a fool, he who dares not is a slave." He bends forward and around to read one he missed, right next to him on the desk: "No word spoken here is ever repeated outside these walls."

Nothing inspirational about that one, Cedric thinks, as he sits back.

The paranoid, monstrous Thomas of the public's imagination comes into view. Words and images that have been bumping around in Cedric's head for weeks—ever since this meeting date was set—come rushing in, one after another—the justice sitting at the Senate hearing table; Coke cans and pubic hairs; Long Dong Silver; "high-tech lynching"; and then Anita Hill's angelic face, cool under fire. He feels his gut tighten. Cedric wonders if he should ask Thomas about Anita Hill. He'd love to, in a way, just ask him, straight out, What went on there? But he dismisses that notion quickly as Thomas's angry face seems to float before him.

A moment later, that image is replaced. "Glad you could come, Cedric," says Justice Clarence Thomas, reaching out a thick, hammy hand. Cedric smiles dumbly, holds out his fingers, and is jerked to consciousness by the justice's crushing grip. He's led through an airlock of huge oak doors that lead to Thomas's chambers and onto a large, blue leather couch. Thomas pulls up a chair for himself. Cedric can't take his eyes off him. The guy is huge—only about five-foot-nine but wide and stacked like a pro football player, his biceps straining the fabric of his white dress shirt.

Thomas begins talking about the *Journal* story, about how he sees and mentors a lot of young people and then about some program he helps run—the Horatio Alger Society—that supports top black students with scholarships. "You know, that might be something for you to get involved with, Cedric."

Sunk deep in the couch, Cedric feels like ocean waves are crashing in his ears. He nods, telling Thomas he'll get involved "for sure. That'd be great."

The justice leans forward in his chair and looks intently at Cedric, clearly able to see the film across the youngster's eyes. "You know, Cedric," he says softly, "I sense that you and I are a lot alike. I have a sense of what you've been through."

Hearing those words, Cedric seems to calm. He meets Thomas's gaze and smiles, feeling his face muscles loosen. "This is quite an office," Cedric says as his eyes wander from the paintings of Booker T. Washington and Frederick Douglass to a picture on the mantel of a young man about his own age, who must be Thomas's son, and then to a foot-high religious statuette on the end table near Cedric's right hand.

"That's St. Jude," Thomas says. "You know what he's the saint of?"

Cedric, unaware of Catholic dogma, shrugs, though he's happy to feel the conversation land on the terra firma of religion.

"Causes beyond hope," Thomas says. "Hope for the hopeless."

"I know something about that," Cedric says, proud to get off a quick quip. Thomas heartily laughs, scrunching his nose in a way that makes him look boyish.

Staring at the statue, he begins reminiscing, telling Cedric how he won it for placing first in the annual Latin Bee at a nearly all white high school—a Catholic boarding school—that he attended in Savannah in the mid-1960s.

"After I won it, I put it on my bureau in the big, open dorm room where we all slept. A few days later, I looked over and saw the head was broken off, lying there right next to the body on my bureau where I'd be sure to see it. I glued it back on. After another few days, it happened again. So I got more glue—put it on real thick—and fixed it again. Whoever was breaking it must have gotten the message: I'd keep gluing it forever if I needed to. I wasn't giving up."

Cedric looks again at the statue—its neck jagged and chipped—and then back at Thomas, trying to imagine what this imposing man, now in his late forties, looked like at sixteen. The dark images of Clarence Thomas are now easy to discard. Instead, Cedric sees a solitary Supreme Court justice who still remembers slights from three decades ago. That broken statue is the same sort of cheap shot that is slung at Cedric each day, he muses, and here this guy has managed to get pretty far despite all the naysayers. Cedric wonders, though, how many of the indignities he's suffered at Ballou he'll still carry with him a decade or two from now.

"Sounds like you had to fight every step of the way," Cedric says, egging Thomas on, wanting to hear more.

Leaning back in his chair, his wing tips on the magazine table between them, the justice is anxious to oblige. He tells about being an illegitimate child, how his mother was overwhelmed and his grandfather eventually raised him under iron codes of discipline. Cedric is prompted to open up about his dad, and the church, and how his mother "tells you to do it once, and never twice." When Cedric mentions how hard he studies—nights, weekends, and summers—Thomas recalls how he learned algebra one summer after he got his hands on an old textbook. And around they go, matching each other—Cedric laughing, Thomas chewing on an unlit Macanudo and waving it as a prop—as an hour goes by, then another.

Thomas talks about growing up speaking Gullah, a pig English that was common among blacks in parts of the rural south, especially along the Atlantic seaboard, and is still spoken on some Caribbean islands. "For me, English was a second language—still is, I guess," he says, and Cedric laughs, realizing that Thomas, who speaks with the practiced precision of James Earl Jones, is joking. "I just worked at it, Cedric, working on my pronunciations, sounding out words. That's why I became an English major as an undergraduate at Holy Cross. I didn't say much in class. I was afraid, afraid of being embarrassed. But eventually, I knew I could speak properly. I got some confidence, but I had to work for it, to earn it."

Having brought up college, Thomas asks Cedric if he knows where he's going next year. Cedric—proud to offer up a Latin Bee victory of his own—tells him, "You bet. I'm off to Brown University."

Thomas frowns and shakes his head. "Well, that's fine, but I'm not sure if I would have selected an Ivy League school." Sliding his bulk down in the too-small chair, he stretches his feet out and rests his chin against his breastbone. "You're going to be up there with lots of very smart white kids, and, if you're not sure about who you are, you could get eaten alive."

Cedric, his brow furrowing, grows quiet, and Thomas chooses his words carefully. "It's not just at the Ivies, you understand. It can happen at any of the good colleges where a young black man, who hasn't spent much time with whites, suddenly finds himself among almost all whites. You can feel lost." Thomas tells him a story about a kid from Georgia who went with him to Holy Cross—"smartest black kid I ever knew"—who "got confused about who he was and ended up getting addicted to drugs and dropping out."

Cedric looks on, pensively, wondering, Why is he telling me this? No doubt getting into Brown was a great victory—it's one of the best schools in America—and Thomas, after all, went to Yale Law School. Cedric remembers Thomas's law school classmates from the hearings. What does he know, Cedric mulls, that I don't?

He leans forward, inching up to the front edge of the couch cushion. Thomas is becoming increasingly animated by the prospect of Cedric going to Brown. He's talking faster now, reaching out his wide arms. "No doubt, one thing you'll find when you get to a school like Brown is a lot of classes and orientation on race relations. Try to avoid them. Try to say to yourself, I'm not a black person, I'm just a person. You'll find a lot of so-called multicultural combat, a lot of struggle between ethnic and racial groups—and people wanting you to sign on, to narrow yourself into some group identity or other. You have to resist that, Cedric. You understand?"

Cedric nods, understanding enough of what Thomas is saying to at least respond, "Like, you mean, that you have to be your own person."

"That's right! That's it!" The justice is rolling, cutting swiftly across the terrain of affirmative action and quotas and something he calls the "liberal elite," his hand chopping the air for effect. But he's not looking much at Cedric. It's more like he's preaching to people who are not here.

Thomas suddenly stops. "Cedric. What are you thinking of majoring in?"

"Math, I think."

"Good. Good. That's what I look for in hiring my clerks—the cream of the crop. I look for the maths and the sciences, real classes, none of that Afro-American studies stuff. If they've taken that stuff as an undergraduate, I don't want them. You want to do that, do it in your spare time."

As he talks, Cedric recalls that there *were* two guys in their mid-twenties who passed through the office while he was sitting among the Lucite messages—could have been Thomas's clerks—but they were both white. Then a third white guy walked by after a bit, maybe a clerk as well. It strikes him . . . of course *they* wouldn't be taking any Afro-American studies. Wayne is clearly some sort of administrative aide, not a clerk. Does Thomas not have any black law clerks? Is it because they don't apply, or because the justice doesn't want them?

"Cedric? Listen, Cedric!" Thomas exclaims, now almost exuberant. "You can't be going out, partying on weekends or going to Florida on spring break. You just have to keep studying, like your life depends on it. Some of these kids will be ahead of you, for sure, but you just have to outwork them. That's the way you'll beat them. It was that way with me, too. There was no safety net. No choice. To fail means to drop all the way to the bottom. It was that way for me. Same for you."

Cedric nods, but his lips are pursed. Thomas's enthusiasm suddenly seems to be gleaming with fury. It unsettles Cedric, makes him feel like he's going off, barely armed, into some sort of battle with white kids. He doesn't want to fight them, he thinks. He just wants to be part of something bigger, with kids—black kids, Hispanics, whatever. With everyone being a top achiever, just like him.

Thomas gets up from the chair and strolls around for a moment, loosening up after the rhetorical workout, and Cedric looks down at his watch. It's almost 4:30. He's been in the office nearly three hours.

Thomas fusses with a few things on his huge, baronial mahogany desk and looks up, smiling sheepishly. An afternoon has passed. Looking at Cedric sitting quietly now on the couch, a sympathetic look crosses the justice's face. He sees that Cedric has been frightened by his dark vision.

"I'm sure you'll do just fine," he says gently, walking slowly toward him as Cedric rises from the couch. "It's just that I understand, in a very personal way, how big a step you're taking. When you get on that plane, or train, at the end of the summer and leave home, you won't ever really be able to go back. But you may find you're never fully accepted up ahead either, that you've landed between worlds. That's the way I feel sometimes, even now, and it can make you angry. But you just have to channel that anger, to harness it."

Cedric, standing eye to eye with the justice, finally finds a sentence forming in his head, a response from down deep.

"Well, you know, I guess I'm just hoping I won't have a reason to become an angry person. That I'll be accepted up ahead for who I am."

Clarence Thomas smiles a warm and melancholy smile as Cedric shakes his hand in gratitude—a firm clench this time—before slipping past the end table with St. Jude and out the door, curiously happy to be headed for home.

May is a month for assemblies at Ballou, a time of diminished class-work and even lower than usual attendance, when there is little to do except gather students in the auditorium. Any excuse will do.

This mid-May Tuesday is called "Awards Day" for the general presentation of awards. At the front of the receiving line in the half-filled auditorium is Cedric L. Jennings: from the Association of Telecommunications Managers and Associates, $1,500; from Omega Psi Phi Fraternity, $1,000; from the Washington Chapter of the American Society of Military Comptrollers, $7,000 over four years; and then there's Paramount's Kings Dominion Scholarship, $1,000. Matching him is the quiet and studious LaCountiss Spinner—with her own cache. James Davis gets a few awards for his all-around efforts, and twenty-two Ballou students who were selected back in junior high by the "I Have a Dream" Foundation (a national network of benefactors who guarantee college tuition to anyone who eventually needs it) walk up to get certificates commending their achievement thus far. LaTisha's in that program, and so is Phillip Atkins, a last remnant of his days as a straight-arrow eighth grader. A middling, earnest student named Lawan Foster who is often homeless (her mother a drug addict, her brother hiding from gang vendettas) gets the "Beat the Odds" award from the Children's Defense Fund.

And then there are kids who are recognized for the achievement of simply participating in various clubs, like the band, ROTC, or the Ballou Sapphire Models—a row of lithe, tight-jeaned girls, hair swirled in impressive fountains, who squeeze by LaTisha, in the aisle seat, on their way up front to receive gold-embossed certificates.

By noon, it's all over and the kids file out, many of them—even some crew members who happened by—shuffling along as they study the four pages of smallish type at the back of the awards booklet, the section called "College Acceptance, Awards, and Scholarships."

Leaning against a wall outside the auditorium, Cedric bears down on his booklet—couldn't very well read it up on stage—matching what he's heard about who's going to college, and where, to what he now sees in type. It fascinates him: a final tally for so many math/science kids he knows and, more broadly, for the 850 or so sophomores who entered Ballou two years ago as the Class of 1995. According to this list, sixty-four students have been accepted into a college of some type, twelve of them into the come-one-come-all University of the District of Columbia. Many of the institutions are black colleges, like Washington's nationally known Howard University and smaller schools like Bennett College and Lincoln University.

Cedric, not necessarily unique in raw talent, shows how he is anomalous in his lofty collegiate ambitions. Under his name is Brown, along with the names of institutions that eventually recruited him, including Duke University, George Washington University, Brigham Young University, and Florida A&M, a black engineering school near Orlando.

More important, each school on Cedric's list has an asterisk next to it, indicating the offer of some scholarship money. Cedric flips through the four pages of student names and sees that plenty of the colleges have no accompanying asterisks. He, like everyone here, knows that that means plenty of the senior class's select sixty-four won't be going anywhere next fall.

Money is crucial. Acceptance to college is meaningless for many kids at Ballou without financial aid. And for Cedric this glorious list means a sort of financial redemption, representing—in the case of Brown, at least—an annual scholarship just shy of $20,000, about what his mother makes a year.

So there it is: his row of asterisks for everyone to see. It's a delicate issue, and Cedric knows to keep his mouth shut. He spots James Davis walking away from the auditorium and decides to check the list before calling out to him. James was accepted to his first choice, Florida A&M. There are no asterisks.

Cedric knows James was hoping for a scholarship. He looks up and winces, thankful that James has vanished in the crowd. Florida A&M's scholarship—a special prize based on both merit and need—is, in fact, an afterthought on Cedric's own sterling list. He wishes he could just give it to James, but he knows it doesn't work that way.

He puts the awards booklet in his backpack and makes his way through the halls, sensing that a largely theoretical separation between himself and most of his classmates has suddenly become painfully literal.

As the day passes, he feels edgy and watchful, detecting some extra bile in the comments and stares to which he's grown accustomed. In the late afternoon, he bumps into Jack Davis, James's equally huge twin, near the boys' bathroom. Jack is usually cordial, due, Cedric figures, to his passing friendship with James. No more. "Brown University," says Jack darkly. "You can't hang there Cedric. You probably won't last a year there. Definitely won't last two. No way. You'll be coming right back."

Cedric says nothing, looking away, just shaking his head. This is the last guy he wants to get into an altercation with, especially on this day of victory.

As May wanes, the whole senior class seems locked in a fitful finale, taking the final tally of dismal achievement and stunted opportunity into the hot summer. It's a bad time for kids to feel desperate and dispirited. When the weather warms and the streets start to fill with kids cutting school and meeting peers who are long beyond formal schooling, the season of mayhem begins in Southeast. Just two days after the awards ceremony, a hail of gunfire was pumped into a parked car—just a block from Cedric and Barbara's apartment building—killing two men and critically injuring a three-year-old boy who later died.

Onto these streets, graduating seniors are about to spill, accentuating the divide between a few haves looking forward to summer preparations for college and a vast army of have-nots, looking at a first summer of official, out-of-school, get-a-job reality.

Cedric, always attentive to potential threats, has spent the two weeks since the awards ceremony with his face frozen in an innocuous half-smile, trying to look utterly neutral and inert, shrugging a lot as though all his good fortune stems from some sort of clerical error. It's just the most recent of many poses Cedric has affected since he got into Brown. Once word got out about his acceptance, he noticed a grimness start to come over his antagonists in the halls. It was easier to be the headstrong monk, a boy on a long-shot mission, before he'd actually won anything. With the prize in hand, he realized his single-minded drive came across as aloof cockiness; his painful martyrdom suddenly looked like self-nomination for sainthood. So he toned it down, not telling anyone about the Clarence Thomas meeting. Not discussing his preparations for Brown. Not talking too much about the awards. Pride, he knows, can get you killed in a place like this.

But with only a few weeks of school left, he's not sure he can keep up this exhausting, aw-shucks facade for much longer.

In Advanced Physics class on an afternoon at the end of May, Cedric—in the front row, as usual—tries to stay focused on his worksheet as Mr. Momen leaves the room.

A moment later, he sees a large hand plunge over his shoulder. It's James Davis, snatching Cedric's Texas Instruments T-18 calculator, a prize Cedric got a year ago from the math department for academic achievement. James hustles to his desk in the back of the room, saying over his shoulder, "You don't need a calculator anyway."

Cedric shakes his head in exasperation. He just can't keep his tongue tied any longer.

"James, I need my calculator," says Cedric, clearly impatient.

James ignores him.

"Muthafucka, give me my calculator," he says, now loud enough that everyone is looking up. "Look, I don't feel like playing all the time, bitch."

Curse words, spoken often between boys of this age in this place, may or may not mean anything. That's for James to decide. And today he clearly decides they mean plenty. His jaw muscles bulge, squaring his wide face. He pushes himself up from the desk and rushes up the aisle, thundering forward, his compressed rage rising like lava until his full bulk is leaning over Cedric, who has barely managed to swivel sideways in his chair.

"Who the fuck you talking to?" James yells, ready to blow.

Cedric is stunned, but it's already gone too far to back down.

"To you," he says, trying to make it sound tough. The words are barely out when James's forty-eight-inch shoulders begin to swivel and a huge, wrecking-ball fist flies forward right into Cedric's heart, as the smaller boy, still sitting, finds the wind flying from his lungs, shoulders folding forward, his chest caving under the force.

A split second passes and Cedric begins to rise, barely, trying to catch his breath and muster some response. LaCountiss and two other girls jump in between the boys. Two boys—one graced with a stamped ticket out of here—standing face-to-face, eyes afire, in this world turned upside down.

At lunch hour two weeks later, Cedric—standing at the entrance to the teachers' lounge—reaches inside the collar of his shirt to touch the bruise on his chest. The bump has gone down and it's now just a dull ache when he presses on it. He looks over at LaCountiss Spinner, sitting with Constance Thompson, an English teacher and senior class adviser who must read over all the speeches for graduation. He keeps his impatience in check, trying to quietly wait for his turn. Her path to sterling grades bore little resemblance to his, insofar as the social codes for girls at Ballou are slightly less restrictive than they are for boys. For a girl to be a "goody" or a "whitey" by wanting to do well and leave everyone behind is not considered as serious a disrespect to the less fortunate as it is for a boy. A straight-arrow boy who thinks "he's better than other people" can get taken down with violence. A girl of the same mien can be taken down with sex, making her a prize for a tough guy who can exhibit irresistible charms. While, as a result, most top students at schools like Ballou are girls, LaCountiss never needed the type of lofty goals Cedric had to hold on to in order to push against a fierce headwind. She will go on to an unremarkable institution— Marymount University, nearby in the Maryland suburbs, which offered her a full scholarship. Never thought much about big, renowned universities. Never had a reason to.

But that's fare for next fall. At Ballou, at least, LaCountiss finishes first in line. Cedric's rear-guard assault—based on acing more advanced, higher-credit classes in the past two years—wasn't enough to overcome a few B's he got in ninth grade. LaCountiss, with straight A's throughout, edged him out by a grade-point fraction for valedictorian.

"That looks just fine, LaCountiss. It's a very nice speech," Ms. Thompson says as LaCountiss, placid and nonconfrontational to the end, smiles softly and slips out.

Cedric plops down in the empty chair and drops his latest draft before Ms. Thompson. He's already seen her three times over the past four days. His speech doesn't seem to be changing much between drafts.

"It's just not there yet, Cedric," she says. She doesn't know Cedric very well, never had him in class, but she knows he doesn't take ultimatums well. "Give it another try. Why not talk, maybe, about some of the friends you made at Ballou."

He nods, lips pursed. "All right then," he says, as they agree to meet later in the afternoon. "But don't expect much."

There is only one day until graduation. Underclassmen are still in school; seniors have been finished with classes, for the most part, for a week. Tomorrow, Cedric is going to have to stand and deliver before the class.

And he has written a spiteful speech.

The question: what to do? The message, quietly passed down a few days ago from the principal's office to a handful of teachers involved in graduation planning, is blunt: he can't stand and give that angry, bitter speech to tomorrow's assemblage of parents, members of the school board, Mayor Barry, and God knows who else. Simply can't happen. Somebody do something.

After lunch, Cedric ducks his head into the classroom of Shirley Briscoe, his senior English teacher. She's sitting at her desk, trying to stay cool in a blue flowered summer dress. It's a sweltering afternoon, and she's grading some of her last papers, their edges fluttering in the breeze from a huge platform fan.

"Oh, Cedric," she says, pleased to see him. She's retiring in a few days after nearly three decades at Ballou, having seen the school slowly deteriorate from a clean, promising place to its current disarray. "I hear you're working on your speech."

He slumps down in a chair in front of her desk, his back to the fan.

"Guess everybody knows it's not going too good," he says with a doleful laugh and passes it across to her.

Her eyes wander down the page, reading his scrawl: "I've had to achieve at Ballou without much help. . . . What did I learn? Watch out for the Dreambusters. You know who they are. Dreambusters are everywhere. Students, teachers, and administrators who said 'You can't, you won't.' . . . Dreambusters follow you all over this part of town . . . you got to fight them . . . you've got to get them before they get you," and on and on.

She looks up. "Maybe you want to start with something positive, something hopeful. What are some other lessons you've learned?"

"Well, be cautious about picking your friends 'cause not everybody wants you to succeed."

"Okay, I suppose," she says. "An important message, I think I'm hearing, is not only to watch out for the Dreambusters, but also, and maybe more important, is that you have to keep those dreams in sight and hold on tight to them."

Cedric considers this for a moment. She opens an English textbook on her desk, spins it, and slides it to him, "Remember this poem from class?"

It's a Langston Hughes poem called "Dreams," and Cedric reads the first line: "Hold fast to Dreams, for if dreams die life is a broken winged bird . . ."

His face softens.

"Yeah, this might work. Uh-huh."

He thinks for a minute. "I guess," he says, trying to summon conviction, "that every person has a dream to walk across that stage at graduation." Even as he says it, he feels guilty. Of course, the other kids have dreams, but over the last four years it was easier not to think about that—it made his big dreams seem bigger and his journey seem more heroic, like he was truly different from the rest of them in some fundamental way.

Ms. Briscoe smiles at him. " 'A dream to walk across that stage' . . . that sounds pretty good," she says, nodding, not wanting to make him suspicious by being too enthusiastic. "I think you'd feel good saying something like that."

Soon he's off to a quiet place to start scribbling. Two hours later, in a conference room next to Dr. Jones's office, Ms. Thompson reads it and gives her assent. "A little rough," she says, anxious to get home, "but it might work. Okay. It's fine to say what you feel, Cedric, up to a point. But you have to think about what other kids feel, too."

Clarence Taylor is neatly lining up just-washed beakers, storing everything for the summer, when Cedric wanders in, befuddled, as though he's looking for something he'd left here.

"Oh, hi Mr. Taylor," he says softly.

"Well, hi there," says Clarence, trying not to sound too surprised or delighted, but hinting at both. Over the past six months, they have grown apart. Cedric thought Clarence was pushing him too hard, not allowing him to breathe and enjoy the victory of Brown's acceptance. And Clarence, a complete workaholic himself, didn't know how to turn the pressure down a notch.

Now, after no contact since winter, they are alone. Cedric's explanation for stopping by is that he'd just gotten approval on his graduation speech and he "has some time to kill." He eases into a favorite desk near the window and Clarence begins puttering around, as always, in perpetual motion. There's so much ground to cover and so little time that Clarence chooses carefully, asking first about his mom, about graduation coming up, and about classes Cedric plans to take next year at Brown.

They joke about some of the younger honor students coming up, mostly girls and one promising sophomore boy. "They keep coming," says Cedric.

"But none quite like you," Clarence lets slip but then catches himself, not wanting to get sentimental. It's his role, he tries to remind himself, to be left behind. It's enough, he remembers telling Cedric last year, that you "get to see them grow, right there in front of you." But he's not letting go—not quite yet.

"Hey! Wait," Clarence chirps. "Did I tell you about the Boston Marathon in April? About what happened?"

Cedric starts to laugh in anticipation. "NO! Oh my Gaawwwd. What?"

It's a doozy, an allegorical gem, and Clarence lays it out sweet and long and full of relish, about how he was coming up past the statue of Johnny Kelley, the ancient Boston marathoner who won the race in the 1930s and ran it into the 1990s ("a hard, 'never say die' old coot, that Kelly") and "I look over and this woman is running alongside me." They'd exchanged nods a few miles back and so then started to talk again, puffing away. She was white and a judge in Boston, and she was tiring. "Oh yes, Cedric, she was flagging, that judge, and she tells me that she's got a friend that lives right near here in one of the nice houses" near the marathon route. And how "she was thinking of running right over to that friend's house right now, getting something cool to drink and calling it quits. . . . And I told her, 'Yes, Ma'am, I'm feeling that way too, sometimes you feel too tired to go on . . . but you got to reach deeper for inspiration.' "

He pauses, savoring it, using every precious second. "And then, Cedric . . . I began to sing to her, right there as we ran."

Cedric's jaw drops in mock surprise and he claps once, egging Clarence on, as the teacher throws back his head and lets it flow:

> When Peace Like a River, attendeth my way,
> When sorrow, like sea billows, roll.
> Whatever My Lot, thou hath taught me to say,
> It is well, it is well, with my soul.
> It is well, it is well, with my soul.

As the teacher begins to repeat the verse—Hymn 189, it so happens, from the *Standard Baptist Hymnal*—Cedric wordlessly gets up and moves to the blackboard, all reflex, it seems, and begins scribbling sine and cosine, X's and parentheses. Clarence squints at the distant chalkboard. The scribbles are the start of a calculus proof.

"The integrating of two whole numbers, I see," Clarence says with the same reverent tone as his just finished hymn. "You still got it! Look at that boy go!"

Chalk is flying, white chips falling on Cedric's head, shoulders, his hand moving in furious arcs, the dark green board filling with arithmetic Sanskrit as it turns olive in the early evening sun.

"I wish all integration was this easy," quips Cedric, nearing the proof's finale. "We'd all be better off."

And Clarence Taylor laughs, loud and long, feeling, for an instant, like he and Cedric Jennings are just starting out.

Beautiful—they drag us halfway across the city and Roosevelt High's auditorium turns out to be hardly any bigger than Ballou's," fumes Barbara Jennings as she glares at Neddy. Her daughter shrugs and seems happy to slip away to chase her seven-year-old, Lawrence, who just disappeared down a hallway.

Barbara is working up a powerful sweat, but perspiration is no great feat with an afternoon high temperature of 96.

"Bishop Long's wife hates being hot," she groans, wishing Neddy would get back here so there'd be someone to complain to—so she wouldn't have to be talking out loud to herself like some damn fool. "I just don't know what Mother Long will do."

Barbara has always been most comfortable and settled when she felt like she was rescuing her Lavar—from infidel drug dealers or his intemperate father, from carping teachers or false idols of peer pressure. Not to mention poverty, despair, and hopelessness.

But on this day of victory—graduation day—there are no demons left to fight, at least not for her. It will only be him, up there.

Soon the Jennings entourage is here and seated, midway in a side section, all in a row: Barbara; then Bishop's Long's wife, Mother Long, and her sister, Skinny, who's anything but; then Cedric's paternal grandmother, Maggie; his half-sisters, Leslie and Neddy; and, on the end, little Lawrence.

The sweltering auditorium at Roosevelt High School—a turn-of-the-century monstrosity with Yankee church spires and crumbling cornices—is filling quickly, and the balcony is now opened. Maggie mentions something about Cedric Gilliam wanting to come but having a lot of work. He was paroled in November and just started working at a new barbershop. Under Barbara's wilting glare, she adds that "he wasn't sure, I don't think, if Lavar really wanted him here."

Barbara takes a deep breath. The man's whole life is an excuse, she starts, but quickly decides it's better—simpler—that he's not here. She turns to make small talk with Mother Long and periodically cranes her neck to watch the crowds of parents as they jam in, women mostly, it seems, rows of them, some casually dressed in jeans, others, like Barbara, more formal. Many are coming straight from work, like she did, but in their uniforms—a nurse, a toll taker, a cop.

Ballou's music teacher silently cues the high school's small band, clustered up against the stage. A solemn "Pomp and Circumstance" marks the arrival of the graduates, with LaCountiss, Cedric, and a few others who will sit on the stage leading the procession down one of the main aisles.

Barbara spots him. "There . . . see him?" she says to Mother Long in a high, almost girlish voice. "Gaawd. Doesn't he look good?"

He does—and everyone can see: the boy near the front of the line, the long gown accentuating his height, girls on all sides. It quickly becomes clear that there will be an absence of the decorum typical of graduation ceremonies. Before the first stanza of "Pomp and Circumstance" is over, people are screaming.

"WE LOVE YOU TANISHA!" is wailed from the balcony. A bunch of kids in their royal-blue silky gowns, with the gold "Ballou Class of '95" sash, look upward and one—Tanisha, no doubt—waves to her family.

Other names hurl from the crowd, whoops and yells for Jameses and LaShawns and Keiths, a thunderous "WE ALL WITH YOU NATASHA," seconded by cries for Jamaals, Latoyas, and Pernells, providing lyrics for the stately processional tune.

It doesn't take long for the graduates to settle into their seats, and Barbara looks down at the program. About two hundred names are listed across three pages, each page carrying a small-print disclaimer: "The listing of names on the program does not imply that students have met all requirements for graduation."

The national anthem and a posting of colors is followed by a few introductions. The place sounds like a rush hour train station, with a low, steady hum of conversation, one thousand or so people all now fanning themselves with the heavy bond paper of the program. Principal Jones, suave as always, sporting a dark, tailored suit, today with a sharp, yellow tie, starts with an admonition, chiding the assembled that "our young people have prepared speeches and if you are quiet, they can continue. . . ."

It is the first of many tongue lashings hurled by the stylishly appointed blacks on the cool, elevated stage—an assortment of school board members, District of Columbia school administrators, $80,000-a-year principals and vice principals. It's not a crowd that takes to ultimatums well. Most of the sweating parents never graduated from high school, much less attended college, and are certainly not going to be reined in at the only graduation many will ever attend by some distant, bourgeois blacks.

Up at the podium, Keisha Ward, class vice president, shouts a short welcome statement through the microphone, asking her fellow students to "look around and see those survivors of these trying years and also see our missing friends, who could not hold on."

Barbara, squeezing some outrage from her reserve tanks, leans toward Mother Long—"No respect at all, these people," she says, "just like at the school," and Bishop's wife shakes her head in stagy disgust. Barbara studies the accomplished suburban blacks up on stage, admiringly. She wants to yell out that it's her son up there, so all those "honored guests" will know that she's different—that Barbara Jennings doesn't belong in this unruly mob.

Cedric belongs up there—that she knows. And Barbara realizes that he's sitting among these accomplished people because she always thought that's where *she* belonged—no matter what other people said.

"Can you quiet down, just a little bit!" exhorts a svelte, smartly dressed female school board member from the lectern. "This is an important day in these students' lives and it needs to be orderly and quiet. . . . Maybe if you're quiet, you won't be as hot."

An obese woman from behind Barbara offers the crowd's reply: "Oh Puleeeeze. A slender lady from up there—and SHE TALKING ABOUT HOT?!" This gets some laughs from the nearby rows and Barbara has to chuckle, despite herself.

Mother Long glares at Barbara from the neighboring seat, a "nothing funny about it" look on her face, and says, "When Cedric gets up there, he better say God has helped you through this, that God's the one who should be thanked today."

"Oh, he will, don't worry," says Barbara sheepishly, before she's drowned out by the Ballou chorus as it launches into a soulful rendition of the old spiritual "Amazing Grace," changes course midway into the Afrocentrically sensible theme from Disney's *Lion King,* and finishes raucously on "got no worries, for the rest of your days, it's my trouble free philosophy, Acunna Motona."

Dr. Constance Brooks, Ballou's vice principal, in a white Liz Claiborne number with a black collar, follows the song with more verbal attacks. "We will have to move people out of the aisles. There are seats in the back of the balcony. Please clear the aisles, or the fire department will move us out of the auditorium." This prompts no discernible movement. Finally, with no point in waiting longer, she murmurs, forlornly, "Ladies and gentlemen, our salutatorian, Cedric Jennings."

Down below, Barbara Jennings's anxiety finally dissolves. She looks up at the stage, transfixed, unspeakably happy to simply be the mother of that boy.

A hundred feet away, Cedric places his glasses on the podium, flips his tassel to the far side of his mortar board, and rustles three pages of typed notes, trying to keep his elbows from locking.

As he looks up and clears his throat, he is certain that the din has actually risen a notch, his ears picking up a few moans along with a mocking "Ceeeeddric" or two. Kids love saying the name. It will always mean "nerd" to them.

He thanks the honored guests for their presence (including Mayor Marion Barry, whose seat remains empty) and turns to thank Dr. Jones, who shifts a bit in his chair and winks in a gesture of kinship, signaling his hope that Cedric will stick to the kinder, gentler text that was approved yesterday.

Cedric turns back to the crowd and begins reading. "I would first like to start by thanking God for giving me the strength and courage to be where I am today. I would also to thank the many people who have had a positive impact on my life, especially my loving mother and my family."

The din is indeed, rising, the crowd having already passed its allot-ment of attentiveness. People who aren't using their programs as fans are noisily flipping pages to see how many more of these speeches are coming.

Cedric pushes forward gamely, keeping his voice loud and even: "When I was asked to deliver the salutatory address I was afraid because it seemed an awesome responsibility . . . many of us who are going on to college, to work, or to the military, understand the feelings of fear and responsibility in our new endeavors . . . but if we, the class of 1995, are to face a new day, we must become self-sufficient, respon-sible, and determined in rising to the challenges of the twenty-first century."

"Blah, blah, blah," says a man leaning close to his teenage daughter a few rows from the stage, and the girl laughs. Cedric hears the whole thing.

He tries to remain composed, again rustling pages on the lectern. "In our high school years, we have learned great lessons that will serve us well in the future. Most importantly, we have learned to hold tight to our dreams, although there have been many obstacles on our way to a high school diploma. . . ."

He pauses and, for the first time, really looks up from the text. The crowd is blurry. He looks quickly to the right edge of the podium and sees his glasses. He forgot to put them on, and he can't stop to do it now in midspeech.

He looks outward again, feeling his throat tighten. The next part he knows by heart. It's the first thing he wrote two weeks ago. It's the very reason he's up here, or so he decided this morning when he added back the next three paragraphs.

"You see," he begins, his voice halting but seeming to sound con-versational, "we have learned how to fight off Dreambusters. Yes, Dreambusters. Their favorite lines are 'you cannot' or 'you will not.' Many of us have been called crazy or even laughed at for having big dreams."

Some in the crowd look up, perplexed, as though they aren't sure what he just said.

"I will never forget being laughed at for saying I wanted to go to the Ivy League. I've been told that I wouldn't make it and, quote unquote," he says, "that I 'couldn't hang.' "

He can hear students mumbling to each other in the middle seats just in front of him, and he imagines what they must be saying: Can it be that the nerd is giving some back? Giving it back to the whole class! Who does he think he is?

He grabs the edges of the podium, intently studies the blur of royal blue while he waits for the room to quiet. He knows some of them are frowning, giving him the dead-eye. But he can't make out their faces, and that makes it all possible, allowing him to see only the indignities, stretching back years—the chiding, the slights, the threats. And finally, he's purging it, spitting it all back. It's a spectacle. People are stunned, silent.

"When one of my peers found out that I was going to Brown, he told me I wouldn't last two years. While they were laughing in the corner and trying to predict my outlook, I laughed back . . ." He pauses, and it becomes clear that he's ad libbing, searching. "I said to myself, 'THERE IS *NOTHING* ME AND MY GOD CAN'T HANDLE.''

The crowd erupts. It's thunderous. A few people are standing. Even the badass kids have to laugh—the human punching bag is finally punching back.

Barbara's up, screaming, "THAT'S MY SON!" loud enough that even Cedric can hear her, and he squints over toward her voice, trying to see—but he doesn't need to. He feels her inside him.

Now the frog prince is flying, up on his toes, preaching, reaching down and, in a flash, he sees his mother standing by the white couch, pointing at him, dropping her finger slowly, like a gun. Remembering every word, he lets it rip.

"For the race is not given to the swift nor to the strong," he signifies, "but to him who endureth until the end!" The mothers, the powerful churchwomen, start to cry out from all corners, and distinctions between the cool stage and the surrounding lowlands are gone as the room thumps as one big tent revival.

Cedric goes on to finish the speech, ending nicely with the Langston Hughes poem, but he knows—even as he recites it—that no one will remember much of the end. All they'll remember is that some boy preached today.

LaCountiss Spinner gives a tame, respectful valedictory speech, mostly thanking a lot of teachers; and Mayor Barry arrives, about an hour late, to present the Mayor's Academic Achievement Award to three students on the stage, including Cedric. As he places a silver medal around Cedric's neck, Barry quips, "Sure is nice to see a young man up here."

Students finally start snaking up for their diplomas. Cedric, suffused with warmth and relief, listens intently as the crowd cheers, like when they all marched in, but more ardently this time. Whole families watch and hug, waving programs, clasping hands, standing on chairs, sweat pouring down their faces. Each family has one of their own up there, after all. Cedric can't help but notice that the loudest ovation is for Phillip Atkins, who offers a gentle nod to the assembled, having traded much for the applause.

Outside, afterward, the air is finally cooling. Everyone floods from the school's portico and into the apricot sunset, glad to breathe again.

Cedric is floating. He sees James Davis, whom he made up with a few weeks ago, being hugged by several girls at once. Cedric laughs, feeling giddy. A few feet in the other direction, Phillip works the crowd, collecting a final round of hugs and high fives from all strata of Ballou's society. Cedric wants to go over to him, congratulate him, feeling like some of his demons have finally vanished, like all that's behind him now.

But he's waylaid. Strangers and people he barely knows are shaking his hand, congratulating him on the speech. Classmates are smacking his back, punching his shoulder, finally accepting him, he muses, now that it's all over.

After a moment, he finds he has drifted toward an oak tree where his family is waiting and overhears Neddy say, "Ma, you've got your life back now that Lavar's graduated and he's ready to move on."

"Yeah, I suppose," he hears his mom murmur, clearly not wanting to think about that now. When she turns, he's already standing close, looking right at her. He's holding an armful of awards against the gown's embroidered chest, saying everything with his smile.

And Cedric Lavar Jennings stands up nice and straight as Barbara—after so many pinched years—finally loses control, letting out a lusty "MY BAAAAABY!" and throwing her arms hard around him.

6

THE PRETENDER

Sitting in the small, sterile offices of Price Waterhouse Accounting LLP in northern Virginia, sorting office keys, Cedric considers how the summer after high school must be a strange in-between period for everyone on the college track—a neither-here-nor-there time.

So it's only natural to feel confused and impatient and a little disembodied, he figures, as he methodically slips four newly cut keys—each with the number 56 for some accounting executive's office of the same number—onto a tiny metal ring and throws it into the cardboard box marked "finished." The drudge work *never* seems to be finished in this summer job, a deadly, dull, $8-an-hour internship obtained through a national program called Inroads that assists promising minority kids.

Boring is boring, no point in stressing about it. It's already July and this job, along with so much else that marks his final days in Washington, will slip gently into past tense when he journeys north in six weeks.

So why can't he seem to relax, he wonders, and simply enjoy the summer? Not that some of it hasn't been okay. He's making a little cash and getting ready to step up to something he's dreamed about for so long. It's just that so much of the good that's befallen him seems to have an unsettling underside. Every sunny expanse seems to have a corner in the shadows.

He roots through the loose-keys box for the fourth number 57 and recalls the moment—almost a month ago—when he was sitting on a curb in front of Filene's Basement department store in Northwest, fretting over the contents of a giant red bag. Inside were two suits—one seersucker, one pale grayish—that were sent by Donald Korb, a Boston optometrist and contact lens inventor who last year became interested in Cedric's achievement.

A benefactor isn't that strange—not these days. Quite a few kids at Ballou have some distant person who makes an effort on their behalf. Phillip and LaTisha, for instance, have the newsletter company magnate from Maryland who sponsors them and dozens of other kids through the "I Have a Dream" foundation. If any of them decide to go to college, their tuition and expenses will be paid. Cedric's guy is a solo player. Dr. Korb read about Cedric in the *Wall Street Journal* story and has paid for periodic tutoring and incidentals, mostly books and some school clothes. A gentle, good-natured Jewish guy of sixty-one—who hasn't spent more than a few minutes with Cedric but has very strong, principled feelings about him—he sent the suits in late May when he heard Cedric would be working the summer at an accounting firm. Sitting on the curb, Cedric mulled over how nice it was for Dr. Korb to do this, while he fretted over his inability to put the garments on his body. They're old white man suits, he muttered as he peeked into the billowy plastic Filene's bag to see if maybe the clothes had somehow changed color and pattern. "Who does he want me to be? Someone who wears suits like this, or who I really am?" Cedric finally blurted out, not even caring if passersby heard him. Half an hour later, he'd exchanged the suits for a store credit of $258, which he used to buy eighteen assorted graduation gifts for himself, teachers, administrators, his mother, and a few friends.

It was a confusing moment, like so many lately. It was a good thing returning the suits and then being able to pass out graduation presents, but he felt like he was between worlds, like he was leaving one world and, at best, merely a pretender in the other.

Cedric finishes sorting a box of keys and suddenly checks his watch. Almost 5:30, quitting time, and he looks down at his delicately checked shirt, smoothing the silky fabric with his hand. It was his first major clothing purchase, made after he got his first two-week paycheck last week. No Goodwill stuff, not this time—the plaid shirt is a Montel Williams label, for $70; the black linen pants were $70; and the black-and-white saddle bucks cost another $60.

Wearing the outfit today, he feels sleek and transformed—a boring job for sure, but look what it gets you. He makes sure he passes the black receptionist on his way out. They had a funny conversation today about how she uses what she calls her "Vanna White voice" on the office intercom. Cedric waves an affectionate "till tomorrow" as he leaves, juking by, nodding at her conspiratorially, to show he knows she's really a ghetto girl.

He has a few hours before Thursday prayer meeting at church, so he trolls a mall in Georgetown. He almost never comes over to this side of town, but last year he visited this mall once—a sumptuous four-story complex with clothes he sees in magazines and a good record shop—and had often thought of returning. The stuff he sees today is truly amazing—fabrics like butter, fountains tinkling in an airy arboretum near the food court, a pair of Versace shoes in one store that he'd give anything to buy. It's so lovely and transporting, in fact, that he manages not to notice for quite a while how salespeople are heading him off before he gets two steps inside each establishment. Not that this is any huge surprise; it happened last time. There are almost no black shoppers here. It's just that he hoped the Montel Williams ensemble would ease his passage, that people might look at him like something other than a threat. By the time he leaves, he wonders if, with his next paycheck, he ought to splurge for a suit, something stylish and a bit more traditional. Maybe it would be easier if he came wearing that, looking more like a young professional.

When he gets home that night, he gets a call from LaTisha. Cedric hasn't talked to her since he saw her for lunch right after school ended. But it was an awkward meeting. At one point, Cedric remembers, he talked about Brown, about his dorm, about talking to his roommate—a white kid from Marblehead, Massachusetts—and LaTisha kind of glazed over, like, suddenly, they had nothing to talk about anymore. It made him uncomfortable.

Tonight, though, there's plenty of news and catching up to do. LaTisha starts by telling Cedric she just heard something terrible about

Marvin Peay, a guy from Ballou Cedric knew pretty well, who was planning to attend a vocational school in Altoona, Pennsylvania. He was working his night job at a McDonald's near the Capitol with two other employees when all three were killed by a fourth coworker, who decided to rob the safe. The papers, LaTisha says, reported that it was the fifth triple homicide in the District in ten months.

Cedric is stunned about Marvin, who was a nice quiet sort. He tells her about an old Jefferson friend of his named Henry Wimbush, who was just killed dealing drugs. He found all this out, Cedric continues, from Torrence Parks, who ended up not graduating from Wilson High because he flunked senior English and his parents—incensed about his failure and his growing affection for Islam—threatened to throw him out of the house. He's now working at Burger King.

LaTisha tells him she saw Phillip Atkins. He's working sorting envelopes in the mail room of the newsletter company owned by the guy who helps fund the "I Have a Dream" program. LaTisha, whose small UDC tuition will be paid by the program, says the mail room job is "like a consolation prize" for anyone who's not planning to go to college. "And you know Phillip," she says. "Real smart, but, like a lot of folks we know, there's no way he's ever getting much past the mail room."

Half listening, Cedric's mind wanders back to graduation. What a beautiful sunny dusk it was, he remembers. Everyone looked so good, smiling in their gowns, and a sort of airborne hopefulness was everywhere. Cradling the receiver with his shoulder while he does the dishes and LaTisha runs through one story of woe after another, he feels that unsettling, in-between feeling again and tells her he has to turn in early.

Trying to fall asleep, Cedric can't stop thinking about the depressing tally, how Torrence will probably still be at Burger King five years from now and Phillip will have long since reconciled himself to being the funniest guy in the mail room. He thinks about how Marvin might have looked after he was shot, and Henry, too, and what Torrence looks like with one of those stupid paper hats. It makes him feel sad and kind of scared, so he runs through all of it again while trying not to feel anything.

———

B arbara?"
    She immediately recognizes the voice on the phone but finds it hard to respond with more than a grunt.

"Ummm, it's me—Cedric Gilliam. Did Lavar tell you I talked to him about a concert, that I wanted to ask you about it . . ." and she listens as he goes through it, the when and where and that there won't be any drinking or drugs.

She's been waiting for this call. Cedric Gilliam is out now, paroled last November after agreeing to get drug treatment and continue with his hair-cutting job. Not that he came to see Lavar over the winter or spring. Just in the last few weeks, though, as his son gets ready to depart, he's made a play at establishing a relationship. The two of them have talked on the phone a few times, and it's been cordial.

Two weeks ago, after one of the calls, Lavar told Barbara about his father's invitation to the concert—something called the Budweiser Concert Series at the D.C. Armory in late July, featuring three of Cedric's favorite singers: Patti LaBelle, TLC, and Mary J. Blige.

While she's become something of an expert on how teenage boys search ruinously for approval from their wayward fathers, she also knows that standing between a father and son can be a disastrous move—the kind of thing that often makes a boy want the companionship of his father even more, as a form of rebellion. She's thought a lot about what to do in the last few days but has been unable to decide.

So she listens as Gilliam rambles on and on. The more he talks, the more she remembers her inability to trust him, to trust anything he says. It's only one month until the race ends, until Lavar is safely settled in at a prestigious university far from Southeast. That single fact underlies everything. She knows this is Cedric Gilliam's last chance to make a connection, to get on the road to some form of relationship with his son. But she'd be a fool to chance an incident at a concert where, of course, there will be alcohol and, of course, there will be drugs and, very possibly, violence.

Finally, she cuts him off. "I didn't raise him to be in that kind of atmosphere," she says, cool, calm, and steady. "I don't want him in that kind of a place. There's just no reason he needs to be there."

It's a total defeat. Gilliam crumbles under Barbara's moral force, and she feels some guilty satisfaction.

"I'm sorry. . . . I just didn't think there was any harm to it," he says, and, a moment later, the phones are returned to their cradles.

She looks over at Lavar, who happened to be in the kitchen when the phone rang and has been wandering in an out of the vicinity throughout the conversation. He just nods, saying that "it was no big deal or anything" in a toneless voice that seems practiced to reveal nothing.

On Cedric's eighteenth birthday, July 24, they eat takeout spare ribs—a rare treat. There has been no other fanfare for the birthday. Cedric mentioned it in passing to people at work, but there was no cake or anything. Barbara has never been much to fuss over birthdays, so the ribs will suffice.

As the days until his departure grow few, Barbara has been mindful to steer conversations toward loose ends—things Cedric may need to know when she's not there. Cedric, anxious about what's ahead, helps her along with a steady stream of questions and requests.

"My last wish," he says, gnawing on a rib, "is I want to be driven to college in an Infiniti. A Q45. I love the Q45. How much can it cost to rent one? You can attach a U-haul on the back."

She smirks at him. "Next summer, when you're working at Price Waterhouse again, you can rent an Infiniti and drive around all summer if you want. On my money, we renting a plain ol' minivan."

The conversation crests this way and that, but the theme of money rises again to the surface, as it often does. "Someday, when you're a man," she says absently, "you'll be paying your own way with no problem."

"I'm a man."

She puts down the rib. "What did I tell you a man was?"

"What?"

"A man," she says, like reciting a mantra, "takes care of himself physically, financially, and spiritually. And I mean, TOTALLY. Nobody else helping."

"I take care," he says, venturing onto uneven terrain.

"Not financially you don't, not yet."

Barbara gets up for a glass of water as Cedric picks through a mountain of rib bones, piled in the middle of the table on the takeout bag. She knows he's anxious for her to finally concede that he's a man, but she's in no rush. That he still relies on her for that affirmation is among her most valuable assets, something she's won, she feels, by mixing her affection with real firmness, by not giving approval or praise unless it's warranted. Sometimes she worries that he'll seek proof of his manhood elsewhere. But not often. He wants *her* to say he's a man, and she'll say it when he's earned it. Not a second before.

The TV is blaring, as usual, offering a ready partner if either needs to momentarily turn away from the exhausting, heart-pricking thrust and parry that sometimes passes for conversation in this cramped apartment.

When they pick up the thread again, Barbara offers a bit of conciliatory praise, about how Sister Sharp, one of her fellow missionaries, told her at church last Sunday that "you were very mannerly. 'I don't know what he does at home,' she said to me, 'but he has very good manners. You done a good job.'

"And, what I told her, Lavar, is that 'when a child knows right from wrong, you don't have to worry about him. And the way they learn is by being told in a way that they really listen. You tell them once and back it up, so you don't have to tell him twice.' "

Cedric moves the conversation over to the Sharp girls, two beautiful, leggy sisters—children of a police detective—who are both flourishing at the University of Maryland.

"Yes, they're peacocks. Lavar, I seen you watch the way they walk and everything. Any man would watch. Attraction like that often leads to other things, to a man making a fool of himself."

Cedric fidgets in his chair. They've stumbled into the eye of the storm—the issues of love, sex, and marriage—and the two of them just stare at each other. "So," he says, moving first, "how do you know what love is?"

"Well, you know because you can be yourself with that person."

"Okay, but how would you know it's not just lust?"

" 'Cause if it's love, Lavar, you won't want to sleep with the person. You understand, it's too precious a thing for that. You need to know who you are and you need to know who they are. And that's enough. Really knowing another person of the other sex can be very exciting."

Barbara has run these lines through her head many times, figuring Cedric would eventually press her on the subject and sort of hoping he would. But, wading in, she realizes she's on anything but firm ground. Looking at him intently across the table, she knows that she can't recall much about the urgent issues of an eighteen-year-old boy. She has little idea what's really going on in her son's head.

The air suddenly seems heavy, and they both turn and watch a few moments of TV. When Cedric starts up again, it's with a diversion: "You know, I'm never gonna fall in love."

"What you saying, fool?"

"I just want to be by myself," he says, clearly playing. "Maybe I'll just adopt some kids."

She can play, too, though she's not as clever as he is at coy asides and misdirection. "All right, then," she retorts, "how would you take care of kids while you work? Think about that."

"I don't know. I'd hire a nanny."

She laughs. "No, Lavar, you'd send them off on a train to D.C. for me to take care of, a long train ride, 'cause you won't be here. You ain't coming back here."

She's not sure how she ended up here, but the light banter somehow brought her to the central issue of her future: will he leave forever? But he dodges it. There seems to be something else on his mind.

"All right then, Ms. Jennings," Cedric says, theatrically. "I must have forgotten to ask you something in our discussion of a few minutes ago. . . . Have you ever been in love?"

She stops, startled. He's been drafting her on the curve and just blew by on the home stretch. She stares at him a moment, as a thousand scenes run through her head, racing backward until she sees herself sitting in a hunter green Cordoba, sunk deep in Corinthian leather. She looks down.

"I thought I was," Barbara Jennings says, barely audible. "I thought I was, once."

In summer, walking any street in the Shaw neighborhood, on the impoverished fringe of Northwest Washington, is to weave by kitchen chairs tucked into the narrow shadow of buildings. People sit in clusters and talk and swelter. Around here, the inside of almost every home is unbearable, the outside just a bit better. Except at Scripture Cathedral, a dark, cool cave—the only air-conditioned refuge in sight.

All of which helps make for a *very* healthy crowd this Sunday August morning, Bishop Long thinks, as he gazes out from his comfy wing on the stage.

As the choir finishes up a haunting rendition of "I'm Gonna Make It," Long scans the transfixed crowd—close to five hundred today— and muses that he already has "made it." Then he shakes his head, cutting it off. He considers such feelings a dangerous strain of self-satisfaction, something God would want him to resist. He is only God's vessel, after all. But the splendor all around is sometimes hard to overlook.

By the summer of 1995, Bishop Long has built a small empire, stretching from the newly refurbished cathedral to his loyal, protective staff, his daily radio show, his TV choir on local cable, and a growing operation that produces pamphlets, tapes, and related religious product lines. Still, there's plenty left for good works, charity, and outreach, with programs for feeding the poor, drug treatment, literacy and adult education classes, day care, and shelters for the homeless.

Not that he's avoided controversy. Bishop Long's comfortable house in Mitchellville, Maryland; his Cadillacs; his finely cut suits; some nearly destitute members of his flock giving their last dime— these drew a few nasty TV broadcasts a few years back, full of unholy clichés. He said it would blow over—and it did—though his competitor clergymen, out of jealousy mostly, sometimes bring it up.

Let them, he thinks, as his foot taps to the music. Why should he be denied a comfortable existence? He works long and hard, and he's saving lives—literally. Judges remand young defendants to his authority. Principals beg him to walk the halls of their schools. He provides a fully formed, self-supporting alternative to the streets, a place a kid can retreat to after school each day and practically all weekend.

"Pop, Pop with Jesus! Pop, Pop with Jesus!" the choir belts out, swaying and stomping, as Long picks up the rhythm and absently claps along. He'll be preaching in a few minutes, so he begins his preparations: looking across the faces in the pews—a thousand life stories he knows by heart—trying to connect, to feel their energy.

The time has come to preach the gospel. He rises, slowly and dramatically, from the chair. Rather than his usual dark suit, today he is resplendent in one of his bishop outfits, a pearl-white robe with blue and yellow tassels and a small, cardinal-style cap.

He greets the flock with a casual smile and makes a few announcements about upcoming events, which is easier to do now than after he's been yelling and sweating for a few hours. Today is Women's Day, a special day of appreciation for the church's bulwark. While Long and his phalanx of dark-suited men are clearly in charge, this is mostly a place for young children and their single mothers—the fierce churchwomen, who do most of the work around here.

Since the beginning of the year, the women have organized countless activities to build unity and, as always, raise money. Later today, he tells them, the top woman fund-raiser will be honored with a queen-for-a-day ceremony, where she'll get a plastic crown and bouquet of roses, toiletries and perfumes, and a free, four-day, round trip excursion to Powerfest, a convention of Pentecostal ministries that will be held a few weeks from now in Virginia.

"All of you women do so much for us here," he says, grinning coyly, telegraphing some levity, "that I'd take you all out for dinner if I could. But it'd bankrupt me—looks like some of you ladies can really eat."

He gets hearty, self-aware laughs from the female infantry—always a nice way to start things off—and then Long cracks his white-leather monogrammed Bible at the bookmark: "Thus the Lord says unto you, 'Be not afraid or dismayed by reason of this great multitude, for the battle is not yours, but God's.'"

And he starts spinning it.

"You may not have a battle with ships of war—like the ancient folks had in this passage from the Bible—but YOU have a combat, YOU have a struggle. Some of you have battles at your home! With your children! With your husband! Battles on your job, with your boss!

"But the battle is not yours, the battle is God's . . . HALLELU-JAH! But before the battle can become that of God, you've got to give it to Him—as long as you're fighting the battle, He won't fight. The Lord has learned how to stay out of battles, unless you give it to Him. Unless you step aside and say, 'It's in God's hands.'

"Don't look at the problem and try to figure it out! Look up, look up to God! That's where the answers are. . . .''

Long stops, mops his brow, and looks out. It's important that to-day's sermon offer pointed lessons to certain people in the room. He needs to know where those people are sitting, so—at the right mo-ment—he can seem to yell right in their ear. He browses the rows of faces until he spots Cedric Jennings: tenth row, right side.

Cedric is one of Long's favorites, along with his mother—been that way since early on. And Bishop knows that today is one of Cedric's last days in church before he leaves for college—for Brown University. The Ivy League is a rarity for a young person from Scripture, and Long hopes it will be seen as a blazing testimony to faith.

He takes a deep breath, launches forward for another half-hour, piling one rhythmic line on the next, ending each with a "HAH," as much punctuation as respiration. "Some of us have battles going on in our mind, because Satan shoots for the mind. HAH! That's why Jesus said, 'I will keep them in perfect peace if they keep their mind stayed on Me.' HAH!''

Then he stops so abruptly that his voice seems to echo. The choir comes up again, on Long's cue, and begins singing, "Give Your Prob-lems to God," giving him a precious few minutes to think about his finale. This is one of the most challenging finishes of any sermon of the year: the tricky, off-to-college speech, one moment when a crack in the church's foundation gets revealed.

The problem stems from a conundrum he's thought through a thousand times. Worldly success—the kind of genuine, respect-in-the-community, house-in-the-suburbs achievement that he finds among his neighbors in middle-class Mitchellville—has never fit well inside the doors of Scripture. And going to college is a first step on that path away from here.

The natural recruits for his brand of fiery Pentecostalism are not those who have gone to college or are expecting to. Rather, they are people at the bottom, who don't know where the path to status, credential, and material gain even *begins*. In his heart, Long knows he mostly gives them a starting point, a place of retreat where they can figure out who they are. Here, at least, they can hand over their already cheapened lives to faith. It helps plenty of them get on the right track and eventually get a little something for themselves—a steady job, maybe even a house. And they remain faithful members, contributors, and true believers as long as they attribute any forward motion—completely and utterly!—to the mysteries of faith.

Yet, it is Long's fate, and that of his church, that the greatest transformations occur among those who usually end up leaving. They're the special few who distill their unquestioned faith in God's power into a faith in themselves and their own power, a faith in their own ability to figure things out, improve themselves, and find their way in the world. And when they get it, there's a subtle, though defining, change of perspective.

It's something Long can detect. When a congregant, probably living paycheck to paycheck, gives $500, winning a trip to the stage for Bishop's own Holy Spirit "touch" to the forehead, it's because that contributor truly *believes* the Bible's assurance that each such gift will return a blessing to them tenfold. But, as the true believer dances on the stage, infused with the Spirit and sure that tenfold—or a hundredfold—rewards are coming, Long might spot some lady in her new dress wince or a newly confident man, fresh from a big promotion, snicker. There are a few congregants who've discovered another way to get ahead, to get that house, and a bigger one after it—the secular way, by studying hard, going to a top college and maybe graduate school, by networking, strategizing, and matching preparation with opportunity. Sure, they still believe in God, but He's got competition now—a belief in the sovereignty of self—and the spell of absolute, unquestioning faith, upon which Long has built his cathedral, is broken.

Despite all he's built, Long knows he can rise only so high as a pastor to the downtrodden. It binds him to the bottom. Even when he profits modestly for himself, his wife, and his kids, the disparities between his life and those of his constituents grow so wide that fingers point at him. The accomplished people, the city's black professionals and leaders of its public life—they don't come to this church. Sure, a few visit—Jesse Jackson and a handful of well-known ministers and black politicians—but they're like him, people whose success is, paradoxically, owed to the needy and the threadbare.

It can all get so bitter. After Long detects the telltale snicker or wince—that sidelong look of doubt—it's just a matter of time. He wants to scream at them, "I remember when you were down and out, when you were sure that no one could love you—with all your betrayals and bankruptcies and sinning—and I showed you how Jesus can cleanse you and God can love you, even when the whole world seems to hate you. Isn't that worth something, if nothing more than loyalty?" But, they just slip out anyway, usually without a word, and later he hears that they're bad-mouthing him, saying he's just about stealing, squeezing money from poor people who just don't have it to give. And, Lord, he tries not to get angry. Those prosperity-bound defectors just don't want to remember their debt to faith, he tells himself.

As the choir finishes its last chorus of "Give Your Problems to God," he wonders if he should lash out, right now.

But why? Doesn't do any good. They still leave, his favorites—the most capable among them—the ones who discover enough faith in themselves that the world suddenly seems hopeful, so hopeful that they feel they don't need a sanctuary. It breaks his heart. He closes his Bible as the choir sits, and he turns his glare on Cedric Jennings—the one he's worried about.

"I know a few of our children will be leaving soon for college. And we're all very proud of them. And we want them to study hard," he says quietly, choosing his words with care.

He sees Cedric look around, like he's worried that everyone is watching him.

Long grabs the pulpit's edges and begins again, speaking softly and deliberately. "I'll tell you something that I don't want any of you children to forget. God is sometimes hard to find on the college campus. Don't you forget that Satan loves a mind that strays far from the Holy Word. And, where some of you are going, you'll be taught to trust your mind, to trust man's theories about history and literature and how the world works. Yes, all you fine students must ask your questions and get your good grades. . . ." He stops and puts a hard eye on Cedric, who is looking back now, frozen in place. "But, never forget—never—that the only real answers lie with God."

The room is silent. Long exhales and looks at his watch. It's 2:30. This service that began at 10:45 is almost over. He, like everyone, can smell the fried chicken's sweet greasy scent wafting up from the basement and causing stomachs to growl.

But no one leaves the room—no one eats!—until they've made their sacrifice to faith.

"Have you given the last $10 in your checking account?!" Long screams. "Have you!? If you haven't, now is the time—see what it feels like to put your trust in the Almighty. I want a line down the middle, a long one, with everyone giving $20 each. And I want all the givers to come up front for a special blessing. Let's Goooo!"

The line starts to snake up the aisle as the pews empty. "It's so sweet," Long exults. He glances over at Cedric, standing in a row that's now mostly empty, looking confused, and he knows that there *are* demons up ahead for this boy, his prize child . . . who's *not budging*. Long decides that he'd better crank it up a notch, and he starts windmilling his thick arms, jumping and yelling, "Jesus is coming! Jesus is coming!" his robes billowing as he whips the faithful to frenzy, uncoupling hope from reason with the swinging ax of faith, and watches the line stretch toward the chapel's rear doors.

Finally, he sees him, his boy, a baby of this church, run up the aisle to drop a crumpled bill in the basket and join a swarm of uplifted arms at the foot of the stage, each hand groping for the Holy Spirit "touch," hoping to feel the surge of God's power. And Bishop C. L. Long, gripping the pulpit, reaches over the crowd—way out—toward Cedric Jennings, who lifts his long fingers for a final blessing.

Washington's Northwest corner of wide, tree-lined streets and brick center-hall colonials has emptied out. The beltway around the city was jammed last night and this morning as the army of lawyers, lobbyists, journalists, and assorted bureaucrats escaped to cooler locales in the mountains of Virginia, the Maryland shore, or favored spots up the coastline to Cape Cod and Martha's Vineyard. The typical itinerary is to begin vacationing this weekend and stretch it through the following Labor Day weekend.

As dusk arrives on Saturday night, August 24, it seems like everyone remaining in Washington is out on the stoop. Despite the heat, there is a festiveness everywhere, with those who remain behind having now won the city by default.

Over at Scripture Cathedral, lights blaze through the stained-glass windows, like there's a bonfire inside, as fifteen hundred black men stand shoulder to shoulder in the pews and the crowded balcony. It is the first official organizing meeting for next month's Million Man March. Bishop Long, proud that Scripture was selected by Minister Louis Farrakhan to be march headquarters, reaches for the hand of a Nation of Islam official—an aide Farrakhan sent down just for this meeting—so they can raise their clasped fists in triumph. And as they do, the throng of black men in dashikis and business suits and worn jeans lets out a roar that so many of them clearly hope will be the start of something . . . anything.

On the northeast fringe of the city, Cedric Gilliam pecks Sherene, his new girlfriend, on the cheek as he slips through the door of the Chateau—a raucous black nightclub—where she works as a hostess. He breathes in the smoke and the smell of beer, not wanting either to leave his nostrils. A month ago, one of the regular parole department urine tests found his urine dirty with heroin—a violation of his probation—and since then a half-dozen federal marshals have been by his mother's house. It's just a matter of time before they overtake him. He had hoped that the intoxicating buzz of this favorite joint—as familiar to him as his own voice—would help drone out the ticking clock he hears in his head. Instead, being here makes him feel like the air is slipping from his lungs.

Across town, on a quiet street of row houses in Southeast, Cedric Jennings is also trying to breathe deeply. Tomorrow he will begin packing for Tuesday's journey to Providence. Tonight is his last big night in town. He exults, slapping tree branches with his up-stretched hand as he walks. It's a night for feeling good.

He spots a few of his relatives sitting on the stoop of his aunt Chris's house, half a block ahead, where a going-away party for him has just started. He breaks into a trot.

"Va, Uncle Va," his nephew Lawrence shouts as he enters the house, and Cedric sees that most of the guests have arrived.

"Hi everybody!" Cedric shouts, looking neat and casual in his long white T-shirt and black jeans.

Aunt Chris pokes her head out of the kitchen and yells, "I hope you're ready to eat tonight, Lavar," and waits until he assures her, "Oh, yes, I'm ready," before she disappears back to her ministrations. Everyone returns to the couch or chair where they were a moment ago, and the room's hive of conversation resumes.

Everyone comes over to greet him, and Cedric looks around the bustling room, lips together in a wet smile. He feels a wash of sentimentality, a nostalgia for the present, and lets his eyes wander back and forth across the room like he might a poem he needs to memorize for an English class—wanting to remember it, every line. Then he settles into a living room chair near the front door.

The only man present is a cousin of Barbara's named Douglas, a computer specialist in his mid-thirties who has had solid jobs but some problems with drugs. He says to one of Barbara's sisters that he's not out running tonight with the other men because "I'm trying to get my life together."

Eating his chicken, Douglas starts into a routine about Barbara's mother telling her father to "bring that big old thing over here"—some sort of sexual reference—and Cedric is soon laughing hysterically along with the table of Jennings sisters. The talk is fast, riffing between subjects and inside references, and Cedric gets seconds, then thirds.

He jumps up, says he can't wait to cut the cake, and opens a large box to see the creamy white rectangle with "Congratulations, Cedric" in blue icing. "Cedric??" he says in mock confusion as everyone turns. "Oh, uh-huh. Cedric, dat's just my professional name." This, as always, gets big laughs.

Soon the little kids are running down from upstairs, having heard about the cake. There's a lightness to everything, a sense that anything is possible. Someone says that Cedric should touch the heads of the children "so to pass on the gift of intelligence." Little Lawrence and the others squirm and dodge as Cedric shouts, "Come here, you," chasing them. He corners Lawrence long enough to tap his forehead.

All the talk of the future, of gifts being passed on, makes Daisy, the oldest sister, want to say a few words. That's why they're here, after all. To wish Lavar well.

"Come on ya'll," she says purposefully. Somebody turns off the TV, and a circle forms around the dining room table as everyone joins hands—Cedric next to his mother—and squeezes their eyes shut.

"God," Daisy begins, her voice searching for a comfortable pitch. "We ask you to bless Lavar. Oh boy, God bless him. . . ."

It is expected that inspiration will arrive, that Daisy will feel the Spirit and the words will spill forth. It takes a moment to happen, and then her voice grows steady and firm.

"Everything that his hand touches, let it turn good. . . . Oh Yes! Lord, let him bring a good report back to his family. Let him succeed, Lord, in this long journey!"

The last fiery words are barely out when Cedric, his eyes closed, feels an ache about the length of the journey—winding and treacherous, into unexplored country—and Daisy seems to feel it, too, because her voice drops to a plea. "Oh please," she says, softly, "we're praying that you shield him and protect him. And let him not be brought down. . . . And even when he is far away, God, let him know that he is loved by his family." It is better that their eyes are closed, better to see beyond this shabby room and their plain clothes, as they all say, "Amen."

After a few hours, the party ends, and Cedric—full from the feast and warmed by a round of hugs—ambles outside onto the lamplit street. He walks a few blocks, smiling back at the black folks who nod at him from stoops or from the doorways of bodegas, and then finds himself checking the street signs.

It's not far from here, he thinks, not far at all. A few minutes later, he's rounding the corner on 15th Street. He wanders a bit, perplexed, having come onto the block from an unfamiliar direction. He's not sure which house it is—even though he lived here, on and off, as a kid and was here four years ago when his grandfather died. He begins studying the front facades, his step slowing.

He walks by a porch where two men are reclining on kitchen chairs and then turns to look back at it.

"Uncle Butch?" he calls out tentatively, and one of the men comes to the railing, watchful and on guard.

"It's me," says Cedric. "It's Lavar."

"Lavar! Damn, I didn't recognize you," says the man, waving on Cedric's approach. "Come here, boy."

Cedric excitedly bounds up the porch steps and Butch—Barbara's younger brother, a federal service worker who took over the house—surveys him in a toe-to-head sweep. "Boy, you got big. You're like a man, now."

Cedric laughs, "I just wish I was wider, more filled out." Butch, a trim, athletic-looking man a few inches shorter than Cedric, is wearing spandex tights with a racing stripe from a day of bicycling. He tells his nephew to "be patient, 'cause it will come and you'll end up being a good-sized man, definitely will."

The company of men is so novel for Cedric that this modest assurance lifts him.

Butch introduces Cedric to his friend, a tall, light-skinned man in his early fifties, maybe, and wide and solid as a tree. "Howdoyado, young man," Cornelius Leonard says, deferentially tapping the brim of his Washington Redskins cap before returning his attention to a Styrofoam cup filled with some sort of punch. Butch has a cup, too, sitting on the railing next to his expensive portable phone. Cedric spots a small bottle of vodka on a corner of the porch.

"Yeah, that's right, I heard there was a party for you tonight over at Chris's," Butch says, and Cedric is surprised, assuming that the crowd of absent uncles and missing fathers in his family wouldn't have even been told about it. "Sorry," says Butch awkwardly. "Sorry, and all, that I couldn't make it."

As Butch talks, Cedric looks at the cluster of men, hanging out and chatting, jaunty and cool. It's a whole unexplored society he's about to leave behind.

"So, you still doing good at school, Lavar?" Butch asks, beckoning Cedric's attention.

"Oh yea," he says, "just about top in my class. And next year, I'm going to Brown University."

Butch squints, clearly having never heard of it, and Cedric helps him along. "It's in Providence, Rhode Island. . . . It's Ivy League and all."

This elicits a meaningful *harummph* from Cornelius, who talks for a moment about how he once was about to go to college—on a football scholarship—"but things went real sour, real fast," he says. He ended up spending a couple decades in prison instead.

Cedric nods solemnly at this—an appropriate response, he hopes—and Cornelius asks Cedric where he went to high school.

"Ballou," he says, trying to make it sound esteemed. "Frank W. Ballou Senior High School."

Cornelius chuckles, thinking it's a joke. "Come on, now, I know Ballou," he says. "Some guys in the joint came from Ballou, and I have a cousin who's a teacher there. Ballou's no place for students."

"He's right about that," Butch follows up, taking a swig of his punch.

"It's just no place," echoes Cornelius, pulling down on the brim of his cap as he glances toward the street. "Just noooo place."

Standing between them, looking one way and then the other, Cedric begins to laugh, and they do, too, and then he's laughing too hard and tries to stop but can't. When he finally quiets, both men are staring at him with wary, glazed smiles, and Cedric Jennings knows, at long last, that the time has come for him to leave this place behind.

7

GOOD-BYE to YESTERDAY

Lavar? Time's up!" Barbara Jennings shouts as she pushes open the apartment door, back from her fourth trip up the three flights from the parking lot. "We've got to go! You hear?"

No response. She stomps back to the bedroom and sees that Cedric's head is under the bed. "I can't find it. It's nowhere . . ." comes a muffled voice from under the mattress. "I just can't go without my calculator. It's got a graphing function and everything."

The long-awaited journey is at hand. Sometime today—a sunny, white-hot Tuesday at the end of August—Barbara will drive her son to what she imagines is the cool, green north: Providence, Rhode Island. At least, that's the plan.

"Did you hear me, Lavar?" she says, not really angry.

"Yeah, Ma," he says, rising from his knees. "I guess, yeah, okay. . . . I'll get a new calculator up there."

Barbara, a sweating tempest with hands on hips, looks around Cedric's room, just now noticing the change. The room, always a mess, at least used to have his presence as its warm center. Now all that's left are empty shelves to oversee a mess of items that didn't make the cut.

Barbara is not feeling sentimental. Early this morning, while Cedric was still asleep (having spent a late night prowling a favorite mall with LaTisha), she thought about other parents of the college bound, her new peers, who, she figures, are probably packing up their cars today in the suburbs. They can be all mushy about their children leaving some happy place where they were raised, a house, she imagines, with a garage, lots of bedrooms, and a lawn. This apartment, though, has not been a site of very many sweet memories. And without them, all that remains is raw, off-to-college tension. She can't wait to get out of here, so she hauled most of the load down to the parking lot by herself.

Cedric, having finally made it as far as the living room, loads up a last shopping bag with a favorite calculus book, his white Nikes, a huge blue Nivea skin cream bottle (to keep his skin from getting "chalky"), and the Brown University course catalogue. He hands the bag to his mother so he can pick up the Sharp Trinitron from the floor. "This was my social life, my date every Friday night," he says wryly, holding the tube, "so she coming with me."

"Fine. You ready?" Barbara asks curtly as they both slip past the plastic "Lord, Help Me to Realize That Nothing Can Happen Today You and I Can't Handle" wall hanging in the front foyer. Without looking up or looking back, she triple locks the door.

In the parking lot, these last items are squeezed into a white 1995 Dodge Caravan. She steps back a moment, surveys the tightly packed van, and exhales theatrically. Thinking back on the past few days of panicked preparations, she can hardly believe she has made it this far.

With her lone credit card at its limit, she had to withdraw cash for the trip and has been nervous for days about carrying around so much money. If she got ripped off, she fretted, Lavar simply doesn't go to college. Not wanting to spend money on long-distance calls to check on hotels in Providence, she went with what she knew—1-800-HOLI-DAY—committing to a budget-straining rate of $96 a night at the Holiday Inn in downtown Providence.

Yesterday, at Thrifty Car Rental in downtown D.C., she felt like she was walking a tightrope. She pulled out $232 in cash and her Visa. "Are you going to put anything on this Visa?" she asked the clerk, barely able to breathe, knowing that an affirmative response could prohibit the entire trip.

"No, it's just in case, just to secure it," he said, and Barbara felt reborn moments later as she slipped behind the wheel of the van.

Now she runs her hand along the grooves of the sliding side door, slams it, and tells Cedric to get into the front passenger seat.

In a moment, they're turning off V Street, catching the highway that crosses the Anacostia River and circles past the Capitol dome. The volleyball courts and softball diamonds near the Washington Monument are a parched savanna, and paddle boats are docked, lifelessly, on the glassy tidal basin. As the van passes behind the Lincoln Memorial, Barbara—feeling much but saying little—is easy prey for Cedric. "I don't know when I'm coming back," he starts.

Acutely aware of everything today, Barbara is ready: "Well, I told Bishop about Thanksgiving break, and he said he's going to send the money up for the trip, to make sure you come home."

"I can't be coming home for everything. Christmas either."

Barbara looks over at him in exasperation. "Well, I'm not making any big Christmas this year. I'll be going to Bishop's house, so that'll be that."

"Fine," Cedric says, knocked backward a step and looking to parry from a new direction. "I won't be calling for a while either."

"You will too, you'll be calling all the time."

"Why would I want to call?" he says, his eyebrows raised. "I'll be busy."

And around they go, working the wound until Barbara makes a move to cauterize it: "Either way, I'm coming for parents' weekend in October."

"Why?"

" 'Cause I'm a parent, it's my right!" she snaps, ushering in a period of silence. They turn from Washington's beltway onto Interstate 95, the road that will lead, seven hours later, into downtown Providence.

They've been on trips before, but this is different. Because one of them won't be returning, the distance they travel is a span that will soon stand between them. Barbara feels each mile and, as the hours pass, reminisces about her life, while Cedric, nervously cracking sunflower shells, has his eyes fixed ahead.

After a quick dinner stop, Cedric's tenseness succumbs to a long nap. When he awakes, just before midnight, Barbara tells him that they're just a few miles from Providence. She looks over at him and wants to tell him that there's nothing to worry about, that everything's going to be fine, but she's not sure how to put it without making him defensive.

Some notion seems to strike him, and he starts rooting through a bag of cassette tapes that he brought. In a moment, Rev. James Moore and the Mississippi Mass Choir is backing up the stunning LaShun Pace, one of Cedric's favorites, as she belts out "Shelter from the Storm," a gospel standard. He cranks it. The van rocks. They put the windows down. It's what has taken them this far, Barbara muses— through apprehension, doubt, even fear. Just crank up the gospel. "I'll be there for you . . ." Cedric sings loudly, and Barbara, guiding the van into downtown Providence, sings along.

The next morning blooms into a radiant, cloudless day, as it ought to be. Freshmen arrive for orientation, ferried by a grand procession of proud parents.

Barbara, tired from the drive, gets a late start and, before long, the day feels harried. It's nearly noon by the time they get to College Hill, a steep slope on top of which Brown sits like a cloud city above the gritty ethnic enclaves, legendary Italian restaurants, and aging factories of Providence.

"I wanted to get this all done early. Now look," she says, sitting in the van near the Brown student union as Cedric, looking at a checklist in his orientation packet, slips out to go get his temporary student ID. "Don't be all day, Lavar," she calls after him, all business, "I gotta get back home."

Cedric has drawn a desirable dorm, Andrews Hall. It's a three-story brick horseshoe on the quieter Pembroke side of campus that was renovated over the summer and now boasts fresh carpeting and new paint. From the Andrews parking lot, they unload the van swiftly, with Cedric helping on this end. While Barbara glances tersely at other parents—mostly white, of course—unloading Lexuses and Range Rovers and Volvo wagons, she notices that Cedric seems to be increasingly relaxed—smiling at some of the other incoming freshmen and offering unsolicited greetings.

"These dorms are nice," Barbara notes over her shoulder to Cedric, who is dragging a trunk full of linens behind her across the second-floor hallway carpet. Remembering Cedric's complaints about last summer's dorms, she adds, "And a lot nicer than MIT, ain't it?"

"Lot nicer," he says, almost shouting. "This place is nothing like MIT."

A small paper square taped to the door of room 216 says "Cedric Lavar Jennings and Robert Burton." Cedric fumbles with the key and opens the heavy wooden door.

"Wow," he says.

"Hmmm, very nice," Barbara confirms.

His roommate, Rob, has already been here, settled in and gone. Barbara moves to the empty bed and starts unpacking while Cedric goes back downstairs for the rest. She carefully places a dozen new pairs of underwear, a dozen new pairs of socks, and six new T-shirts (clothes bought with money she didn't have to spare) onto closet shelves, and she begins a ritual that she figures is being repeated at this moment in hundreds of rooms across the campus: a mother making her child's bed for the last time. It's not like Barbara made his bed back home, she muses, but it doesn't matter. She made a thousand beds before she was twenty, and now she meticulously presses flat a fold of sheet, tucking it tight. Cedric returns, carrying his CDs, and crosses the room to check the unfamiliar titles in Rob's collection as Barbara lays the blanket and smoothes it.

With the van unpacked and their stomachs growling, Barbara decides they should walk to one of the dining halls for lunch. Soon, she and Cedric are strolling the campus, through archways and across neatly edged rectangles of thick grass.

While Barbara is delighted that Cedric, so tightly wound yesterday, is now buoyantly bouncing as he walks, an unwanted self-consciousness is welling up inside her. She'd rather not notice the cars other parents are driving, the clothes they're wearing, and the ease with which they move. She knows, of course, that the typical Brown parents probably went to college and on to some professional status that their offspring, by virtue of this Ivy League acceptance, are now bounding toward. Here, it's a day for her to be proud, but she can't help staring at them— these smiling, polished people—and overhearing their jaunty melody of generational succession: a child's footsteps following their own, steps on a path that leads to prosperity's table and a saved seat right next to Mom and Dad.

Barbara, watching Cedric demolish a ham sandwich at the dining hall, tries to figure out what she brings to this place, where she fits. It's her day, too, she resolves, looking across a dining hall filled with effusive, chatty parents and freshmen, though her song is flat and elemental—an old, familiar harmony, really, about sacrifice and denial and a child venturing where the parent never could.

"Really is a whole 'nother world up here," she says quietly across the table as Cedric reaches for her untouched sandwich, barely noticing that she's there. In that instant, she realizes how afraid she is that she might lose him.

It's almost two o'clock when they head back to the dorm. Near the new, soaring brick medical school, Cedric spots a bumper sticker on a parked car: "Your Honor Student Was Beaten Up By My Kid" it says, a play on the honor student bumper stickers that are especially popular in the inner cities.

"That car must be from D.C.," he jokes, and Barbara puts her arm around him as they laugh.

A tall, thin Caucasian girl with hazel-blue eyes, a row of earrings, and a shaved head strolls by. "Isn't that awful," Barbara murmurs to Cedric after the girl passes. "Must be chemotherapy." He nods sympathetically.

A few blocks ahead, passing a lovely Victorian house just north of Andrews dorm, Barbara admires the wide, circular porch and an apple arbor alongside it. "That fruit could feed a lot of hungry people," she says as they walk the last few feet to the dorm. Inside Cedric's room, they're puttering around when the door opens. It's a smallish white boy with dark hair, a faint Van Dyke beard, and sandals.

"You must be Rob," says Cedric with a wide smile.

"You must be Cedric," he echoes back in a soft, cheery voice.

Barbara nods a hello at him and rises from Cedric's bed. She knows that the time has come. In a moment, she and Cedric go down the elevator and outside and begin walking the last block to the van. She doesn't want to lead and senses that he doesn't either, so their pace slows until they're almost weaving—like they're not going anywhere, really. But as he looks down at his feet, she's able to glimpse the side of his face without him knowing. And Barbara Jennings can't help but hear echoes of her earlier self, holding a baby a little too tight, saying, "I'll save you, and me, too."

At the bumper of the van, he looks up.

"You be good, okay?" she says.

"Yeah . . ."

"Come here," she finally says, holding her arms out wide, and the two fall together as she presses her cheek hard against his.

"Trust in God, let Him guide you," she whispers.

"I will, Ma."

They hug for a good, long time. She's not been a mother to show him much physical affection in these latter years. The situation demanded strength. She had to be a father, too, as best she knew how, and maybe that hardened her touch. So, as they pull apart, she finds that her cheeks are flushed. She shakes it off.

"Okay, now," Barbara says. She reaches into the back seat and gives him a Frito-Lay assortment pack, uneaten from the trip. He nods. She gets into the front seat and waves once, and Cedric begins ambling down the hill toward the dorm.

"Wait!" She spots his deodorant in the space between the seats and yells through the open window. He runs the few feet back to get it.

"All right, 'bye," she says, and he turns, briskly walking back to the dorm as she watches him in the rearview. He doesn't look back.

Barbara is quiet as the van eases into gear and drifts onto the quiet street. She told herself she wouldn't cry, so she tries to occupy her eyes, looking at things she passes by. That Victorian would sure be nice, she thinks to herself, heading past the wraparound porch.

But something's wrong. She snaps to attention. The money!

Next thing, she's back in the dorm parking lot and then running up the stairs, taking them two at a time.

The door to room 216 bursts open. "I forgot this," Barbara says, panting, and squeezes three neatly folded twenties into her son's hand. Already, though, the room belongs to Cedric Lavar Jennings, a Brown freshman, and that nice white boy on the other bed. She feels suddenly unsure. Cedric is smiling broadly but like he's looking right through her. "Well, good-bye Lavar," she says simply and slips out. Doesn't hug him this time. She'd think a lot about that later.

It takes a moment for the heavy oak door to swing on its hinge. And when it slams, it's like a thunder clap, leaving her alone with the smell of fresh paint.

Cedric, sitting lightly on his taut blanket, looks across the dorm room at Rob Burton, who is slumped on *his* mother-made bed, looking right back. It's one of life's storied moments of forced intimacy.

"So, ummm, is your house real close to here?" asks Cedric, making sure he smiles.

"Well, Marblehead is just in Massachusetts, about an hour and a half," says Rob. "My mom dropped me off this morning. My dad has someone covering for him so he's on Cape Cod this week. He's birding," says Rob. "They and my sister, she's at Harvard, will all take a trip down next week to go out to lunch or whatever."

Cedric looks at him blankly, all energy diverted to internal processing: Covering. Doctor? Cape Cod. Summer house? Birding . . .

"Birding?" he asks.

"Yeah, you know, bird watching."

"Oh, right, uh-huh."

"What music you got over there?" Cedric asks, hopping up and crossing the room to examine Rob's CD collection. "I've heard of these names—REM, Sting—but I don't know any of their music. Smashing Pumpkins? What, they sing Halloween songs?"

"You never heard the Smashing Pumpkins?" says Rob, courteously suppressing his surprise and then discounting the group. "Well, yeah, they're some band. You know, they're just okay."

Cedric appraises Rob from the corner of his eye as they stand—side by side—pawing through forty or so CDs in Rob's little slotted carrying case. Rob's a half-head shorter, maybe five-foot-six, but seems comfortable standing in tight. Cedric, who has always thought white people, in general, don't like being too physically close to blacks, feels himself loosening up. "I like Aerosmith," he chuckles as he slips the group's CD back into a slot. "So, at least I know one of them."

Then they're over at Cedric's collection—thirty-one CDs that he's carefully, lovingly collected—and Rob offers reciprocal curiosity. "What's SWV stand for?" he asks, inspecting a CD cover with three black women posturing in slinky red.

"Oh, right, that stands for Sisters With Voices," Cedric says, laughing, "with, you know, 'sister' being slang—like for a black woman."

"That much I could figure out," Rob laughs, clearly enjoying the cross-cultural riffing. "I mean, I'm not a *complete* idiot."

With matters moving breezily, they talk about how to organize the room. The beds are already against opposite walls, with double windows running most of the room's length between them. Under the windows, they push together the two, university-issue, white pine desks, so their outside edges touch, making a double-wide plateau that stands between their facing chairs. Each then begins to clutter his half with desk lamps, calendar mats, bookends, pencil holders, and whatnot.

Moving furniture, unpacking books, and plugging in digital clocks is an ideal follow-up to their delicate, though cordial, first chat. A burst of activity, and some sweat, seals their union. Despite obvious differences, this is a nascent moment when their interests are identical: get settled, be friends.

With goodwill suddenly married to survival, decisions are swift and simple, starting with an agreement to share Cedric's Sony CD cassette player and to put it on Rob's trunk.

"And, hey!" Rob says as Cedric spins, "we can share my fridge—no problem."

Cedric looks down at the small square brown fridge at the foot of Rob's bed—the sort of item seen almost nowhere in America outside of a college dorm. "All riiiiight," he says, surprised to find himself reaching out to shake Rob's hand. "We made it."

On the Brown campus, this is a prenatal period—six days of dense, carefully planned orientation activities for freshmen before classes start next Tuesday. The freshmen are divided into units, organized through dorm assignments, of between thirty and sixty students. Cedric's unit, two corridors of rooms in the eastern wing of Andrews Hall, is among the smallest, with only thirty-three kids.

By Wednesday night, only a few hours after the parents have left, Cedric has already pored over the large packet of orientation booklets, pamphlets, and fact sheets—more things, he thinks, than he'll ever need to know about Brown. He's especially drawn to figures about the racial/ethnic composition of the school's 5,559 full-time undergraduates. It's a strange list, he thinks. The terms are so complex: white, non-Hispanic, 66 percent; Asian or Pacific Islander, 15.3 percent; nonresident alien, 6.6 percent; black, non-Hispanic, 6.5 percent; Hispanic, 4.8 percent; American Indian or Alaskan Native, .3 percent.

At a quick unit meeting later that night, he looks around the second-floor lounge and does a quick head count: two blacks, including himself. The other one is an attractive dark-skinned female, who looks to him like a city girl. Cedric sort of nods across the room to her—there's not a chance to do much more—and he quickly does the math: two blacks out of thirty-three, or 6 percent. Just about the school average. Beyond the white kids—more than half the unit—there's a mixture: three Asian Americans, plus a girl from Singapore and another from Hong Kong; two Indian Americans (as opposed to Native Americans); one Arab American; two Hispanic Americans; a boy from Israel, another from Geneva, and a girl from Bosnia—more or less reflecting the percentages Cedric read about for the rest of Brown's undergraduates. One exception is that Brown's student body is half female but two-thirds of the unit are women.

As he passes the next day with this crowd, Cedric slips into his polite but wary game face, responding quickly when questioned, avoiding extended conversations, taking in more than he is giving out. He's taking mental notes on every discussion of who hails from where and what they've done, every hand raised in a group discussion that's not his, every offhand late-night reference to Hemingway or John Grisham, to Beethoven or Bob Dylan. From the collected references, he tries to decipher patterns of behavior and custom. It's exhausting. Periodically, he breaks from the crowd, retreating to his room to unwind, feeling like he's been cramming for a test.

The campus activities of these first two days are meant to instill pride of acceptance. Ceremonies large and small welcome each youngster to the exclusive society of the Ivy League. It starts on Wednesday evening at the incoming freshmen dinner as President Vartan Gregorian tells them they're the "best, most intelligent, most diverse class to ever enter Brown," an address he or his predecessors have given (generally called the "best ever" speech) to every incoming freshman class. The admissions numbers—measurable proof of specialness—are cited at intimate nighttime dorm meetings and in a grand speech by the admissions director at a class meeting on the green.

At this embryonic point, the unit moves as a pack, holding on to each other as they cross unfamiliar terrain, sure only of their specialness. They go to dinner in a roving band of fifteen.

On Thursday evening, Cedric's cluster bumps and jostles into the Ratty, the cavernous freshman cafeteria on the far side of campus. They settle into two long, rectangular tables.

Phillip Arden, the Geneva-bred son of a millionaire British mine owner and industrialist, looks up from his plate of pork chops with milky mystery gravy. "I probably got the lowest SAT score here," he says loudly, to no one in particular. Conversations along the table jerk to a halt. Cedric, who has been concentrating on the pork and mulling the idea of becoming a vegetarian, looks across the table at Phillip—a pleasant-looking, brown-haired boy. He exudes a sort of wide-eyed openness that Cedric already senses some of the women find endearing and the guys, mostly, naive. "And, you know," Phillip continues, "I got just over 1200."

Cedric puts down his fork, his heart sinking. He's been fretting over this moment since last year. Only a day into school, and it's already upon him.

Around the table they go. Almost all of the kids are, in fact, in Phillip's range, something Cedric—shooting daggers across the mystery gravy at the young mining heir—is sure he must have known. At the high end is Evan Horowitz, an intellectually ostentatious student from Stamford, Connecticut, who scored a 1430. At the low end is Sonya Garza, a lower-middle-class Mexican American from Sanger, California, who scored 970.

The wheel comes round.

"I, uh, got a 960," Cedric says, like he's mentioning the weather. No one reacts. There's a forced casualness to this conversation, as though no one much cares, but Cedric instantly realizes that he could, right now, recite back everyone's score, like it's some sort of identity number, and that they all could probably do the same with his 960.

"I'm not ashamed of it or anything," he says, not sure what tone he should affect, as others around him go on eating, pretending not to hear.

By Friday at dawn, a preemptive panic has set in. Maybe it was last night's SAT exchange. Maybe it was not knowing who Freud was in a lunchtime discussion Thursday or hearing that Phillip Arden's father owns an island near Bermuda. Or maybe it was the umpteenth exchange where he wasn't sure what to say, so said nothing. All he knows is that his suspicion that he lacks prerequisite knowledge and acquired poise is metastasizing as he squints into the early morning sun, unable to fall back to sleep. As he's lying there, dread is hatching a plan.

Throwing off the covers, he grabs the orientation booklet off his desk. Activities for Friday morning include scheduled meetings with academic advisers. Also today, professors are holding short classes to explain courses that are geared to freshmen.

Cedric gets dressed swiftly. He looks over at Rob, still asleep, and begins searching, quietly but furiously, for his temporary ID card. He must have left it at the dining hall last night. So breakfast, sitting in the silent dorm lounge, ends up being a bag of Fritos from the snack pack his mother left him. Looking over the course selection booklet this summer, he had figured on playing to his strengths in the first semester: calculus, of course, and Spanish. Now he revises that plan to match his strengths with a path of least resistance. He took Brown's Spanish placement test yesterday afternoon and got a 30—not great considering he's been taking Spanish since seventh grade, but enough to place him in second-, or even third-, semester Spanish at Brown.

He rushes from the dorm and seeks out a professor for second-semester Spanish. "Check out the textbook, see how it looks to you," she says, in English, thankfully, allowing him precious scheduling flexibility in which level class he'll take.

Math will be trickier. This, after all, is his métier—his passion and his expected major. He stops by the office of Professor Jonathan Lubin, who teaches Math 10, a third-semester calculus class, mostly for freshmen with a year of high school calculus and good advanced placement test scores.

Professor Lubin snatches a copy of the syllabus from his desk and hands it to Cedric.

"How does it look?" asks Lubin.

"Hmmm. I know some of this," Cedric mumbles, mostly to himself, regretting each word as it leaves his lips.

"Really. Like what?"

"Well, L'Hopital's rule, I mean I already had that," says Cedric about a rule to define the limit of functions, which he worked on at MIT.

"Really," says Lubin. "Look it over. What else?"

"Ummm. Techniques of integration, too." Cedric stops. He realizes he's dabbled in quite a bit of this stuff already.

"What kinds of grades did you get in math in high school?"

"You know, A's,"

"Of course, even if you've done these things, they'll be done in more depth here. But I think you certainly belong in this class, young man," says Professor Lubin, smiling broadly. Cedric finds himself gazing at Lubin's teeth, which might as well belong to a great white shark.

"I guess . . . well . . . I don't know," Cedric mumbles, backing out of the office.

"I'll be seeing you later," the professor calls out.

"Yeah, 'bye," waves Cedric, already gone, thankful that he didn't have to mention his satisfactory calculus advanced placement test score—a three out of a possible five—which would land him in this class for sure.

He looks at his map for the physics building and, after a few wrong turns, ends up at the office of his academic adviser, Professor Robert Pelcovits.

"Do you have a minute?" Cedric asks, ducking his head in.

Pelcovits, a nervous, birdlike man, looks at his schedule book. "Who are you?"

"I'm Cedric Jennings."

Like most other freshman academic advisers, Pelcovits has eight students to meet today, each of whom was given a meeting time on a slip of paper in their orientation packet. Cedric lost it.

"Well, sure, I guess I've got just a few minutes right now," says Pelcovits, searching around for Cedric's file. "Yes, here we are."

Cedric takes a deep breath and begins his pitch, trying not to worry about what's running through Pelcovits's head as he studies the file.

"I just feel I need to figure out where I stand," Cedric begins, steadily, having rehearsed this line at sunrise this morning. "I don't want to get in over my head."

Five minutes later, he gets Pelcovits's signature, approving his enrollment for Math 9, a second-semester calculus class a notch lower than the one he just attended. For English, Cedric opts to take Writings of Richard Wright, a freshman literature course. Its prime attraction is that he's already read and written book reports—in both eighth grade and twelfth grade—on the course's core text, *Native Son*. As to foreign language, Pelcovits, sensing Cedric's uneasiness, says he might as well look at both Spanish 1 and 2 and see which one he's more comfortable with.

Cedric still has one more class to sign up for to get his required fourth for the semester. Pelcovits suggests one of Brown's liberal arts fortes, maybe Political Theory.

"I'm not sure. It would have a lot of reading," Cedric says hesitantly. "But I'll check into that." He then turns the conversation to the last issue on his agenda, telling Pelcovits he's planning to take all his classes satisfactory/no credit, or S/NC, Brown's parlance for pass/fail. It's an option students tend to use for one class or two, tops, out of the four classes required each semester.

"Are you really sure about that?" the professor asks.

Cedric looks at him for a moment. Which way to go? Inside, he feels his pride being challenged by a choking fear of failure. Maybe they made a mistake by accepting him. If he winds up getting crushed in an academic defeat, he might be forced to return home, shamefully. Pride quickly dissolves, allowing Cedric a clear glimpse at what he needs to fall back on in order to clinch this approval. "Well, I didn't come from that good a school and all, a real bad city school," he says, forcing himself to look down, forlornly, feeling a bit nauseous.

Pelcovits accedes. For better or worse, Brown gives Cedric the upper hand. A defining feature here is student autonomy, the so-called open curriculum, which students won during demonstrations in the late 1960s. Students, in theory, can take everything satisfactory/no credit. The concept is noble: to encourage students to take intellectual risks, to try out some classes in unfamiliar disciplines they might otherwise avoid for fear of a bad grade. The intended message is to indulge your curiosity, challenge yourself, experiment.

Cedric has fashioned his own message: duck. He leaves Pelcovits's office having charted a slightly less taxing path, one that will allow him a few extra moments to stop, breathe, and fill what he is increasingly certain are gaping holes in his preparation. Walking back toward the main campus, he feels compromised but relieved, and his mind finally turns to food.

Cedric emerges from the stairwell swinging a Snapple Lemon Iced Tea bottle like a blackjack and sees a crowd gathering in the doorway of the second-floor lounge, just next to his room. It's 7:30 on Friday night, and a seminal moment of Brown's right-minded indoctrination is about to commence: the all-important diversity orientation session. Official title—"Community Values: Pluralism and Diversity."

The diversity workshop is actually the second such meeting of the day. Between 3:30 and 5 P.M., they all sat through "Community Values: Alcohol and Other Drugs, and Community Safety." But that was more a reading of the rules, without too much student participation. Still to come on Sunday night, "Community Values: Sex without Consent— Implications for Brown Students."

Rabbi Alan Flam, a university chaplain, head of Hillel (the student Jewish organization), and, for fourteen years, a facilitator of unit diversity meetings, welcomes the group as they settle into the lounge.

"To me, these meetings are one of the most exciting challenges of being here at Brown," begins the rabbi, a husky man with a trim beard and a passing resemblance to the actor Richard Dreyfuss. "Tonight is the beginning of a conversation that I'm hopeful will continue for your four years, or five, or eight years at Brown—however many you might spend here—and for your life after college. We'll have a conversation that goes to the core of what being a Brown student is about. So I welcome you."

With that portentous introduction, the students grow attentive as the rabbi and his student facilitator, Vida Garcia, a Hispanic third-year resident counselor from San Antonio, Texas, explain the first exercise: cultural pursuit.

It's a takeoff on the board game Trivial Pursuit. Students get a list of twenty culturally loaded questions (like "Knows what 'Juneteenth' is"; "Knows what an upside down pink triangle symbolizes"; "Knows the significance of Cinco de Mayo"; "Knows who Rosa Parks is") that they are not allowed to answer themselves. Instead, they have to find a different classmate for each answer, a classmate whom they think will know the answer, and get him or her to respond. The desire to get everything right, deeply ingrained in these reflex achievers, should force them to rely on stereotypes about who will know what.

And it works. Cedric walks up to a Latino-looking girl for the Cinco de Mayo response—gets it, checks a box on his page—and then is barraged. A steady stream of classmates approaches him, one after another, for the Rosa Parks response. Afterward, back on the couch, his head is spinning. He feels uncomfortable, manipulated, singled out solely because of his skin color. Sure, it's happened my whole life, he thinks, but he hated it then as he hates it now.

Students talk a while about their mixture of pride and resentment. Cedric, like everyone else, recognizes what just happened. The exercise forced students to act on prejudices—often drawn from obvious characteristics—that they'd rather not acknowledge having.

After a short break, they move to the next step: kids are given a small slip of white paper and told to write one word that tells who they are. Pick an identity—just one.

Cedric looks at the blank piece of paper in his hand and remembers the furious diatribes of Clarence Thomas. Everyone reduced to one-word definitions. So, he thinks, this must be how you end up so angry.

After a moment, Vida—standing beside a huge pad that rests on an easel—asks for people to call out what they wrote.

There are a few last stabs at resistance. A top-achieving Korean American girl from Massachusetts offers a flavorless "tennis player" as her identity. A girl from Singapore demurs, in halting English, that "I don't feel very cultural identity." Rabbi Flam tries to bring her around, probing, "Isn't Singaporean a culture?"

"Well, note really," she says, racing through her limited English vocabulary. "Thing is . . . I'm just me!"—a comment that draws applause, albeit tentative.

Kim Sherman, an earthy, artistic girl from Tennessee, searching for the common ground everyone enjoyed an hour ago at the dinner table, asks sheepishly, "What about 'Brown student,' isn't that an identity? I mean, after all, we've been here almost three days." There are chuckles, but not carrying the light-hearted "We are the world" esprit that defined the first few days.

Cedric, like the rest of them, feels that spirit quickly dissipating. After Vida scribbles "Brown student" on the easel, she pauses and gazes with dissatisfaction at her short list. The idea is that students, if forced to choose only one word, will probably pick the most obvious identity, the one they may well have been tagged with in cultural pursuit. Ten years back, the easel would have been filled at this point with ethnic and racial designations, with everyone happy to offer their own hyphen. But tonight's freshmen clearly have arrived knowing that the multiculturalist credo—embrace diversity so that every personal characteristic is cause for pride, not shame—has been criticized for sort of institutionalizing divisiveness. They gag a bit as the medicine goes down, uncertain third-day freshmen not sure what to say or do and not wanting to commit. Vida sees the hesitation and is unfazed, like she expects it. She artfully changes course: "Well, what is interesting are the identities that didn't show up."

People start looking up from their shoes, their faces registering relief. Rabbi Flam nudges them. "What about HIV positive?"

"Absolutely," Vida chirps. And up it goes.

The kids pick up the cue. Through various meetings, they've already ingested the sexual codes. Almost in unison, they tick them off: gay, lesbian, bisexual, questioning, transsexual, transgender.

Rabbi Flam: "Don't forget queer."

All go up on the easel, including "queer." Rabbi Flam continues stoking the fire: "What about being a survivor of sexual abuse?" he asks cheerily. The list expands. The neophytes are in groupism freefall.

Weight? one says. Oh yes, says Vida. Anorexia, another offers. You bet! Age? Sure, agism. Learning disabled. Vida's scribbling madly. Handicapped. Yup.

Ira Volker, a garrulous, politically ambitious Los Angeleno, tries to pull the brake cable: "I have a big problem with that. I think overcoming a handicap would define someone's identity. But being handicapped or being learning disabled is not an identity, it's how you deal with it, how you overcome it that would create the identity."

John Frank, son of a Manhattan psychoanalyst, parses that, saying that "Ira's point might be partially true, but if I were deaf, then absolutely it would affect everything I'd ever done, it would be who I am."

"But, I mean," Ira responds, in a final grope, "you couldn't overcome some particular limitation if you're sort of agreeing with it, sort of accepting it as who you are."

From a couch across the room, Cedric listens intently. That last thing about the danger of accepting limits strikes a nerve in him. He looks down, his mind racing. While his blackness is the identity carrying the highest voltage in this room, or almost any room in America, the sheet in his hand is still blank.

"It's not that complicated," Cedric says suddenly, his voice high pitched with frustration. All eyes turn to him. "Your identity, I think, should be something that you are proud of. I wouldn't be *proud* to say that I had only one leg and I could just barely walk, you know, on one leg. That may be true, but I wouldn't let it define who I was."

Everyone begins talking at once.

"Please be quiet!" Vida shouts. "One at a time."

She turns to Cedric, perplexed. "Say that again?"

"Okay, ummm, I said I think your identity should come from something you take pride in. It shouldn't be something that just sets you apart from other people, it should be one of those things that, you know, people generally understand is a good thing, something we all share, rather than what separates us. I mean, the things that make up identity are deeper things than skin color or whatever. Things, I don't know, like character or our faith or how we treat other people. And if we talked, instead, about *that* stuff, I'm sure we could agree on what was good or, at least, on the way we ought to be."

Vida and Rabbi Flam look at Cedric quizzically as the room grows quiet, the kids turning to their facilitators for guidance.

After a moment, Vida attempts to wrestle Cedric's point about shared values and common ground back to the preordained narrative. "What you said about pride really sparked something for me," she finally says, "because I know people who are handicapped who are extremely proud and that's who they are, or it might be something that is just a part of them, or, you know, the idea that an identity isn't necessarily positive or negative. But I think it shows all the different ways we think about who we are . . . umm . . . and also about how the outside world imposes negative and positive elements on us."

Nods all around. Cedric's brow furrows as he tries to understand what she just said, while his point disappears in the thicket. Everyone returns to the deepening groove of identity designation for another hour, with the discussion moving from whether it's fitting to be "really proud of something you never had a hand in, just the way you were born" (that from the provocative Los Angeleno, Ira Volker) to why no one mentions Caucasian as an identity. "Because someone might think you're racist—Caucasian is the oppressor group," says Kim Sherman, quickly picking up the multicultural lexicon. "Instead, we stretch for something distinctive, you know, being a minority—in who you are or how you act—or being some sort of victim. That's what gets you status."

Why would anyone want to embrace being a victim, Cedric wonders. Even though he's probably the only true victim of circumstances in the room, being a victim is the last thing he'd want to celebrate. He looks down at the unmarked paper in his hand. One word? A thousand words wouldn't do justice to who he is, he decides, and crumples the scrap into a tiny ball.

Rob Burton opens the door, delighted to see that the room is empty. It's Saturday, early afternoon, and he's ready for a little down time. He played soccer for a while on the green near Andrews dorm in the late morning, and, with lunch now in his belly, he's feeling whipped. It was a late night of partying last night—drinking beer mostly, cruising around the campus, and then talking until all hours on the third floor with some of these new guys.

Flopping on his unmade bed, he remembers that one of them—a guy named Billy who got 5's, highest you can get, on all of his achievement tests—said he went to a private Catholic school in Baltimore.

Just like me, Rob thinks. Head propped on his pillow, he admires his corner lair. Got it just so. On the wall to his left are two glossy photos he tacked up yesterday. The nearest one is of him dancing, sweaty and close, with his girlfriend at his high school prom. He starred at the school, a private Catholic academy in Marblehead, his senior year—newspaper editor, varsity tennis and soccer player, second in the class. And a cute girlfriend, too. He broke it off with her this summer, and it's just as well, he realizes now, that he doesn't have an HTH (home town honey) like some of the guys. It would make things so complicated. He looks at the other photo, also a prom shot, of him and his best buddy in a drunken tuxedoed hug, and laughs. What a nut. Got to send him an e-mail later today, he thinks.

His mind wanders back to beloved Marblehead, a sumptuous seaside exurb of Boston where he could drink a bit, do some experimenting with his girlfriend in the back seat of his car, and then set off on his path to college and beyond. Rob's father is an obstetrician; his mother is a longtime emergency room doctor turned occupational physician. There was never any question about whether he would use his quick mind and good manners to excel. It was assumed in everything that cosseted him. His house is a stunning five-bedroom clapboard colonial, ten minutes from the blue Atlantic.

He misses it, but not terribly. He feels a sense of closure about it all after another excellent summer running a skiff at the Marblehead Yacht Club, hanging with his buddies, and going on a few trips with the folks. Sure, there was a sense that an era of his life was coming to an end. But it was time, no doubt, to take the next step.

He rolls onto his side, figuring he'll catch some sleep, and looks just to the left of his pillow at his favorite recent *Rolling Stone* cover—neatly taped up—a shot of Sting, all blond ease, gazing off remotely and effortlessly, very cool.

He lies there for a while, finds he doesn't really feel like napping, and sits up. Resting gently on top of his canvas bookbag, which is teetering on the edge of his desk right near the bed, is a letter home he started writing two days ago.

He snatches it, seeing if maybe he feels like finishing it.

"Dear Mom and Dad,

This is my first letter, one of many I can guarantee. It's August 31st, Thursday. I've been here approximately 24 hours and I'm beginning to slowly realize I'm here. I'm slowly touching down to earth.

All is going well. After saying good-bye to Mom, I returned to my room to find Cedric and his mom unpacking. We are getting along well, although our tastes in music couldn't be more different. . . ."

Cedric. He pushes a pile of his sweaty clothes from this morning's soccer game away with his foot and puts the letter down on a cleared spot of floor. Well, college is supposed to be broadening, he muses, and there's no doubt he'll get broadened this year with a roommate like Cedric. But it'll work out. Casual and nonconfrontational, upbeat and accommodating, Rob can get along with anyone—it's a point of pride for him. If people are reasonable and open-minded, conflict always dissolves. Even if they just agree to disagree, at least they will have agreed on something. Not that he won't be challenged when it comes to Cedric. He's never really been close to a black guy, barely known any. The few encounters he's had were characterized by caution, by him feeling like he was walking on eggshells, not wanting to offend, inadvertently, with an inappropriate tone or casual remark. Last night with the guys, when all the talk shifted to roommates, Rob said to everyone it was going fine. There's a lot of interest in Cedric from the other kids, him being a black city kid and all. Everyone agreed that none of them had spent too much time with a person like that and, God knows, there aren't all that many of them here at Brown.

He looks across the room at the empty bed, at the hospital corners and fluffed pillows, everything in order, like a fortress. It seems like he and Cedric couldn't be more different, he thinks, looking at his mess of socks and papers and empty juice bottles. Different, it seems, in every way.

He grabs a pen, bent on finishing the letter. It's dated two days ago, he should get it done.

The door opens.

"Hey, Rob."

"Oh, hi, Cedric," Rob says, looking up from the notebook on his lap with the letter on top. "Where you been?"

"Lunch."

"Yeah, me too," Rob says, wondering if Cedric saw him there and thought that Rob might have snubbed him because they didn't sit together. "I didn't see you."

"Oh, no. I had to go to the corner and get a sandwich. I lost my temporary ID. I'm just living off this money my mom gave me. It's baaaaaad. I can't eat on my meal plan. It's like I don't exist." Rob commiserates and says he'll steal stuff for Cedric from the cafeteria if he wants.

Cedric putters around for a bit, hopping over to his chair and looking at some scheduling forms on his desk, while Rob turns back to the letter, not making much headway.

"Do you like mopping floors?" Cedric asks, after a bit.

"No, I don't *think* so," Rob says mawkishly, thinking it's some sort of joke.

"I just want to take a mop to it once a week, just to keep this place clean," Cedric says.

"Sure, you can do that if you want," Rob says, not thinking until a moment later that Cedric might have been hoping for more participation.

"You know, Rob, your feet smell bad."

"Oh come on, they do not."

"Do too! Man, walking around in your bare feet . . . that's disgusting."

Rob, accustomed to cut grass, thick pile carpets, and clean beach sand, has no idea what he's talking about. "Cedric, everyone walks barefoot."

"Maybe where you're from," Cedric says, raising his eyebrows. "Not where I'm from."

Cedric sits on his bed and turns on the TV, flipping the channels, looking for something to watch. Rob doesn't watch much TV and told Cedric that the first day. Now, with the noise, he can't seem to concentrate on the letter.

Instead, he grabs a novel he's been reading over the summer and flops on his bed, trying to ignore the blare. After a while, he drops the book and decides to see whom he can find to hang out with up on the third floor. He'll let Cedric enjoy the company of his TV.

"I'm outta here," he says to no one in particular as the door slams. For the first time, he notices how nice his bare feet feel on the hallway carpet.

Waking up just shy of noon on Labor Day, Cedric is gripped by hunger. Barbara's cash gift ran out yesterday. It's now a matter of survival; he needs food.

A few minutes later, next up in line at the registrar's office, Cedric gathers his strength for combat with the clerk on duty. He explains that he lost his temporary ID but understands that the permanent ones are ready. She tells him that to get the permanent ID (a student's passport to everything from the library to the dining hall to the bookstore), he needs to hand in his temporary one.

"I told you, I lost it."

"Well, let's think," says the clerk, a prim, brown-haired girl with glasses, probably a student. "Then, you need a picture ID of some kind, like a driver's license. Pretty much everyone has one of those by now."

Cedric closes his eyes as he shakes his head. "I don't have a driver's license . . . nothing like that."

He tries not to yell. The line is lengthening behind him. His eyes wander to a set of long file boxes on her desk with alphabetical dividers separating cards with laminated photos. The IDs.

"Cedric Jennings," he pleads, pointing to it. "Just look at the picture in there. I'm telling you, you'll know it's me!"

She looks up at him, showing just enough sympathy to paw through the H's, I's, J's.

In a moment, he's outside, holding high the prized card. He runs down the hill to the Ratty, where he bumps into a dozen Unit 15ers gathering for the morning meal. It's 12:34 P.M.

Over powdered eggs and undercooked hash browns—no coffee, at least not yet—they talk about last night's karaoke party in the dorm, where Cedric, at that point weary of solitude, made a brief appearance and sang a few songs.

The breakfast crowd—clearly delighted that the standoffish Cedric is here—talks about how stunned they were by his voice. Someone asks if he's considered trying out for one of Brown's many singing groups. Cedric, munching on toast, eschews that idea with a humble nod but is delighted that someone noticed something about him beyond pigment.

Sitting next to Cedric is Zeina Mobassaleh, a tall, doe-eyed Arab American from Potomac, Maryland, hailing from the exclusive Holton Arms school. She looks across the table and admires Rob Burton's hat, a canvas Australian job with a dangling strap. Rob, as always, is a vision of ease and cool: wraparound sunglasses, sun-bleached T-shirt, sandals, a tiny metal half-sun, half-moon hanging from a woven leather necklace.

"Couldn't survive without it," he says. "This hat kept the sun off my face while I was working on boats at the yacht club and . . ."

"Wally. . . . Wally," Cedric interrupts from across the table. Rob smiles, his nonchalance broken, but that's okay. "Wally Cleaver, *Leave It to Beaver*. That's you."

Sure, an old reference (for years, Cedric has devoured old sitcoms), but it's right on. Lighten Rob's dark brown hair a touch and he's a dead ringer for Tony Bill, who played Beaver's older brother.

Like so many inner-city kids, Cedric knows that his notions of the distant, white world—of two-car garages and dads home for dinner—have come largely through the television, with all of its vivid distortions and unintentional verities. After days of sitting on the sidelines, not being able to enter conversations because he couldn't offer anything in context, he has discovered a way in. Everyone knows TV. That's one place, Cedric realizes with glee, where he has a Ph.D.

He turns to Zeina. "You know, and you're like Janet, from *Three's Company*."

"Oh no. People think I look more like Sandra Bullock, from *Speed*," Zeina protests. "Janet is such an anal-retentive wimp."

"No, she's not," Cedric says, stopping Zeina with his earnestness, as though the TV character is a dear friend. "She has surprising strength. Yes, you may look a little like Bullock. But Janet is your double."

Next to Zeina is her roommate, Corry Mascitelli, a smooth-skinned blonde girl from Southbury, Connecticut. Cedric pauses a moment.

"Marcia Brady." Bingo. The table is hysterical.

Quiet Billy Mosberg, the Catholic-school kid from Baltimore, with a thin nose, glasses, and a cap pulled down over his high forehead, awaits Cedric's designation. "George Bush's son." More laughter.

Phillip Arden wants one, too. "What about me?"

"Give me a few days," says Cedric, smiling broadly, feeling a first blush of social acceptance—he might possibly make some friends up here. "I'll get it. I'll come up with one for you, too."

They disperse into the midafternoon sun, with much of the day having already passed. Classes start tomorrow, Tuesday, and there's a bustle on Thayer Street, College Hill's main drag of latte bars, used-record nooks, boutiques, bookstores, sandwich counters, pizzerias, and copy shops. Like a small town hurrying to prepare for the harvest, everything here is left until the Labor Day sunshine starts to cast long shadows.

With his new ID, Cedric meanders into the huge, three-story Brown bookstore. He needs to buy books for the courses he's signed up for—Spanish, Calculus, and Richard Wright—and look for a fourth course in catalogs they have at the store's resource desk that include candid course critiques from student surveys.

He waltzes onto the second floor, through long rows of books marked with yellow index cards noting course titles. With each step, his anxiety about gaps in his current level of learning seems to grow. He begins to wander, gazing at titles and authors: Sylvia Plath's *The Bell Jar,* Hemingway's *For Whom the Bell Tolls,* a biography of Theodore Roosevelt, another of Woodrow Wilson. All people from another country. Some of the names sound vaguely familiar. Most draw a blank.

A short girl with dark curly hair is standing next to him in front of *Beowulf.* He notices her intermediate Spanish 1 book, the low-intermediate section he's figuring on joining. "You taking that Spanish?"

She turns, surprised but pleasant.

"Yeah, and some of this other stuff," she says, lifting her fresh stack of books for Political Theory 101 and, for her freshman English seminar, The Sentimental Novel.

"That's so much reading," he says weakly. "You sort of an English person?"

"I guess, I like to read," she says. She's very sweet.

"Yeah, I wish I did, too," he says. "I wish I had started liking it about ten years ago."

She laughs and says maybe she'll see him in Spanish as she strolls to Jane Austen and the Victorians. He looks to his left. Martin Gilbert's new biography *Churchill, A Life* piled five feet high, topped by a tilted copy, sticking Churchill's bulldog mug right in Cedric's face.

Oh God, he thinks, I should know who he is. He grabs the book and flips through. "Churchill," he whispers after a moment, committing it to memory. "Prime minister of England during World War Two." Then he gently replaces the book, looking up to make sure no one has spotted him.

Standing there amid the bustle, he lets out a deep sigh, a thank you—to God or whomever—that he opted for lower-level classes and pass/fail. Pride, he mulls, can get you in big trouble.

He looks at his watch. The bookstore is closing soon. He still needs to figure out his fourth class and sprints over to the resource counter, grabbing the course books with student ratings.

Flipping through, Cedric rates them simply as to risk of failure. Philosophy of Science? No way. Moral Philosophy? Too much reading. Anyway, philosophy is boring.

He spots a pile of textbooks at a nearby table and figures he might learn more by flipping through them.

Elementary Psychology: An Introduction to Mind and Behavior. He fans some pages . . . much too technical. "Should it be so technical?" he murmurs. He grabs a Physics 3 textbook. Pelcovits, his adviser and a physics professor, told him to avoid it in the first year. Still, he flips through, realizing that Mr. Momen taught him lots of this material. Confidence boosted, he rushes back to the information desk, where two twentysomething employees are sitting near piles of course catalogs.

He asks one—a fat white kid with moppy hair—if he knows what courses are already full.

"Huh?" He's just there to tell kids where books can be found. Out of the corner of his mouth, he says sarcastically to his partner, a short, chubby girl with bad skin, "Do we know which courses are full?"

She rolls her eyes and addresses Cedric in a Shari Lewis Lambchop voice, like you might a five-year-old: "Maybe the registrar knows."

Cedric knows the white girl is dissing him, but there's no time to fret. He just shakes his head and grabs another course book. The page splays opens: Religious Studies. He looks for a moment at the long list of selections—Religious Ethics and Moral Issues; Introduction to Islam; The Darker Side of Human Existence; Religion, Colonialism, Nation Building. Provocative topics, all, but he stops. There's a voice in his ear . . . Bishop Long. God knows, he doesn't want to be learning something that directly contradicts what he's learned at church.

Or does he? He remembers Bishop's warning of two weeks ago—almost word for word—about the perils of trusting reason too much.

Cedric, ushered here mostly by adrenaline and faith, realizes he's now facing a living, breathing, credentialed counterpoint to his revered Bishop. Nothing theoretical about it. Around here, nothing is exempt from dissembling questions and critical examination—not even religion itself. He can see Bishop's one eye, looking through him, and hear the words, "The only true answers lie with God."

He discards Religious Studies and cracks the catalog back open: Education Department. The courses seem attractively neutral, more about the "hows"—how knowledge is passed. Staring right back at him is History of American Education. Prof. James. That's it! The fourth course. The bookstore is closing in ten minutes. He quickly grabs what he needs for Spanish, Calculus, Richard Wright, and now History of Education, as he runs—past Freud, Jung, Nietzsche, Kant, Faulkner, Shakespeare, the whole Western Canon—for the cashier, feeling like he'll escape intact.

But he's not out the door yet. Pulling out his ID and bookstore charge, he realizes that another famous dead white male is staring at him. It's from the cover of *Rolling Stone,* on a rack right near the Dilbert books—a black-and-white headshot of a guy with long gray hair, a beard, and glasses; two dates are listed under his chin, like when someone dies. Cedric looks intently at the face, snatches the magazine, and flips it open. "Thaaaat's right," he whispers to himself, feeling forearmed and slightly strengthened. "Jerry Garcia, Grateful Dead."

At eleven o'clock the next morning, the bell above University Hall rings and a bagpiper begins playing a generic Scottish march. Four students—one black, one white, one Asian, one Hispanic; two boys, two girls—hoist a large "Class of 1999" banner, brown with red piping, and lead a snaking line of chatting, mostly backpacked students through the ornate iron Van Wickle Gates, the uphill entryway to campus from downtown Providence. The tradition is to carry that banner out the same gates four years from now as this, the last class of the twentieth century, graduates.

Few ceremonies as grand and formal as this are to be found any-where outside of the Episcopal Church. As a bell from the clock tower joins the one from University Hall, 219 professors, in their gowns and caps of crimson, royal blue, and deep purple—like a sedate Renaissance festival—follow the incoming freshmen onto the main green. A forty-two-piece wind ensemble plays Schubert.

The convocation speaker is Elie Wiesel, the 1986 Nobel Peace Prize winner, Holocaust survivor, scholar, poet, philosopher, and all-around conscience for hire. He reminisces for a while and throws out a few light aphorisms before turning bleak and discussing Bosnia and balkanism, victims of wars, and conflicts across the globe.

"Unless one wants to lie," he says, brow furrowed, the breeze lifting his comb-over skyward, "I am rarely truly hopeful."

After the speech, students wander off in the warm breeze to opening-day classes, where syllabi are passed out, first assignments are given, and little else is done.

Cedric is especially enthusiastic about the instructor in his Richard Wright seminar, a black graduate student named Stephan Wheelock. "He seems really cool and smart, you know, and relaxed," he tells Rob as they walk to the cafeteria for dinner.

Rob talks excitedly about biology—his probable major—and how it's okay that he can't get into Biology and Gender, a hot-button course at Brown, because he can get into Marine Biology, one of his passions. "With classes starting, something's changed," he says quietly, suddenly introspective. "You know, like we've slipped out of our shell, or shed our skin," and Cedric nods, thoughtfully.

A few moments later, the Unit 15ers gather at two long tables, and Cedric, feeling heady from his conversational victories at lunch yesterday, throws out a line. "I can't believe that people take a shower without flip-flops on," he says. "It's so dirty."

Sitting across the table, the black girl from his unit (he's found out that her name is Chiniqua Milligan and she's from upper Manhattan) smiles like she understands him. "I wear flip-flops, too," says Chiniqua's roommate, red-haired, freckled Maura McLarty. "I wish everyone did." She, Chiniqua, and Cedric all nod affirmations at each other. The desire to belong is palpable, with everyone looking for connections. Any link will do.

The hypergregarious Ira Volker passes by from a neighboring table, doing a random survey of who's drinking milk versus soda. "Look, he's like Casey Kasem—just skinnier," Cedric says, pointing at him, another flawless TV connection, prompting a round of giggles. Ira continues with data collection: "I've polled everyone, and we're all getting along with our roommates."

Cedric says, "I have *big* roommate problems," and Rob, at the far end of the table, eating an ice cream cone, slumped down in his chair, offers up a sly smile—closing off any inference that his roommate might not be joking—and Cedric returns the favor by smiling back.

After the long years of self-exile and, often, isolation, Cedric is now drunk with freedom. "Maybe I'll read Richard Wright tonight or we'll call some girls and have an orgy," he says later, settling back into the dorm room as Rob flops on his bed, chuckling.

Cedric is just grinning, speechless. He has finally arrived. And at moments like this, with too many jumbled and onrushing emotions to tag with words, he sometimes feels that songs help him make sense of things.

Cedric begins to sing an old Boys II Men tune called "It's So Hard to Say Good-bye to Yesterday." It's a slow, sweet rhythm and blues number, a favorite that begins with the lyric "I don't know where this road is going to lead me." Rob looks up, quietly astonished.

8

FIERCE INTIMACIES

The freckled blonde girl sitting to Cedric's right in History of Education—8:30 A.M. to 9:50, M, W—is leading the class . . . in sleep.
It's a mere ten minutes into this morning's lecture, the last in September, and she's already gone, chin buried in her collar, head bobbing
gently.

Public sleeping has a way of spreading across a lecture hall. Someone hears soft, steady breathing from a neighboring desk and soon
offers an accompaniment, which is why eyelids are drooping at desks
near the blonde in what soon will become an informal sleep study.

Professor Tom James, a sort of opaque, soft-spoken man in his early
forties, is no match for the lack of natural light and the humming
ventilation system in this basement classroom. Still, he pushes forward
gamely—there's a lot of ground to cover in this survey course—and by
8:55 he's tying social characteristics of late-eighteenth-century American progressives to the emergence of public educational institutions,
schools that carried, he asserts, "an evangelical fervor in what they saw
as the serious business of educating youngsters, especially the hoards of
immigrants."

Cedric looks over at the sleepers and shakes his head. "How can
they sleep?" he murmurs under his breath. "They must already know
this stuff." He turns back to his notebook and scribbles "immigrant."

"How many of you have been to Ellis Island?" James asks, drawing
ten hands out of the thirty attendees, a high ratio among the conscious.
Ellis Island is not a core concept in Southeast Washington (it is, in fact,
the sort of white people's history often passed over in favor of Afrocen-

tric studies), and Cedric has never heard the reference. He jots the word "Ellis" on his pad. It floats on a white sea, without context.

"What happened to that evangelical fervor?" James asks the class. "Have we lost it along the way?"

On Cedric's left is his unit-mate Maura McLarty, a red-haired Irish girl bred in the strong public schools of Andover, Massachusetts, daughter of an administrative judge. Already on her third page of precise notes, she listens intently as a talkative student in the first row parries with James on the "evangelical fervor" question. The religious metaphors, meanwhile, prompt Cedric to put down his pencil on a thin half-page of scribbles and daydream of Scripture Cathedral.

One month into this new world of higher education, Cedric Jennings's chin is barely above the waterline. So many class discussions are full of references he doesn't understand—he often feels like a foreigner, like one of those Asian kids he sees in the math lab who can barely speak English but integrate fractions at blinding speed. By now, he understands that Maura *knows* what to write on her pad and the sleepers *will* be able to skim the required readings, all of them guided by some mysterious encoded knowledge of history, economics, and education, of culture and social events, that they picked up in school or at home or God knows where.

Class is dismissed, and Cedric nods a farewell to Maura and moves quickly for the door, happy to be alone as he walks across campus to Spanish, a class that offers a brief respite. There, at least, everyone stumbles along on the same uncertain footing of *cómo estás* and *bastante biens* and he doesn't feel as conspicuous or obtuse or ill prepared as he does in education class . . . and almost everywhere else he goes at Brown.

The day is sunny and splendid. Blazing yellow and red leaves that draw peepers to this part of New England are crunching under his Nikes. The thing he loves most, he decides, is walking between classes, a time he can feel purposeful, like he's on his way somewhere.

After Spanish, he affords himself an indulgence. Dr. Korb sends him $200 on the 15th of each month for miscellaneous costs and spending money. The money tends to go fast, but today he still has a little left from the September check, and he decides to go out for lunch.

All it takes to eat well at Cafe Paragon on Thayer Street, where the eavesdropping is superb, is $10. Every stratum of the Brown society is represented here—from godlike tenured don to midlevel administrators, assistant and associate profs, grad students and lowly undergraduates. The atmospherics are mixed just right. The music is Euro-funk, edgy but quiet enough to allow for easy conversation at the closely packed mahogany tables. The waitresses are a carefully selected sampling of the university's comeliest females in all-black outfits, the skin-snug tank tops provided by management. Here, gentleman profs can drink musty Warsteiner Ale or Italian Perini Beer (both $3.25) to wash down a thoroughly adequate burger ($2.50). For undergraduates, meanwhile, the Paragon is a just affordable luxury of theoretical adulthood and an escape from Food Service cold cuts—though, usually, freshmen get carded.

On this sunny, unseasonably warm Wednesday in late September, the place is jammed. Of the many issues to discuss, affirmative action is proving the ideal back-to-school subject. Stoking long-standing disputes on the subject, there is news of late, starting with July's decision by the California Board of Regents to end preferential admissions based on race and this fall's demonstrations at the University of California at Berkeley and elsewhere by minority students.

At Brown, like most top private institutions, affirmative action is offered to "less qualified" and "underrepresented" minority students. Yet, like at its peer institutions, Brown's bold initiative doesn't go much beyond the offer of admission. Once they arrive, affirmative action kids are generally left to sink or swim academically. Brown offers plenty of counseling and tutoring to struggling students, but, as any academic dean will tell you, it's up to the students to seek it out, something that a drowning minority student will avoid at all costs, fearing it will trumpet a second-class status that he or she may fear classmates have suspected from the first. Not surprisingly, dropout rates among minorities, particularly those of lower income, tend to be higher than the rest.

On all sides of this carefully parsed, middle-ground policy are encampments of passionately intense discussion. At the cafe today are several exchanges on the subject. Cedric, settling at a table inside, orders a ginger ale and trains his ears to a table immediately to his right.

Two professors, both white, are leaning in close over a pair of Anchor Steams.

"Are we doing a service to young people to boost them above their academic level and then not offer the services they need?" asks the squat one with flying gray hair. "Because, who really can? Who can offer that sort of enrichment? You can hardly blame the university. It would take years, and money, and a whole different educational track to bring some affirmative action students to a level where they could compete. There's no choice but laissez-faire, sink or swim. They should be going to middle-rung universities. There's no right, as far as I see, to go to an Ivy League institution. If they work hard, their kids can come here. Hell, it's what everyone else had to do."

As his burger arrives, Cedric listens and pretends to read the *Brown Daily Herald,* the student newspaper. Eventually, the professors are drowned out by loud conversation at the table on his other side. It's all Cedric can do not to respond. Their words make him think of Leon Trilling and what he said. He imagines telling them about his long journey, that his struggle has built in him a kind of strength—a conviction about his ability to overcome obstacles—that other kids don't have. But of course that strength is hard to measure, and lately he's become uncertain if it will be enough to get him where he needs to be.

The loud people pay their check and leave. The professors, meanwhile, have moved on to the companion controversy about hiring minority faculty members. "It's a mockery," the other professor, a tall, distinguished-looking guy, spits, ticking off the names of a few minority professors around campus. "A lot of them are good teachers, sure. But they're unpublished, not respected, not scholars. What do they bring? Their passionate, oh-so personal 'perspective.' Nothing special about that. Jesus, everyone's got one of those."

Faculty club interlocutions over "publish or perish" or how affirmative action exacerbates the conflict between the magnetic lecturers and the dogged scholars are not on Cedric's radar. He manages to be dismissive, digging into his burger, his $2.50 indulgence.

A few minutes later, he emerges from the restaurant and passes a clutch of wrought-iron tables on the sidewalk, favored spots in the warm sun. He spots Stephan Wheelock, his Richard Wright instructor, twenty-four and black and bursting with passionate personal perspective. Stephan is eating a barbecued chicken sandwich with a friend, a thirty-something white guy who's visiting Providence. Cedric waves and offers a cursory hello as he passes.

Stephan nods back a greeting and then continues talking excitedly with the friend as Cedric waits for the light to change before crossing the street. "At least, you know, Brown is a socially conscious place. But, you see, it has been a huge transition for me coming here, being brought here under the guise of equality," says Stephan, graduate of Tougaloo College in Mississippi, a black school not far from Oxford where his father is a preacher and his mother a librarian. "I am constantly having to play catch-up with guys who've spent the past five years speaking three languages, visiting Europe, and reading all the right books. Here, at Brown, they say, 'Don't worry, you're all equal, starting on the same footing. Ready, set, go!' They just don't get it. Where I come from, people don't go to France to study. A trip to France is a big deal. I haven't been reading all the right books since I was twelve and then have some Rhodes Scholar Daddy tell me the rest. I didn't have that kind of access, access that could empower me."

Throughout the day, the overheard conversations at lunch echo in Cedric's head. More than the specifics, he recalls the intensity of the dialogues. At this point, affirmative action is the last thing he wants to hear or think about. During dinner and studying that evening, he finds himself responding to the professors under his breath: So, he got in. If he fails, he fails; if he makes it, he makes it. Why does everyone have to draw conclusions about an entire race from that, or take sides. He wanted a chance; he got one.

The next day, Cedric awakens with renewed ardor, a determination to compete on an even footing, to meet Brown's academic rigors head-on. After lunch, he strides into his Richard Wright class. Stephan Wheelock smiles at him—"Helloooo, Cedric," he says theatrically—and Cedric offers a grim nod.

He is counting on this class about the familiar novels of Richard Wright—some of the few books he's previously read—to help teach him the thinking and writing skills he so desperately needs.

Up to now, it has not been happening. One short paper—an

ungraded one-page autobiographical essay he wrote in class on the first day—came back last week with few comments. With all sixteen students, about half of whom are black or Hispanic, now settled around the seminar table or at desks lining the walls, Wheelock goes over a few "scheduling changes," cutting assignments off the syllabus, like he did last class and the one before, lightening the class's requirements. Then he starts the discussion with an overview of Richard Wright's signature 1940 novel, *Native Son,* which the class is supposed to have read by now.

Cedric, sitting against the wall, opens his copy of the book. He knows it cold. He watches Wheelock—light-skinned, with stylishly thin bifocals on the end of a small, thin nose—going through a brief synopsis of the plot. The book's central character, Bigger Thomas, is a laborer whose days of poverty and brutishness and frustration lead to the killing of a white woman. After discussing the basic plot for fifteen minutes, Wheelock advances his literary deconstruction by mentioning the novel's oft-noted companion essay—"How 'Bigger' Was Born"— in which Wright tells at length about the creation of his main character, about the five "Biggers" he's known since his childhood.

"Why did Wright decide to put this essay at the back of the book?" Wheelock asks portentously, as most of the class begins flipping through its 1993 edition of the book. "Back in 1940, Wright made a literary decision as to where to put it. Clearly, he put it at the end for a reason."

A half-hour of discourse is launched. Cedric looks around the room. There are plenty of black faces. It may not be calculus—his love—but he really knows this book. If he doesn't raise his hand now, then when? His arm shoots up. "All right, yes, Cedric?" Stephan says, delighted.

"Umm, I think Wright wanted you to figure things out for yourself, so you wouldn't be thinking about all these larger forces, like racial repression and violence right off," Cedric says. "He had to put the explanatory essay in the back . . . otherwise you'd sort of know the answer before you asked the question."

Stephan nods agreement and other students follow up. Cedric exhales. That wasn't so hard. The discussion winds along another few minutes until Brandon, another black in the class, raises his hand. He seems confused.

"Professor Wheelock," he says. "I have an earlier edition of the book and, well, the essay, 'How Bigger Was Born,' is in the front rather than the back. It runs, you know, before you get into the actual novel."

There's silence. Air seems to escape from the room. Everyone instantly sees the mishap, which reduces half an hour of vigorous discussion to a waste of breath. Some shake their head, disbelieving, trying not to laugh.

A dazed Wheelock nods once, wordless. His mind seems to race, looking to grab anything to halt the freefall.

"Well, okay . . ." he says finally, trying to recover. "So, the question, then, would be why did the powers that be in the publishing world decide to put the essay in the book's back, you know, in the edition most of you got?"

The frantic rebound gets little response, and in a moment he begins shuffling assignment sheets in front of his chair.

"Let's see," he says, forcing a smile. "What do you say we get out a little early today?"

Cedric, sitting at a desk against the wall, looks across a roomful of slackened jaws and stunned gazes—white, black, Hispanic, and Asian—and puts his head in his hands.

In room 216 of East Andrews Hall, being alone in the room means the automatic granting of "music control." As agreed upon and enacted on the last day of September, if the other roommate comes in, he has to wait, silently and without complaints—no matter how long it takes—for control of the music to be ceded. Music control is ceded only when the controlling roommate leaves the room. The roommate left behind then immediately assumes control. If one roommate leaves, then returns to find other roommate playing his own music, too bad. Simple enough?

Rob is sitting on his bed. Cedric, on his.

"Agreed," says Cedric, curtly.

"Okay, agreed," says Rob, and the two say nothing more that

night. They just sit there in the silence. Since neither of them had "music control" at the time of the agreement, the only way it could be granted was for one to leave. So that night, no one moves and no music is played.

It has not been a good first month for Cedric Jennings and Rob Burton. First, there was the issue of cleanliness, born of a cultural collision between one boy who grew up in casual comfort with a cleaning lady twice a week and the other who spent his life scrubbing dishes and toilets to stave off squalor. Cedric has always been fastidious about his person. Though his room on V Street, his one private place, was often a mess, he always has been neatly dressed and exhaustively scrubbed in public. Now, nothing is private. Just like his person, his room is constantly on display; he might as well be wearing it. The message sent from Rob is the opposite. Rob's impulse—getting stronger as he feels less and less inclined to give in to Cedric—is not to care about how messy the room is. He doesn't mind the disarray, why should anyone else? Because his coolness and self-confidence is subterranean, springing from beneath his casual demeanor, it's important that surface issues, like how clean you keep your room, are afterthoughts.

Meanwhile, if Cedric focuses on what he considers Rob's faults—his messiness, and, now, his taste in music—he doesn't have to think about how Rob is a popular kid, at ease, easygoing, and reasonably good looking with his ice-blue eyes. He also tests well; comes from a strong, loving, *Leave It to Beaver* family, and can be sort of funny in the arch, smug, iconoclastic way college kids need to be.

People are constantly coming by the room seeking Rob—to go out drinking with him at the Underground, Brown's on-campus club, where beer is served; to go to this party or that; to stroll over to the Gate, the favorite campus eatery just a few feet from the dorm, for a late snack; or just to visit, because he makes them feel comfortable.

Cedric knows *he* makes them feel uncomfortable. And he is fast on his way to becoming a hermit—or so he thinks one night when he's alone with coveted music control and answers several knocks on the door, like Rob's social secretary.

Cedric is not malicious. Deep down, he sort of likes Rob. He's just up to his eyeballs in confusion and fear of failure and loneliness—and he feels worse when he sees the fun everyone else seems to be having.

Clearly, some East Andrews residents are spending serious time and energy having fun. They're doing all the things that college freshmen have been doing, under various guises and with various aids, since the first tenderfoot left home for Harvard in 1636.

Despite Brown's self-consciousness about each student's individuality, the four preferred pastimes are the same here as they are at most every other college: drink beer, smoke pot, dance to deafening music until you drop, and, on the rare occasion, get naked with some other warm body.

Possibly the best explanation why Cedric Jennings is in Brown's class of 1999 is that he managed to steer clear of the buffet table of adolescent experimentation, believing—rightly, it turns out—that in his neighborhood most of those dishes were poisoned. This was an extraordinary feat, considering how peer pressure at Ballou was backed up by violence and the almost irresistible urge for teenagers to salve deep despair with sex, drugs, and music.

Cedric knows all this, just as he knows his resistance was made possible, back when, by Barbara's fierce code, Pastor Long's admonitions against all such licentiousness, and the constant reminders of Cedric Gilliam's broken journey, testifying to what can happen when someone without hope of personal betterment discovers drinking and drugs. But, eventually, something else took root. Cedric, needing to justify his monkish routine night after night, developed a genuine belief that sacrifice, hard work, and extremely clean living would lead to rewards, including a scholarship to a top college.

But now that he's made it, the guideposts are gone and all around him smart kids are getting high, getting drunk, and screwing. Even the real smart ones, kids who can eat Cedric's lunch in almost any subject.

Sitting alone on his bed one Saturday night, there's a knock on the door and a few kids from down the hall crowd in, rosy with anticipation of a night of some drinking, an off-campus party one of them has heard about, and then, who knows, maybe some late-night pizza.

"Hey Cedric, come on," one of them says.

"Naaaaaw," says Cedric, declining nicely, trying to show he appreciates their asking. "I just don't do that kind of stuff." And everyone nods meaningfully, though Cedric can tell they don't really understand. In a moment, they're gone.

Just as well, he thinks, half meaning it. Self-denial and a strict code of dos and don'ts are, at this point, knitted into his very being. "It's who I am," he says to himself, over and over. "I can't change now." He gathers up his laundry and spends the next two hours in the first-floor laundry room, flipping through an issue of *Billboard* he's already read—a Saturday night with the spin cycle, just like the last two, hoping someone from his unit will happen by and then hoping they won't. Back upstairs about midnight, his clothes folded and the dorm empty, he fusses with his CDs, playing and replaying beloved tracks, singing the songs with perfect inflection. One of his favorites comes on. He begins a dance, one step, then slides and spins. But, twirling around, his reflection is framed in the closed window—a young black man dancing alone in his room—and he feels like a fool.

Two days later, on Monday night, October 1, he can't take the solitude anymore and ventures out into the hall. People passing in and out of rooms are, invariably, friendly. He imagines that they view the quiet, tallish black student as an oddity, a curiosity. Whoever gets to know him first, really know him, will have stories to tell and the rapt attention of others. So Cedric, sensing this diffident fascination, smiles at all comers but offers few openings.

At the end of the hall, a door is open and both roommates seem to be hanging out. It's John Frank and Zayd Dohrn's room—two guys with many options. If the social life of this unit were a tennis tournament, John and Zayd would be the number one seeded doubles team.

John was born to thrive here. He's Jewish and conventionally handsome with brown hair and green-blue eyes—bright, affable, and engaging. Beneath that and a three-day growth, he's also shrewd and sophisticated. Among the thirty-three kids on the second and third floors of East Andrews, he's off to the fastest start, already a member of the Brown Derbys, the widely known Brown a cappella group whose mixture of song and shtick draws big crowds. He's also probably the first to get laid, groveling with a unit-mate after one of the first weekend's parties.

"Hey, it's Cedric," John says, genuinely surprised, ushering him in. "Entrez!"

Cedric wanders around, taking in the room. John's side is a disaster, even messier than Rob's lair, with clothes piled so high and wide that the bed looks like a plateau on top of a lush fiber mountain. "My Gaaawwd," Cedric says.

"Just got done cleaning," says John, his standard line.

The other side of the room is as neat as Cedric's—a few books stacked in one corner of a spotless desk next to a bottle of hand cream, a few avant-garde posters, several pairs of stylish shoes and boots perfectly aligned on the closet floor. Reclining on a bed with tight hospital corners is Zayd Dohrn.

"Yo, C," he says. " 'Bout time you dropped by."

"Oh, hey Zayd," says Cedric, who has had a few brief hallway encounters with the tall blond. But his attention is elsewhere, at what must be the largest CD tower in the unit. It's John's three-hundred-CD monstrosity of spinning shelves, a tower that the two roommates share, standing like a lighthouse above the mess. Cedric is drawn to it, amazed.

"That's quite a CD collection. Wow," Cedric says. "Just look at it."

"They're mostly John's CDs," says Zayd.

"But the ones Cedric's admiring are yours," says John.

Cedric spots plenty of familiar music. Hip-hop artists, rappers, soul, rhythm and blues. "You got 'Ready to Die,' by Biggie Smalls? I mean, you know, a white guy with this stuff?"

"Yeah," says Zayd, "I think he's great."

For the first time, Cedric's stark notions about white America are blurred. He looks at Zayd, back at some other titles, and then at Zayd again. Yup, still white.

Then it's like there's no one else around and the two of them are just talking, real easy and natural, about hip-hop artists they like and lyrics that really hit home. Zayd is not only informed and interested, he actually defers to Cedric's knowledge.

"You know, Biggie is married to Faith," Cedric says, mentioning the female R&B artist Faith Evans and plucking one of her CDs off the tower.

"What? Really?" says Zayd.

"Yeah," says Cedric, offering up some choice morsels. "They sometimes refer to each other in the music. Oh, it's a whole thing."

"For real?" says Zayd, adding a touch of street to his voice.

And Cedric grins, "Fo' reeeeeal."

Later that night, lying in bed, Cedric is still sort of smiling to himself. If he is a hopeful kid by nature, it may be because in his darkest moments some glimmer of light has often appeared. He's not certain—not yet—but he thinks he may have found his first friend at Brown.

In the darkness, he tried to think back across the previous few weeks to any brief encounters he's had with this Zayd—from Chicago, Cedric thinks—trying to fill the outline with some more color.

One moment comes into focus. It was the very first week of school, when everything was loose and open, before cliques started forming. He was standing in the hallway with Kim Sherman, the artistic girl from Tennessee, and Zayd. They were right near the door of Mimi Yang, the senior psychology major who is the unit's peer counselor, looking at an envelope taped to her door that was overflowing with condoms and latex gloves, a sort of low-rent safe sex dispenser.

"What's that glove for?" Cedric asked.

"It's for fisting," Kim said, and told him how homosexuals sometimes use their fist for anal sex and that it can transmit the HIV virus.

"Yeah, right, fisting," said Zayd. And then to Cedric, "You never heard of fisting?"

"Naw. Gaaawd. It's gross. I mean, it's worse than oral sex," said Cedric, venturing to the limits of his sexual knowledge.

"What's wrong with giving a woman oral sex?" asked Zayd.

Kim added, "Listen, Cedric, just about every guy tries that."

"Not where I'm from. Black guys don't do that, except crack heads or something. Why would you want to be down there?"

Kim giggled and looked over at Zayd, whom she kind of likes.

"Oral sex is my forte," he said, as Cedric stared at him, astonished by his candor. Zayd shrugged. "Hey, I'll try anything."

Yes, Cedric remembers it all clearly. What kind of person lives by such a credo? This college sure is one strange place, Cedric laughs to himself. Zayd? What kind of a name is *Zayd*?

Chiniqua Milligan rushes into the reading room of Brown's sprawling modernist Rockefeller Library, searching for a familiar face. Across a carrier deck of linoleum, she spots the group of boys chuckling at a table tucked between the towering periodical racks. She speed walks across the room. "Sorry I'm late—can't believe all you are still here," she says, huffing.

The male quartet from Wheelock's class—Cedric, two other black students, and a student from Japan—is delighted. Cedric jumps up, " 'Bout time you made it," he says, smiling, and helps her with her chair as the other boys look her up and down, real quick.

It's the first meeting of the Richard Wright study group. Tonight's task is to plan a class discussion on *Native Son*—a discussion this group will lead next class—but little was accomplished by the guys in the hour before Chiniqua's arrival.

Once she settles into her chair at the reading room table, work commences quickly. Questions are listed, and one of the black guys says he'll type them up and print out copies. In a few minutes, everyone is dispersed.

Outside the library, on one of the first cool evenings of autumn, Chiniqua and Cedric begin the long walk back to the dorm. As the only two black freshmen in Unit 15, it's no surprise that they've managed to size each other up pretty well over the past month.

Cedric, who has been looking futilely since he arrived for someone fitting his profile, sometimes jokes—when he and Chiniqua bump into each other and no one else is around—that she's a "ghetto girl in disguise." She laughs politely at this. But Chiniqua Milligan is actually more of a paradigm of what's possible in urban education when commitment is matched with real money. Her father is a bus driver, and her mother is a teacher's aide. Chiniqua and her sister were raised in an apartment in a black working-class neighborhood of upper Manhattan called Inwood, forty blocks north of Harlem. As a studious sixth grader, Chiniqua was pulled out of line and offered a stunning gift. She entered Prep for Prep, a much hailed Manhattan-based program that identifies promising black and Hispanic sixth graders from the New York City public schools. It offers them tutoring on one weeknight and on Saturdays and then places them into the city's top private schools as seventh graders. Cedric has already bumped into a few Prep for Preppers at Brown and is certain he'll meet more. He's heard they're all over this campus.

For them, Brown doesn't have to offer affirmative action. It's already been handled, long ago. Chiniqua, who scored an 1100 on her SATs, received years of counseling—both academic and social—to assist with the collision of cultures she ingested each day crossing fifty blocks of Manhattan.

She rose through the exclusive Columbia Prep, a cocoon for the children of Wall Street chieftains and assorted celebrities, including Woody and Mia, Robert DeNiro, and Bill Cosby. She beat out nearly everyone, graduating third in her class. At Brown, she's thriving in a tough pre-med program and manages a heavy schedule of classes.

The O.J. Simpson acquittal was yesterday afternoon, and the university is embroiled in racial discussion, though not *between* the races. It's all intramural, as it is throughout much of the country, with whites moaning to whites as they feel the bite—in many cases for the first time—of being clobbered in what escalated into a racial contest. And many blacks, so accustomed to being routed by whites, feel a swell of jumbled, out-of-context pride.

Chiniqua feels some of that pride and senses that Cedric must, too. Out of all the kids in the unit, however, they can discuss such sensitive racial sensations only with each other. "So what'd'jou think?" Cedric asks. "Him getting off. You think he's innocent?"

"All I know is that it's over and a lot of people I spent the last couple hours with are crazy angry—though they won't say nothing around me."

Tonight was Brown's traditional response to the divisive national or campus issues: a mandatory "outreach" meeting held in all the freshman dorms. Chiniqua tells him that's why she was late to the library.

"Oh yeah, the race outreach," Cedric says sheepishly. "I just didn't go. I just decided I wasn't."

"Well, I went," she says with a how-could-you look. "I was the ONLY one there."

"Was it bad?"

"No, just like always. All of them just talking. No one says anything. Everything's fine, everything's good. He's acquitted, so what. It's nothing special. . . . We is all saints here, anyway.

"Only about half the unit showed up, even though it was supposed to be mandatory," she continues, moving easily between black-speak and flawless diction in her usual speedy canter. "Some other people were there, some facilitators, and we did these exercises. They asked us questions, like, when we were kids, were our dolls of many colors, or all one, you know in terms of their skin tone. And you stand up if yours was a certain kind of doll . . . people didn't know what to do."

They walk for a while in silence. Cedric looks over at her, catching a glimpse of the side of her face, with its high cheekbones and large, dark eyes. She's compact, about five-foot-six, with a lean figure that's adorned artfully in a short leather skirt and turtleneck, wide belt, and midcalf boots. She knows he's looking and likes it, looking forward at nothing and looking good.

"Oh yeah," she says, remembering one other thing. "I told the facilitators I had to leave early, that I had this other meeting. They were so deflated. It was like the whole thing was going to collapse with no black person to look at." She laughs lightly at this, reconciled over years to often being the lone black in any room.

Chiniqua is sophisticated—for better or worse—in ways that she knows Cedric is not. Close contact with whites is no novelty for her. She's been a passing friend and fierce competitor of white kids for years. She knows some are nice, some are not—just like blacks—and they're no more gifted or graced. It was she, after all, who wrecked the grading curves in high school. White kids? There's a lot about her that they can never, ever understand and not much hope of any breakthroughs anytime soon.

Like a lot of black and Hispanic kids who come here from integrated settings, she finds herself already drifting toward her designated racial enclave. Much like the assimilated Jewish kids drawn to orthodox Sabbath services at Hillel House, Brown offers Chiniqua—who was reluctant to attend militant black rallies in Harlem or troll clubs on 125th Street—a sterling opportunity to reestablish her racial bona fides and validate her blackness. Safely inside these gates, she can now pick up a dose of black culture pasteurized by ambition, whether it's a tweedy, just tenured black professor talking about radicalism at a coffee clatch or fellow black achievers partying hard this week because next week is already blocked out for studying.

In the past two weekends, she's been going over to dorm room parties at Harambee House, Brown's lone black dorm, and has tried to lure Cedric over. They've definitely become friends. He's a little awkward, she thinks, but kind of nice and not bad looking. It could develop into more. But he's hard to size up. A few weeks ago, he said something about having spent his whole life with blacks and wanting to see if there's a place for him among nonblacks.

"So you coming with me this weekend to Harambee?" Chiniqua asks, managing to make it sound casual. "Just people hanging around, you know, like us. . . . It must get mighty lonely just being by yourself so much."

"No, it's okay," Cedric says as they get off the elevator at the second floor—he breaking away toward his room; she, toward hers. "I'll be fine. Really, I will."

She knows he's lying, so she makes sure the invitation is left standing.

"Well, maybe some other time."

Cedric takes the other path a few nights later, when he ventures out of his lair and finds himself a racial stranger in many rooms. Mostly they're dorm rooms on the second floor of Andrews, where freshmen, here like elsewhere, spend an unfathomable number of hours sitting on their beds—heads against the wall or propped pillows—semistudying or not, listening to music, catching a little TV, sending off e-mail messages while flipping through yesterday's student newspaper and talking about "you know, nothing," which means everything. Just plain being is pretty damn interesting in these first few months of stay-up-as-late-as-you-want independence.

John and Zayd's room, with the unit's top CD collection, is a favored place to hang, and there's often a crowd inside. When Zayd's there, Cedric feels comfortable dropping by, so he frequently takes a route that passes by the room on his way in and out of the dorm after dinner.

One evening in mid-October he sees Zayd combing his short, dirty-blond hair in the mirror near his open door. They've seen each other a few times in the past couple of weeks, walking back from classes in the late afternoon or catching a midnight slice of pizza at the Gate.

"Hey, it's been a couple of days. What's up?" asks Zayd, and soon the two are sitting on Zayd's bed, some Boyz II Men on the CD, and Cedric is filling the room with his talk.

For Cedric, each encounter with Zayd is an opportunity. As a trustworthy white peer—Cedric's first—Zayd is a sounding board for questions and comments that Cedric has harbored for years, notions about white America that reverberate endlessly in the echo chamber of Southeast.

"So, do you think the cops framed O.J.?" Cedric says, prodding.

Zayd, who by inclination and rearing is sympathetic toward the so-called oppressed, nods along but is reserved. "Do cops frame black suspects? Absolutely, all the time. Did they frame O.J.? I think there's just too much evidence to fabricate. I think, though, that O.J. was helped by all the black guys who've been framed for all the years."

Cedric nods at this judicious response and wants to know Zayd's thoughts on other black martyrs. Midway through his list, John wanders in. By then, Cedric has made it to Marion Barry, whom he says "was completely framed by white cops." John jumps in with the standard white counterresponse, "Look, he did it. Right? He was smoking the crack in the room with the girl. Doesn't matter if he was targeted or not."

"But, like, that's the point," says Cedric. "He was a suspect from the first day he became mayor, 'cause he's black. A black is a suspect, no matter who he is. And eventually they got him."

Zayd nods at this. "Yeah, definitely, blacks are racial suspects and that skews the equation."

Around they go, hashing it out in this freshly painted, drywalled holding pen, with its little mirror and sink, where kids hashed things out last year and will again next year and the year after. It's just that this year an exotic bird is among them, an authentic ghetto kid who, for whatever reason, made it through the urban inferno without donning an armor. Cedric can take his off. Once he finally starts talking, he's open and transparent.

He's a draw. The room usually fills when Cedric is around and, soon, Ira Volker is here, along with Florian Keil, his soft-spoken German roommate whose father runs a Boston arm of the Goethe Institute, the German government's cultural ministry abroad.

Neither says too much. But as they listen to Cedric's speech—his black urban expressions, sometimes wrapped around an inappropriate infinitive verb or dropped suffix—a little street creeps into all their voices, part accommodation, part unconscious imitation. Cedric, whose ear is sensitive to such inflections, is not sure if he should be flattered or offended.

Without offering much about himself, Cedric senses their ardor to make him part of the group. His blackness and his standoffishness, his unwillingness to party with them, seems to make everyone worry that there's an unspoken racial subtext: that he doesn't like them because they're white or something. Cedric knows everyone will feel better once he shows that he likes everyone else, proving that goodwill at Brown crosses racial lines. This bothers Cedric, and yet the desire to make himself belong actually intensifies as word spreads of the disputes with Rob. Well-intentioned fellow unit members try to intervene. A few nights after the racial discussions in Zayd's room, Zeina Mobassaleh gets Cedric alone in his room and makes a plea for reconciliation. "Cedric, why don't you and Rob just talk it out. Rob is really a nice guy. The problem is communication."

"Zeina, look, he and I are just so different, and us being across the room from each other, there's gonna be bad stuff," Cedric responds, shutting off her efforts.

Cedric doesn't want to get into the nuances of the conflict, but the situation is clearly souring with each day. His fatigue from acting as Rob's social secretary causes some mishaps, albeit unintentional. One night he forgets to pass on a phone message and Rob is understandably upset about it. Cedric, knowing he screwed up, manages to apologize.

Then it happens again. Someone called about not being able to meet Rob for a chemistry study session. Cedric took the message but then forgot to pass it on. A few hours later, while Cedric is reading his education textbook in the lounge, Rob storms in. He stood outside the chemistry building for an hour, waiting for his study partner. Eventually, he got the guy on the phone and felt like an idiot.

"You didn't give me the message, and it screwed up my whole night. I was standing out there for an hour," says Rob, barely suppressing a shout. "I mean, are you doing it on purpose?!"

"No, look, I was wrong," Cedric says, regretful. "Really, I'm sorry."

But Rob keeps going. He points his finger at Cedric and glares, hard-eyed. "Don't let it happen again." He stomps out of the lounge and back to the room.

Maybe Rob would have said the same thing had his roommate been white or Asian or Hispanic. But Cedric can't be sure of that. He sees condescension. He sees effrontery. He sees things that blacks see and maybe whites don't. A second later, he's rushing back to the room on Rob's heels.

The two of them square off in the middle of their room. "Don't you talk to me like I'm a child or something," Cedric shouts. "Talking to me like I'm less than you, like you have no respect for me. You don't know me, so don't speak to me like that."

"You don't know me, either," counters Rob, not practiced at confrontation the way Cedric is. "Listen, you're seeing things that aren't there."

"All I know is that if you talk to me that way again, I'm gonna fuck you up. I'll kick your ass."

"Just try it!" Rob shouts back, right up in Cedric's face, clearly knowing the proper response to that one. "Just fucking try it!" This time Cedric, who hasn't punched anyone since eighth grade, storms out of the room.

Roaming the halls, he searches for someone to talk to about the confrontation. Rob, it seems, is a friend of nearly everyone on the hall. Cedric knocks on Chiniqua's door. No answer. She's been visiting friends at Harambee a lot lately.

He runs down the hall. Zayd understands the dynamics of the unit, and he's not close to Rob. Zayd will understand. But while Cedric— pounding Zayd's locked door—has few cards in his hand, Zayd has many. Standing there, Cedric tries to figure out where Zayd might be. He could be visiting Bear Beinfeld, a popular sophomore who is Zayd's childhood friend and offers easy access to a more diverse, nonfreshman world. He could be visiting one of many women, lots of them in upper classes, that he already knows. He might be meeting a professor on Thayer Street. No way to find him; he could be anywhere.

Deflated, Cedric writes a note on Zayd's message pad with the grease pencil. "Zayd, Need to talk, quick,—Cedric. It's IMPOR-TANT. YOU CAN COME BY LATE!" Then he flees from the dorm, walking for hours around the dark campus, feeling like a fugitive and wondering what it would be like if he just dropped out and went home.

Cedric Gilliam stands on the edge of a graveyard at 19th and E streets, Southeast, Washington, and checks to see if he has time for a cigarette. He's a little ahead of schedule this warmish autumn eve-ning, and he leans against the cemetery's low brick wall, slowly sucking and tasting each puff while he runs through the string of events that landed him here.

Maybe he lost his head a little, let things get out of hand. Every-thing was going so well in the first few months out, his hair-cutting and a little side dealing balancing out just fine, the women happy that he could now stay the night, an open-ended expanse of freedom up ahead. The problem was the heroin, or not so much the beloved stuff itself as what it did to the rest of things. He started doing a little too much of it. Just a little extra. And, by spring, things were starting to fray with him and Leona, where he was living. They got in this huge fight—she doesn't do drugs or anything—and she threw him out. He thinks she also tipped off his parole officer, because right after that fight, it so happens, the guy brought him in for a surprise drug test, which he failed. Then the guy was all over him, all righteous, and he had to go into a program and get tested all the time, until he got his last chance to test clean at the end of June. When he failed that one, there was nothing to do but lay low. By then he was living with Sherene, who's been real nice to have him, considering the U.S. marshalls have already been by his mom's house. Real nice, that is, until last Friday, when she told him she's got too much to lose—a nice new apartment and a new job—to risk having him around, having marshalls come by her apartment or office looking for him. Not that she was ready to abandon him; she just told him it was time to turn himself in.

He yelled and cursed at her, all the time suspecting that she was right. Last weekend, sleeping where he could, looking for friends to shack up with, and scratching up just enough cash to get by did its part in nudging him along. But there was something else. Over the long weekend he also thought a lot about Lavar. They had some good talks over the spring and early summer. Real friendly. They laughed a little and would have gone to that concert if Barbara hadn't stood in the way. He thought about all that, and how the boy's a little bit like his ol' dad. Not that he's tough in the usual ways, but he's got a tough craftiness about him. Figures out where he wants to go, figures out a way to get there. Doesn't back off of things—goes right at them. And thinking about that on Sunday, sitting on a stoop in an out-of-the-way part of Northeast, he started thinking about Brown, how that boy is sort of showing him up by managing things—handling classes at a famous university and getting settled, far from home—while his father is running away, ducking and hiding. And that was it. Yesterday, he placed a call to Captain Roy Grillo, a parole supervisor he has known since he was a guard at Lorton in the mid-1980s. They set a place and time.

The cigarette is only half finished when an unmarked blue sedan from the D.C. Department of Corrections rounds the corner on 19th at 6:15 sharp. Cedric considers snuffing and pocketing what's left—a prison habit but something he hasn't done in the last ten months of freedom and relative plenty. He looks intently at the butt for an instant, not sure what to do, then drops it, and stamps it hard under the heel of his freshly shined shoe.

"Man, you sure this is what you want to do?" says Grillo through the lowered passenger side window as he pulls to the curb.

Cedric looks at him a moment, surprised by the question. "Yeah, ummm, I guess," he says finally. "I just want to go ahead and get this shit over with."

He thinks about that exchange—about how Grillo seemed to offer a free man's choice and how he opted for the responsible course—a thousand times over the ensuing month. At first it felt sort of good being the stand-up guy, taking his medicine. But week to week it gets harder. For one, it seems like knowing that he could still be outside hustling, eluding the U.S. marshalls, actually makes his days back at Lorton feel harsher, more depriving, than any time he can remember.

Then there's his placement—a bed in the most dangerous facility in the complex, a miserable, medium-security zoo where he's cut off from all the scams and good contacts he built up in minimum security over most of the 1990s. So he talks to almost no one and counts the days.

At three o'clock on a cold morning in mid-October, he hears the fat night guard's boots tapping along on the cell block's concrete floor between a row of beds. "Don't worry, I'm already up," Cedric says in a loud whisper, sitting up, as the wide silhouette nods from behind a flashlight's glare. "I don't need the high beams, I been up for hours."

There's a lot on his mind. Today, finally, is his parole revocation hearing. It will be a long, tense journey through the D.C. criminal justice system. Depending on how things break, it could mean a few more months in prison . . . or a few more years. During the morning's preparations and bus trip to D.C., Cedric's mind locks onto strategic either-ors, multiple-choice answers to hypothetical questions and considerations about how much he'll be able to lie. It's not until 9 A.M., when he's led into a waiting area near some hearing rooms in the D.C. jail, that his furious calculations momentarily stop.

"Sherene, baby," he says, standing there in his orange jumpsuit, sounding more breathless than he'd like to. "Real good to see you." He bends forward and pecks her on the cheek, smelling some perfume she's wearing and feeling dizzy, his just uncuffed hands fumbling forward.

She pulls away, looking at him with mock disapproval, and introduces a tall slender black guy to her left in a black suit and boldly patterned tie.

"Idas Daniel," he says, giving Cedric an overly hard handshake. "I think we're in good shape." Cedric had heard about Daniel from someone in minimum last year, and Sherene had to pay him $300 in advance to handle this hearing—something she's complained mightily about. The lawyer loops a long arm around Cedric's shoulder and starts whispering something about dirty urine and various D.C. drug treatment programs and how Cedric should keep quiet in the hearing, but Cedric barely hears. His head is buzzing. He thinks about how a hit of heroin would be bliss at this moment, just to ease him out. But there's no time to think, or talk, or even hug Sherene again. Cedric Gilliam, 158706, is the first hearing scheduled this morning.

A guard leads the trio into a tiny cork-walled room where a leggy black woman in a short skirt sits next to a fortyish Hispanic guy in a brown suit. The guy must be Enrique Rivera, the parole board member, Cedric figures, and the woman is clearly some sort of corrections assistant who'll implement whatever Rivera decides.

Rivera? Rivera. His mind races. Inmates pass time discussing the board's five members, analyzing their tics and prejudices to make informed predictions about what might happen in these tiny hearing rooms. The inmate handicapping of Rivera: he's supposed to favor Hispanics over blacks. There are no cordialities, and Cedric can't meet Rivera's gaze as he sidesteps through the doorway and sits. The leggy woman begins reciting Cedric's criminal history and various incarcerations, highlights from the forearm-thick folder, or "jacket," on inmate 158706. He already knows every word of that file—every arrest record, court filing, psychological assessment, and rendition of his troubled family history.

His mind wanders, flipping backward until he fixes on something from way back, thirty years at least, that's always bugged him. A lady from child welfare visited his house and wrote that Maggie, his mother, was a "bitter, discontent, distraught individual who took out her frustrations on the children with various forms of rejecting behavior." It's in a report he once read. The social worker added that Maggie encouraged authorities "to 'put the boy away,' with institutionalization being viewed by her as the only meaningful alternative for her son." He always remembers that, every word.

The leggy woman is almost up to the present, talking about how Cedric checked into drug detox in April, was given a last chance to stay clean by his parole officer, then failed the urine test in May.

"The basic case," says Daniel, "is my man couldn't get off the stuff." Rivera nods along, and they discuss how hard it is to place an inmate in one of District's crowded drug treatment programs. Cedric watches the men chat, chummy and complacent, his eyes darting from one face to the other.

"I'd like to say that the violation committed by me was wrong!" he blurts out, drawing Rivera's gaze. The man stares at him, saying nothing, and Cedric starts rambling. "I maintained a job, cutting hair, a regular job . . . and tried to clean myself up . . . but, you know, being incarcerated, it's a point of fact, that the Department of Corrections facility is drug infested . . . and that's why I'm asking for an inpatient program . . . where I can get away from everything that's a problem for me."

He stops abruptly. He knows he should have let Daniel do the talking instead of babbling on, looking like what he is—a desperate man not ready to be on the outside. Daniel murmurs something compensatory, trying to redirect, but Rivera is just looking at Cedric, like he's trying to dig inside him with his eyes. This time, at least, Cedric looks back, but—goddammit!—his left eye starts to twitch and he can't stop it. Fighting the spasm, he hunches forward, looking like he's going to say something, and everyone seems to wait on him. He looks once around the room. "I'm basically asking to be given another chance," he croaks finally, feeling the breath go out of him.

Rivera smiles a sort of melancholy smile, a smile of pity. A moment later he's making a recommendation that Cedric go back to Lorton until his needs can be assessed and a slot in a one-year inpatient drug treatment program can located.

And then it's over. Leaving the room, Cedric nods thankfully toward Rivera. He feared it would be worse, that he'd be reprimanded and sent back to serve more time. But this is different, an order that he be placed in a treatment program—the kind of program he's needed—soon as that can be arranged. Daniel, grinning and jokey, huddles with Cedric in a foyer area outside the hearing room.

"They're gonna have a real tough time finding a year-long treatment program, with cutbacks and all. But that's what Rivera will recommend anyway. So when they talk to you at your assessment at Lorton, be flexible that six months is what you really need. It'll be easier for them to find you a bed that way." Cedric listens, trying to find in Daniel's tone and inflection a confirmation that this was a victory. Yes, it is a victory, he decides, and spots a guy he knows from minimum security in an orange jumper, waiting for his hearing. "Joe, Joe, can I have a cigarette?" he asks, and he snatches the cigarette the guy passes to him, artfully slipping it into his breast pocket. Of course, the cig's not free—nothing is around here—and Joe wants some intelligence about Cedric's hearing, about which board member is on today.

"It's Rivera, and I was worried, because he supposedly favors the Puerto Ricans. But he was okay. For me, it was dirty urine, and it'll mean six months, I figure," he says, gathering sensations in a prediction. "Yeah, six months, tops, in an inpatient drug treatment program, and then I'll be out."

It's time for Daniel and Sherene to be led out, and Cedric moves toward her quickly, grabbing her hand. "You'll party tonight, be celebrating and all?" he asks, smiling, and kisses her cheek again. She pulls away, but not briskly like before, and purses her lips, playfully. He wants confirmation. "Well, will you be?"

"Okay," she says, giving in. "I guess so." Savoring this small victory, he nods. "Well, then, I can think about you being out, having fun."

It only takes a few weeks back at Lorton for Cedric Gilliam to feel mocked by the idea of a celebration. Celebration? Celebrating what? he mulls, lying on his cot one evening as November approaches. He's checked on the availability of one-year inpatient slots. It's a joke. Inmates are waiting three months just to be assessed for placement, and then it's another six months, maybe even longer, to find a bed. Rivera ordered something that's not findable. Cedric's not going anywhere.

Sherene visited yesterday and they just sat on the little, mustard-colored plastic chairs in the visitation hall—a big gymnasium—not saying much. He tried to describe to her how dangerous this place is, how there was a stabbing a few nights ago, and how he feels like he's lost his bearings. These young guys, some doing endless time on three-strike felonies or murder raps, are just looking to exact some punishment, to take it out on somebody. A few weeks ago, they had four stabbings in one night. Guys are making shanks out of toothbrushes, bits of metal, table legs. Some guard got busted for smuggling in guns. Maybe being out for almost a year made him soft, maybe it's just age and fatigue. But he's not sure he has the energy anymore to put up a deterring facade, to spot potential threats and fend off attacks. All he knows is that he's tired of always being jumpy, with no trusted guys over here to back him up and no connections to score drugs.

Sherene didn't seem to want to hear any of it. She just kept looking up and down the rows of facing chairs, with inmates hugging and kissing the girls visiting them, people wrapped up in each other like pretzels.

"Aren't you happy to see me, after I've come all the way out here? What, you're just not in the mood?" she asked, after a long silence. He just grumbled. It's hard to get "in the mood," he mulled darkly, when you know you'll have to leave the gym floor in a few minutes, walk behind a screen on the stage, and take off all your clothes. You want a cold shower? Try having some guard running his rubber-gloved hands all over your cold body and then ordering you to bend over and part your cheeks. The only thing worse than having it done is having to talk about it. So he said nothing. Sherene left in a snit, and he, of course, walked behind the screen to peel off his sky-blue jumpsuit.

The days start to run together. There's nothing to do here. Movement is tightly restricted, unlike at minimum, where you could get a pass to go to the library, or some class, drug treatment counseling, job training, or whatever. A little excursion like that can make a whole day. Here, there are no programs to speak of. Cedric spends every day bumping around cell block 18, a fifty-man open dorm area. Once in a while he plays Scrabble with a guy named Zack. But they're not all that close; Cedric doesn't even know why he's here or for how long. On good days, he might score a newspaper to read—that helps—but they're scarce.

It's raining hard today, a day in early November, cutting off the option of going outside into a small courtyard near the cell block. There's nothing to do, simply nothing, and Cedric bums a piece of notebook paper from a guy across the room. He takes it to a bare table near the blaring TV, pulls a plastic pen from his hip pocket, and sits on a metal chair with a torn fabric seat.

He sits there a long while, staring into the whiteness. He can't remember the last time he did this. Years, at least. He draws a line on his palm, to make sure the pen is working, and then presses it to the paper.

> *"Dear Lavar,*
>
> *I know I haven't written to you in a real long time, but I was thinking about how things were going for you at college. It's not so good for me here. For the first time in a long time, I'm really feeling down.*
>
> *But I was wondering about you and how it is going. What classes you are taking. What the other kids are like. I know the Ivy League must be hard. But I'm sure you'll do good because your studious and determined."*

He reads over what he's written a dozen times.

> *"I remember when you visited me here when you were 12. You said you wanted to go to Princeton. I remember thinking that you were crazy, shooting too high."*

He stops. No need to rush it. He wants to get the words just right. Thinking back on that Princeton thing—maybe it *was* more than six years ago—sends him into a minefield of memory and regret. It ends further back than he usually reminisces, to when he was just a kid—

maybe thirteen—and his father, Freddie, visited from Philadelphia. Hasn't thought about that forever. That's what getting depressed will do, he thinks, unearth stuff you forget about. The old man had disappeared when he was seven. Left town, no one knew where he'd gone. Then all of a sudden, he's there, coming by the house and saying he's in Philly now, like no one ever got beaten and nothing ever happened. He took Cedric down to a flea market on H Street. Bought him a round cap, checked, with a nice fabric, that kind of hung to one side. It was the early '60s, and that was a very cool hat. Had to cost $10. Then he was gone, just like that—no forwarding address, just vanished. Whole thing made his mom crazy, like he'd never seen. She threw the hat away in some garbage someplace, where he couldn't find it. God, he loved that fuckin' hat.

The buzzer rings for dinner. Guys start easing toward the locked cell block door, slowly lining up to go to the mess. Cedric just sits, taking his time, easing out of the recollection. Thirteen years old, just a little shit. He shakes his head. That was about the time he started getting in trouble.

He looks down at the letter's two scratchy paragraphs. Who's he to be writing this letter, he muses, a letter from prison to an Ivy League college; sure they don't get much jail mail in the Ivies. He reads it again, slowly, thinking that the tone of it bothers him a little. It's sort of apologetic, like he's apologizing to Lavar.

He frowns and folds the letter into thirds, then again lengthwise, and roughly shoves it in his pocket.

Cedric Jennings stares at his midterm paper in Calculus and finishes off a third box of Golden Grahams for lunch at Vernon Wooley Dining Hall, called the VeeDub. The grade is a 94. He looks up. Chiniqua and her roommate, Maura, are sitting across from him. He shows them the paper. They're effusive in their praise.

But it doesn't cheer him. He's told Chiniqua, at least, that this is just one level above beginner math and that he shot low out of fear.

Still, when she smiles at him, he smiles back. The two girls pile plates and glasses on their trays to go, and he pours another box of Golden Grahams. It's a cereal he ate a lot of at home, sometimes when there wasn't much else to eat. In the last couple of days, since midterms ended, he's been eating a lot of it.

"Cedric, how many bowls you gonna eat?" Chiniqua says.

"As many as it takes," he says, trying to make her laugh.

"Takes for what?" she says, rising with her tray. And then she bends in close to whisper, "You should eat some real food."

A frenzy of studying for mid-October's midterms gave Cedric a break from the fixating strife with Rob. Everyone, Rob included, had other things to worry about. Cedric, nonetheless, did most of his studying in Rockefeller Library to avoid his roommate. Not that he had that much studying. Calculus was a walk in the park, and his only other midterm test was in Spanish.

He didn't need to worry about bumping into Rob in room 216. His roommate is all but living on the third floor, dividing evenings among rooms of various friends.

Cedric—with sound strategic instincts from a lifetime of confrontation—forces himself not to retreat from the group of white guys so he can't be characterized for everyone by Rob. He tries to stick with the group and shake off his confusion at their strange habits. For one, the white guys are more physical and affectionate toward one another than he's used to seeing among the black kids from high school, who were so wrapped up with burnishing their hard exteriors. Black kids from his school and neighborhood might have hung together endlessly but rarely showed the sort of self-deprecating, carefree vulnerability that's common here. He's not sure how to react. No one here is boastful. They all make fun of themselves—and each other—though their underlying confidence never seems jilted. It's the precise opposite of what has passed for normal his whole life, one spent around those whose underlying self-confidence was easily punctured.

One weekday night in Zayd and John's room, seven or eight kids, including Ira and Florian from across the hall, start teasing each other in a way that Cedric can't abide.

It's homosexual banter. Black guys just don't do it.

As the white boys start in, Cedric feels his gut tighten. "Come on, bend over and let me fill your gas tank," one says to another, and everyone starts to crack up. "Come on. You know you want it."

Cedric's not laughing. He can't. He becomes noticeably grim. They don't understand.

So they treat him just like he wants, deep down: just like another guy. Under those rules, anyone who shows uneasiness becomes the focal point. Comfort here is practically a moral concept. Visible discomfort, on an issue like this, brings a *Lord of the Flies* response: haze it out of him.

"Hey, Cedric," says Ira. "Bend over, and I'll fill your gas tank."

Cedric gets flushed.

"Come on, Cedric," says John, a sort of natural class president among the group. "It's okay. I'll bend over and you can fill up mine." Guffaws go around. Even Zayd can't resist the riptide.

Cedric jumps up from Zayd's bed. "I don't like that kind of talkin'," he says, loud and firm but still under control. He doesn't know what else to say. He looks down, pushes out the door, and races back to his empty room.

His door stays locked. Hours pass. At midnight, he has to go to the bathroom and ventures out, cracking the door first to see if anyone is in the hall. And then he sees it. On his grease pad is a neatly written message that anyone could walk by and read.

"Hey Cedric, Meet us later tonight in private and we all can have some real fun. Love, Ira and John."

Cedric blows up. In a second, he's pounding on Ira's door, and then they're nose to nose in the doorway. "Don't be leaving that mess on my door so I have to wipe it off."

"I didn't write anything," Ira counters. "I don't know what you're talking about."

"You're just doing this to annoy me, Ira! To get me going!"

A crowd is gathering in the hallway.

"Look, I do what I want to do. And I'll do what I want to do to you," Ira bellows. "So get out of my room."

Everything's in the open now, a spectator sport, a free feed.

"You can't just accuse Ira of doing it unless you know he did," says

Corry—Cedric's Marcia Brady—out in the hall from a neighboring room. "You don't know it was Ira."

"I know it's him," Cedric rants. "He's done stuff like that before. Don't tell me. He's always saying stuff like that."

Zayd tries to diffuse it. "Everybody's not against you," he says, keeping his voice quiet and even. "You think that, but it's not true."

Cedric halts. He looks across the corridor, now filled with mostly white peers and a few of color. All eyes are on him. They know about Rob. And now this. Everyone just stares. All he wants is to get back to his room and never come out.

John, at Zayd's side, ends it. "Jesus, Cedric. You ignore people just to get attention, and then you get the attention and you don't want it."

Cedric looks, dazed, at John. His ringing ears are shutting off everything. How the hell did he end up here? While everyone stares, he walks back to his room and softly closes the door.

A few days later, Zayd is sitting on the moist grass of Brown's main green, on an oddly warm, short-sleeve October day, talking to his buddy, Bear, about Cedric.

"Other kids wonder why I'm his friend, what I see in him," he says, his smoothly muscled bare arms wrapped around peaks of bony knees. "And it's strange. We're like opposites. We're so different in so many ways, but I just find him so interesting."

More than any other student in the unit, Zayd has the luxury of autonomy. While John masters the fierce intimacies of a freshman dorm, Zayd seems to stand above the fray. He's considered a touch aloof, in part because he won't simply offer the full, instant disclosure that is common currency among college freshmen.

People, including Cedric, don't know much about him. The few things they do know are intriguing. Zayd starred at the Laboratory School of Chicago, a progressive private school run by the University of Chicago, and took some courses at the university. He went to Northwestern University film school two summers ago, when he was just sixteen, and has written a play called *Phallacy,* which he calls "a sexual farce."

One other thing is known about Zayd. He's a slender, wide-shoul-dered six-foot-two, with carefully cropped, pushed-back hair, high cheekbones under blue eyes, and the perfect proportion of eyebrows to slender nose that is the hallmark of male models. This, combined with his mysteriousness, causes some substantial sexual frisson among the women in the unit and his various classes—energy he casually harnesses in frequent, though usually short-lived, sexual liaisons.

But the most important quality that draws people to him is invisi-ble. Zayd is the embodiment of an ethos that, more than anything, defines merit around this campus and many elite institutions like it: constant, fearless, rigorous experimentation—both social and intellec-tual. The more daring, the better. By that measure, Zayd is muscle bound.

Zayd Osceola Ayers Dohrn emerges from a reactor core of such headlong thinking: the elegant Chicago brownstone of two fiftyish col-lege professors on the city's integrated and edgy south side, just a few blocks from the University of Chicago. Writers, artists, and savants of America's progressive vanguard have, for years, passed through his liv-ing room, pollinating him and his two brothers.

His prime directive, as he mentioned in Cedric's presence that first week of school, is "I'll try anything."

Which is why Zayd, among all the broad-thinking kids in this right-minded university, is the only one with the daring to knock on Cedric's door, which has been mostly locked—locking out the world—for a week since the much discussed hallway detonation. Zayd gets no answer and writes a provocative note: "C—Came by, heard music inside. I guess we're not friends anymore or something. Zayd."

He passes by again as October nears an end. It's now two weeks into what seems like Cedric's permanent hibernation, and Zayd won-ders if it may end with a transfer application and a bare mattress. The doorknob clicks open. Zayd walks in, talking casually about some new album by Tupac Shakur, the controversial and glamorous rapper, talking like nothing ever happened. Cedric, parched with solitude, can't resist the company. To be sure, it's a strange, wild CD Tupac just released.

"You know, Tupac's uncle was this guy, Zayd Shakur, a radical black activist who was killed by the cops in the early '60s," Zayd continues. "That's who I'm named after. My mom and dad knew him—or, I guess they knew some Black Panthers who knew him."

"For real?" Cedric asks.

In a few days, parents will be coming for parents weekend, and the two of them talk about that for a while, sitting on Cedric's bed. Cedric says he doesn't know whether his mom will make it. It's a long way, and she doesn't have a lot of cash. Zayd nods, knowing not to ask too much, and says, "It's going to be very weird having all those parents around."

He pauses. "Remember my mom came by a few weeks ago—she might want to come by to say hi," he ventures, "if that's all right."

"That'd be fine, no big deal," Cedric answers easily, clearly relieved to be edging out of exile. Then they walk down to the corner to Sam Goody's to buy a CD, figuring they could share it.

9

BILL PAYERS
on PARADE

Crunching leaves with her high-heeled boots, Bernadine Dohrn arrives at an irrefutable confirmation of middle age: the visiting of a child for parents weekend. She knows this must elicit smug smiles from those who know her or know of her, the latter being anyone with the slightest memory of the 1960s.

Let then snipe, she thinks. She's happy to still be visible in the mind's eye as queen mother of America's once fearsome radical counterculture, through which she stomped in her leather miniskirt, shouting about racism and classism and exhorting her fellow travelers to bomb, pillage, and "freak out the honky establishment."

In a fuzzy sweater, pleated skirt, and Aztec-flashy earrings, she's wandering around the Brown campus with her husband—once her companion on the FBI's Most Wanted List and fellow Weather Underground leader, Billy Ayers. Today they're just another pair of sentimental, fiftyish grownups searching for the right dorm.

It's a national hobby to track celebrated '60s hellions—to gloat over their wrinkles and gray hair and business suits as mile markers of a generation's lost ideals. Yet, because Bernadine and Bill are so famously anachronistic, a plain fact is obscured: they were suited to their times then and they are, likewise, suited to their times now, as middle-aged baby boomer parents.

"You remember when I talked to Zayd on the phone right after he got here?" Bill says to Bernadine. "He said, 'Dad, it's like my first seventeen years were just a preliminary stage, just getting me ready for this moment. I was born to be in college.' And I said, 'Like, hey, what about me! I'm your father. Those first seventeen years were everything to me.' "

Bill, his once illustrious shoulder-length blond curls now graying, cut short, and tucked under a baseball cap, makes a mock wounded face and Bernadine laughs heartily, as does Harriet Beinfeld, Bear's mom. She's an old "movement" friend who helped hide the couple and their toddler, Zayd, during the couple's seven long years underground, fur-tive years when Zayd was born. Harriet is still walking beside Bernadine and Bill, except this time it's through the wrought-iron gateway entrance to Brown's main green.

"I think we're all feeling that it sure would be nice to be eighteen right now," Bernadine says wryly to her companions.

Yes, they're all feeling it—she, Bill, and Harriet, along with many other parents wandering on this Friday afternoon at the start of a week-end's visitation. Summing up generational zeitgeist, after all, is some-thing Bernadine has always done. Bill, too. Striding across the Brown campus, clicking the concrete with high heels that show off her cele-brated legs, Bernadine expounds about events and issues writ large—just like when she was in college—describing a conference on violence against women she just attended that showed her "how we can't prose-cute violent men with Mark Fuhrmans as our allies . . . how the opponents of racism and the opponents of violence against women are natural allies in the struggle."

At this point, she and Bill are working well within the system. She's a lawyer who runs a center for juvenile justice at Northwestern Univer-sity. He's a trailblazing professor of education at the University of Illi-nois who often works at solving the dilemmas of educating the urban poor. And, like so many parents—both liberal and conservative—traipsing around campus today, this pair is hooked on mass behavior and sweeping public issues in a way that their children are not.

Bill picks up Bernadine's conversational thread, responding swiftly, breezy and hyperarticulate, about seeing the O.J. verdict in a juvenile detention center with some hardened kids who were "high-fiving and screaming that 'I want that Johnnie Cochran as my lawyer.' " They could go on like this all day.

But, a little way across the Brown campus on the long walk to East

Andrews, Bernadine's galloping high-pitched Judy Holliday voice grows softer and less certain. She haltingly recalls what it was like taking Zayd and Bear out to dinner on an impromptu "business trip" through Providence three weeks earlier. They talked that night about Kiekegaard concept of dutiful love versus passionate love—something the boys had just learned in Philosophy—and she turns to tell Harriet "how the boys were making a case for dutiful love as being superior. I mean, my God, they're so young and they've already lost confidence in passion. It's part of their cautiousness about politics, about ideology, about all sorts of things that I just don't understand. If they don't feel a little reckless, romantic energy when they're young, then when?"

"Lately," she continues, after a moment, "I'm not sure about how much of what we stood for, and still stand for, will actually survive us. It's their time now, and they're so different from the way we were." Her voice trails off as the others listen sentiently.

Bill and Harriet start chatting with Bear, who's tagging along, and Bernadine's mind wanders to Zayd, to her anticipation of spending this weekend with him. He's her pride, her heir, and, in some ways, her nemesis. He's discovering his talents, like she was at his age, but using them in ways she thinks are narrow and, sometimes, frivolous. Signing on to sweeping social movements? Fighting for larger causes? Forget it. It's all so fragmented with these kids these days, she mulls. Everything focused on personal behavior and group identity, inward fixations; everyone a one-man show, displaying themselves through consumerism and fashion. Yes, they believe in things, but nothing they'll sacrifice for. There are no overarching principles that Zayd or any of his peers seems to embrace. Take women's rights. Here she is, fighting against the dehumanization of women, and Zayd, using all of his sexual sway, treats them like targets. Drives her crazy! She told a friend recently, "What Zayd needs is a beautiful, brilliant girl to kick his ass." A girl sort of like she was, at twenty.

She sighs. She's not going to get into arguments with Zayd, not this weekend. His counterattacks—about the price she and Bill paid for losing themselves in ideology, about how you should take care of yourself and your own fulfillment before you start saving the goddamn world, how the two of them never want to grow up—leave her spent.

No, she's going to be good. Of course, it could be worse, Bernadine thinks. Her friends with girls who are Zayd's age moan that every last precious daughter has already had a dorm room lesbian encounter.

Bernadine walks quietly for a moment, then perks up again, remembering one moment from her recent visit that has heartened her: getting to meet Zayd's new friend, a boy named Cedric Jennings. She tells Bill that after her dinner with Zayd and Bear that night, "Zayd wanted me to meet Cedric. But he told me that Cedric is 'really hard to deal with, really out there,' and I told him I can act appropriately. So we went to Cedric's room. And I said Hi to him . . . that I'd heard a lot about him and that I wanted to meet his mother during parents weekend. 'Well,' he said, kind of sheepishly, 'you know, she doesn't say much.' And I told him, 'No problem. I can handle that.' And then we left. I mean, I think it's terrific that he and Zayd have become friends. At least that's one good thing. Zayd may not be committed to much, but at least he's been taught to venture out, to experiment a bit." Everyone nods at this and she smiles, looking up at the brick horseshoe of Andrews dorm just ahead.

Yes, her Zayd is an experimenter who clearly shares his mom and dad's penchant for knowing which way the wind blows, being as fitted to his generation's awakening as they were to theirs. Bernadine and Bill, of course, enlisted in their era's "try everything" mania and pushed it to the limit. Appropriately, Zayd's oft-spoken "try anything" credo takes him in a different direction. Bernadine knows its full text is more like, "I'll try anything . . . that my searching, mush-brained, never-grow-up parents haven't already tried."

They arrive on the second floor of Andrews and spend a few minutes searching for Zayd. They knock on Cedric's door, but the room is locked. Then Bear, who ushered the grown-ups across campus, realizes there's been a mistake. They'd told Zayd to wait outside for them at a distant entrance to Andrews Hall. He runs off to retrieve his friend, who appears a moment later.

"Oh Zayd, we really fucked you over!" Bernadine yells across the hall, past a few parents picking up their kids as dinner hour approaches. "Didn't we? We fucked you up leaving you out there."

Zayd's face tightens as he weaves toward them. She knows he hates it when she curses like that in front of other people, like she's still nineteen or something. "Yeah mom," he says softly. "You really fucked me up."

The rain is thunderous, flooding dirty downtown Providence as the night train from Washington arrives at noon on Saturday. Barbara and Neddy, dragging suitcases and Hefty bags, emerge from the porticoed escalator and slump into a wooden love seat in the train station's central atrium.

"Lord, Neddy, it's been a trip," murmurs Barbara. "Can't believe I'm here."

"This is about the craziest thing I've ever done, coming all the way up here to see Lavar for just one day," says Neddy.

Barbara laughs along, but she doesn't agree. "Naw. It's worth seeing him, even if it's just a day."

A creeping disarray in Barbara's life back home conspired against her plan to bake sweet potato pies for Cedric. She missed a Bible study class on Revelations that she planned to attend at Scripture Cathedral early yesterday evening. Then she missed the train—Amtrak's 10:30 P.M. sleeper from Washington to Providence. At 11 P.M., Neddy was still waiting in the messy apartment on V Street while Barbara packed. The next train was at 3 A.M., so the two of them spent the next hours knocking about, collecting odds and ends. They boxed up Cedric's Supernintendo along with as many strewn-about game cassettes as they could find and watched TV to stay awake. A friend of Neddy's drove them to Union Station just in time for the 3 A.M., landing them in Rhode Island a few minutes shy of noon.

But, no matter. They're here now. Barbara is in an embroidered jean skirt and shirt and a small khaki rain hat. Neddy, next to her, primps, smoothing wrinkles on her pumpkin-colored shirt and straightening her stylish silver necklace.

This is the longest Barbara has ever been away from Cedric, and, with the central focus of her life absent, there's been some dangerous drift over the past two months.

She had thought her life would change, that it was time to find some happiness for herself, maybe even a man. Nothing too romantic. Just someone to be around, to be a friend, to give as much as she has to give.

For the first few weeks in Washington, Barbara floated forward between work, church, and the living room couch. Figuring she needed to start looking more attractive, she bought a few dresses on a new charge card. She never got around to paying the bill.

Then she ran up her phone bill with calls to Cedric in late August and early September. Then Cedric couldn't call her at home because her phone was disconnected in early October. When he called her work number, she was out sick. Weeks passed, and Cedric, growing concerned, finally reached Neddy one night to ask if their mother was okay. "You know, Neddy, you know how she can get when she gets down."

He was right to worry. She was down, low down—sleeping a lot, missing work, even missing church functions. Neddy started coming over to rouse her, bringing by little Lawrence to cheer her. Nothing seemed to boost her. By mid-October, though, she began to look ahead to parents weekend, figuring that a trip to see Lavar could get her on a new footing.

In a last conversation before the phone got cut off, Cedric told her that he didn't want her to come, like he was ashamed of her. She wasn't sure if he was playing. But she couldn't worry about that. She had to get there. So Barbara withdrew all her remaining cash and bought a train ticket she couldn't afford.

The rain drips down Barbara's back after five minutes standing outside the locked East Andrews door. She doesn't have Lavar's number to call upstairs, so she and Neddy wait, huddled together.

Evan Horowitz's family pulls into the Andrews dorm parking lot in a black Chevy Blazer with Connecticut tags, driven by Evan's investment banker dad and carrying his mom, brother, and Evan's girlfriend from Tufts University in Boston.

Evan lets Barbara and Neddy inside. He knows who they are, but he doesn't introduce them to his family as they all head up the stairs.

Barbara, with Neddy in tow, wanders the second-floor hallway, mostly vacated, looking for a familiar door. Chiniqua, just out of bed, emerges from her room in robin's-egg-blue pajamas. "Hi there," Barbara says impulsively, delighted to see a black girl. A startled Chiniqua blinks a greeting and slips down the hall into the bathroom.

Barbara stops at the door of Mimi Yang, the peer counselor, and looks at the envelope of condoms. "I know this ain't his room," she says, rolling her eyes. She's still uncertain until Rob opens the door on the adjacent hall and slips out. "Oh yeah, hey," he says, fleeing quickly, and she says, "Hi, Rob," to his back.

Inside, the room is dark, shades drawn. It's half-past noon. Cedric, in his pajamas, sits up quickly. "Oh God. What time is it?"

"I can't believe you're still in bed," Neddy chirps. "You still in your pajamas."

"Turn on some lights in here," Barbara says.

"PLEASE, NOOOO . . ." he cries, laughing, ducking under the covers.

The women prowl the room proprietarily, Neddy fingering through the CD collection, Barbara poking around the laptop computer, while they gently bust on Cedric in the familiar, sometimes affectionate, call and response that they've been at for years.

Cedric lies there with a dazed smile while mother and daughter turn resolute and industrious, with Barbara heaving the suitcase up onto the foot of the bed. "Oh Ma, don't put that wet thing up there."

"Just shut up." She pulls his leather jacket out of the suitcase and chucks it on the bed. "You wanted this?"

Neddy goes straight for the Supernintendo. "Lavar, where the other remote control? . . ."

"I don't know, in the drawer, I think."

"You didn't cut your hair," chides Barbara, looking him over. "Whatchya doin'?"

"You should have done that yesterday, Lavar," Neddy follows, "for our arrival."

"Nuh uh," Cedric mutters, finally rising from the bed. "I gotta do it today. . . . I need to get some new electric clippers for my hair."

Barbara nods, delighted. That's one mission for today—something for her to do. Get new clippers, "Get dressed, Lavar, let's get going," Barbara snaps.

There's no hugging or touching, just this good-natured fussing, and Cedric bids for a bit more. "You didn't even say 'hi' to me or 'I miss you' or nothing."

"You ain't said 'hi' to me either," Barbara curtly counters.

"I did say 'hi'," he mutters, walking over to the sink. Then, more gently, "You wet?"

"A little bit," Barbara says, now gentle herself. She looks him over as he washes off his face at the sink. Looks like he put on some weight and maybe an inch. So this is where he lives. Her eyes take in every detail of the room. She's been worried about him not having a church up here and has worked up a provisional plan, which she now springs.

"Talked to Bishop on Thursday and he wants you to call him at his home, make sure that you're staying right with God. I got his number with me."

"You serious? He does not want me to call. He said that?" Cedric is flattered and surprised, but the prospect of a call seems to make him anxious, which concerns Barbara. Bishop warned about drinking, drugs, and strange white customs. If Cedric doesn't want to talk to him, Barbara wonders, it might mean that he's struggling with temptations.

"I ain't got no money to be making no calls."

"He said you should call collect," she's says, trapping him next to the sink.

Cedric slips away and sits back on the bed. He says, "I just don't think my calling him is appropriate. . . ."

She's on him in an instant. "Appropriate?! You know, you're getting toooo smart." She starts smacking him on the head and back, and he's laughing, trying to grab her hands, but she's too fast, and she's now laughing, too, light and airy.

"Okay, Ma, stop," but she keeps it up. "Okay Mommy," he says, affecting a little boy's voice, and she pulls back.

"Don't give me that 'Mommy' stuff. Listen, Pastor expects you to call him."

"What do I say?"

" 'How you doing? . . . I'm fine . . . Praise the Lord.' That's all. You just scared to call him, Lavar. Admit it."

"Yeah, I guess you right."

Barbara sits down in Cedric's desk chair and watches her children argue over some rhythm and blues singer she's never heard of. She would just as soon stay in this room until tomorrow's departure rather than venture out among the other parents and students, with their luxury cars and American Express cards. She thinks about Cedric not wanting her to come, about how he may be ashamed of her and ashamed about where he comes from, but she pushes the thought away.

Cedric is now a Brown student, at the threshold of full citizenship on behalf of lots of Jenningses. Jenningses who would want her to make a good showing. She's a Brown parent, after all.

"Come, Nanette, we should let him shower and then he'll need to get dressed in private," she says decorously, rising and gathering herself. "Cedric," she says, calling him, maybe for the first time, by his "professional" name, "you do what you have to, don't worry about us. We'll be waiting outside."

Though Brown has set up parents weekend programs—seminars and coffees, just like at orientation—they're sparsely attended. No one wants to stay around the campus. The idea is to locate the lost child and get him OUT OF HERE.

The abducting has been going on steadily since Friday morning, when Dr. and Dr. Burton—Rob's parents—arrived to attend some of his classes. Both sturdy Ohioans who came East after medical school, they sat through Political Theory, trundled off to Chemistry, and soon stole Rob off to go mountain climbing for the weekend. They managed to not encounter Cedric. The casual and wealthy Phillip Arden, who lately has been getting "come hither" e-mails from girls who've met him around campus, greeted his father—who flew in on his Lear jet—with an unwelcomed development; mononucleosis, just diagnosed. After sheepishly passing on the news, he retired to his dad's suite at the Westin hotel for a weekend of sleep.

The few kids whose parents didn't show—like Sonya Garza, the Hispanic girl from far-off Sanger, California—tended to be adopted for a lunch or dinner by the parents of a roommate.

By Saturday, Thayer Street—with its five-block run of shops and eateries and boutiques—has the harried concentration usually found on the last shopping days before Christmas. It's an army of bill payers on parade. Every shop is jammed, with smiling, ruddy parents wielding plastic.

Each parent is a paying customer of the university, and the grounds have been clipped, mowed, spackled, painted, and adorned for all their money's worth. Even the cafeterias are offering uncommonly strong fare—meat loaf and veal parmigiana, beef stews and lemon meringue pies—just in case parents join a child for a real taste of college life.

As Cedric takes his sweet time showering, Barbara and Neddy go to a drugstore a block from the dorm to pick up an economy size Nivea lotion for him. Barbara looks down Thayer Street—overrun by hoards from Westport, Grosse Point, and Palo Alto. "It's a mob, look at them all," she says to Neddy. "I don't want to be any part of that."

And she won't be. A little later, the family catches a ride to some nearby malls and they pass the afternoon strolling through familiar discount chains like Ames, Duane Reade, Payless, Marshalls, and the Dollar Store, not buying much except a $19.95 ConAir hair clipper for Cedric to shave his head.

Cedric doesn't say much, but Barbara senses that he's content just to listen to the language of home and news of Southeast. "Some Asians bought a store near my house," Neddy tells him as they finger through a huge sock bin at Marshalls, "and they be jacking up the prices and hoarding money and, now, they selling malt liquor. They don't sell malt liquor in Georgetown, but they sell it in my neighborhood, and it keeps black people down."

Barbara considers this for a moment, examining a pair of argyles, before offering a counterpoint. She's talking to Neddy, but, like everything else she says this weekend, she's most mindful of what Cedric is hearing. "Well, they work hard and do whatever they have to do to get ahead, to get to the next step. The problem with black people is that if someone gets a little more than them, everybody jump on him, saying he think he's better and all. For Asians, it's a goal that everybody get better and everybody get in on it. They come over here, living fourteen to an apartment!"

"There are a lot of Asians at Brown, and they stick together here, too," Cedric mumbles, letting Barbara know he's been listening, as he pulls on a leather hat that no one at Brown would be caught dead wearing and looks at himself admiringly.

By nightfall, everyone is back on the terra infirma of College Hill. It's the big Saturday dinner rush of parents weekend, and Barbara, wanting to do what Brown parents are supposed to do, asks Cedric about restaurants. He's heard of a place called Adesso, and soon she leads the family there. It's the area's restaurant of choice just off Thayer, with blond wood, ficuses, California stylish cuisine, and a fifty-minute wait.

The Jennings contingent leaves its name with the hostess and walks back into a long alcove hallway lined with chairs, almost all filled with laughing parent–child clusters, mostly white. Barbara spots an elegantly dressed Hispanic family a half-dozen seats away, a mother and father talking animatedly to a daughter. A black family is vacating a table and making for the exit, the father folding his credit card receipt and putting it in his wallet.

Barbara sees some faces of color but feels little comfort. There is nothing to match the conspicuousness of poor and black—the lot, she is certain, of only one family she knows among the dozens here.

Eventually their name is called, and the Jennings family is led to a table. Barbara looks at the menu and then looks again.

"I never spent this much money on food, ever," she whispers to everyone and no one. "What could they do to the food to make it worth this much?"

But the hive is buzzing all around—chattering clusters seeming to close in from all sides—and she pushes down the list of wood-grilled entrees.

The waitress, a platinum blonde practicing her pronunciations, arrives and describes the specials. Barbara orders the shrimp and scallops on angel hair pasta special; Cedric, shrimp and chicken over rigatoni, off the menu; and Neddy, the half-moon spinach-stuffed pasta with mascarpone sauce.

As the waitress leaves, everyone sits in silence, breathing lightly. Barbara looks at the yellow pansy in a flute vase on the table.

"Is that some kind of red sauce on that flower?" she says, and everyone looks. Seems to be marinara.

They all begin looking for things, trying to find seams in the restaurant's elegant fabric to ease their discomfort. A complimentary appetizer comes and is set near Cedric.

"This is beet flan," the waitress says, and everyone nods meaningfully at the news until she's gone.

Barbara looks at it, perplexed, and then at Cedric. He takes her cue and begins gazing at the little round plateau of reddish mold. "What'd she say it is?" she riffs, leading on the others. Cedric pokes at it with his fork. "Oh Gaawwd. It moves!"

Evan Horowitz and family are within earshot at the next table, talking about plans for their upcoming winter vacation in Hawaii, Evan's classes ("a piece of cake," he chortles) and goings-on at home in Connecticut, one long stretch of unself-conscious discourse suited to this place, Brown University, and the presumption of ongoing success.

Meanwhile, at the Table of the Marinara Pansy, the discreet charms of the upper-middle class have been shrunk to the manageable notion of beet flan.

"Go ahead, Lavar, try it," Barbara says. "You the family pioneer." He ventures a spoonful.

"Alpo," he says. "It tastes just like Alpo," and they laugh good and loud, not caring who hears them. The waitress comes by to check if everything is satisfactory, and Cedric asks her, "People actually eat that beet stuff?"

The blonde looks both ways and leans in conspiratorially over the table's corner between Cedric and Barbara. "If you wanna know the truth," she whispers, betraying an up-the-hard-way East Providence patois, "we've been scraping it off the plate all night."

A small victory won. Barbara offers a warm, winking smile to the waitress and seems to settle into her blond-wood-and-polished-chrome chair. The Jennings clan, she feels, has something to bring to this room, as well.

The entrees come and everyone eats hungrily, while Barbara talks between bites of shrimp about Cedric's graduation speech. "Oh, how Dr. Jones's face changed when you started into that Dreambusters thing."

"Everyone's always hearing about how well Cedric did, when you did good yourself," she says earnestly to Neddy.

"Back then, they didn't even keep the grades as GPAs," Neddy says with mild disinterest as she spears a half-moon and pushes it through the cheese sauce.

"Yes, you *were* good," Barbara continues, undeterred. "You'd a gotten a 3.6 average or something, if they'd figured it up."

Neddy wipes her lips with a coral cloth napkin and smiles sympathetically at her mother. "Let's be real. I was a B to C student. I wasn't like Lavar."

But Barbara presses on, spinning a story from her own youth. "I used to pass my math homework around the room to the other kids, so they could get the answers all right, too. And the teachers never caught me."

From across the marinara pansy, Cedric beams. "You were good, too, weren't you?" he says, his eyes locking onto hers, his face rosy with pride.

They are the only people in the room. "Yes, Lavar," she says. "I was good, too. I was very good."

By Sunday morning, Barbara and Neddy are already thinking about Washington. They both have to work tomorrow, and it's seven long hours to D.C., so they angle to leave before lunch. After their one night at the Holiday Inn—Barbara's funds now all but depleted—they pack up the suitcases and catch a cab to Cedric's dorm for a brief farewell.

Other than last night's dinner, there has been no interaction with the weekend's army of mostly white baby boomers, so many of whom are coming full circle to beloved campus life. The spirit, for those parents, was summed up by one mother Barbara overheard in the Adesso waiting area last night: "It's a funny feeling being back at college," she said to her daughter, "but I guess you never can go home again. Isn't that Thomas Wolfe, dear? Or someone?"

Such sweet sentimentalities, felt by most parents now packing up their cars, are as foreign to Barbara as the 1960s counterculture—a mostly white phenomenon, after all. "Negroes" and their plight were, of course, part of the progressive discussions that swept campuses and helped set political and moral codes for this huge generation. Yet blacks made up only 6.4 percent of the U.S. college population in 1968.

Barbara, poor as a teenager during the 1960s and as an adult in the 1990s, has spent her life on a parallel plane. Threading her way through packed cars in the dorm parking lot, she reflects that she doesn't connect with any of it.

Ascending the eastern stairwell of the Andrews dorm, Neddy tagging close behind, she looks up to see an attractive white family descending.

"Are you Barbara Jennings?" says a high, clear woman's voice.

Barbara blinks and stops on her step.

"Hi, I'm Bernadine Dohrn."

Barbara looks at her dispassionately. "Oh, hi," she says, befuddled.

"It's very nice to meet you. I'm Zayd's father," says Bill, sensing that Barbara may not know who they are.

"We admire your son enormously," Bernadine adds. "He's a great kid."

"Yeah, uh-huh," Barbara says, perplexed by such cloying, white-hot affection from people she's never met.

"This is Zayd," says Bill, pulling his son forward by the arm. Zayd bows his head toward Cedric's mom and smiles wanly.

Barbara, though, seems genuinely pleased. She knows Cedric likes him. "Oh, yes, Zayd! It is nice to meet you," she says warmly before she and Neddy move purposefully by the contingent and continue up the steps.

"Well, maybe next time we'll get to see you, spend some time together," says a clearly dispirited Bernadine to Barbara's passing left shoulder. She gets a sidelong nod as response.

Up one flight, Barbara turns to Neddy, feeling a residue of fatigue from the weekend's low buzz of tension from not belonging here, from worrying that she may embarrass her son. "You know, I think I'm ready to go home," Barbara says softly. "It'll actually be nice to get back."

10

A BURSTING HEART

Five blocks downwind of campus, just before the road curves to the gritty row houses of East Providence, is a pillared neo-Georgian mansion. The oldish building, cut into honeycombed medical offices, has a winding staircase, milky glass partitions, and strange medicinal odors. It is filled on most days with senior citizens on Medicaid.

But, once an hour or so, a frazzled student can usually be seen sitting in a corner chair of the waiting area, counting seconds and looking out a tall window onto the parking lot. He is here to receive $40-an-hour academic life support: upstairs, quick right, second door on the left.

The office is small, eight feet by ten feet, and Helaine Schupack, the tutor, likes it that way. She and the student are never far apart, hovering, shoulder to shoulder, over her narrow desk, mercilessly dissecting a term paper or gleaning the five trenchant points from a thirty-page chapter of gobbledygook. The walls are bland and mostly blank. No distractions. Nowhere to run.

Helaine is a very good tutor—the lucky students end up here. She is known around Brown by administrators and professors (her husband, Mark, is an emeritus professor of economics), and referrals come, randomly but steadily, from around the university's circumference. Maybe a student is dragged to an academic dean's office by an especially attentive dorm counselor. Or some eagle-eyed professor realizes that the drooping wallflower in the last row is going to fail the midterm. Or, possibly, a savvy parent detects the scent of suppressed panic in a late-night phone call. Those and countless other instances often lead to a skulking, furtive trek for kids ranging from foreign students with language problems to, as Helaine often says coyly, "some kids of the famous."

No names, please. She knows they don't like to come here, any of them. So they don't tell anyone.

Tardiness and missed appointments are common. She looks at her watch: it's 4:19 P.M. on the first Friday in November. "Is his name pronounced Cedric or Ceeedric," she mutters to herself. Whichever way, he'll soon be twenty minutes late.

Helaine—a wiry bantamweight of an indeterminate age above fifty, just over five feet with a gray moptop, the gaze of a hawk, and quick, precise hands—pulls a thin file marked "C. Jennings" from a drawer. She reads a letter in it from Donald Korb. He's been trying to get this student to see her since early September. Helaine remembers Korb well. When she was helping run a learning disabilities center through Massachusetts General Hospital a few years back, she tutored Donald's son, David. He was in high school at the time and hitting some academic shoals. Donald was delighted with the results: David went on to the University of California at Berkeley and is now working for Citibank in New York.

Donald was acutely concerned about Cedric being overmatched at Brown. At least that's what he told Helaine when he called in mid-September in his effort to set up today's meeting.

There's thumping on the stairs. A tallish black student, breathless and murmuring apologies, stumbles in. Helaine looks up at him. He's a little gawky, with a gentle, open face, but a nice-looking boy without the standoffish pose she sees in a lot of her black students. "You're lucky, you're my last of the day—I can stay late," she says, clipped but affable. She taps him on the shoulder to sit down.

In a moment, she fires off a long list of questions, her clipboard poised: any allergies? any family members prematurely gray? any relatives who stutter? She then asks Cedric to write a sentence so she can carefully examine the way he holds his pencil.

These are some of the strange, medicine-man tests to identify learning disabilities. For most of her charges, she quickly identifies some strain of learning disability (a broadly applicable label) that allows them special provisions for test-taking and general classwork.

"Have you ever had any trouble in school?" she asks, because she hasn't hit any obvious LD markers. "Always a good student?"

"I guess," he shrugs.

"Well, in any case," she says, putting aside her clipboard, "let's talk about your writing."

In a phone call earlier in the week, she told Cedric to bring some papers on which he is now working. Today's session comes a few weeks after midterms, and he's carrying two major midsemester papers that are due next week. He tells her he's been working on the papers since early October, writing and rewriting, and he's even gone to the student writing office to spruce them up. He hands over his latest draft of the shorter one, an analysis of a Richard Wright short story, "Fire and Cloud."

"Are you satisfied with this?" she asks after reading it.

"Naw. Not really. It doesn't say what I want real well," he mumbles.

"Well, it's really not too bad," she says. She's heard from Donald that his writing has moved from abysmal to poor and she figures he must have been working furiously on prose since he arrived.

She begins reading the paper aloud in the reedy, Hepburnish voice of a diction coach, picking up a few grammatical errors, tense changes, and some sentences that need reworking. The paper is only two pages, and she soon crests toward the end. Wright's main character, Reverend Taylor, brings the short story to a climax when he leads a march of blacks and whites through a small town.

Cedric, having been fed a rich brew of Martin Luther King integrationism by Barbara since birth, responds to the story's finale in a heartfelt way.

" 'When Wright wrote this,' " Helaine reads from Cedric's conclusion, " 'the idea of strong whites and strong blacks, marching side by side, was wildly implausible. The story is intended to be inspirational, like a dream of what could be.' "

She pauses, letting that last, moving line seep in. "Cedric, I think that's a nice paper."

He laughs like he's embarrassed, but she detects that it's really relief. They work over some changes she's noted along the way, and then she says, emphatically, "Show me another!"

He pulls out the big midterm paper for History of Education. She asks who his professor is. "James," he tells her.

"Oh yes, he's very good," she says, and again reads it to herself and then aloud. The assignment is to elucidate and analyze your "family educational tree."

She immediately sees that this gives Cedric another sterling opportunity to write passionately—to simply write what he feels. He opens with the journey north by his grandparents, who, Helaine reads aloud, " 'thought little about education. Marriage and having a family were enough. In 1940, my grandparents were united in holy matrimony. From this union there were ten children, five girls and five boys. With only a third grade and grade school education, respectively, Grampy and Granny had nothing to offer their ten children but God, love, and a roof over their head.

" 'At sixteen, my mother got pregnant with my older sister, Nanette Jennings,' " she reads aloud. " 'The pregnancy came at a crucial time in her life. She was beginning to get her life together and realize her dreams. Education was her only way out. When the teachers and principal at her school found out she was pregnant, they forbade her to come back. They thought that it was a disgrace and that she was setting a poor example for the other students. So she dropped out of high school in the middle of her junior year and ended up on welfare.

" 'At twenty-five, she got pregnant again with my other sister, Leslie Jennings. This time she made up her mind to go back to school. During this time, high school graduates were the only recipients of decent jobs.' "

"Cedric, you can make it tighter by cutting, 'During this time,' " Helaine says, crossing out that phrase.

"Okay, then," he says.

" 'She was going to do whatever it took to take good care of her children. After six months she earned her GED. This opened up many doors for her to gain work in the government. After passing the civil service test, she received work at the General Accounting Office.

" 'At this time, my sisters were well into grade school. That's when she began dating my father. Cedric Gilliam was a guy from around the neighborhood. He was very intelligent. In addition to graduating from high school, he has a bachelor's degree in urban studies, business management, and ecological studies from the University of the District of Columbia.' "

Cedric begins to laugh, high-pitched and nervous. Helaine looks back down at the page.

" 'He had also been incarcerated for narcotics distribution and armed robbery. That was not smart,' " she reads, dispassionately.

"That was crazy," Cedric blurts out. "Right?"

It's a tragic story, and she feels his embarrassment.

"Yes, Cedric, that was crazy," she says, softly.

" 'In 1977, I was born. My father was long gone and my mother was left with a broken heart.' "

Helaine stops reading. Her detachment has dissolved. She glances up at him, but he's already staring at the blank white wall, looking a little flushed. She takes a deep breath and pushes on.

" 'In search for strength and restoration, she attended a revival meeting. It was there that she accepted Jesus Christ as her personal savior. She then became actively involved in church activities. Because of her strong interest in God and the way she lived, I was imparted with the same beliefs. She is a social missionary and sings in the choir. Even if I had not been interested in church, she would have still made me participate. My Christian heritage and education go hand and hand.' "

"That should be 'hand in hand,' " she says quickly, not wanting to stop the flow of her reading.

" 'I was always taught in church that education is the way. My pastor would always say, people fail because of a lack of knowledge. This knowledge included God's world and important information that can help anyone better society. I consider myself blessed because, between me and my sisters, I am the first to graduate from high school and go on to college. . . . I thank God for giving me a mother who could give me discipline and at the same time help me find answers to my dreams.' "

Helaine places the paper on the desk, cocks her head, and squints at him.

"This is a beautiful paper. Yes, there are a few problems, grammatical things, some sentence structure, some punctuation, but, on balance, it's very strong and compelling."

"You really think so?" Cedric asks. "You really do, don't you?"

Helaine helps him rewrite a few awkward sentences and sets up a time for next week. In a moment, he's out the door and rushing off to dinner.

Later that night, while she's loading the dishwasher in her kitchen and her husband is upstairs in the third-floor study with his econometric tomes, she turns Cedric's two papers over in her head.

She realizes it will be difficult to keep her distance from this one. She recalls a phrase from the first paper—"a dream of what could be"—and smiles. In the second, he gave all credit to his mother's discipline and the transforming qualities of faith, which is something most kids would feel self-conscious writing about. It's exciting to work with a kid who is so devoid of irony, so unguarded. And also terrifying. While it's not going to be easy to get him to where he needs to be academically, Cedric simply can't afford to fail. He's got everything— God, mother, faith—riding on making it. The thought makes her short of breath.

No, those papers weren't the type of smart, dispassionate exposition he'll need to excel, not the kind of collegiate prose that attaches carefully qualified examples to broad principles. Yet, because Helaine is granted access to the shadowy realm of how professors actually grade papers, she knows a secret, and it offers her some conditional hope. Affirmative action can be subtly woven into grading. Cedric will get good marks on both papers because he found a way to squeeze his inspirational feelings into each assignment. To mark him down would be to mark him down as a person.

While the more typical Brown students will need to master the models for smooth explication and elegant grammar to excel, Cedric can ride on his strong and unique "personal perspective." A tale of overcoming oppression sells here and almost everywhere.

She turns out the kitchen light, grabs a handful of papers from other students that she'll review in bed, and begins to ascend the steps. No, in future classes on more diverse and unfamiliar subjects, Cedric's advantage will certainly decrease, she decides. At least for now, though, he's been able to find ways to rely on his bursting heart.

An addendum is needed to the music rules. An exception, really. Both Rob and Cedric know this, but they've held out, not sure how to bring it up. The problem is bladder size. If one of them leaves the room to go to the bathroom, he risks losing music control. So, one evening in the second week of November, with Sting's "Fields of Gold" quietly playing, Rob brings it up, and they quickly agree that bathroom runs don't count.

On the rainy afternoon of November 14, Cedric wanders back to the room after finishing his Richard Wright class, visiting the science library, and running a few errands. He throws his bookbag on the desk and flops onto his bed, his head near the TV.

Cedric's face becomes hard and tight, like a death mask, when he glances at Rob. Phillip and any number of kids who taunted him through Ballou's hallways left their scars. He knows that, just as he knows that those days are slipping further into memory. But Rob seems to be picking at the scars, even though his white, doctor's son demeanor couldn't be further from that of tormentors of the past who were always in his face.

Rob just ignores him. And that seems, somehow, worse. There he is, just sitting on his bed doing a chemistry homework sheet and listening to REM, the Georgia rockers on *his own* CD player.

A week ago, Cedric took his CD player from the trunk in the middle of the room and set it up on a shelf over his bed. He mumbled that Rob's "side of the room" was "such a disaster that the stereo could get broken over in all that mess."

Rob didn't argue. He went home that weekend to the large colonial in Marblehead and brought back two stereos, one for his side of the room and another he can carry to the lounge or wherever he pleases.

With that act, Rob completed a division of property, of once shared items that included Rob's hair clippers and the phone (Rob now makes and receives calls from friends' rooms).

But they can't go back to being strangers.

Cedric looks at his watch, five o'clock on the nose. He turns on the TV. Much of his free time is spent in front of the tube. The P.T. Barnum–like talk shows—at their lurid peak in the fall of 1995—are a staple. He has first-name relationships, sometimes admiring, sometimes acrid, with Oprah, his favorite, and also with Montel, Sally, Jenny, Richard, Gordon, Jerry, Tempest, and Ricki, whom he now flips to.

"Cedric, could you turn it down a little," Rob says, not looking up from the chemistry worksheet resting on his legs. Cedric turns it down a barely discernible notch.

Rob leaves the room for a moment and leaves his music on. Cedric assumes it falls under the bathroom exception, though Rob didn't abide by subprovisions about notification. Cedric takes advantage of this gray area and momentarily turns up his beloved Sharp Trinitron. Rob returns, notices the amplified TV, and turns his stereo up a few clicks as he passes it on the way back to bed.

Cedric, his ear practically against the screen, turns the TV up a tad to compete with Rob. Rob gets up and turns his stereo even louder.

Cedric looks up. Rob, nonconfrontational to the last, is already back on his bed, as though nothing has happened. Like Cedric is invisible or something. He purses his lips.

The volume knob on the TV goes to full blast. Ricki's whining voice blares across the open air. The agile Rob leaps up and cranks his stereo to pain-decibel levels.

The Trinitron can't compete, but Cedric knows what can. He jumps to his feet and flips on his stereo, blasting a local hip-hop radio station. LL Cool J's "Hey Lover" overwhelms REM's "Losing My Religion."

The walls are shaking as the two boys stare at each other, wide-eyed and stunned.

Rob busts into the hall and disappears, while Cedric, shaken, flees for the peer counselor's room.

Cedric is fortunate to find Rachel Edy sitting at her desk. She's

called "Rock" by Unit 15ers and is the most respected of the East
Andrews counselors. Rachel is solid and attentive, a natural listener.
She knows that penetrating a roommate dispute is roughly equivalent to
getting inside a failed marriage: next to impossible.

But some matters need to be dealt with immediately. And they are.
She and Cedric talk late into the night. And a week later, Cedric has
New York Undercover, a Fox TV favorite starring a black detective,
cranked to a healthy volume. Rob hums contentedly on his bed, wearing $100 earphones.

As the end of November nears, Zayd is busy. A racy script he wrote
in intermediate playwriting drew raves, and he's been telling people
that a pretty brunette junior in the class "made it known that she's
available." Then, there are the ongoing social demands of "Bear's
posse," a group of sophomores who hang around Bear and are always
itching for adventure. Beyond that, there's professor Bernard Reginster,
the youngish, Belgian philosophy professor who wears black boots,
black jeans, and stylish little octagonal bifocals. Zayd (like most everyone in the three-hundred-seat lecture hall for Existentialism) thinks
Reginster is about the coolest human being anywhere. He's trying to
figure out a way to bump into him somewhere, in a real casual way, and
talk about philosophy.

Still, there's time to knock once in a while on the door of room
216 and pull Cedric out. "Come on, C," Zayd says on a chilly Sunday
night a few days before Thanksgiving break. "Let's get off College Hill
and hit a mall."

Bear and his white 1992 Chevy Blazer are otherwise occupied, so
they catch a ride with another friend. Zayd is in the back seat, humming along to "Gangster's Paradise," the new hit by Coolio. Cedric
bobs along to the rapper with Medusa-like hair.

"You ever think about things you went through when you were
little?" Cedric offers, head nodding to the beat.

Zayd loves it when Cedric asks innocent questions like that; they
draw out memories or feelings that Zayd has shelved as unsophisticated.

"Sure, all the time," says Zayd. He spins into stories about when he lived on 127th Street and Amsterdam Avenue in upper Manhattan around the time his parents were coming out of hiding. His mom had been arrested for suspicion of having some involvement in the Brinks truck robbery in Nyack, New York, where two cops and a security guard were killed. Mostly, it was just that she was friendly from her revolutionary days with Kathy Boudin, a radical who'd been involved in the robbery. Bernadine was released after a year without charges— not long after she did an exclusive interview with Phil Donahue from her jail cell—and she and his dad started on the path to getting the credentials that would ultimately serve them well in the years to come. But it was a slow start. They lived in a gritty apartment, and Zayd was one of the only white kids at a tough P.S. on the edge of Harlem. He tells Cedric he was "thoroughly trashed by this kid who was two years older than me, a black kid who was huge. And I remember when it came time to move up to fourth grade and about half the class was held back, and he was one of them, I was so happy."

While the attention of a white listener might be piqued by the idea of half a class of black third graders being held back, Cedric, familiar with such pervasive failure, sees something else.

"How can you get beat up by all these black kids but not end up hating black people?" he prods.

Zayd simply loves fielding Cedric's prickly asides, many of them full of explosive charges. It makes him feel like he's walking an exhilarating minefield between racial encampments.

"You can't hate everyone because of what *some* people do," says Zayd. "Everyone's different. They could've just as easily been tough white kids."

"Yes, that's true," Cedric says coyly. "There ain't no real difference—there are black people that don't like other black people as much as they don't like white people."

Both smirk at that, Cedric spinning the all-people-are-the-same idea on its head. "Take Clarence Thomas," Cedric says. "He seems to be upset at a whole lot of people."

Zayd just loves this, too, the way Cedric takes him on a tour of what Zayd figures is the "real" black viewpoint.

A bit later, eating chicken fingers at the mall, Cedric lets on that he's actually met Justice Thomas, and Zayd, having met his share of celebrities, knows how to be reserved in his reaction ("Oh, really?") but then artfully prods Cedric for more: "Did he talk about his penis?"

"Just shows, you going after the black man again," Cedric says, and Zayd knows he's playing.

"No, he talked about coming up, about being poor, talking 'gitchee'—which is like a country slang—when he was young and how he had to learn to talk properly and how hard that was." Cedric pauses and glances over at Zayd, who looks at him anxiously, waiting for something choicer. "Oh yeah," Cedric relents, "and his hair was beady."

Zayd: "What's *beady* mean? It that like nappy?"

Cedric: "No, no. With nappy, your hair is clean, just shooting out all over the place. Beady is when you don't brush your hair. They call it buckshot. Like you're not clean. Like your hair is all oily. And he was wearing one of those cheap shower watches, like a Casio—one of those five-dollar things. I couldn't believe it, here's a Supreme Court Justice wearing this."

Cedric adds: "You know, he's married to a white woman."

"She's an ugly woman," Zayd says definitively, though he can't remember what she looks like.

"And he wears these squeaky shoes," says Cedric, "and smokes these cheap cigars."

"Sounds like a seedy character," Zayd says, only half joking, and Cedric lets it lie.

To Zayd, Cedric seems so authentic in his feelings, his faith, his resentments, his finely woven codes of right and wrong. He seems to have these dense, profound dilemmas, where Zayd just dabbles in anything he can find. And there's one other thing: Zayd likes the way Cedric reserves friendship until it is arduously won. It makes everything, now, seem more valuable.

By now, Cedric has confided in Zayd—told him things he has told no one else at Brown. About his father being in jail, about moving year to year as a child, about the blistered drug supermarket of V Street where he ended up. Zayd respects these confidences (though unit mates are anxious to know more about Cedric), and he makes his own

offering in return. Dropping by, sometimes after a late night of partying, alcohol on his breath, he tells Cedric about his ongoing adventures—a fight he almost got into with a townie on one night, an older
girl, a senior, who invited him back to her apartment for a very private
party on another—taking Cedric along in a way. So a dialectic is established between one kid with no boundaries and the other with nothing
but.

They walk through the mall together, ducking into a Nike store
and then wandering through the atrium of ferns and benches. In a few
days, Zayd will be flying home to Chicago for Thanksgiving, and he's
wondering about two girls, Cami and Camoun, two stunning French
girls who are friends from high school. He can't seem to choose between them. He tells Cedric that "Cami told me that if I see Camoun
again, she won't see me anymore, but I really like them both. I mean, I
think I can pull it off and see them both, I just have to be careful.
They're both just amazing girls. . . . I showed you the pictures,
right?"

"Yeah, they're fine looking," Cedric says, nodding his head in
assent. "But that's not the point. You should make a choice and stick by
it. Listen, trust is something you have to practice. Someday you're
going to fall in love with someone, and you need to understand what
trust is all about. What you're doing now is developing bad practices of
betraying people's trust."

Amazing, Zayd thinks. Where does Cedric come by this stuff?
How? He laughs, shaking his head. "Come on, C, there's a Record
Town around the corner. Let's go put on some earphones."

Which is what they do—hopping for the next half-hour through
new releases at the CD listening stations that rim the walls at Record
Town.

They'll have to be heading back soon, so they grab a couple of
Cokes and drink them at a candy-striped table in the food court. Zayd
is feeling expansive and tells Cedric about Thanksgiving: a big show at
his house, with thirty-five family members and friends, and how every
year he likes to go with his father out to shoot a quail or a pheasant.
Zayd's grandfather on his dad's side (a patrician who was chairman and

CEO of Commonwealth Edison Power) taught Zayd how to hunt. Zayd's dad doesn't much like the pheasant hunting—and Bernadine, a strident gun control advocate, thoroughly hates it—but Zayd keeps it up anyway, pressing his father to go. "It's a family tradition and all, so they have to let me do it—but it drives my mom and dad a little crazy," Zayd says with glee, neatly wrapping the whole story around his core issue of how to rebel against two legendary rebels. "Shooting the gun is wild—the boom really pops in your ears."

Cedric begins to laugh hysterically. Zayd looks at him uneasily, toying with a suspicion that his winding tale seems frivolous to Cedric, who struggles with diamond-hard dilemmas.

But Zayd quickly realizes Cedric's amusement with him is genuine. It's just that beneath his friend's eager smile, lava flows.

"Talking about all that shooting," Cedric says, riotously, practically falling off the white, curled-iron chair, barely able to breathe. "It made me think . . . yeah . . . think how I miss Washington, I miss the gunfire, I miss the guys on the street corner. I miss my miserable neighborhood. . . ." His eyes are tearing with laughter. "Oh yes. 'Bye Washington! I won't be back for Thanksgiving this year. . . ."

Cedric pauses on the top step and looks to the right of the wide, carved-oak door. KORB, it says, in four-inch letters on a golden plaque. He looks left and right down the empty corridor of the tall brick houses of Brimmer Street on Beacon Hill through the branches of sycamore trees lining the cobblestones. Then he gently reaches out, running his long fingers on the straight back of the *K*. It must be gold, he figures, what else? He snaps out of the trance and lifts the heavy door knocker, letting it drop once. In a moment, a short, owlish man is standing before him.

"Cedric!" he shouts, loud enough that a house full of people might hear. "Welcome. Come, come in."

He waves Cedric across the threshold and reaches up to hug him.

"Hi, Dr. Korb," Cedric says with a bemused smile. "Thanks for having me and all."

"Oh, Cedric," Donald Korb says, pulling back from their embrace. "Having you for Thanksgiving is an honor." His *o* stretches in a thick, upper-crusty Boston accent. "You are our special guest."

Those words are barely out when Cedric suddenly realizes there are twenty people—at least twenty!—jammed into the foyer, and more coming down the wide staircase to greet him.

His smile freezes at its widest arc. With only a few seconds before they descend on him, Cedric slips out of his furry black vest—Donald quickly grabs it—and drops his bookbag full of clothes.

Then he's surrounded and nodding vigorously, receiving each well-wisher as they clutch his hand, or both hands, a few hugging him, everyone glistening as though they're being reunited with an old, dear friend.

They all know *of him*. Donald talks about Cedric often. Cedric tries to keep names straight but gives up after half a dozen and floats upstairs on a wave of back slaps and bursting smiles.

"Oh, hello Cedric," says Donald's attractive wife, Joan, her back against the marble peninsula counter in the second-floor kitchen. "It's so nice to see you. Can we get you something to drink?"

"Ginger ale would be just fine. And, yeah, and thanks for having me, Mrs. Korb. . . . I mean, I can't believe I'm here."

It's Thanksgiving afternoon, 1995, and Cedric Jennings has never been this far from home. From the bottom of America to the top. Inasmuch as Southeast Washington or Harlem or Watts is a shadow in the minds of most Americans, Beacon Hill, along with Park Avenue and Knob Hill, is well known as a sunlit peak.

While the Korbs' neighbors include Stephen Roosevelt, FDR's grandson, and Edward "Ned" Johnson, chairman and, with his family, majority owner of mutual fund giant Fidelity Investments, Donald is part of the new wealth on the block. He went from very comfortable to beyond that around 1978, when one of his companies (and its patents, which improved the production process of soft contact lenses) was bought by a company that is now part of Hoffman-LaRoche.

That was when he started, in earnest, to buy roomfuls of fine antiques, transforming four stories and eight thousand square feet of homey spaciousness into a palace.

Donald is a busybody and gadabout, priding himself on knowing more people from more strata of society than an "old money" neighbor would meet in three lifetimes. And he somehow manages to keep in close touch with most of them.

Including Cedric. He called Brown three days ago to make sure Cedric was coming for Thanksgiving. Cedric hesitated, but Donald insisted he come. The optometrist, in fact, calls Cedric every couple of weeks and, on the fifteenth of every month, like clockwork, sends Cedric a check for $200.

He also sends notes—lots of them. Though Donald travels often, raising money to seed new ventures for his latest company, Ocular Research of Boston, he manages to launch a flurry of missives to Cedric. For a man who enjoys soaring rhetoric and winding philosophical discussions, he is oddly precise. Makes copies of everything.

The notes to Cedric are particularly winning and affectionate. They might contain some thought Donald had in passing when, say, he was teaching a course at the University of California, Berkeley, last year or traveling to Australia to meet potential investors. They all end with little boosters like "Be Strong!" or "Never lose faith" and always the salutation "Love, Donald."

But beyond that, he and Cedric have only met once, when Cedric was at MIT. Donald came by and gave him a pep talk about getting conditioned for the academic competition ahead, just like a fighter might prepare for a fight.

This afternoon is their second face-to-face encounter.

"You know, Cedric's mother went on welfare for a few years when he was two," Donald tells his brother-in-law, Jerry, a doctor, as Cedric stands mutely between them in the living room. "When I heard that, it just spun everything on its head. Just look at the outcome. She had her priorities right."

Cedric realizes they're both looking at him—wanting some response—and he nods an enthusiastic affirmation. He takes a sip of ginger ale and looks over his right shoulder at a ten-foot-high oil painting (from his midcalf to the ceiling) of a plump boy in a gold-leaf frame. It's like the ones he saw in museums as a kid, he thinks, old portraits with puffy, pale people staring straight ahead. He's eye to eye with the painting's imperious, princely lad. "What you lookin' at?" he murmurs to the fat face.

". . . I agree, it's just so awful that there's so much division in our society," Jerry says to Donald, but to Cedric, too.

"Oh yes," Cedric says, spinning to attention, his face a mask of earnestness. "So much division."

Donald excuses himself and moves to a central spot in the sumptuous living room to give a toast, holding out his crystal glass of white wine. He thanks "everyone for coming, for partaking of the bounty, including our special guest . . ."

Cedric—his black jeans and long-sleeved black pullover shirt conspicuous in a sea of khakis and blazers, a long piece of celery with goat cheese (he hates goat cheese) dangling from his long fingers—offers a sickly smile to the unctuous eyes.

Toast completed, Donald sees his special guest standing unaccompanied before the painting and hurries back over, asking about Barbara, about what she's doing today.

"I think she might still be at home," Cedric says. In a moment, the portable phone is coming his way and Cedric is reciting the number—a new one Barbara just got when she finagled back her service.

"Hello?"

"Ma, it's me."

"Lavar? Where you calling from? You at Dr. Korb's?"

"Yeah . . . it's real nice and all."

Cedric asks what she's got planned and she says she'll be going to church and then to her sister Chris's for some dinner—but he already knew that from a conversation they had just two days ago following Dr. Korb's call.

"Remember what I told you, Lavar," she says. "Watch what everyone does first. Which fork they use on what, how they manner themselves. Okay? Then do what they do."

"Yeah, I know," he says, looking up furtively, wondering if anyone can decipher what his mom's talking to him about. She listens to the self-conscious silence, and neither of them say anything as he presses the receiver harder against his ear.

"You know I love you, Lavar," she says.

"Yeah, me too." He's unable to say more. "Okay, well 'bye." And he passes the phone to Donald, who wants to talk to Barbara, too.

Soon, the crowd ambles downstairs to the first-floor dining hall and settles into two tables, one a traditional dining room eight-seater and the other a long Arthurian monstrosity. It has room for a dozen on each flank, and Cedric slides into a middle chair next to Donald's twenty-six-year-old daughter, Cindy.

Many of those seated at Cedric's table are youngish Korb cousins—college age or slightly older—who launch into cross-table discussions about their college majors or first jobs over the pumpkin soup appetizer.

Cedric looks down at the soup, then at Cindy to his right and, to his left, at a young, dark-haired woman, either Spanish or French, he's not sure, who looks like one of those Euromodels he sees in magazines. Okay, big one's the soup spoon. He takes a taste of the orangish puree, doesn't like it, cleans the spoon on the napkin in his lap and puts it back next to the teaspoon.

"So, what's your major, Cedric," asks Donald's niece, Caroline, a tall blonde at the University of Pennsylvania. "I mean, do you have one yet?"

Cedric pauses. Every eye at the table is on him. He feels like a circus act. His mind races. Of course, he hasn't really decided.

"I'm triple majoring," he says. "Computer science, math, and education."

Swoons up and down. Whoa. Wow. "Hey, that's amazing," says Caroline's brother, the hunky, good-natured Jonathan, a senior at Middlebury College. He brushes back the brown hair that hangs over his oxford button-down collar. "God, you must be soooo smart."

Nods and harrumphs all around, and Cedric smiles, feeling like an impostor.

An avalanche of food follows—all the traditional favorites, including a thirty-two-pound turkey, stuffing, cranberry sauce, and candied yams. Cedric nibbles, quietly, his appetite blunted by the knot in his gut.

The Euromodel asks: "So, do you like your roommate?"

"No, we don't get along."

From across the table: "Cedric? Do you usually have a big turkey for Thanksgiving?"

"No, ummm, well, like a chicken sometimes and potato salad and macaroni and cheese . . ."

At that point, Cindy begins chattering at him nonstop—about her life, her hopes of becoming a TV news reporter, asking Cedric questions but not waiting for answers. Cedric thinks, God, she talks a lot, but he's happy to just smile and nod his head at her for cover.

Suddenly, she stops. "Do you have enough to eat, Cedric?"

He looks down at his plate, still half full. "Yeah . . . I'm fine."

A minute later, he's asked again, this time by Joan Korb, passing by with a turkey platter. "No . . . No . . . Mrs. Korb, I'm fine, really."

He starts to lightly perspire, feeling the wall right behind him, his abdomen against the huge table, chairs tight on both sides. His brain catches fire: Is everyone worrying whether the poor black kid has enough to eat?!

Dusk arrives and things loosen a bit as people get up and mill about in a break before dessert. Donald slides in next to Cedric and talks easily with him for a few minutes, asking about problems with Rob, Helaine's sessions, how classes are going, whether a particular paper Cedric mentioned has come back. Cedric exhales a bit and talks unselfconsciously. He likes Dr. Korb. The older man's relentless good works and attentiveness has provided him passage across Cedric's minefield of trust. Cedric is always honest with Dr. Korb. Well, almost.

"So, how did you like those suits I sent you, the ones from Filene's?"

Cedric looks back at him in disbelief, thinking, Did he really just ask me that? What a day.

Already numb from the festivities, he lies like a pro. "Oh, the suits. . . . I love them. They were great. I mean they *are* great."

Donald goes off to talk to Jerry and another guest, and Cedric catches an ancient woman sizing him up from across the table.

It's Donald's aunt, Miriam, a ninety-two-year-old white eminence in a black shawl who, during introductions hours back, mentioned how she was "a pioneer, too," as one of the first women to graduate from New York University Law School in 1927. "I only went there 'cause the jerks at Columbia didn't accept women."

As he looks at her now, Cedric is reminded of some of the very old black women at church, whose wisdom seems to grow the older they get, as they keep watching the world pass.

"I sure would like to meet your mother," she says, smiling at him. "She must be quite a woman."

Cedric feels a warmth come over him. "Oh yes, Mrs. Korb . . ."

"Miriam."

". . . Okay, I mean Miriam, my mom is something really special," and he talks for a while about Barbara, about Thanksgivings they've had, sometimes just the two of them.

"I bet you miss her today."

"How d'jou know?"

"Because we old ladies have nothing else to do but get smart."

Cedric lets out a big heaving laugh and, for a moment, he feels completely comfortable.

"So what's with a freshman having three majors," she asks coyly, having overheard the earlier exchange.

"I sure like saying it."

"You keep saying it, and let all their jaws drop. Saying things can sometimes make them happen."

"All right," he agrees, and, with that, Cedric gets his bearings back. Enough, at least, to get him through dessert—the Indian pudding, pumpkin cheesecake, and pumpkin pie.

During languid second and third cups of coffee and tea, David Korb tells everyone a raucous tale of a Spanish emigré friend—Juanito, who once attended Thanksgiving here—and how he got lost in New York, "running uptown and downtown in his yellow shorts, yellow T-shirt, camera strapped around his neck dripping with sweat . . . yelling to himself, 'Where am I, how did I get here?' " The room descends into hysterics, and Cedric laughs overly hard, doubling over, to make certain no one will suspect he's been wondering the same thing all night.

People finally leave the tables, clustering off, some to watch football or flop into deep, soft chairs. Cedric goes to the bathroom, giving everyone the slip, and then tiptoes into a hallway near the front foyer where he half listens to Donald talking to his brother-in-law Jerry and another adult guest: "What is the ultimate expression of a man's egotism?" Donald asks, not aware that Cedric is nearby. "I mean, some egotism may be wrapped up in what I do for Cedric, what I do supporting kids who need it. But no! The ultimate egotism, more broadly, is a belief in the existence of God . . . though, rationally, there is no way to get there from here. Faith, in a way, is egotism. I know it's at the center of Cedric's life, what keeps him going. But ultimately, it can't get him where he needs to be . . . he needs to find his place through reason, not faith, a place in the world of men, not just in some imagined kingdom of heaven."

Cedric's ears perk up when he hears his name, but he's not sure what the point of it is. It's okay that Donald talks about him—he's allowed to, he's given a lot to Cedric and deeply cares about him—but so much that the older man says is indecipherable.

Soon it is time to go. Donald is going to give him a ride to Cambridge, where Cedric will visit some friends from the MIT program at Harvard. Everyone rouses from their sated, full-bellied stupors to say good-bye, and, this time, Cedric moves quickly through the line. He's grateful. Really. Everyone does wish him well, and they seem to care about him, especially Donald's wife and children. But appropriate responses and emotions are bottled up in him, jumbled and inaccessible, and it makes him feel guilty and anxious to flee. He slips on his fuzzy vest, grabs his backpack, raises a hand of farewell to all, and turns toward the door.

Miriam is blocking his exit. He looks down—she can't come much past his belly button. She reaches up her arms as he bends way forward. "You're gonna be fine," she whispers in his ear, and he really hugs her.

He straightens up after a bit, thankful to be facing just her and the door. And then he's out into the cool November night.

The trip to Harvard Square is swift, just across the Charles River, and he and Donald make small talk. Donald's complex advice about achievement and self-awareness often leaves Cedric vexed, but his gravelly voice sounds soothing to the boy and makes him feel at ease. He'll call in a few days, he tells Cedric as he drops him off. They hug, awkwardly, across the Saab's shift.

Harvard Yard is all but empty tonight. He's looking for Thayer Hall, but there's no one to direct him. Like at Brown, most students can manage a brief trip home, and the ones who can't are usually adopted by roommates or friends. Those left behind tend to be poor kids who live far away, many of them minorities.

And so Cedric races around the echoing yard, searching the labyrinth of dorms for a few such refugees—namely, Mark McIntosh and his twin sister, Belinda.

After half an hour, he's becoming frantic. It's not just that he's supposed to sleep there tonight. It's more than that. He feels like he's been on a strange journey—confusing, exhilarating, bizarre—and home is wherever black people are.

Fifteen sweaty minutes later, he thinks he's bumped into the right dorm. He punches a room number on the intercom plate alongside the locked exterior door.

Nothing. Then a grainy sound. It's Mark's voice coming through.

"NIGGER?!" Cedric screams, a word he never, ever uses. "That you!?"

"Yeah, it's me," Mark says through the static. "Calm down."

"I'm stranded out here. Oh Gaaaawd, come get me!"

Professor Tom James cleans his desk, preparing for office hours and a steady stream of students. Now, at the end of the semester, there's always much to do: students wanting advice on final projects or wanting to argue, in advance, about expected final grades; advisees stopping by for counseling; or students majoring in education who simply need his signature because he's chairman of the department.

"Buenos días," Franklin Cruz says, ducking his head in.

"Hola. ¿Cómo estás," says Tom, delighted.

"Más o menos," Franklin says, offering a shrug, though Tom knows he's just being modest. Franklin is Tom's freshman advisee and a star student. His family emigrated from a rural section of the Dominican Republic to a neighborhood on the edge of Harlem, and Franklin was tapped as a sixth grader into Prep for Prep. He went on to thrive at the exclusive Collegiate Preparatory School in Manhattan.

Getting comfortable in Tom's office, Franklin floats an idea for an independent study project for next semester—the classifying of urban minority students as "special needs," a technique that allows educators to steer toward them funds that are guaranteed by federal statute for handicapped children. "Terrific, it's a very provocative issue," says Tom, who mentions some studies that are already underway on the issue. Eventually, they discuss Franklin's final project this semester about comparisons of integrated secondary schools with segregated ones. When he gave an oral presentation on it last week in class with his partner, Cedric, Franklin was at his light-footed, multilingual best. He managed to match the hues of his own journey with those of a wider American canvas, bloodlessly and analytically connecting his own experiences with broader trends.

It's what Franklin does so well, Tom muses, as he listens to the polished student expound. Not that Franklin denies his Latino heritage—a mortal sin at a place like Brown, where group identity is celebrated by 160 different student groups, many of them aligned along ethnic or racial lines. But, take it one level down, and Franklin, like most students at Brown, is artfully accommodationist in his character. In just a few months, Brown has helped him to intellectualize his Latino status, to make it portable, something he can take out, and wear, when needed. Here, he's encouraged to wear it a lot, whether in class discussions or social engagements. But underneath the public posture, Franklin, like so many of Brown's upwardly mobile minority students, is becoming skilled in the many dialects he'll need to get ahead. He's slowly cutting away some of his cultural ethnicity as he cuts a deal with the broader American society he expects to enter. The process is gradual but steady, causing changes he may not notice until after he's graduated. In the meantime, he can assuage assimilationist guilt by hanging

out with Latino kids at the VeeDub and going to salsa dances at
Machado, the Spanish House.

All of it fascinates Tom. For years, he has written scholarly tomes
about education of the minorities, from analysis of how the children of
Japanese Americans interned during WWII were schooled, to a complex assessment of how statutory changes at the turn of the century
allowed immigrant minorities—in those days Jews, Italians, and Irish—
access to education. Thick books, respected in the field. But some of
his freshest insights come haphazardly, from observing students who
pass through his office and classroom.

Later that afternoon, after meeting with a procession of students,
Tom has a free moment to poke along the aged cedar shelves lining one
wall for a book he's been thinking about.

He sits back down with *Joining the Club: A History of Jews at Yale* and
flips through some favorite parts about how certain professors at Yale in
the 1920s and 1930s reached out to ostracized Jewish students, ushering
them into Yale's pristine hallways. He skims through a section about
how the Jews arrived, giving up their religious orthodoxy to adopt a
sort of liberal cosmopolitanism, giving over, in a way, to the same
assimilatory currents that Franklin is being swept forward by. It wasn't
entirely a one-way street. Ultimately, Yale had to bend to accommo-
date new ways of thinking and learning from a more diverse student
body. It was a dialogue, a push and shove. And it's going on today, as
black, Latino, and Asian kids try to match their cultural perspectives
with rigid standards of merit that predate their arrival.

Tom admires those old Yale professors and desperately wants to fill
a similar role for outsiders of his own time, students who, he thinks,
carry a heavier burden with skin color than their predecessors ever
faced with their less conspicuous ethnicities.

As he prepares to leave in the late afternoon, there's a knock on the
door. Tom looks up. "Oh, Cedric. Please come in, sit down."

The student seems sheepish. He enters gingerly and slips into a
wooden armchair with its varnish worn to an aged gloss.

"Professor James, you see, I'll be leaving for home in just a few days
and I just need you to sign this request for me to be in that Fieldwork
and Seminar in High School Education for next semester," Cedric says.

"I think it'd get me off College Hill and, like, it might be good to do researching at a school in Providence, which, I guess, is what you do in that class."

"I think it would be just right for you, Cedric," Tom says as the student passes a form across his desk.

"How's your semester been?" he asks with a by-the-way casualness as he looks down to sign the form.

"All right, I guess. I'm taking everything pass/fail and I'll pass everything . . . but I feel kind of lost sometimes."

"That's not uncommon for a freshman at this point," Tom says, looking up, trying to be encouraging, though he knows—and suspects Cedric does as well—that what this student faces is far more confusing and complicated than most. "Just stay with it and it will become easier."

Cedric smiles. "Yeah, right . . . ," and then begins rambling about maybe majoring in education along with math.

The juxtaposition of Cedric and Franklin causes Tom to squirm. He knows Cedric mostly from his papers, especially the family tree paper where he so boldly revealed how faith is at the center of his life, and from a few times he's spoken up in class. Cedric is not accommodationist. He is black and urban, a church kid from the inner city and, at this point, still culturally fixed, always in his shoes. He can't step away from it, can't intellectualize it, because it's still too close, too visceral. It's why so many kids like him—passionate, sometimes angry kids—fail here.

". . . so, Professor James," Cedric finishes up, "I was thinking maybe of education as part of a dual major might be good for me."

Tom nods and looks closely at the student, scanning the bags under his red eyes for clues to his inner life. He imagines how obtuse and disconnected Cedric must feel. He wants to ask if he's found a church in Providence, about how things are going in the dorm, but he feels uneasy prying into those realms.

"I think that would be just fine, Cedric, but it's still early to declare a major. Let's keep talking about it as you go forward."

Cedric has what he needs and rises, putting the signed form in his bookbag.

Tom rises, too, fumphering. "You'll come see me, right? If there's anything, any problems or anything you want to talk about," and Cedric nods halfheartedly as he turns and begins walking for the door.

"Don't forget how much you've accomplished already, by making it to Brown," Tom says, keeping his voice even but betraying some urgency.

Cedric turns, expressionless. "It's a little hard to remember all that now." He seems to force a smile of gratitude as he strays out the door. And Tom James spends what's left of the day replaying the dialogue in his head, wondering what else—what better—he might have said.

11

BACK HOME

A sheet of ice blankets Washington. Cedric sits on a dinette chair in striped pajamas, leaning close to a radio on Barbara's kitchen counter.

"Montgomery County public schools, closed; District of Columbia public schools, two hours late; Alexandria public schools, closed . . ."

He flips it off and dials a familiar number. "Hi, it's me, Cedric Jennings," he says expectantly to a secretary answering the phone at Ballou's office. "I was wondering if 'Alumni Day' is still on? It's supposed to start at 9:30 but with the two-hour delay, school won't even be starting until 10:45 . . . uh-huh . . . okay, then. I'll be there, for sure . . . yeah, 'bye."

He walks across the cluttered room and slumps onto the white couch in the empty apartment, Barbara having already left for work. It hasn't been such a terrific three days since he arrived home for Christmas break, but he has sort of been looking forward to today's return to Ballou. Just before graduation last year, Ballou's librarian, Marilyn Green, asked if he would be there and if he'd be willing to speak. He said he would. And during those dark lonely days of the fall, when he often felt friendless, having committed to a date gently provided a counterpoint to his flagging confidence. He would have to face them all if he had to drop out of Brown by then. Through November, he'd sometimes see his old teachers sitting in the library, like they were waiting for him, counting on him. And it would summon something in him—not pride, exactly, more like self-preservation.

Cedric indulges in a long shower this morning, thinking over his speech. He needs to be upbeat but realistic, he thinks, and, with so many things he wants to say, he has to be careful not to ramble. He decides that in talking to his audience—seniors thinking about college—he needs to try to be absolutely truthful about what it's really like to be in a big college, far from Southeast. He owes them that.

Such candor hasn't been easy in his first few days home. Two hours after the night sleeper from Providence arrived on Sunday morning, Cedric was already in church, with Barbara beaming and a hundred pairs of eyes on him.

He never did get around to calling Bishop Long after parents' weekend, so the pastor had a little surprise in store: he called Cedric and another college freshman onto the stage to ask them a few pointed questions—things he knew the congregation would want to know.

"As Cedric's spiritual godfather," Long said, jauntily holding the hand mike like a talk-show host, "I'm obligated to ask how things are going at Brown University."

Cedric paused. He had thought about this on the train ride. He knew people would ask, and he knew they'd need an answer that wouldn't leave them confused and deflated. On his way to a good, concise answer, he took a few logical detours: (1) even taking everything pass/fail, he knew that his grade in Calculus would have been an A, and (2) in his other classes, he simply doesn't know what his grades would be. With the benefit of such forethought, his response on stage was clarion clear: "I have a 4.0 average."

"A four point oooooh!" screamed Bishop Long, turning to the flock and waving his free hand as they rose in a standing ovation.

Once the clapping died down, he moved to the other key issue. "So, Cedric, have you found another church up there?"

"No, sir, ummm, there aren't many churches up in Providence . . ."

"Not many churches?" said Long, casting a skeptical look. Relieved to be past the grade-point issue, Cedric proved to be as light-footed as a politician on the stump. "I just know there's no way I could *ever* replace Scripture Cathedral."

Long snapped his head toward the audience with a "that's-my-boy" grin, showing his delight and compelling thunderous applause.

Just shy of 10 A.M., Cedric walks through the metal detector at Ballou's front door (a new addition this year) and into the school's front foyer. It's empty because of the late opening, giving him a chance to quickly check which teachers might be around. He glances at the wall clock and sprints down to the math wing, first floor.

"Ms. Nelson, it's me," he whispers, ducking his head in the first-floor classroom.

"Oh, Cedric, you made it," she says, and she hugs him.

A moment later, he's at the room of Ms. Wingfield, his ninth-grade math instructor and homeroom teacher for four years.

"I got your letters," she says as soon as she sees him striding in, all aglow.

"Got yours, too," he smiles back. "That was a nice card."

"So, how did it go?" she asks.

"I'm doing good, 4.0," he testifies, feeling less guilt saying it than he expected.

"Oh, come on," she says.

But he doesn't flinch. Walking these hallways, the performance pressure is, if anything, rising. He can't back down now. "The good are delivered," he says to her, slightly under her breath. "Yes, the good are delivered."

In an empty, unused annex of the library, teachers have already gathered around a cafeteria table with a coffee urn, juice bottles on ice in a large plastic punch bowl, and a few plates of donuts and muffins.

Cedric feels awkard walking in, clumsy and outsized, not sure, suddenly, how he's supposed to sound when he talks to them all. He grabs an orange juice and hovers close to the table, making small talk.

"Someday, you know, I'm coming back to be the principal of Ballou," he says to a couple of teachers with whom he's been chatting. "After, of course, I become a software designer and make my fortune."

They both smile at him, warm, sad, soft smiles, making him suddenly feel boastful and transparent, and he finds his self-confidence rapidly eroding as everyone moves into seats.

Alumni Day, as much as anything at Ballou, is an act of imagination. The icy day notwithstanding, the turnout is bleak, as it has been for years, with ten or so seniors, half a dozen returning graduates, and maybe twenty teachers.

Dr. Jones, having traded in last year's starched white shirts and colorburst ties for a black turtleneck, stands at the plug-in, desktop podium. Cedric already heard from Ms. Wingfield that the violence and mayhem at Ballou have been rising steadily, and Dr. Jones looks weary. Any optimism he had during his first year as Ballou's principal seems to have vanished in his second.

"Ms. Green has been planning for this day almost the whole year now," he says, looking slightly stricken as he gazes at the small gathering. "We look forward to you, alumni, coming back, an effort for you to have a continuity, a continuum, for you to help someone else who's been in your place and knows what it's like to go to Ballou." He pauses, looking down momentarily at his fingers curled around the podium's edges—like a fighter asking his arms to decide whether it's worth getting up off the canvas.

He straightens them and swiftly wraps it up: "Because I want those young people who are still here to see the success that you, the alumni, have had . . . and know that they can do that, too. So, right, you can dream and you can fulfill your dreams . . . okay . . . good morning and have fun."

Cedric watches it all, feeling disembodied. Slumped in his chair with arms folded, long legs stretched out, and ankles crossed, he gazes around the room, noticing how small this library is (hell, Jefferson's was bigger), how few graduates showed up, and how the teachers, mostly standing along the spotty shelves of books, don't dress nearly as well as the professors at Brown. He sees James Dans, in a wrinkled green army jacket, slip into the back of the room looking grim. He feels an urge for the two of them to get out of there and talk about old times.

The first student speaker, a girl he barely knows who graduated in 1993 and goes to Howard University, starts off predictably, talking about how she was fourth in her class at Ballou but was overwhelmed as a Howard freshman, practically failing most of her courses until she discovered Jesus . . . "and He became my study partner."

She launches into a stunning testimony of how "Jesus taught me when to study, taught me how to study, taught me what to study, told me exactly what was on every test," and boosted her average to nearly 4.0. "I just got one B in French, and that was my fault."

When she cites Jesus as the source of her federal educational grants, Cedric starts to chuckle, shaking his head. He attributes everything to Jesus, too, but federal loans? If only it were that simple, he muses, as Ms. Green returns to the podium and his moment approaches. Then he's up front, tapping the mike. He tells them his name, that he's triple majoring in math, computer science, and education, and that he wants to talk about "practical things."

He crests through some of his going-it-alone, against-the-odds mottos, like listening to yourself, to your own heart, in deciding about college and not what other people ("some of whom are scared to do what you're doing") expect of you. Then he recounts how people warned him about going to a "big white university with lots of private school kids" and notes that he's proven them wrong by being "very happy at Brown and very successful at Brown, with a four point average."

As the clapping dies, he tells the seniors to take advantage of Ballou's "contingency of great teachers who hold your hand because there's nobody gonna be holding your hand when you get out there in the world. It's hard to believe I'm saying this, considering what Ballou can be like, but, in some ways, this is a shelter for you, a protection against some of the real obstacles to achievement, some of which are real complicated. Once you get out there, you have to build your own protection."

He pauses for a moment, realizing that these teachers and administrators must recall how he stood proud nine months ago and told them that "there's nothing me and my God can't handle."

And it jars him. The memory of that line makes his chest ache, and he knows that his front is crumbling, that every word, now, is taking him further from that rallying cry.

"To really shoot for the stars," he continues, unable to match the phrase with an upbeat tone, "you must fully accept the challenges of life—to face them honestly and head on—because life is not an easy road. It's very hard. . . ." His voice catches on the last word. The library seems silent, a roomful of unblinking eyes. "You need to work hard, very hard," he begins again, desperate just to finish. "And put your trust in the Lord and not man—because man will let you down—and you can succeed in life." He flees back to his seat before the brief applause ends.

After a few more short speeches, most teachers wave farewells and hurry back to class.

By now, the school day has started. Cedric notices James has already disappeared, and he wanders out into the halls, not sure what to do. He peers into a few classrooms, thinking that everything seems the same but weirdly far off, like he's watching it on TV. On the first floor he walks past a cluster of boys who should be in class—they look sort of puny to him—and then he stops, reaching out to touch his first-floor locker. It's someone else's now, but he turns and leans his back against it and tries to sketch outlines of the previous owner, the angry boy who ran a gauntlet in these halls and preached at graduation. But he can't. The only thing around him that stirs any remembrance is the thing that, back then, he struggled to overlook—the very ruin of the place, the fading light in teachers' eyes, the bleakness all around. Maybe he didn't notice it as much when he was here, or maybe it was the blight, closing in, that kept him running, and he saw it only in passing. Now he smells despair everywhere, and it makes his nostrils burn.

He rouses himself, pushing himself off the locker. Shake it off, he thinks, and he starts to walk again, this time more briskly, trying to affect the purposeful gait that wore down hush puppy soles on this linoleum. He figures he'll run upstairs to check whether Mr. Taylor might be free.

But on the way to the second floor, he stops. There's something red on the step. Its dried and all, but you can tell. He'd heard that two girls got in a knife fight just a few days ago. Must have been here.

He stares at the blood for a long time, he's not sure how long, until his mind goes blank. Then, Cedric Jennings, salutatorian, class of 1995, turns silently and descends the stairs, knowing only that there's no need to ever come back to this place.

LaTisha Williams looks across the table at Cedric at a home-style restaurant seven blocks south of Scripture Cathedral. She sips her water and says, dreamily, that she still "feels real tingly" and he nods, but not with nearly the enthusiasm that she'd hoped for.

It's January 22, and Cedric just took LaTisha to the Sunday afternoon service at Scripture. In the midst of whooping frenzy, LaTisha got the Holy Spirit.

Well, she may have, anyway. She herself isn't exactly sure, so she decides to talk a little more about how it felt going up on stage and having Bishop Long strike her on the forehead. What's indisputable is that she was up there five minutes or more, feeling faint, crying and waving her hands, sighing, "Oh Jesus, Oh Jesus," over and over, while Long's deputies held her up.

"All I know," she says, "is it was such an amazing feeling."

Cedric listens to her with an almost clinical detachment. "Generally speaking," he notes, "when people get the Holy Spirit, their whole life changes, with them getting settled and feeling this kind of bliss all over—and it lasts a while, at least a day and usually a few days. I just remember from when it happened to me when I was thirteen."

"Well, isn't it different for everybody?" she says, suddenly feeling sour. "Isn't it a personal thing?"

"Oh yeah, no doubt," he says, giving a little ground. "Look, what I'm saying is that, clearly, something powerful happened to you up there—I'm just not sure if the Holy Spirit actually entered your body or not."

A cheeseburger with fries is slid before her, a breaded catfish with salad before him, and she lets the issue of spiritual authenticity lie, at least for now. They quietly eat, saying little.

It's a day of high hopes for LaTisha. She'd never been to Scripture before but long anticipated going. She knows the church is at the center of Cedric's life and, in some ways, holds a key to his drive, to his sense of mission.

She found she missed him more than she expected when he left for college and, in the weeks between phone calls to Providence, often thought about why. Their bond, she decided, was both more and less than a traditional romance. While they were never officially dating, or each others' "boo" (as she sometimes joked with him over the phone), he was, clearly, a focus of her life. She'd spent years uncovering his young, black, male minefields—the array of buried explosives so many boys at Ballou seemed to carry about issues of trust and respect, about achievement and toughness and manhood. And, in that often exhausting, day-to-day effort, she'd inadvertently invested her heart.

Between bites, LaTisha breaks the silence by asking what he's been doing for the three weeks of winter break, why he didn't call. He offers no explanation other than saying he's been "just sitting around the apartment, watching videos" and that he's been getting up early every weekday morning—about 5 A.M.—to watch a show on local cable where a math professor, standing at a blackboard, goes through a college-level calculus course.

Feeling like she might as well confide in him, she's candid about her problems at UDC and how she'll just take two classes next semester and start working. She already has something lined up in the mail room of United Communications, the newsletter company, right next to Phillip Atkins. "You know," she says, trying to sound self-reliant, "I could use the money."

He nods, like he's sympathetic, but she's sure she detects an appraising look, something she hasn't seen from him before.

By the time dusk arrives, both are back at Scripture in metal folding chairs set up in long rows across the basement for a smallish prayer meeting of about eighty. Bishop Long, dressed casually in slacks and a yellow sport shirt, talks across a wide range of topics with animated enthusiasm, joking, telling stories, loosely quoting Scripture. He talks about how ladies, with "figures like Coke bottles, sometimes get dressed for church like they're going to a show" and how people should look "presentable coming to church, if that's within their power, but not be showy, trying to turn heads."

LaTisha listens, arms folded, slumped in her chair. Cedric leaves for

Brown tomorrow, and this day didn't turn out quite like she'd hoped. Sure, at Scripture she felt a surge of something—a taste, at least, of the steady, spiritual energy she's so long detected in Cedric. Thinking ahead, she decides that she'll call Barbara in a few weeks and maybe come back here for another visit to church, this time with her.

As for her relationship with Cedric, this special day is rapidly feeling like a disappointment. She purses her lips, trying to assess matters: she knows she's a big-hearted person, she knows she's been there for him when no one else was—and would be again in a moment, if he'd let her.

She looks over as he listens raptly to Long, even though he told her on the way back from the restaurant that his enthusiasm for church and the unquestioned power of faith is slowly ebbing.

If he's having some doubts, she mulls, maybe she could find her faith and help *him*. She decides she'll pray for him, but the idea makes her remember how she used to pray at her old church that God would steer her to a boy, any boy, who would be her friend. She hadn't thought about all that in more than a year, or the adjoining recollection: her prayer that Cedric was the one. And, as LaTisha's mind wanders backward, her chin comes to rest against her breastbone's high ridge, and her eyelids drift shut.

Almost an hour later, at 9:30, she feels a nudge from Cedric. The service is over. Time to get back home. She fights to rouse herself from a deep sleep, and they wander quietly toward the front of the church to catch a ride home with another congregant at tonight's service.

LaTisha, sifting through a jumble of emotions and knowing their time is short, tries to quickly engage him, criticizing the last thing she heard Long say before she dozed. "I don't agree," she says, "that you always have to be looking your best at church, dressing up and all. Everybody, whether it's a bum or whatever, should be welcome here—it's the Christian way, it's God's will."

They both slip into the car, ignoring the driver, as their discussion of this obscure point drifts into discord. As LaTisha turns from her front seat to continue the debate, Cedric fires from the back with zeal: "It's not what he said, LaTisha! Bishop Long said you should look as good as you are able—without being provocative or flashy—because this, after all, is a house of God."

"Don't worry, I hear what you're saying and all," she retorts, talking fast and feeling, at this instant, that she's not to be trifled with. "My point is different. My point is simple. In the supposedly perfect world of the church, it shouldn't matter how you look, or what you wear. If you're fat or skinny or come wearing a Hefty bag. Look at Jesus, look what he wore, how he looked. If you're a person of God, it just don't matter!"

Cedric glares at her as the car snakes toward Southeast: "You don't understand anything, LaTisha. He's saying you take care of yourself. All right?!"

There's no controlling it now. Both are screaming at each other, regret and anger gushing out, until desperation creeps into LaTisha's shriek: "It don't matter how you look, Cedric—it's what's inside, the spirit in you. That's what matters, that's what matters!"

But he's yelling too—even louder—and suddenly she feels herself being overwhelmed by a ferocity she's never seen in him: "Listen to me! He's saying you don't let yourself go! All right?! You make yourself look as good as you can! You hear me? What I'm telling you—you just don't let yourself go!"

They fall silent, and she realizes that this shouting match has nothing to do with Bishop Long. It's about the two of them, offering a glimpse at how Cedric must see her now. Sitting silently, exhausted from the screaming, she thinks back on that appraising look at dinner. Yes, it was cool and distant, a look of judgment, sizing her up as an overweight, clinging black girl with few prospects and regret growing like kudzu, stuck, maybe forever, in Southeast D.C. Which is, after all, what she is. But still, she hates that any of that matters, that those circumstances mean anything. Cedric used to know that they didn't—none of them—back in the days he could look right inside of her and see all that was good. She glances at him in the rearview mirror and can make out the side of his face in the passing streetlights. He seems expressionless, gazing out the front window, unaffected. And, as the car twists toward Anacostia to take LaTisha home, she forces herself to recognize that Cedric Jennings really doesn't live here anymore. He's just passing through.

The auditorium is casually filling when Cedric arrives, a fresh note-book in hand, and glances down at his imitation DKNY wrist-watch. Great, a few minutes early, he thinks. He flops into the aisle seat of a long, empty row of worn oak chairs, bolted onto the sloping concrete, and considers, with some astonishment, how happy he is to be back at Brown.

Being here makes him feel settled and curiously disconnected—like he's very much on his own but now more comfortable with it. Looking back, the month at home was nothing like he'd expected. Sure, there was an initial, warm blast to the senses when he first returned in mid-December—the smell of air freshener in the bathroom, the taste of the fried chicken Barbara made on his second night back, the feel of his mattress, with dips and gullies in just the right places—but then it all felt too familiar, lending a dull tension to his drifting, uneventful days in the apartment. Infrequent outings—to church, mostly, and one small family gathering at his grandmother's house—only ended up making him feel more obtuse, as people he'd sometimes known his whole life asked off-target, generally uninformed questions about his new life in Providence.

His new life in Providence? He considers the phrase and grunts a laugh that echoes faintly across the empty seats. He's noticed a jocular, familial air to the hallways of East Andrews, a feeling (more relief than resignation) that this place, in some official way, has now become home for all of them. At least that's the way it felt when everyone returned and began hugging and talking excitedly, laughing at nothing.

Cedric's shoot-low curriculum, born of fear last fall, was a one-time deal. If nothing else, his fabrications at church and at school over his nonexistent grades confirmed what he'd already figured: he can't take everything pass/fail ever again. This semester he'll take higher level classes for grades. He also knows he won't get the benefit of the doubt that many professors extend in the first few months of freshman year.

This semester, he mulls during a last moment before his morning class starts, everything is about to "get real."

Cedric squints to get a better take on the tiny, distant figure of professor Billy Wooten, just now adjusting the podium microphone. He eventually makes him out as a thoroughly average white, middle-aged guy of average height, with a conventionally professorial demeanor and an unremarkable lecturing style—all of it squeezed into a standard-issue tweed jacket.

"Welcome," says the distant figure, "to Elementary Psychology, the introduction to mind and behavior."

Cedric opens his notebook, pulls out a blank sheet of paper, and poises his pen as Professor Wooten describes what will transpire over the next fifteen weeks. It's the fabled freshman survey course: a bread-and-butter staple of college. Though Tom James's History of Education was a survey course, there were no tests; it was small enough that Professor James could take a special interest in Cedric, and, most important, it covered areas that allowed Cedric to indulge his passionate perspectives on race and education for credit.

Half an hour into today's lecture, Cedric can already feel the difference. He's written down a slew of loaded terms, from *sensation* to *perception* to *interpersonal attraction.* He glances over at the syllabus, just passed out. There are two multiple-choice midterms accounting for a big chunk of the grade and then a multiple-choice final. A once-a-week lab section will look at methodologies to study these mysterious terms. Lots and lots of terms. He looks up as Professor Wooten prepares to show some slides and instructs a teaching assistant to dim the lights. Sitting in the shadows, Cedric realizes that, in here, he's faceless, just a number, like a walking, breathing SAT score in Nikes. Walking out into the late January sun a few minutes later, he makes a mental note to get that textbook—today!—and start reading it, cover to cover.

Going from class to class over the coming day, the semester's lineup takes shape. In the Calculus 10 class, he scans the syllabus and sees some material he covered at MIT and plenty that he didn't. The teacher is a wiry, awkward, fast-talking Ph.D. candidate named Peter Berman, an oddity among the mostly Asian grad students who teach this course. The class, though, is almost identical to last semester's: a diverse crowd of mostly nonmath majors, many of whom are expecting to use this class toward a major in one of the sciences. Surveying the room, Cedric decides to display his mastery and answers a question about inverse trigonometric functions. He can feel the eyes of other kids sizing him up. It feels good, so he answers another. A few minutes later, his arm goes up to nail a third.

He knows he's showing off, but it feels wonderful, a cooling salve to ease his fear of being revealed as academically unworthy. As Berman scribbles ahead toward logarithmic functions, Cedric wonders if he's wrong to be so proud, and his mind slips back to something Long had said a few weeks ago in a Sunday sermon about the sin of pride, one of Bishop's favorite subjects. "He that is of a proud heart stirreth up strife," Cedric recalls Long commanding, quoting Proverbs 28:24, "but he that putteth his trust in the Lord shall be made fat." Where, he wonders for the umpteenth time, does using one's talents to bring "glory onto God" end and the much maligned "pridefulness" begin? He hauls out the threadbare response he's been dragging around for years: that everything you are comes from God, that He deserves credit for it all. Obviously. God created everybody, and all the black winners on the Oscars and Grammies and MTV awards are always thanking God for everything they've accomplished, like they're not allowed to take any credit for themselves lest other blacks jump on them for being haughty. But if God created everyone, Cedric mulls, tapping his pencil eraser on the desktop, what ultimately differentiates the winners from the rest? Take the kids who made it to Brown. Some are people of faith, most are not. But, one thing he's noticed: very few of them arrived by simply putting their trust in God and praying everything would work out. Took a lot more than that.

He looks up at the blackboard, trying to focus on the equations and get his head back in the lesson. But it's no use. Why is he so good at calculus? Because he worked long and hard to master the thoroughly earthbound puzzles of integration, slowly building a faith in his own abilities. And hadn't that effort been driven, in so many ways, by a burning desire to have something—anything—for which he could be proud? Where's the sin in that? Is he just bringing glory unto God with his God-given talents, or does it have nothing to do with God?

He rests his head in his hands and rubs his eyes. Too much to think about, too much to figure out. Spending so much time over the holiday in church, where everyone is ranked according to sacrifice and faith, and then returning to Brown, where everyone is ranked strictly by achievement, has sparked a real shock.

He thinks for a moment about his classes this semester. There will be the second half of his yearlong Spanish class—no big deal. But there's this class—an education fieldwork seminar, where he'll visit some school in the inner city of Providence, keep a journal, and write a couple of papers—that is sure to present its own distinct challenges. It will undoubtedly tap, for better or worse, into his own fiery experiences at Ballou on the axis of race and achievement.

Sitting in the opening session of another class he's thinking of taking—Computer Science 22, Discrete Math—he spots one of Brown's nerd-gods, an eager Asian kid who answered two questions in the last five minutes. And it suddenly dawns on him: at Ballou, that was Cedric. He was the one with the unshakable confidence, at least in the ordered realm of mathematics, the one, often the only one, who could always figure his way out of a jam—or at least give it one hell of a shot.

Then he came to Brown. Losing his pride last fall for those first cautious steps into a white world—dropping onto a lower academic track of beginner classes and pass/fail—didn't work very well, he decides. At the time, he thought it would. He thought about pride being a sin, like Bishop says, and not being something that was central to his journey. If he just did the best he could to cross that lowered bar, he recalls thinking, he would still bring glory onto God and feel okay about himself. Or part of it might have just been sober common sense—maybe this was the only way to avoid crushing failure.

But, in the end, after the months of rewritten papers and late-night cramming, it felt sort of lousy. He left Tom James's office in mid-December feeling exhausted, slightly soiled, and strangely unlike himself.

The key, he finally realizes, has always been pride. Over years, it had quietly knitted itself into his core. But, just like at church, it was sort of a sin in his neighborhood and at Ballou. Though he'd never actually use the word, kids must have sensed it in him when they always attacked him for "thinking he was better than everyone else." He ended up building all those convoluted rationales for lofty ambition, saying he needed to go to a famous college, a place everyone had heard of, to justify all of his painful sacrifices. It's all clear now: that was just a cover. It was pride—pure, simple, in-your-face, shining breastplate pride—that got him to this place. And, after making it this far, he'll be damned if he'll swallow it now.

He smiles, almost laughing, like he's made a discovery. How could he have forgotten that? He looks across the room in this upper-level course and decides, then and there, that he'll sign up for discrete math—*and* stick with all the other classes. That'll give him five courses for the semester, one more than the per-semester requirement most students stick to.

After class ends he feels strengthened and purposeful, and he stops by the Brown bookstore to load up on textbooks and supplies. The campus seems festive as dinnertime approaches. With everyone back but little assigned work, it will certainly be a Thursday night of partying and reunion. He walks up Thayer Street lugging books, returning the smile of one passing kid from last semester's calculus class, and then there's the girl, whose name he doesn't know, who smiles at him sometimes in the tray and silverware line at the VeeDub.

"Five classes," he says to himself. "Have I lost my mind?" It actually feels kind of good to say it. He remembers what Miriam, Dr. Korb's aunt, told him about how "saying things can sometimes make them happen." Yes, this is a bold plan that won't just draw him even with the other kids, with their measly four classes, but might take him a notch above. It's an intrepid act—maybe his first since arriving here—that, somehow, seems to liberate him.

He turns the corner near a flower shop on the north end of Thayer and into a parking lot that edges into the shadow of Andrews dorm, his arms now straining with the bags of thick, fresh, unopened books.

He sees the dorm loom up ahead. Thinking about Zayd and Chiniqua, about Evan and even Rob, he begins to run. He can't wait to tell them, in a casual, offhand way, of course, that this semester he's taking five—count 'em, five—classes. So, take that, he thinks, bounding to the second floor two steps at a time.

The Gate reaches its blooming, buzzing peak by eleven on Thursday night—a prime-time, weekend's-coming effusion of see-and-be-seen activity, fueled by overcooked roast beef on cardboard sub rolls, slices of barbecue chicken pizza, Cool Ranch Doritos, and up-half-the-night vats of fountain Coke.

Cedric assesses Zayd's brown boots, crossed and resting on the mirror-topped table.

"You didn't buy those boots until you saw mine," he says.

"I didn't?" replies Zayd, arching a brow. "All I know is I bought them 'cause I liked them."

"No," says Cedric emphatically. "You saw mine and said you didn't like them, that they looked like a girl's. Remember, we were over at the shoe place?"

Zayd shrugs, rotates his gaze around the room once, and then turns back. "Okay, so they grew on me."

"Just don't you make it sound like you thought of it yourself," says Cedric. "It's just important, you know, that we clear about what's what."

Zayd seems to ignore this, scratching a blotch of dirt off the edge of his raised sole, then offers a carefully tailored response: "I mean, Cedric, I respect your sense of style and, naturally, some of it's gonna rub off on me. And some of mine, on you. I'm cool with that."

Cedric blows on the tip of his barbecue chicken pizza slice, takes a bite, and throws Zayd a skeptical look. "You mean some of my authentic, been-in-the projects style is gonna rub off? Yeah . . . ," he shakes his head in mock disgust, ". . . right."

Zayd lets it lie. He takes a swig of his designer juice—Nantucket Nectar's Guava Passion—and then looks away. Cedric, sure he detects impatience, something he rarely sees in Zayd, eases off a little. "Well, all right," he mumbles halfheartedly, "I guess you got worse projects there in Chicago than we do in D.C. . . ."

Zayd, swiftly attentive, meets him in the middle. "For sure," he says eagerly. "You ever read that book, *There Are No Children Here*, about those two little black kids growing up in Henry Horner Houses in Chicago? That may be the worst housing project in the entire country."

Cedric frowns. "What, your college professor dad get you to read that?"

"No," replies Zayd, his voice oddly tentative, a puzzled look on his face. They're both just looking at each other, and Cedric decides not to avert his gaze or fill the silence. A host of unwelcome and unfamiliar emotions seem to be welling inside him—he can't quite make them out—and he roots about for another pitch, the last one not having worked very well. "Don't give that affluent, white liberal stuff," he says finally, stunned that a smug, cynical, college-boy line just passed his lips.

Zayd seems stunned, too, and their tension shatters into laughter.

It's cold and wet outside. The Gate keeps filling, and no one's going anywhere. Other kids from the unit stop by, fold themselves into the duo's conversation, then alight at some other table, leaving Cedric with the one person everyone knows has managed to be-friend him.

Along the way, the two of them settle into a discussion of music—the realm of hip-hop, rap, and R&B—the one address they both seem to share. Just before dinner, Cedric bought the new CD by R. Kelly, the hip-hop star, with $12 he borrowed from Zayd, and Zayd asks if he's listened to it yet. Cedric hasn't, but they talk about R. Kelly anyway, and then about whether Zayd should get his chin pierced—Cedric is against, Zayd equivocal—and then about Chiniqua's tight new braids, both agreeing that they look very, very good.

"What kind of hair do you think looks best on a black girl?" Zayd queries philosophically, "other than her just trying to be white, like Mariah Carey, just straightening her hair?"

Again, Cedric feels his face and mood darken, but Zayd wheels around before Cedric can answer as Abby, a girl from the unit, drapes her arms over his shoulders. Cedric surveys the two of them flirting as he tries to pick through the last hour of conversation, in an effort to isolate what's gnawing at him, making him feel volatile, like he's pressing something down. Abby spots someone across the room, cheerily says "See ya" to the two of them, and turns to leave.

"She's always so happy," Cedric says as he watches her snake across the room toward a wall-mounted TV where David Letterman is double-taking to Paul Schafer. "I hate that. It's unnatural."

"I know what you mean," Zayd replies easily. "For any thinking person, it's untenable. If you're a thinking person, you're upbeat sometimes, sad sometimes, whatever."

Cedric nods, inspecting every word and feeling, like he often does. He has a jealous admiration for how light-footed and unencumbered Zayd is, how dilemmas of all sorts seem to vent right through him. "Sometimes, I keep things inside and it eats at me," Cedric says quietly, trying to take things a level deeper. "Like, remember I told you about when I visited my father that time in jail, how he did nothing but talk to my cousin and how it just ate at me for the longest time.

"It wasn't so much what he said that day that stuck with me," Cedric continues, "as this feeling that I had trusted him—invested emotions, or whatever, in him—and that he betrayed that. You know, that and other stuff I been through, makes it hard for me, sometimes, to have faith in people. Like the closer I get, the more I worry about being abandoned."

Zayd is attentive, fascinated by Cedric's emotions in ways few others are around here. "You got to have faith in people," he says, importantly. "People are all we got."

Cedric resists sniping What's that? Something from a greeting card?—and instead takes a last swig of his ginseng iced tea. Zayd is trying, after all. Trying to help, Cedric mulls, the poor black kid with few friends and all these troubles. Cedric, just back from a disquieting vacation in D.C. and newly committed to his bold five-class plan, is particularly impatient with his poor black "specialness" tonight. He wants to change the subject, to air things out. He tells Zayd he should take psychology with him, "you know, so I could stay awake in class."

"Maybe I will," Zayd replies, skillfully noncommittal. "As a neurotic Jew, at least on my mom's side, I'm supposed to know all that psychology stuff. It might be nice to at least know what all the terms meant."

Cedric knows that's a "No" and bears down on the hard crust of his pizza. A few minutes later, Zayd's friend Jake stops by and the two begin chatting.

"I shouldn't be seen with two white guys," Cedric says acerbically. "I really should be going. If people from D.C. saw me here with two white guys, they'd say, 'Oh, the brother's selling out.'"

Cedric watches as Jake quickly apologizes for interrupting, and Zayd's smooth features start to cloud. He feels a moment's hesitation. "Well, I guess, just for tonight, it'd be okay," he mutters.

"Thanks," says Zayd, who manages a thin smile. They sit and say nothing, neither moving. After almost a minute, Zayd spots a tall black kid near a bank of video game machines across the room and waves to him.

"Sister Souljah says that just because white people may be around you," Cedric says, mentioning the female rapper's news-making barb as he turns to look hard at Zayd, "it doesn't mean they are for you."

"I could be," says Zayd softly. "You're for me."

"Who told you that?" Cedric says, as he watches Zayd's expression become pained. He waits another moment, letting the silence speak. "I'm not saying I'm not," Cedric says finally, surprised at how flat and hard his voice is. "I'm not pretending to like you, or not like you, I'm not pretending to *be* anything."

The muscles in Cedric's jaw clench, his mind racing: so Zayd wants to talk about it, about blacks and whites, about the fascinating racial dialogue, about how two opposites, one black, one white are friends and ain't that fuckin' cool. So, now, we're talking about it all in such a way that, maybe, he won't want to talk about it so much anymore. So, maybe, we'll get past always looking at each other's skin, and just be friends—friends without category headings.

"Whatever Sister Souljah says I know, ummm, that I'm white and I like you. Shouldn't that be enough?" Zayd asks in a plea, as Cedric— letting the question hang—rises to go.

"I guess it should be," he finally says in a voice without inflection, glancing down at the top of Zayd's dirty blond head. "All I know is I already got a lot of studying to do. I'm gonna get back and get started. Maybe, I'll see you around."

12

LET the COLORS RUN

The bus rumbles along a ravine that winds down from College Hill onto a wide asphalt plain of pawn shops, convenience marts, and vacant stores. It's a part of Providence that Cedric has never seen, and he looks intently out of the bus's scratched, cloudy window. Everything they pass is gray, from the dirty mounds of frozen snow to the steely clouds in a murky sky to the people—white and then, increasingly, black—who scuffle along, their faces obscured by wraparound scarves or tightly tied hoods as they try to get somewhere before the cold gets them.

Ten minutes on, after a dozen turns, he wraps his fingers around the bar of the seat ahead and pulls himself up straight to get a better look out of the wide front windshield. That must be it, he surmises, spotting a sorry-looking box of red brick with white limestone archways and ledges: Slater Junior High School.

It's February 6 at ten of eight, a forbiddingly cold day with a stiff dawn wind that seems to have kept the sun from rising on the first day of Cedric's Fieldwork and Seminar in High School Education course. Arrangements have already been made by the seminar's professor for an undergraduate to attend classes here two mornings a week, so there are only a few formalities at the first-floor principal's office before Cedric can go to the classroom he'll be observing on the school's second floor.

Clutching a visitor's pass, he wades into the early morning swells of seventh and eighth graders on their way to first-period class, all of them looking very young and innocent to him. He knows otherwise, of course, because he knows this place without having to open his eyes.

Though he's spent most of his life in schools similar to this, he knows he's supposed to reach beyond that now and also become a dispassionate observer. So, feeling clumsy and outsized, like some sort of black Gulliver, he clomps forward, noting the exposed pipes running along the twenty-foot ceilings, the bulletin board with homilies to build self-esteem, and the rough mix of students, more than half of them either black or Latino. The white kids, though, don't seem to be any better off than the rest, a poorer version he's never seen. He overhears a cluster, passing in the opposite direction on the stairwell, speaking in a foreign language that sounds like Spanish. Upstairs, he checks room numbers on the cross beams of door frames until the right one appears, and he ducks his head in.

"You must be Cedric," says a fortyish white guy in khaki Dockers, a white button-down, striped tie, and brown Timberland bucks. He has a thick mop of longish graying hair and a full beard. "I'm Mr. Fleming. Welcome to eighth-grade mathematics, also known as the funny farm."

Cedric laughs, surprised to be looking down slightly at the teacher, who is consequential and wide-shouldered, and must be about five-foot-ten. With a precious few minutes before the first-period bell rings, Cedric offers a thumbnail résumé—noting his interests in math and education, his hometown, how Brown is a "great school and all"—and Mr. Fleming lets him in on the most important things he needs to know about Slater: "A lot of the kids you'll be seeing have troubled lives at home . . . the neighborhoods around here are poor . . . the prospects for these kids are not very good." Then he sweeps through a cursory overview of guns found in lockers and concealed knives as he studies Cedric's face, searching, it seems, for a clue about whether he's looking at a black college student who knows of such mayhem or someone, like almost everyone else, who's only heard about it.

Cedric is not about to let on. "I understand what you mean," is all he says, barely nodding, as half the desks in the room fill and class starts. Mr. Fleming tells them that Cedric is a Brown freshman who will be observing the class for the next two months. Cedric, sitting at a utility table near the door, finds himself nodding to the kids—almost all black or Latino in this, the lowest of nine math sections in the eighth grade.

Mr. Fleming proves to be loud and acerbic and sometimes coyly wiseguyish. He keeps a semblance of order by raising his volume when needed. It's a game of cat and mouse. One girl pulls another girl's hair. A boy kicks another boy's shin across the aisle. Notes are passed and laughter suppressed. One kid sleeps soundly near the window. Mr. Fleming runs through basic math exercise on the board, reducing fractions, asking for answers from the class, though he seems to not call on certain students. Cedric notices one in the back, a slim black kid who never raises his hand but seems to instantly know all the answers, often just blurting them out. After a bit, Mr. Fleming booms at him, "DID I CALL ON YOU!? WELL, DID I?" The student is unfazed, and after Fleming has moved on, the slim kid turns to Cedric. He can feel the boy's eyes sizing him up. Others are quietly studying him as well. And Cedric is studying them back, and studying Mr. Fleming, too, taking notes on a piece of loose-leaf paper. He pushes forward, though the whole affair seems bizarre: them all looking at him, him at them, searching for answers. Answers to what? Answers for whom?

The class ends, and a few kids cluster around his chair, their eyes almost even with his. "You really a freshman at Brown like he said?" one of the black girls asks with a tone of disbelief.

"Yeah, why's that so surprising?" he chuckles, as he spots the slim black boy shuffling slowly around the periphery.

"Just, you know, not that many people I heard of going there," says another black girl in the group, as several of the kids and Cedric nod at once, no one having to talk about things they all seem to understand.

After the classroom empties, Mr. Fleming sits on the edge of the utility table, wanting to talk to Cedric in the few minutes before the next class arrives. There will be three more classes before Cedric leaves at twelve, "all of them tough, but none tougher than this one you just saw," he says, noting that a lot of those kids were classified as "special ed" for emotional or behavioral problems, like about half the students at the school.

He leans in toward Cedric, conspiratorially. "You know," he whispers, "I can tell the ones that will die when they leave here, when they leave this school. I can see them. You look at them hard enough, long enough, and you can tell. You really can."

The words slice open a blister of confused emotions that bubble from Cedric for the rest of the morning. Other classes come and go. Cedric takes more notes, most reflecting on how Mr. Fleming passes judgment with his booming admonitions and cutting asides. "One false move and Marlin gets it," Fleming says at one point, putting his finger against the head of one boy in the midst of some elaborate criticism. "Listen, there's no way you checked this over," he blares later at a girl who tries to hand in a worksheet early. "Carelessness will get you killed in here." Cedric's pages fill with notes. And by the time he silently slips out, just before the last class ends, he finds himself murmuring fantasies about what Mr. Fleming will say to him next time, or the time after, that might offer an excuse "to put my big black fist in his face."

After the long bus ride back and a quick lunch in the cafeteria by himself, Cedric retreats to the eighth-floor stacks of Brown's computer science tower. Sitting in a carrel near the window, he splays out his notes, looking them over and letting the rage simmer through him. He can tell the ones "that'll die when they leave here." How can he tell? They're just kids! He's writing them off before they even get a chance. Sure, some of them have behavioral problems—what else could they have, growing up the way they live!—but Fleming treats them like they're worthless, like he's looking right through them.

He pushes the note pages aside and opens the black-and-white-speckled cover of his "A-Plus Compositions" notebook. Carefully, in the upper right corner, he writes 2/6/96, marking the first entry in his journal.

Below him, the Brown campus seems small and distant, like a fragile scale model of brick buildings and domes, squares of grass and tufts of bush. Yes, this is where he lives now.

He turns away from the window, grabs the black pencil, and writes, with point-breaking pressure, the first line of his journal: "As soon as I walked into the school, I felt at home."

Brown University?" asks the man with a smile that reveals his surprise. He's a middle manager at the Department of Agriculture's division of food inspection and safety. "An athletic scholarship?"

Barbara Jennings looks evenly at him—a slight fellow, born in India, she thinks, who has long been boastful about the academic prowess of his daughter, who just started at the University of Maryland. A fine school, of course, but not Brown.

"I don't believe they have athletic scholarships in the Ivy League," she says, giving her tone just the right mix of condescension and impatience. "Anyway, he's *there* because of his academics."

With a nod, she continues down the hall and turns into her cubicle, not feeling as good about her tart reply as she expected she would. It's a late afternoon in mid-February, and she settles in for the last hour until quitting time. She no longer answers her phone by saying "Process Products," and the branch's new name, "Food Safety," may not last either. There's been lots of turmoil at cumbersome federal departments like agriculture lately—more restructuring, though, than actual cost cutting. A few promotions she'd hoped for never came her way, and a slot that recently opened above her went to someone younger. It once might have bothered her, stirring memories of how many college graduates she's trained over the years, mostly white men, and then watched ascend. But fretting about her advancement, at the office or elsewhere, is not something she's inclined to do much of these days. She types some figures on meat inspection onto her screen, part of a report on food safety to be presented at a Congressional hearing by a deputy agriculture secretary, then turns to one of her friends at a nearby desk.

"So, you ever think they'll do that slave museum thing?" Barbara asks.

The woman chuckles, "I know they ought to, that's for sure . . . and make you the curator," a comment that compels a laugh from Barbara, something she welcomes these days like sunlight. Talk about "the slave museum" has settled into running commentary for the division's mostly black female support staff since they moved into this office six months ago and learned that it was once a slave quarters and transport station, a place where slaves were housed from up and down the coast or just off boats from the ports of Washington and Baltimore and auctioned. Apparently, some artifacts from those days are in a warehouse somewhere.

Rich fare it is, indeed, for the black ladies of the typing pool, especially the ones who long ago learned to swallow their ambition and

sometimes still feel it growl in their stomachs. Ladies like Barbara. Not
that she was always that way. When Cedric was still at home, she'd
conscientiously report to him about any small bump up in her pay, or
any added responsibility she'd assumed, wanting him to feel like she
was on the move too, just like him. That was a long time ago. Every
day it seems she discovers something she once did, some way she once
acted or thing she once said that was designed to put up a good front or
send Cedric a message she thought he'd need.

Not much point in facades anymore. He's getting older, and it's
harder for her to hide things. He found out that she didn't end up
going to Chris's house last Thanksgiving, like she said over the phone
when he called from the Korbs'. She just ate some leftovers and went to
bed. Christmas wasn't much either, and Cedric seemed a little disappointed, though he didn't say so. In fact, over the winter break, Cedric
didn't say all that much. Everything was cordial, and it was nice to have
him with her at church—everyone so proud of him—but the privacy
zone that once extended to the borders of his small bedroom had
grown to envelop a whole mysterious life in Providence. She tries,
always will, to give him bits of advice, telling him not to worry about
what other kids are doing, partying and all, not to lose trust in God and
to stick with his studies. But she's not sure whether he listens or, in her
very darkest moments, whether he ought to.

The day is done, and she wanders outside in the cool, cloudy late
afternoon. It's a church night, and she's looking fine in a new paisley
patterned dress and maroon shoes. Her shoes are the only thing that
gives her much joy lately. The floor of the closet in her room is full of
them, every shade, stripe, and style.

A few hours later, she enters the sanctuary and chats with some of
the missionary ladies she's known for years, many of whom have noticed she's been looking good lately. "You all turned out tonight, Barbara," one says.

"Oh, this old thing," she replies, always mindful of how delicate
issues of material success can be Scripture.

Tonight's sermon is about temptation. Long says it's about "how
we all stray from the Word of God in our lives, and how only repen-

tance can show us the way back." Barbara opens her Bible to a verse Long cites in Kings. But after a moment she finds herself looking at the bookmark rather than the text. It's a postcard she got a few months ago—a mailer, but addressed to her, from a travel agency in Florida. It offers a package trip, a "nine-day Florida and Bahamas vacation," costing only $398 for two people. Four years ago, she went on one of these cheap cruises to the Bahamas with Valerie Hobbs—a daughter of her godmother—and they had a real time. She looks to her left and right in the pew and turns the postcard from upright to horizontal, flattening it against the open book so no one can see. She looks at the palm trees and the soft, pale white beach. Nine days . . . $398 for two. But whom would she go with this time, she wonders. She gazes into the wide center section of the church, passing over the familiar faces of women and a few men. No one from here—no one from this place of public piety and sacrifice—seems suitable. If there was a special man, that sure would be nice, but no candidates in these seats. She tucks the palm trees back inside the worn black covers of the King James.

Barbara gets her usual ride home and ends up back at the apartment at about ten, a little earlier than usual. It started raining sometime during church, been threatening all day, and she brushes off the moisture from her shoulders. She gets the mail from the lobby lock boxes and climbs the stairs.

She often feels settled and ready to sleep after church, but Bishop's message tonight about temptation didn't move her; in fact, it left her feeling unrequited and a little edgy. She throws her raincoat over a dinette chair and fingers through the envelopes. Mostly junk, a few credit card solicitations, bills from some of her store charges, and a letter from Barac Realty. Through the translucent oval in the envelope she can see the block letters "Notice of Eviction."

March is coming, and obligations brim like a lake above a dammed river. She has learned, over many years, how to not think about the crush of bills, how to turn off the debtor's dread so she can get through her days without throwing up. Even now, it feels like another person's eyes are looking down at the notice in her hand. The letter generated by a computer comes every few weeks to remind her it's just a matter of time. She places it in a stack on the dining room table and sits down in the chair, feeling wetness from her slung raincoat seep through her dress at the small of her back.

It's time to take stock. She needs to do something about the whole mess. A month ago, she felt like she was confronting the debt of back rent head on, and maybe even cutting a path to solid ground. On January 28, there was a hearing at Housing Court, a special subsidiary chamber of the civil courts system that mostly handles landlord-tenant disputes. It was a few days after Cedric went back to college, and Barbara was deeply thankful that she didn't have to go while he was there; she'd managed to conceal her dire situation from him. Barac sent one of its men to lay it all out: how Ms. Barbara Jennings failed to make her $452 payment on December 1 and, on December 15, Barac initiated eviction proceedings. On the day of the hearing, Barbara was actually almost three months behind. The judge asked what happened, and she thought about going through it all, describing how she was just making her bills at the end of October but then needed to withdraw money for parents weekend. But instead she just said she'd "fallen behind on a few things, your honor, and I can get back on track." The gavel slammed: she was ordered to make a two-month payment on February 1 and another on March 1 to get even. But a few days ago, on February 15, no check for $904 had arrived at Barac, and the landlord restarted the eviction clock.

Running through it all again puts her stomach in a knot. Not that the ticking of debt and disaster ever completely leaves her mind—it's always running on some just audible track, continuous play. She can ignore it most times, as long as she keeps focused on the day-to-day matters of office politics or squabbles at church or a pair of shoes she's been eyeing. But then there are nights like this, once every couple of weeks, triggered usually by a letter or a dunning call, when everything flips and the din of obligations is suddenly deafening.

She grabs the letter and opens it on her lap—$1,352 currently owed in back rent, plus $340 in late fees and court costs. Then she looks past the letterhead to her lovely maroon shoes. A swell of defensiveness rises in her, and she indulges it. After all, it's not like she's been living like a queen; an extra $100 a week or so in her pocket, rather than the landlord's, has meant that her other bills are finally on time and that she can start paying off old debts—some of them years old. And, yes, there have been some shoes and dresses, and contributions, of course, to church, but nothing all that extravagant.

She drops the letter on the table and shuts her eyes, fighting the familiar urge to let herself off the hook, and then she rises with a groan. Her mouth feels parched, and she gets a drink of Coke from the refrigerator before collapsing onto the couch and propping the pillows. Lying back, eyes wide, she thinks of a phone conversation with Cedric a few weeks ago. He was going on about some of the problems with Rob. Having heard much about this during the first semester, Barbara had been thinking about what she might say to help him—and that night she got her chance.

"You know, Lavar," she had said, "I think Rob is a test that God has put before you. That, even though he couldn't be *more* different than you, you have to somehow see what's godly in him. It's a test all right."

Cedric seemed to really listen, which made Barbara feel good for days afterward. Thinking about it now makes her smile and feel slightly strengthened. "Getting that back rent, that's my test," she whispers. "He's got his test. I've got mine."

And saying the words so God might hear them, too, is just enough to buy her some sleep.

Hey, you want to go to breakfast?" Rob asks, moving toward the door on his way to the showers.

Cedric, putting on his socks, looks up. "Ummm, sure. Why not?"

There has been a thaw. There had to be, or it would have ended with punches thrown. Both of them knew it.

So today it's "Want to go to breakfast?" Just like that. Amazing, Cedric thinks, as he laces up his Reeboks.

Small calibrations were already occurring in their relationship in the last days before winter break, though Cedric didn't realize it at the time. They talked one night during finals like regular roommates. It was late and the lights were out—that must have helped. It was real casual. Rob asked about Cedric's high school, what it was like, and Cedric went through it, laying it all out simply—the gangs and the violence and how he was singled out—and Rob listened closely, asking a few thoughtful questions.

"I never had to deal with any of the kind of stuff you did," he said quietly. "Must have been pretty rough."

"Yeah, wasn't too great," Cedric said, fatigued by then from the conflict and ready for a temporary truce. He knew that a lot of tough finals were avalanching on Rob, who had been haggard and unshaven for days, his wool hat pulled half over his ears, looking like a smooth layer had been burned off of him. He seemed different, more open. So Cedric, looking up at the dark ceiling, ventured a bit further. "I guess we really make quite a pair. Huh?"

"No doubt," Rob laughed softly. "You know, Cedric, we should have had a conversation like this the first week of school."

In the month since their return from winter break, relations have been cordial, if not exactly warm. It's not like they're partying all night. But breakfast this morning goes well, just the two of them. They talk about classes this semester and goings-on around campus as Cedric downs a few bowls of Golden Grahams. Rob mentions the "Wall of Shame" scandal that's getting ink in the *Brown Daily Herald*. Cedric says he doesn't read the paper much, so Rob fills him in on the object of controversy: a wall in one of the boys' bathrooms with graffiti listing the names of black guys who date white girls. It's sparked a controversy about "keeping with your own and all that," Rob says earnestly and adds, "It makes me really angry, a real outrage, you know?" Cedric smiles at this. "Yeah, makes me angry, too," he says, appreciating Rob's effort.

As Rob gets up to leave, he mentions that a couple of kids in the unit are getting together at Cafe Paragon at eight for his nineteenth birthday. "It's just us," he says, with a sort of studied casualness. "You should come by."

Cedric, surprised by the invitation, can do little more than nod out a maybe. Sitting alone at the long table, he pours another bowl of Golden Grahams, thinks about Rob's awkward description of the Wall of Shame, and realizes how far he and Zayd traveled in their dialogue.

Yes, it was tiring to always be talking about race, about black views of this or white views of that, but at least it was talking. A few days after their edgy Thursday night exchange at the Gate, they had it out. It was the last Sunday in January, and Cedric stood in front of Zayd's TV while he and Bear were trying to watch Zayd's copy of *Pulp Fiction*. That got things started, and eventually there was screaming about disrespect and some money Cedric owed Zayd for the R. Kelly CD—all of it just an excuse to yell and go their separate ways.

They haven't spoken since, and Cedric now realizes that the timing of the split was lousy. February is a bad time to be estranged from your best friend—a month when freshmen tend to distill and discard some of the unfamiliar, insecure elements of the first semester that kept them all holding on to each other, traveling in large, safe groups. Now that everyone has been through one round of finals and a revealing month at home, it's time to make some choices about who your close friends will be and how you'll define yourself under Brown's implicit guidelines, as first laid out in the diversity workshop.

Though most of the Unit 15ers still have one foot planted in some tight, vetted clique on the hallway, plenty of them also have the other foot searching for solid ground elsewhere. Without Zayd, Cedric prowled around the campus through February, mostly by himself, observing the segregation. The white girls formed the feminist camp, boasting a force of numbers that make it Brown's most formidable interest group. Along with rape crisis meetings, awareness sessions, and there are the larger formal events, like evening lectures led by professors from the Women's Studies Department or visiting feminist dignitaries.

One night, walking by an auditorium one floor above the Gate, Cedric peeked into one. A black woman was talking about "empowerment." Had to be an audience of five hundred, all women as far as he could see, and he spotted a couple of girls from the unit. Eating breakfast alone the next morning, Cedric found an article about the speaker in the school paper, about her being a lesbian and all. There's a big interest group overlap there—between the feminists who also happen to be lesbians or are experimenting with it and this other big crowd, the LGBTQA, or the Lesbian, Gay, Bisexual, Transgender, Questioning Alliance. March begins their appreciation month, and there are posters everywhere about upcoming events. Cedric looked at one posted in the math building and shook his head. A Gala Leather Lunch, Queer Dress-up Day, gay porno movies—real stomach turners, for him, but not as shocking as when he first arrived. Actually knowing people who go in for this stuff has made it increasingly difficult to remain as judgmental as he once was.

For one, there's John Crews, a black sophomore who's the minority peer counselor for the unit. In an angry memo he slid under dorm room doors in November about poor attendance at some sexual preference outreach, he told everyone he was bisexual. Cedric and Zayd hooted about it for a while, saying they didn't want to see him in the shower, but after that faded, Cedric had to admit that Crews wasn't such a bad guy. And then there's Molly Olsen, the bald girl that Cedric and Barbara passed at orientation and thought was undergoing chemotherapy. She and Cedric talk sometimes. Her head, of course, was shaved on purpose, she told Cedric, because she "didn't want to be held captive by male notions of female beauty." He sees a lot of girls with shaved heads. Cedric knows they don't hang with guys and presumes they're toying around with lesbian stuff, but he never bothers bringing it up with Molly.

Then, of course, there are the racial and ethnic groups. At lunch, right after President's Day weekend, Sonya Garza, a Latino girl in the unit, talked about this class called Hispanics/Latinos in the United States that she said "completely changed my life." There are mostly Latino kids in it, and she has been spending a lot of time with the Latin American Students Association lately, or La Fuerza Latina, or one of the other Latin groups. They have salsa dances and special dinners. The Asian kids in the unit, Cedric also notices, are suddenly spending more time with their various groups. There seem to be a million of them— Korean Students Association, one for the Japanese, one for students from Hong Kong. The list is endless. Even Zeina Mobassaleh, the hypergregarious girl from Holton-Arms School in D.C. who's sort of like the unit's social director, has vanished into something called the American-Arab Anti-Discrimination Committee, one of the big Arab groups. She may even be an officer.

Though there's a group for every ethnicity—sometimes loosely presided over by a professor who teaches in that cultural discipline—Cedric has noticed that the black students have a special place in the firmament. For one thing, they have their own dorm, Harambee House, which offers a physical nucleus. That's where Chiniqua has disappeared to. She still asks Cedric to come, and he still holds back, feeling like going over there and disappearing into that huge clique would represent some sort of defeat, a retreat from what originally brought him to Brown. Lately, though, he just doesn't see her around much and sometimes wonders if he should just go one day to Harambee, just to find her.

That leaves the mostly white, heterosexual guys—"the oppressor group," Cedric remembers Kim Sherman saying at the diversity workshop—who have nowhere to go. They might branch off into little bands, like John Frank singing with the Brown Derbies, but basically they just wander about unlabeled, serving nicely as props for all the other groups.

Cedric figures a few of them will be wandering over to Cafe Paragon tonight for Rob's birthday. All that's left to do, as he strolls down to Thayer Street after dinner, is decide whether he's going to go.

It's been a strange, solitary month, different from the bitter isolation and ostracism of the fall, where he felt out of control. By now he realizes he's learned plenty about how to mix with the other kids and about ways he's slowly changing, discarding some of his fears and doubts and forming attachments.

All of which makes his current exile mostly self-imposed, a remnant, maybe, of long years when he became accustomed to being alone, convincing himself that it meant he was special—and maybe better in some fundamental, godly way—than the other kids on the street or at church or at Ballou. He had to tie his identity to that notion of separateness; it was the only way he could stay on course and keep his sanity, really, as they hurled insults at him about racial betrayal or insufficient maleness and foolhardy optimism. Here, no one is really hurling anything. They're just all going about their business—everyone in their own little show—and he has to find some other way to feel special. Being alone doesn't seem to be working.

He mulls over all this as he walks, haltingly, down Thayer, looking at his watch and realizing they're probably all at Cafe Paragon already. It's a cool but brilliantly clear evening, stars out, and he pulls closed the neck of his bulky green parka.

He sees Cafe Paragon a block down the street, bustling with people flowing in and out the door. It's really a bar at night, with lots of noise and drinking and smoking, the kind of place he's been warned against visiting his whole life—by Bishop and his mother—a licentious spot where anything might happen and the last place a holy person, a special person of God, ought to be.

Just a few feet away from the entrance, he hesitates and veers right into the College Hill Bookstore, grabbing a *Billboard* off the rack. He quickly flips through the top 40, top 20, Top Albums, Top Singles, total revenues, CD sales figures, and realizes he's already memorized all of them from a *Billboard* he bought a week ago. He stops, gently closes the magazine, lays it back on the rack, and just stands there, feeling a sudden nostalgia for his shut-in's life of television, CDs, and friendships with two-dimensional images. It's clear (so achingly clear as he hovers, empty-handed, near the wall of glossy magazines) that he'll need to start unfolding in some fresh and frightening ways to keep moving forward.

The inside of Cafe Paragon is smoky and as loud as a train station. Everyone hails a welcome as he plunks down in an empty chair at the end of a long row of pushed-together tables, conveniently near the door.

It feels fine to be in here, sort of energizing. Everyone except Cedric orders food—he's already eaten and has no money, anyway—but the conversation, ricocheting across the table, offers plenty of sustenance. It's mostly guys from the unit, six of them—plus Maura McLarty, Zeina Mobassaleh, and Corry Mascitelli—and Cedric doesn't feel he needs to say much. His presence alone seems to be appreciated. Ira Volker, sitting cattycorner to Cedric's left, eventually engages him in a heated discussion about the unavailability of Tupac Shakur's latest CD single. Ira is digging in with the position that since it's not being stocked at Sam Goody's up the street, it can't be bought. Cedric, grinning, slams him with knowledge about CD packaging and distribution, capping it with, "I study music, do you study music?" When he looks around, Cedric realizes everyone at the table is taking delight in his show, and he laughs airily. In this warm wash of ease, Cedric then listens intently to the talk of national politics and summer internships, even though he doesn't care much about either subject.

As nine o'clock nears, everyone starts pulling out driver's licenses or fake IDs to try to order beer, and Cedric feels an urge to go. He doesn't have a driver's license, something he's embarrassed about, and drinking beer is definitely something he has no intention of doing. So he sings a verse of "Happy Birthday" to Rob and rises.

"Thanks for coming, Cedric," Rob says.

And Cedric nods, "Thanks for asking me."

Walking back to the dorm, he senses that he's taken a step, albeit small, in an intriguing direction, and the brisk night air feels good on his face. Back in the dorm room, still feeling the bracing air in his nostrils, he sticks to his evening plan. The Grammy Awards are on tonight, a show Cedric watches every year. He flips on the TV and settles in. Despite a great gospel number—where Shirley Caesar is joined by Whitney Houston, prompting Cedric to leap from his bed and sing lustily—the Grammies end up being a disappointment. Mariah Carey, one of his favorites, is aced out on best album, the second to last award, leaving her with no Grammies despite six nominations. Cedric watches her dispirited face flash across the screen and turns off the TV, not so much disgusted by her losing as with him being a person who would care so much.

He opens the door, pokes out his head, and then leans against the frame. Zayd walks by with Bear on their way to Zayd's room. Neither looks his way. Sonya Garza and her white liberal Minnesotan roomie, Nicole, are on the carpet arguing, good-naturedly, about politics near where Evan, at the end of a phone line stretching from his room, is telling his girlfriend from Tufts that "we're not really growing together." Rob runs into the room for a moment, having just called home for his birthday from the third floor—respecting Cedric's viewing privacy in a way Cedric suddenly wishes he wouldn't—and mentions how his Dad "just thanked my Mom for that moment nineteen years ago" before he skips out into the hallway to wrestle with Abby over an ice cream cone, the two of them laughing flirtatiously.

Watching the whole circus, a smile plastered on his face, makes Cedric feel gloomy and, at the same moment, strikes him with an overpowering desire to break free from himself and dive into the flow, to not be so conscious, all the time, of how he looks and where he's from, to get past whatever it is—anger or envy or just otherness—that seems to be holding him back.

He retreats into the room, letting the door slam shut, and sits down at his desk. He's supposed to write an entry in his journal tonight about Slater and flips through his pages of notes—rantings, really, of his out-rage at the way the kids are treated, about the injustice of it. He reads them once, then again, but writes nothing in the journal. Tonight he can't seem to locate his fury.

Larry Wakeford stares in silence at the blonde, butch-cut, mischie-vously cocked head of a student—a delightfully contentious senior named Leslie—and notices a ray of late afternoon sunlight reflecting off her nostril stud. He chuckles.

"Listen, Leslie, I'm not sure if I'm actually exercising some sort of tyranny or not. I'm just giving guidelines for an assignment," he says while leaning forward, fingertips on the edge of the seminar table, in a purposeful pose. "I think we need some sort of rubric, some sort of accepted criteria for our work in this class . . . or there would be chaos. We all can agree on at least that, can't we?"

Murmurs ripple across the room, a lovely, high-ceilinged address on the second floor of stately Sayles Hall, with dark wood paneling, aged to perfection, narrow twelve-foot windows, and twenty students in Fieldwork and Seminar in High School Education who are just limbering up.

The issue du jour involves "rubrics," or how the format of an assignment can favor the strengths of some students and highlight the weaknesses of others or, in any event, how it can stifle creativity. The subject, discussed theoretically in previous classes, has circled around to delicious relevance on this early March Monday's discussion of the upcoming midterm paper. It is noted simply on the syllabus as "five pages, typed, double-spaced, on the topic of diversity in the classroom, using observations from each student's fieldwork."

Larry is certain of one thing: his winking suggestion that the syllabus line may just be a starting point, that the students may actually search for "some sort of criteria" that "we all can agree on" and have it stick, will mean a few minutes of edgy, vigorous discussion. He crosses his arms, leans his back against the chalkboard, and lets them have at it, winning a respite, after an hour of lecturing, to watch how various kids might connect educational theory to their passionately held views about grading and fairness.

"Why couldn't we, for instance, write a three-act play that deals with issues of diversity in the class we're observing," says a thin white boy, one of only three guys in the class.

"Well, let's not forget you have to include observations from your journal *and* some attendant analysis. But—a play—hmmmm, maybe," Larry shrugs, keeping it going as a girl near the far wall discusses various writing styles that might be "untraditional, yet, you know, appropriate."

As he watches, he gets the "this-is-what-I-came-to-Brown-for" rush. He knows he's an oddball around campus: a fifty-one-year-old assistant professor, nontenure track, whose appreciation of teaching on this hallowed academic ground is heightened by long years of deprivation, twenty-five, in fact, slogging through eleventh-grade biology classrooms and assistant principal jobs at public high schools.

Sure, there were years he loved it, especially the eleven years in Chapel Hill, where professors' children from the University of North Carolina mixed with a manageable minority, 20 percent or so, of black and Latino kids from the town's poorer sections.

Then it fell apart, all at once. His marriage of twenty-five years collapsed. That was the main thing. Unattached, with his kids already off to college, he followed the Chapel Hill principal to Cincinnati and spent a year as an assistant principal at a well-known magnet school in the city.

That's where he read an ad in *Education Week* magazine about three-year teaching stints at Brown, with possibility of renewal. High school teachers were encouraged to apply. Larry immediately realized that competition for the fellowships would be fierce, but, beyond being a damn good teacher, he had some reasons to be hopeful. He'd had Ted Sizer, Brown's famous education professor, back when he was getting his master's in education at Harvard in the late '60s; his mix of teaching and administrating might intrigue them; and he "presented" well, with his easy, affable manner, accessible good looks (much like the fatherly, gray-haired actor William Windom), and the slightly rumpled demeanor of a professor, all tweed and oxford cotton and rep ties. He looked like he belonged at a university. People always used to say that.

He's up for renewal for a second three-year stint in a few months. He looks at his watch—5:25—about five minutes left in today's class. Better rein it in. "I think the key element some of you are not considering is the issue of skills: that you're not only here to freely express yourself on a particular subject but also to build certain time-honored skills, like clear expository writing and analysis. That's a big part of what you need to be evaluated on."

The class quiets, considering this.

"I mean that doesn't work all that well for me," says Cedric. Larry looks over. Cedric and a Latino girl from modest, inner-city origins are the two students that most intrigue him in the class, kids who are now observing life at the kind of awful schools from which they sprung. "What do you mean it doesn't work for you, Cedric?" he says softly, trying to draw out Jennings, who doesn't talk much in class.

"I don't know," Cedric says after a moment. "It's just that the things I see at my junior high school get me so angry, so passionate, that it's hard to be all intellectual, or whatever, about it."

"Why don't you write a poem about it!?" chirps Leslie from across the room, as everyone, Cedric included, begins to laugh.

"Well," Larry says, checking his watch again, so they'll all know time is up. "I'll leave it this way: if anyone wants to propose a different rubric for this midterm paper, they need to clear it with me first. Otherwise, five pages, double-spaced. See you all next time."

On a Friday afternoon a few weeks later, Larry closes the door to his small office in the education building, sits back down at his desk chair, and gazes at the phone-book-sized stack of midterm papers. Best to just shut himself in and push through the grading, however long it takes. He promised he'd hand back all the papers on Monday. By dusk, after a few hours hunched over his desk, he's well over halfway done. Most of them are what he expected—kids lifting observations from their journals, mostly mentioning exchanges between the teachers and their students, then weaving in some footnoted passages about diversity or tracking from the three books they've had to read thus far in the semester. In a few papers, he sees an occasional bit of original analysis. He marks a B at the bottom of the paper before him, scribbles a few comments, and puts it in the completed stack.

He looks down at the next one. "Oh God," he laughs, a full page of verse. Actually, he realizes, flipping it over, two full pages. He turns back to the first page and looks to the top right—"Cedric L. Jennings."

Shaking his head, he lifts his red Flair pen and begins to read.

As I gaze into this rainbow of kids
I often wonder what nature will bid.
Girls embellished in jewelry and fads,
It's hard to distinguish them from the older lads,
Boys wear earrings, pants below the waist,
In society's eyes they're indeed a disgrace.
Although these kids are in their teen years,
many have had to shed grown-up tears.
Rape victims and welfare recipients are in this array,
sometimes they're the brightest in this display.
Yet, I can no longer glory in this beautiful rainbow,
the teachers are telling them that it's time to go.
They line up in their single files,
many saying good-bye to their pals,
And, as I look a while longer, I become confused.
What was supposed to be a rainbow has become misconstrued,
There was one line of kids, who each had books.
The others were only concerned with their looks.

When the talking finally stops, they began a long procession.
Will the teacher or the kid be giving the lesson?

Walking through the halls can lead to dismay.
"Just say no" is the slogan of the day.
There's a poster for each case, one on every wall;
Over there's the room where they dump them all.
Inside, problems from past and present cause distress.
Is it something the teachers are really able to address?
Teachers don't have time to analyze each dilemma,
so they group the kids with proscribed curricula.
These curricula are not based on intellectual ability,
instead they target students who lack behavioral stability.
It's not that easy for these kids to behave;
Many of them, teachers think, are headed for an early grave.
But does a kid's knowledge depend on his behavior,
or should he depend on the teacher as his savior.
To meet the needs of each kid is hard,
that doesn't mean they should be called "retard."

Larry looks up and rubs his eyes; page two still to go. Jesus, he mulls, it's an epic poem. God knows he didn't expect this, but maybe he should have seen it coming. There were kids like Cedric, he recalls, at the magnet school in Cincinnati, a school that was about 60 percent white, 40 percent black. Plenty of the black kids arrived there from toxic inner-city junior high schools and were creatively gifted but short of basic skills. He used to see poems a little like this—verses, raps, or whatever—from the kids who could no more step back from the fiery elements of their poverty and blackness than some Vietnam combat vets could from the war. Everything was passed through the stark prism of their experiences and they just bled onto the page—sometimes awkwardly and, God knows, far from iambic pentameter—but often with a stunning inventiveness. Not that anyone expected their insightful effusions to take them very far; not, the joke was, until they included sections for poetry writing and personal testimony on the SATs. How,

he wonders, did this Jennings kid manage to get to Brown? He flips to
the second page:

For teachers, hostility is not on the prescribed diet,
but hope will keep the kids from causing a riot.
Calling kids stupid is not the right way to go;
this will stop the continuous educational flow.
These kids are brighter than the teachers think.
Some can audit someone's taxes in just a blink,
Instead their minds are deteriorating with their kind,
leaving educators in an ever tightening bind.
These kids are crying out for attention.
The answer is not always found in detention.
So, will grouping them in sections solve the mystery?
The answer may be obtained by looking at each kid's history.
Their minds are eager, can't you see,
these kids are yearning for real diversity.
But teachers are always telling kids, "no you can't,"
So the kids end up fighting and darken their chants.
They want to be challenged, but their brains slip into ease,
withholding their knowledge is like being a big tease.
All this yields is a lack of respect.
Homogeneous grouping may be the prime suspect.

I must admit I'm not pleased with this picture,
Nor the time it's taking for this painting to configure.
But a true artist must possess patience.
Developing new ideas for his latest creations
Yes, red, yellow, and orange will do,
But there's something still missing to create the perfect view.
Always looking at same hues is really no fun,
Maybe I'll just let the colors run.
This is, indeed, a great idea:
This mixture will be named the picture of the year.

With others I won't conform, to prove my expertise
My God, have I created a masterpiece?

On Monday afternoon, Larry waits until the last moment to pass out the midterm papers, not wanting the kids to be looking at them during class. He hands back Cedric's without any marks or a grade. As the class sifts out, the student comes forward.

"Why don't you come by and see me in my office and we'll talk about your paper," Larry says, making sure his tone is upbeat. "My office hours are three to five on Thursday afternoon."

Cedric stands there, stricken, holding the paper out in front of him like a burnt offering Larry might still, somehow, accept. "Don't worry, Cedric, it's nothing bad," Larry says finally, and then watches ruefully as the student slips out.

Over the next three days, Larry finds that the "poem predicament," as he dubbed it to a colleague, is regularly floating to the surface of his thoughts, making him reflective about his role as an educator, his twisting career, even his late '60s stint in the Peace Corps in Colombia, South America. He remembers how wise some of those so-called primitive villagers were, people that he, a pink-skinned young man from Harvard, was sent to help.

Sitting in his office on Thursday afternoon, he knows he needs to arrive at some decision and unearths the basic boilerplate of his role as a college professor. The rules are clear: it was a passionate, evocative poem, maybe even brilliant, but not the assignment. Yes, someone in class made a light-hearted comment about writing a poem, but he clearly stated that anyone wanting to alter the assignment needed to get it cleared first. This effort utterly disregarded the assignment. That means a C or maybe even an F. He chews on this prospect for a moment and looks to shore it up, meditating that the upholding of accepted academic standards is precisely what enables institutions like Brown to offer a diploma that has meaning, a seal showing that the recipients can master valuable skills of reasoned discourse, of deduction, exposition, and logical thinking, abilities that will help them to approach any subject, no matter how foreign, throughout their lives.

He sits for a few moments, trying to get comfortable in this posture. There's a knock on his open door. "Cedric, come in," he says, rising, and the student sits on the edge of the office's only other chair. "You know, I've thought a lot about your paper in the past couple of days," Larry opens, warming up.

"You didn't like the poem, did you?" Cedric suddenly elbows in, swallowing the last word. Larry's planned monologue is disrupted, and he discards it. "Actually, Cedric," he says softly, "I loved it. I was moved by it."

A pursed smile, almost like relief, crosses Cedric's face, and he and Larry just look at each other for a moment. The room seems warm and very quiet, and Larry, after such a long, bumpy journey to this place, suddenly feels younger and more trusting than experience should allow.

"I'm going to give you a B," he says haltingly. "But you have to understand two things. Your final research paper, which has to be according to the assignment, may carry more weight than normal in your overall grade."

Cedric nods, saying nothing, waiting for the second thing. Larry looks out the window, wanting to get it just right. "If you're going to make it here, Cedric, you'll have to find some distance from yourself and all you've been through," he says after a moment, as he leans forward, making sure their eyes meet. "The key, I think, is to put your outrage in a place where you can get at it when you need to, but not have it bubble up so much, especially when you're asked to embrace new ideas or explain what you observe to people who share none of your experiences." He stops, sensing this may be futile. "Maybe I'm not making myself clear."

"No, no, you are," Cedric says, with an eagerness that startles the teacher. "I'm understanding more about that all the time. I really am."

And Larry Wakeford, watching him go, is surprised to feel his reasonable doubts about this student's future begin to lift.

13

A PLACE
UP AHEAD

Cedric looks down at his copy of the poem and then passes it across his cluttered desktop to Zayd, who's sitting in Rob's wooden chair.

"Tell, me what do you think, I mean which parts you like the best or whatever," Cedric says as he watches Zayd begin to read.

They're talking again. Cedric was the one who broke the ice, calling Zayd one night last week, one dorm room phone to another. "You know who this is?"

And Zayd replied, "Well, I used to have a buddy who talked a little like you, whoever you are."

During the month of silence, Cedric missed having Zayd around, though he'd never tell him that. In fact, he doesn't want to come right out and tell Zayd lots of things he's realized lately, especially the nascent insights discovered from the writing of his wrenching sixty-eight-line poem. Cedric, of course, knew that the assignment was supposed to be a dispassionate analysis of diversity in the classroom, with examples and quotes and all that, and he tried writing such a paper. About eight times. But each start looked worse than the last, a bland paragraph or two that barely touched on the ferocious emotions that had been unearthed by his visits to Slater.

By early last week, forced into action on the night before the paper was due, some verses arrived in his head just like song lyrics sometimes do. It was just after midnight. With few alternatives, he began to fuss over opening lines and rhymes, trying to squeeze some concepts about tracking and homogeneous grouping into his own format. By 4 A.M., bleary, with lines sixty-seven and sixty-eight beginning to swim together, he finally slumped off to sleep. It wasn't until a few days later that Cedric read a copy in the clarity of day and realized that the poem was as much about his journey, his anger, and his regret as it was about the kids at Slater. Much of it, he recognized, might have been written for, and to, the kids at Ballou. That was mostly what he saw rereading it, that the poem was sort of a letter back to all of them, even his tormentors, telling them that he understood how, in the same way he needed to push against them, they needed to lash out at him.

But there was another thing he noticed: how a few lines spilled out about his own bottled-up yearnings that change occur more quickly than anyone could hope for, that he make it to a cool, easy place of acceptance he's sure that he's glimpsed up ahead. He wonders if Zayd can see it in there, too.

He looks over and clears his throat. Zayd has just finished reading. "It's great, Cedric. I mean it's poetry, really."

"So?" Cedric presses.

"So what?"

"So, which line did you like the best, which part, you know, really said something to you?"

Zayd looks down again at the paper, glances across the ridge of his furrowed brow at Cedric, then down again, clearly understanding that this is some sort of test. "That's easy," he says after a moment, offering a tense smile as he holds the paper up to read it precisely.

" 'Always looking at same hues is really no fun,/Maybe I'll just let the colors run.' " He throws the paper on the desk. " 'Let the colors run' . . . that's some very fine shit."

Cedric can't help but let out a little laugh. "All right," he grins. "That's my favorite part, too."

So it's settled. The next day, after lunch, they troll Thayer Street with an air of casual ease, like whatever prompted the rift was in some previous, forgotten stage of their friendship. But there has been a subtle change, an added attentiveness that strengthens their bond. At Sam Goody's they fence over the worth of various artists: "Funkmaster Flex, that's a '70s guy," Zayd says dismissively.

"Yeah, but he's got 'Busta Rhymes' and new stuff on here," Cedric retorts. And then they argue about some other singers—D'Angelo and Monica—and who's going in what direction on the *Billboard* chart. But there's not really an edge to it. It's like, Cedric thinks, they're both trying to figure something out—in this case, about their original lingua franca of music—and it doesn't matter who gets to the right answer first, or even if there is a right answer. Not that either one really has forgotten what happened. After Zayd lends Cedric $15 for a few mini-disk CDs, saying, "Listen, that's all the money I've got," Cedric remembers to say, "Thank you, Zayd . . . and don't worry, I can pay you back tomorrow."

"I'm not worried about anything," Zayd says with a casual nod.

It's a busy time, with midterms coming, followed by a week of spring break, and they pause on the corner near Goody's to break off. Nothing personal, just so much to do.

"I got to study for calculus," Cedric says, holding the bag of CDs. "We're doing integration series now."

"Oh God, I hate that—S1, F1—I did so bad in that in high school."

"Oh, right," Cedric says, prodding him. "Listen to you, 'I did so bad but I still got an A.' "

"No, actually, I got a B in calculus."

"I thought you told me you got straight A's in high school."

"Nope, one B."

Cedric laughs, "All right, then," and Zayd murmurs about some pressing reading to do for his media deconstruction class before they slap hands. "I'll talk to you in a little," Zayd says casually over his shoulder.

"Definitely!" Cedric calls back as he walks toward the Computer Science library, mulling over why it should now be odd to feel like Zayd's peer, his equal. And, after a moment, all that's left is to wonder what it was he was feeling before now.

There's an air of expectation in the psychology lecture hall as two hundred or so kids trod in, feeling none of their traditional lethargy. Last class, they were told that the first of two midterms will be coming back today.

Nothing focuses a collegiate mind like a returned test, the kind of numerical measurement of worthiness that is rarely repeated in later life. For the freshmen majority in this survey course, a new score will, in moments, be factored into each student's personal approval rating: a tracking poll on the issue of whether their acceptance to Brown was, in fact, some sort of terrible mistake.

"If I had them handed back in your sections, I could guarantee that half of you would forget to bring them to lecture," says Professor Wooten, nodding toward a table lined with boxes to his left. "So I've devised a system for you to get them right now." Students begin to file toward the stage. Graded tests are grouped alphabetically and placed in five boxes spaced across a wide table on the stage; lines form, and students quickly snatch their papers and return to their seats. Coming down the steps, stage left, Cedric glimpses down at his score, "30 percent, F," and almost trips. He feels dizzy.

Once everyone returns to their seats, Wooten rolls over his stand-up blackboard. "The highest grade was a 98," he says, writing the number in full-blooded sweeps of chalk. "And the lowest, I'm sorry to say, was a 30," and that goes up too, as Cedric, slumping in his seat, just stares at his score, huge, up on the board, as he feels nausea rising. An imprimatur of shame. Moments later, an Asian kid, pretending to ask Wooten a question, lets on that he got the 98, and Cedric glares at him, feeling homicidal urges. He decides right there that he has to switch this class to pass/fail—and passing will be a struggle. He must, simply must, get a higher score on the second midterm in a few weeks or he'll have to drop the class.

But he can't afford to, because he'll probably have to drop CS 22—Discrete Math. He decides to wait until after that class's midterm, but he's already reconciled himself to abandoning the course. It's just too much. Where he has killed himself on a few homework assignments he's done fine, proving to himself he can do the work. But, right now, his mathematical learning is not strong or diverse enough to compete, get a decent grade, and leave time for his other subjects.

Not everything is in crisis. Spanish, this semester like last, is a nonissue. It's a basic language course, taken pass/fail, and he'll easily pass. In the fieldwork seminar, meanwhile, he just has to be thinking of the final paper, still a long way off.

Gradually discovering some confidence in social interactions may be crucial to his sense of self-worth, but a companion measure of self-worth, the one tied to academic performance, will be tested in the coming week's midterms. This is survival.

As the campus library stacks and late-night eateries fill with midterm studiers, he stops by Discrete Math to pick up the take-home midterm. Walking back to the dorm, flipping the pages, he feels himself shudder: it's filled with cryptology, systems of decoding numbers for use in a computer, and esoteric mathematical proofs that seem to have no connection with anything tangible. He'd have to work a solid week on this to get an acceptable grade.

He flips the midterm into a wire wastebasket outside the cafeteria and the bold, five-class gambit folds with barely a whimper. It doesn't feel as bad as he thought, not like a retreat so much as a reasonable fallback position. Far different from the swallow-your-pride, lowered bar of the first semester, he decides a few minutes later over a bowl of ketchupy tomato soup. The five-class charge, he realizes, served a modest purpose: getting him off to a strong start in January. He felt like he was going for it, that he was as good as anyone, and maybe better, that he wouldn't accept limits or impose limits on himself out of some fear of failure. Sitting across from him at the cafeteria table is Evan Horowitz, the unit's math whiz whom Cedric has chatted with from time to time about Discrete Math. The guy, after all, is already working as a tutor in the computer science department. Cedric debates whether to tell him he's dropping the course but opts not to and is thankful that it doesn't come up as they make small talk.

He polishes the soup, gulps down a pancake-flat grilled cheese, grabs his tray, wishing Evan a sporting "lotsa luck" on his midterms, and slips out, feeling purposeful, focused, and a little short of breath. With his option of dropping one class now exercised, everything that remains must work out, starting with his forte, calculus, his big midterm test.

Any prepatory advantage he had in the subject has been lost, and he has been working increasingly harder as the semester has progressed. At least here, the effort is bearing dividends. This class has two midterms as well and, a few weeks ago, he scored a 94 on the first. He usually gets 100s on the weekly homework assignments and quizzes.

Last week, Peter Berman, the instructor, told the class they were going to do a project—an involved calculation from a several-pages-long word problem—instead of taking a second midterm, as originally planned. Cedric, who had already started studying for the second midterm, complained. He'd prefer a test, he told Berman, to a long, labor-intensive calculus project. The instructor agreed to let him take the midterm from a section that meets at the same time a few doors away.

Now, with that test two days away, the crunch is on. Arriving back at his room, Cedric packs items into his bookbag like a survivalist bound for the woods—his black calculus loose-leaf notebook, with color-coded pages of notes and carefully filed quizzes and homework; *Schaum's Outline Series,* a college-level cram book; his Texas Instruments TI-82, with graphing function; a pack of fresh pencils in the bookbag's front pouch; and the glossy, hard-covered *Calculus,* a thick tome of 480 pages (most of them untrammeled at this point). The text, a painful $89.90 at the Brown bookstore, is required for the course. Some other math professors at Brown have murmured that it's dense and pedantic almost to the point of being unusable or, as Berman warned some students, "definitely not self-serve."

Nonetheless, Cedric shoves it in his bookbag, at this point straining at the seams, and then pivots toward the shelves above his bed, snatching an ancient, battered favorite from the row of spines. He looks at it, pursing his lips into a thin line, and runs his hand across the wobbly cover—*Theory and Problems of Differential and Integral Calculus.* He sits on the tightly made bed and flips through the book. It's beaten to hell, for sure, but concise and accessible, with bold headings, simple prose, and everything lined up in a perfectly logical procession. He bought it at the Indian Head Thrift Store, down the street from Ballou, just before he left last August. Cost $1.04, including tax.

He flips forward to the chapter on series, an odd digression from the mostly tangible issues of calculus dealing with force or velocity or the trajectory of objects as they bump and bounce through the world. Series, the subject of the midterm and an area virtually never taught in any depth before college, are different, representing a systematic way of getting a numerical value by successive approximations, getting as close as you need to get but not necessarily arriving at a definitive answer. Looking up from that definition, Cedric frowns. He remembers reading this page in the fall. He sometimes does that—just reads ahead in this book to areas he hasn't yet covered in class. Tries to figure them out himself, like in the old, solitary days, and it relaxes him, making him feel he's shoring up defenses. He remembers reading this and thinking then, like now, how his attraction to math has always sprung from its conclusiveness, the way you could, on your own, get to a lone, irrefutable answer—something no one could take away—and how this series stuff is something else, how it's all about just getting close. "Just an approximation," he murmurs as he wedges the old book into his yawning bookbag and makes for the door, wondering about whether a particularly secluded carrel is free in the Rockefeller Library stacks. "Just getting close. What the hell good is that?"

After two days of junk food and little sleep, Cedric wanders into his regular Wednesday morning calculus session. It's a few minutes early; only Berman is there. "Cedric?" he says, looking up from some work at the front table. "I thought you'd be taking the midterm now with Mr. Chin. His class meets around the corner."

Cedric looks ashen. "I'm scared," he says, managing the miserable words with a weak smile. "I mean, I'm nervous. I want to do well so badly. I need to." There's no way he can describe to Berman his unfolding vision of dire warfare—the surrender in CS 22, the imminent rout in psychology, the searing issues that seem to envelop him in education—and how, studying maniacally over forty-eight hours, he felt like he was preparing for a titanic assault on his last stronghold. He knows crippling doubt is on the march. He must turn it back. A draw is not enough. It needs to be a clean victory. Cedric clears his throat, recovering a modicum of poise. "You know, this stuff is tricky, and I'm thinking I should have just stuck with the project . . ."

Berman, an awkward, high-strung guy with gaze aversion, comes out from behind the table. "Listen, just do your best," he says, looking past Cedric at the wall under the clock. "I mean, I'm sure you'll be fine, so don't worry. I mean, just don't worry." Cedric looks at him for a moment—how small and nervous he seems—and then nods glumly. No sanctuary to be found here.

In a moment, he enters a classroom in an adjacent hallway and takes a packet of six stapled pages from a table near the blackboard. Kids are already toiling away—same kind of crowd as in his class—and Cedric finds a desk near the wall.

He looks at the clock: 10:06. He has until 10:50. Five questions. Speed is important, and the first one is cake, a straightforward, "evaluate the limit" question. The next two, though, are ticklish—one dealing with various series equations and whether their functions would converge or diverge; on the other, he needs to locate the power series in two functions.

He flips to question four, his hand sweaty and cramping, and reads it with astonishment: "Find the 2nd degree Taylor polynomial and the remainder at A = 0 for the function $f(x) = 3(x + 1)$." His head jerks up. Berman's barely mentioned Taylor polynomials in his class. This calculus section must be a little ahead of his. He thinks about getting up to mention it to Mr. Chin, but he's left the room for a moment. A clean miss of one whole question will at best mean a cliffhanging B, and most likely a C or worse. He closes his eyes and takes a deep breath. No turning back, no plea for mercy. After a moment, something starts to take shape. That's right, last fall he read a few pages about this in his thrift-store book. While the series, with its system of approximations, closes you in on the actual answer but never gets you there, the Taylor polynomial is a way of figuring out how far you still have to go. He remembers that—he remembers how he liked that idea, that at least you can come out with a number, a remainder, a measurement of the distance yet to travel to the answer. He opens his eyes and bends forward, his pencil racing through a line of $f(x)$ functions, until the clenched muscle of his jaw line loosens to make way for an admiring smile.

The next day is Thursday. Tomorrow he leaves to go home for a week of spring break. He must know the outcome. He spends the day refiguring the problems from memory, racing through functions and equations, looking for his errors and convincing himself that he made several large blunders. He calls Berman three times before he finally picks up.

"Professor Berman, can I still do the project because I think I did really poorly on the exam?" Cedric implores, trying not to make it sound like a plea.

"Let's just wait and get the exam back and see the results," Berman says. "It's not even graded yet."

On Friday morning, he buys an Amtrak ticket for that night's sleeper to Washington and trundles off to Calculus. Berman is off on a new lesson about some tricky integration, but Cedric can hardly hear him, feeling the breath enter and leave his lungs, looking up every minute or two at the pitiless clock. The class ends, and he sits frozen at the desk, waiting for the last kid to straggle out.

They're alone. "I got your exam back," Berman says, looking at Cedric, then quickly away. Cedric rises with a grunt.

"I think you did a little better than you think you did," he says, facing a far wall.

"I figured I failed, so I guess that'd be a D," Cedric mumbles as he floats forward, unaware of his feet.

Berman looks intently at him as he thrusts the test forward.

Cedric spins it in his hand and looks at the cover page's grid:

Problem   Score

#1   15
#2   19
#3   20
#4   20
#5   24

_____

TOTAL   98

His jaw goes slack. "OH MY GAWWWD! A 98. HOW DID I DO THAT?"

He looks up at Berman in astonishment. "That thing you did on the Taylor polynomial question—we hadn't really done that in class—and you somehow figured it out on your own," the teacher says, looking at Cedric reverently. "Just amazing."

Cedric just shakes his head, speechless, and slowly raises his arms toward the drop ceiling, paper clutched in one hand, his eyes closed.

"Sweet Jesus," he whispers. "Take me home."

Cedric looks in his dorm room mirror as he's meticulously dressing on an evening in early April and thinks for a moment about home.

Spring break was last week—the final week in March—but it's already slipped into idle, indistinct memory . . . mostly of sleep. Arriving home, he was simply exhausted, wrung out from tension as much as actual exertion and ready to pass a few days doing nothing. Church services on either end framed the intervening spread of inertia—a few phone calls, an outing to a mall in Silver Spring, some psychology reading for the class's dreaded second midterm in April, and plenty of TV. Barbara gets cable and Cedric doesn't. So there was lots of catching up to do.

His mother seemed glum and pensive. Slipping on a long-sleeve gray shirt, he remembers that he saw a late payment notice of some kind on the dining room table. But she's been getting them for years. He steps back and examines himself in the mirror, stands up straight, and smiles, showing off his perfect teeth. As ready as he'll ever be.

It takes a while, at least a half-hour, for him and Chiniqua to really get comfortable. It seems, in fact, like the farther they get from the dorm, the more at ease they grow. And eventually they end up a hearty half-mile from campus at a midrung shopping plaza on College Hill's west fringe. It's a place rarely frequented by Brown kids, who tend to stick to Thayer Street, where every establishment (no matter if it's the sparkling, two-story Gap or the splintery Hole-in-the-Wall Records and Tapes) carries a gleam of college-townness in decor and demeanor.

This place is different. "No one can say I don't take you out nice," he says as they cross the parking lot toward Coconuts, the record, tape, and CD store.

"Oh, we doing it all right. . . . Hey Cedric, let me make my stop in Popular Club first, real quick."

And they do, him holding open the double door as she passes inside the bland storefront, giving him a chance to look her over inconspicuously: all cute and casual in her tight blue faded jeans, black low-heel boots with a delicate, pointed-toe, and an oversized BROWN sweatshirt under a black leather jacket, collar up. She'd bought some shoes here a few weeks ago, and hearing that they'd be coming this way, she brought them with her to return.

He likes that—her returning the shoes and all—so it's not like some big formal date or anything. If anyone asks, they can just say that Chiniqua was returning some shoes, then they decided to catch something to eat and a movie. No big deal. Considering that any hint of romance between the only two blacks in the unit would be the gossip sensation of the month, Cedric figures he might need a cover story.

It's crowded inside the store this late Friday afternoon, with women, mostly black, toting small children and picking up this item or that they've ordered before the weekend arrives. Phone-book-sized catalogs from Popular Club, a discount catalog merchandiser, are stacked in piles along the walls, and Cedric and Chiniqua each grab one. They flip through the pages of off-brand clothes, shoes, and household items as she waits for her number to be called. She points to a dress. "Uh-huh, you'd look mighty good in that," he says. They're both familiar with Popular Club, an establishment that has grown fast in inner cities by mugging the pose and product lines of nationally known chains that won't locate in low-income areas. Every bit as much as a soul-food restaurant or an A.M.E. Baptist church, this storefront is a branch office of home. Cedric, glancing up from his catalog as Chiniqua returns her shoes, notices that a spandex-clad woman about their age, holding a newborn and jerking the hand of a resistant toddler, is sizing her up from across the store, probably noticing Chiniqua's sweatshirt and wondering, he figures, *what's she doing here?*

He steps next to Chiniqua—just getting her credit slip at the return counter—and glares at the woman as he takes Chiniqua by the arm. "Come on, time we got going," he says, and leads her out and next door, where, in a moment, they're wandering contentedly through Coconuts, an even cozier realm than Popular Club, bumping along, shoulder to shoulder, through the ample CD selections of hip-hop, gospel, rap, and rhythm and blues. Even though the big tent of black music is a spot where folks of all races stop by nowadays, and even though the enthusiasms of hallmates like Zayd and Maura are, indeed, welcomed, it's understandable that the two black members of Unit 15 feel a bit proprietary about this fare. Moving through the rows of CDs, they gently feel around for a place to stake their claim, stopping, after a bit, at the white polyurethane divider marked Keith Sweat.

"You know, I grew up with this music," Cedric says, pulling out an old CD, *Make It Last Forever,* from the R&B pioneer whose best days are long past him.

"What year was all that?" she says, then answers herself "Oh yeah, it was fifth grade and all. I used to sing him all the time. Oh, I had a big crush."

"Wait, here it is," he says, flipping it to check the copyright. "It's 1987. Right, fifth grade."

"Like, no one in the unit knows anything about people like Keith Sweat," Chiniqua says, smiling. "It's kind of nice, you know. You have to be *real.* You have to have grown up with it like us, to really know it."

Cedric just smiles, and around the room they go, pulling up obscure CDs and humming songs and reminiscing. Chiniqua's urban upbringing, Cedric knows, was something of a departure from his. Her parents are working class—her father, a bus driver; her mom, a teacher's aide; her brother, a New York City cop. And the Inwood section of upper Manhattan where they live is a mixed neighborhood, predominantly blacks and Latinos, especially from the Dominican Republic (and a good bit of crime), but also a clinging minority of Irish and Italians and even a few Jews. But hovering over an old Bobby Brown CD, both of them can sing "Every Little Step" with the same lilts and dips they sang it with seven years ago.

"Right, this music is who we *is,*" Cedric says, puckering his lips and juking a step as he slips Bobby Brown back into its row.

"Who we *are*," Chiniqua says, smirking.

"Whatever," he mumbles, feeling a first, light breeze of self-consciousness about the right tone to affect—actually being on a date and all—but remembering to smile.

It is, clearly, a date. And it *is* just the two of them. Cedric has never really been on a college date (something he's ashamed of and would never admit), and he wants to make certain Chiniqua doesn't suspect it, never suspects that the protocols of how to act alone, with a woman, in this context, are all new to him.

So he drifts a few steps away from her, slipping into a gentle pimp roll, and roots through publicly available images about appropriate behavior for a fine and studly black man. Nearby, in the movie soundtrack aisle, a heavyset white guy with watery eyes and a long, mottled army jacket provides a foil. The guy mumbles, "You're gonna have a bad day . . . ," maybe to himself but in the general direction of Cedric, only five feet away across the jazz section divider.

"You don't know me," Cedric says, jutting out his jaw. "You don't *want* to know me."

This seems to encourage the army man, who bellows, "You're gonna have a bad day," and then faster, "You're gonna have a *very bad day*."

Cedric, leaning across John Coltrane and Miles Davis, shouts, "You don't know me so you better not mess with me!" with enough volume that even he's startled.

"Oh God," he hears Chiniqua from behind, "I don't want to get into this." He turns to see her retreat toward classical, plenty of confirmation that the tough black dude pose—taking no beef from no man, especially a white one—seems to work only in movies and music videos.

A second later, with his chest unpuffed and the manager already escorting the mottled army man out, he joins Chiniqua near Bach and tries to regain the ease of a few minutes ago, talking about wanting to buy R. Kelly's album *12-play*—a misguided conversational selection, he immediately realizes, because it's filled with explicit lyrics and sexual asides.

"Why you want all that nasty, confrontational stuff," Chiniqua sighs. "I'd never buy it. No way."

Cedric, wishing they could just talk again about Keith Sweat and fifth grade, summons some saving grace, shrugging, "Well, you gotta give a guy a chance," enough to compel from her a reluctant smile.

A half-hour later—past the Radio Shack, Staples, a local no-name supermarket, and down a long incline of parking lot—they settle into a booth at McDonald's. With Donald Korb's monthly check for $200 not due until mid-April, this is all Cedric can afford. But, like the low-rent shopping center, it seems to be just fine. He gets two quarter pounders, the second one for free because pickles were wrongly put on the first one (he *specifically* said no pickles).

"Tastes better when it's free," he quips, as he plucks off the pickles and glances up at Chiniqua quietly slipping one of her two cartons of chicken nuggets into her jacket pocket for later before cracking open the other one. They eat, not saying anything, and he wonders if she might be feeling funny about pocketing the nuggets, the kind of thing, he figures, she might not do around anyone, up here at least, but him.

"Why not, before the movie, we stop by the supermarket and pick up stuff," he says, his month full, "like drinks and candy and whatever, and sneak it in under our coats—you ever do that?"

She laughs lightly and seems relieved: "What? You do that stuff?"

"Oh, showaaaaah," he says, laughing. "Me being a real hustler and all." They both crack up, though Cedric stops so he can watch her laugh. He notices how her left ear is pierced three times for a silver hoop and two studs, and how the top stud has this cool blue dot in it. Yes, she looks good, he thinks, and tonight is going well, better than he imagined. Soon they're both hunched forward over the table, talking conspiratorially. They agree that a movie about the dorm would be called "Clique," and then Chiniqua does most of the talking, mentioning how lots of white kids in the unit go on ski trips together and how "it would be nice to try going skiing, I mean, black people like to ski, too."

Cedric listens intently. Chiniqua, after all, has had so many experiences with white kids that it boggles his mind. He nods as her monologue moves to how "even some freshmen and sophomores drive around in BMWs and Mercedes and Lexuses . . . but it doesn't bother me . . . I know it's just Daddy's money." She pauses, sipping her diet Coke. "I mean, I went to high school with kids who had cars like that. It don't mean nothing, deep down. They wished they had my grades."

She stops, suddenly seeming self-conscious. "What's wrong, what you looking at?"

"Your hair's different, it looks really good." Cedric notices she's actually blushing as she turns her head, offering a better look at her carefully spun rows of mini-dreads.

"Did it myself," she says softly, and Cedric feels warmth coming across the bolted-down table that makes him feel anxious and short of breath and, all in all, just fine. But also uncertain enough that he finds himself becoming boastful, talking about how many CDs he now has collected and his trip last semester to Boston.

"I was walking through Boston and I think some of the areas weren't so great, but being pretty big now and black and all, I wasn't scared. It was, you know, different."

Chiniqua distractedly dips her chicken nugget in the sweet and sour, letting him ramble on down this dead end, and then tries to change the subject—talking about going to MIT recently to visit some friends—prompting a final smooth-guy gambit from Cedric.

"Why didn't you ask me to go?" he asks, all smirky. "Damn, girl, we could have spent the weekend."

"Give me a break," Chiniqua counters impatiently. "I've asked you to go to about one thousand things. I can't figure you out . . . you never want to go!"

Cedric, his cards called, folds the suave-guy hand. "Yeah, you're right," he says gently. "Well, maybe I'm ready now."

As he says the words and sees Chiniqua's angry brow soften with understanding, he remembers something he thought about a month ago, about his being like a nocturnal animal, blinking in the light. He thinks of that a lot. And he realizes, as the two of them sit quietly, easily, not having to say anything, that his eyes may finally be adjusting.

The date spins swiftly forward, light and carefree. The movie, a Martin Lawrence vehicle called *A Thin Line Between Love and Hate,* is the story of how Martin, a womanizing, hip-hop brother, manages to seduce the wealthy, corporate executive (Lynn Whitfield), then betrays her and feels her titanic wrath. But, like so many "black" films of this era, the movie is full of code about dilemmas du jour over race and class, with Martin's down-to-earth, devil-may-care, ghetto scoundrel getting the stamp of black authenticity to highlight how Lynn Whitfield, with her college degrees, corporate status, flawless diction, and foolish desire for monogamous love, has really succeeded only in losing touch with her true black soul.

Of course, it's not until the lights come up that the encoded messages hit home, leaving Cedric and Chiniqua silent and contemplative as they journey back to campus. As he walks, Cedric is reminded of the "wanting to be white" taunts at Ballou, about the stereotyped notions that so many people hold (movies are certainly good at pointing up *those,* he mulls) and how far all that is from the real issues and interactions he's grappling with. A few blocks from the dorm, Chiniqua mentions another recent movie, *Waiting to Exhale,* which deals a little more subtly with some of the same race/class/ authenticity issues. Cedric says he saw the movie, too, and they discuss a scene where the married Wesley Snipes goes up to the hotel room of a single woman, played by Angela Bassett.

"Well, he's wrong. He shouldn't have been up there if they weren't married," Cedric says, reflexively, mimicking Barbara's zero-tolerance stance on premarital sex, which helped usher him through the urban minefield. "Shouldn't have even been in that damn hotel room."

Chiniqua looks at him quizzically. "Why not? They're both adults," she says, catching Cedric with a dizzying broadside as they cross onto the dorm's parking lot. His mouth goes dry. His mind races.

He just smiles wanly at her and reaches for the dorm's heavy exterior door, thankful, suddenly, to be back at East Andrews, where he and Chiniqua will certainly separate before they arrive on the second floor to, as always, meet everyone's prying eyes. Their evening, thereby, ends smoothly and naturally, giving him an out to consider what, in God's name, someone named Cedric Jennings does next!

What the hell is Rob up to, Cedric wonders as he glances over at his roommate—a vision of shabby prep in his torn khaki shorts, faded Marblehead Yacht Club T-shirt, and sandals—hovering near Cedric's CD player like he's looking for something.

"I really like this, I mean it's growing on me," Rob finally says, snapping his fingers. "Who is it?"

Cedric pushes aside his psychology textbook and looks over, astonished. "You like it?!" he laughs. "No lie?"

"Yeah. So . . . are you gonna tell me who it is or make me guess?"

"It's Hezekiah Walker and the Love Fellowship Crusade Choir. The song is called 'I'll Fly Away.' "

"I'll Fly Away," Rob says, nodding meaningfully as he turns to go. "It's, you know, great."

The door slams, and Cedric leans back in his chair, bemused, shaking his freshly shaven head. Rob has actually been borrowing some of Cedric's CDs lately, and Cedric is developing a passing interest in Alanis Morissette, one of Rob's favorites. Crazy.

April, he decides as he cranks Hezekiah a notch, is turning out to be his best month, even if it's only one week old. He's still daydreaming about his Friday night out with Chiniqua. Meanwhile, all's well with Zayd, who beat him last night in Supernintendo, on Cedric's TV, at that. Word is out that the marquee musical act for spring weekend in two weeks is the Fugees, so they joyously blasted the group's music in honor of the announcement and talked until late, first in Cedric's room and then in Zayd's. The fact that Zayd got their first CD last year, when they were unknown, combined with Cedric's casual aside last winter that he thought the group's curious mix of hip-hop and soul and rock was at best "derivative," gives Zayd bragging rights on having discovered them first. He's crowing over this small victory, something that would have irritated Cedric a few months back. But not so much anymore, Cedric muses, closing psychology for today and stretching some kinks out of his lower back. That Zayd gets straight A's and has pretty fair musical tastes doesn't intimidate Cedric anymore.

Everything seems to be getting easier. He recalls last semester, when whatever the other kids said or did, the way they acted and addressed him—or, for that matter, ignored him—felt like some form of slight. A judgment on his unworthiness. Cedric's not sure what, specifically, has changed, but actions and words, in the dorm or the cafeteria or the classroom, seem to carry less weight, less personal charge.

With dinnertime approaching on this Wednesday night, he picks up the phone near Rob's unkempt bed, dial's Zayd's number, and soon they're scarfing lasagna at a long table in the VeeDub.

Talk shifts to girls, and Cedric is delighted to finally have something to offer. Not wanting to disclose much about Chiniqua, even to Zayd, for fear everyone in the unit will be gabbing about it, he mentions another girl who's caught his attention, an Asian girl from psychology lab named Anna, who's "really fine," he tells Zayd. "I've talked with her a few times and I'm thinking about asking her out," he continues excitedly, before an admonition from Bishop Long suddenly echoes through his conscience. Searching for rebuttals on such issues, Cedric experiments with a head-on assault: "I don't know Zayd, you might say, she has one of those Coke bottle bodies." He gets a whoop from across the table.

Zayd, after suggesting various romantic tacks, brings up his own dilemma. He's met a girl—"smart as hell," cute, confident, blonde. "This one I really like. She's different."

Cedric puts down his fork, pauses thoughtfully, and takes a deliberative sip of Sprite. "This may be the one, Zayd. The one that's worth going slow, real slow, with. You know my advice. Don't try to sleep with her. Go out five, maybe six times, before you even think about it. Let a real relationship form, real respect, first. By then, you may find out that she's the one and you'll want to wait even longer."

Zayd smiles, and they high five above the dirty plates, hands meeting in the middle. "You may be right this time, C. Yeah, you may be right."

Spring, of course, is the season most suited to college life—to the budding senses of emerging adults, to the carefree promise of growth, to the far-from-home feeling of being unbound. Especially in universities of the north, where winters can come hard, the fit is so neat that it's even possible to believe that sun and warmth and soft grass possess transformative powers.

And Brown, in the mid-April lull between midterms and finals, is bursting with flora on the freshly cut main green and students convinced that they are, finally, at their best.

The university's officially designated party weekend, with at least one big-name musical act, starts on Thursday, April 18, with the following Friday beginning the reading period for final exams. But Spring Weekend also draws townies from Providence, along with kids from colleges in Rhode Island, Massachusetts, and other states along the East Coast, a crushing crowd of foreigners that alters Brown's social character. Instead, it's this weekend, April 12 and 13, that many students consider the true pinnacle of Brown partying, a weekend when all quarters of the university seem to be working furiously to entertain themselves, turning the campus into a vast progressive dinner party, with each house on the street serving a different dish.

At lunch after Friday calculus, Cedric picks at his macaroni and cheese with one hand and, with the other, a pile of 3-by-5-inch squares of colored paper: little, shove-in-your-pocket fliers that campus groups make to advertise events. Today the table is blanketed, making for good lunchtime reading.

The gays and lesbians are staging a weekend of parties, culminating in the "Vote Queer, Eat Dinner" fete on Sunday evening, called a town meeting, for "TNT, LGBTA, BITE, QUEST, Hi-T with Q, SORT, B'GLALA, RUQUS, and all other queer folks" to party and elect officers.

The Students of Caribbean Ancestry call one and all to their SOCA Cookup '96, because, a pink flier boasts, "Dis Food Nice!" while a nearby yellow flier shouts: "Celebrate Latino History Month with this Semester's LAST SPANISH HOUSE FIESTA!!! . . . Salsa! Merengue! Cumbia! Free Sangria, Beer and NON-ALCS!"

A white flier trumpets "A CAPPELLOOZA II," an a cappella

competition that Cedric knows lots of kids in the unit will be going to—Zayd's roommate, John Frank, will be singing with the Brown Derbies. Under it, a pale yellow one about tonight's Brown University Chamber Ensemble at Alumnae Hall. There are plenty more—bashes, Friday and Saturday, by fraternities and feminists and anyone else you can imagine—that Cedric glances at and dismisses as he rises with his tray.

The multicultural miasma, with its fixation on group identity and loyalty and authenticity, still unsettles him, though not quite as much as when he arrived last fall. Back then, he saw it solely in centrifugal terms, as something designed to distill and separate rather than unite. Now he knows it's more complicated. Walking back to the dorm, he thinks again of his date with Chiniqua, of them talking about Keith Sweat and laughing and reminiscing. There is an almost irresistible comfort to being with your own, being able to share what's common and familiar, to be with someone who really understands. Through high school, he spent so much energy trying to get away from people like him, and now he sometimes feels the opposite urge, the urge to finds others who are at least somewhat like him, which is really all the gays or the Latinos or the Asians are seeking. This morning, Chiniqua mentioned a blowout party tomorrow night at Harambee and Cedric considers, as he has ten times today, whether to go. He calls forth, also for the tenth time today, his one-line rebuttal: I didn't come to Brown to be with only black people. I've already done that.

Rob's in the room, and they talk amiably, still a welcome change after the long months of strife. Rob says he's staying in tonight—or at least has committed to—considering that he still "feels completely whipped" from "Funknight" at the Underground, Brown's student-run club. Cedric knows why Rob is mentioning the Underground. Last night, Cedric almost went with the regular Thursday night delegation from the unit. It was all very natural. Rob asked him to come along. Cedric said sure, and Rob nodded like it was no big deal, even though both of them knew it was. The Underground, especially on Thursdays, has been the unit's most regular haunt. Cedric has been asked to go dozens of times. He's always demurred and later heard stories of drunkenness and wild dancing. In one way or another, he's let people know, starting around September, that it's the last place someone who doesn't drink and doesn't dance (at least not in public) would want to be—precisely the sort of place, in fact, that Bishop Long and his mother have spent two decades warning him about.

Such warnings ultimately made their last stand in the line that formed last night outside the door of the dark, noisy subterranean cave, a line in which Cedric was standing—the last of six kids from the hall—and then suddenly wasn't.

"You were there, right behind me," Zeina Mobassaleh told him at breakfast this morning. "Then I turned around and you'd vanished."

The whole thing, already lore across the hall, was just plain embarrassing. Cedric, grateful Rob didn't directly razz him about it, rises to get a piece of Wrigley's spearmint gum from his desk and looks out the window, thinking it all through again and realizing how his stern, righteous solitude of last semester must have just looked like terror to everyone else, like someone afraid to join the world. Afraid, afraid of what?

Rob sends off some scatological e-mail to a high school friend at the University of Massachusetts and, swiveling in his desk chair, rosy with delight from his missive, asks Cedric if he's going to go to the "Sexual Assault and Spring Weekend" dorm outreach in a few days. " 'Cause, you know, it could be pretty interesting, how, without even knowing it, you can get into a bad situation."

He's just making conversation, but Cedric, desperate to shore up the miserable image of how he fled from the nightclub line, reaches for a cold bucket of rectitude, one of those discussion enders Barbara used to summon when dangerous issues arose.

"I think it's really simple with sex assault or whatever. It's like AIDS. You have sex one time, you can get AIDS, so you just don't do it. Same with sex assault: you don't try having sex, you won't have to worry about something like that happening."

Rob looks at him, clearly befuddled. "But, you can't go through life not trying anything. What's the point of that?" And Cedric, feeling suddenly transparent, folds with a glum, "Whatever."

His real response, for what it's worth, comes later that night, when Molly Olsen (the fast-morphing, once-bald modern dancer) knocks on his door, asking him to come with her to the Underground to see some local comedians. He shrugs. He's got nothing better to do, he says. It ends up being a cinch this time to just stroll in, so much easier than last night when he could feel all those kids from the unit wondering if he'd pull it off. He sits down at a table with her and his tall glass of ginger ale, dead center in a room filled mostly with white kids drinking watery beer, and waits for some expected discomfort to fade. Or rather, to arrive. After a few minutes and a second ginger ale, though, he realizes that nothing untoward is bound to happen, that, instead, he feels loose and sort of relaxed here with the always provocative Molly. And, soon enough, he's laughing at the comedians with everyone else, having completely forgotten to consider how he must look.

Just after noon on Saturday, Cedric rolls into a column of sunlight that has crept onto his pillow and stirs awake. Lying in bed, barely conscious, he tries to remember the swift-flowing sensations from the night before. After a few minutes, he settles on a hazy recollection of himself, sitting in the smoky nightclub, feet cleaving to the beer-sticky floor, head back, mouth foolishly open in a hoot, drunk coeds all around.

He snaps upright, trying to shake the image away. After a moment, he's surprised to find his thoughts racing backward to an in-class writing assignment on his first day of school last fall—a first-person autobiography in Wheelock's class. He started it: "Who is Cedric? I am a very ambitious and very religious person . . . ," but, sitting here, it seems to have been written with someone else's hand, someone he barely knows. Looking down at the hands resting on his thighs, he raises his palms to cover his eyes. "Who is Cedric?" he murmurs. "Who is Cedric?"

An hour later, he's walking briskly down an extension of Thayer Street, where the fashionable shops give way to low-rent housing, and then cuts left toward a working-class section of town. He needs to get away from the university, to clear his head, to get his bearings.

He has ventured a few times before to this part of Providence, just beyond Helaine's office and the Georgian brick homes of professors:

fifteen or so square blocks of turn-of-the-century row houses and squat apartments, broken by clusters of sole proprietorships, jewelers, drugstores, and barbers, in buildings charging modest rent. It's urban and threadbare and a little grimy. And, as he walks, he feels solemn but grounded, a little like he used to feel strolling Martin Luther King Avenue in Washington.

Just past a fenced park where some homeless men are splayed on wrought-iron chairs, is a boxy brick building, the Salvation Army's local headquarters. Cedric ducks into the store, lingering at the trash can full of scratched snow skis, then the one with tennis rackets, before losing himself in aisles of men's overcoats and plaid sport jackets, picking through them expertly. Eventually he emerges onto the street in a beige wool overcoat with a high, turned-up collar (a real '70s Superfly number, he thinks, for only $15) and struts eastward toward a few shops clustered around a pizza joint with some outdoor tables. The sun, spotty until now, breaks clear, so he buys a ginger ale and sits in the empty row of tables. Turning left, he catches his reflection in the plate glass window. "My God, I look like my father," he murmurs. The resemblance is unmistakable—especially in the coat—to the way Gilliam used to look, all slender and stylish, when Cedric was a kid.

The visage is both alluring and unnerving, but he indulges it, thinking of what Gilliam might be looking like these days (back at Lorton after a good long drink of freedom) and how difficult it will be to find solid work when he gets out, whenever that will be. He'll have to start a business or something, Cedric decides, because who would hire him? "I wouldn't," he mumbles to himself, and laughs hoarsely. He abandoned me at the start and then did it again and again, Cedric reflects, trying, with little success, to muster his customary rage on the subject. He wonders, instead, if his father is still doing drugs (Barbara once said there are plenty of drugs in jail) and whether the drugs make him sick.

He slips off the coat, flings it over the empty chair across from him, and roots around in his pants pocket. On a slip of paper he retrieves is scribbled 1-800-USA-FIND, an organization he saw on one of the shows (Sally or Montel, one of them). You send the organization $80 and they try to find a certain person you're looking for. When he jotted it down off the TV, he was thinking of Jamal McCall, his elementary school friend, his first real buddy, who left suddenly after a week at Jefferson. The whole matter is vexing. Here it is, his best month, a time when he's emerging and finally figuring some things out, and here he's thinking about going back to find Jamal. How bizarre, he thinks. But, looking at the number, he recalls again going to the porch on U Street, where Jamal lived, and cupping his hands on the cloudy window as he looked in at the vacant rooms. No word, no forwarding address, no good-bye. He shoves the paper back in his pocket, grabs the overcoat, and begins a meandering walk, here and there, stretching for hours. Just walking, trying to keep his bearings through unfamiliar streets, feeling edgy and contemplative and a little wild. At a mom and pop jeweler, he tries on some white gold rings he can't afford (a nice complement, though, to the pimp coat) and then, at a nearby corner, approaches a man idling at a red light in his cream Infiniti Q30.

"I love that car, how much does it cost?" Cedric asks, approaching the open driver's side window.

"Umm, about $55,000," sputters the man, a distinguished, white fiftyish guy with salt-and-pepper hair who then steps on it, as though he's worried Cedric's next request will be for the keys. Cedric just watches the rounded back end speed away.

"Wow," he murmurs, "got to have one of those someday."

As the afternoon wanes, he circles in a wide arc back toward campus. Reviewing his curious, searching day, he wonders about why he needed to get away on his own and reminisce. After a bit, a line pops into his head that he first heard in high school during one of the many black history months and then had to write an essay about at MIT. Hell, thinking back, he's probably used this quote in a half-dozen papers. It's one of those classics from W.E.B. DuBois, the black philosopher and critic, the one about the black man having no "true self-consciousness" but rather a "double-consciousness," which DuBois says is a "sense of always looking at one's self through the eyes of others, of measuring one's soul by the tape of a world that looks on in amused contempt and pity."

He chews on this for a while, turning it over in his head, and finds himself agreeing with the basic idea of blacks having a "double consciousness" but wondering if seeing yourself "through the eyes of others," which everyone, after all, does to some degree, means you can't also have a "true self-consciousness." He feels like he's getting one of those—a truer, clearer sense of himself—as he finally pushes forward out of his solitude and mistrust, through his thicket of fears and doubts. Part of that process, he figures, must include days like today, where he's forced to backtrack through a thrift shop of memories where, no doubt, some demons are hiding in the racks. Who knows, he mulls, maybe to slay those demons is the reason he has to keep going back.

He's getting close to Brown, only six or seven blocks ahead, and up to the left is the Eastside Market, an old, modestly priced independent supermarket, a rarity, that he's visited a few times to buy food.

Finals will start in a couple of weeks and he figures it's a good time to load up on provisions, cheap and bulky fare for when he gets hungry, studying late—something to sustain him in a pinch. Walking across the parking lot, he suddenly laughs loud, causing a passing lady to stare. What he really *needs:* Oodles of Noodles. A couple of packages. The dreaded Oodles (a staple to stave off starvation in the lean days of his youth, a dish he swore he'd never, ever buy when he grew up) are what he feels a sudden craving for. He may even down a bowl when he gets back to the dorm. Just thinking about it reminds him of one last thing he's worked hard *not* to think about lately, and he silently commits to calling his mother, whom he hasn't talked to since spring break.

Dinnertime is approaching, and East Andrews is bustling, everyone revving up for Saturday night. Cedric, striding through with his bag of groceries, feels curiously renewed from his journey, ready now for almost anything. Balancing the groceries on his knee, the coat on his arm, he grabs the pen dangling from Chiniqua's memo pad and writes, "Hey, what time's that party at Harambee tonight? Call me. Cedric."

The groceries are barely unpacked onto his closet shelves when the phone rings.

"Hello."

"Cedric? It's me, Clarence. I'm in Providence."

"Mr. Taylor?! What are you doing here?"

"I stopped through on my way to the marathon, you know in Boston. I'm so happy I got you."

They make a plan to meet, and Cedric hangs up, thoroughly astonished. What a day, past and present colliding, and now Clarence Taylor! Fifteen minutes later, on the far side of Brown's main green, he spots a white Cutlass Ciera and breaks into a trot.

"Cedric Jennings, as I live and breathe," the teacher shouts.

"Oh Gawwd. Mr. Taylor. I can't believe you're here," Cedric says, panting, and they hug, the student now towering over his old teacher.

"My oh my, you're really growing up, look at you," exults Mr. Taylor. Cedric has never seen Clarence in this context—sloppily casual in his hooded gray sweatshirt, jeans, and sandals with no socks, far from home and with his wife, who nods politely from the far side of the car.

After Clarence grills him a bit on academics and Cedric talks a little about his searching day, Clarence opens the car door. "I got something for you." He reaches into the back seat, behind the Styrofoam Gatorade cooler and a bag of pretzels and pulls out a Bible study magazine. "Here, I brought this."

Cedric looks at it blankly and says earnestly, "I'll read it as soon as I get back."

Clarence looks over at his wife and tells Cedric, "We're going to have to get going soon," but his visit wouldn't be complete without a recitation. He's been saving this one up.

Cedric smiles benignly as Clarence plunges into Romans, chapter 8, verse 35: "Whoooooo," he intones, "shall separate us from the love of Christ? Shall tribulation or distress, or persecution, or famine, or nakedness, or peril or sword? As it is written: 'For Your sake we are killed all day long; we are accounted as sheep for the slaughter.'" He pauses for dramatic effect, preparing the punchline. "'Yet in all these things we are more than conquerors through Him who loved us.'"

Nodding along with each verse, Cedric knows Mr. Taylor wants him to say something, something profound and scriptural. "Well, Mr. Taylor, you certainly got every word of that one from Romans right," Cedric says, mostly to fill the silence. "But, you know, I think I like it better when you get a few words wrong, like you used to." Clarence's expectant smile fades a bit, and Cedric says the thing that just dawned on him. "Remember when we were in your classroom that time, me and LaTisha, and she was busting me about putting all my faith in making it to the Ivy League, to a place I'd never seen, where I might not be welcomed? And you said that thing, remember? About faith, you know, how the substance of faith is a hope in the unseen. You botched it and all, but in a good way," he says as Clarence squints, trying to bring the memory into focus. But Cedric pushes forward—there's almost no one else he can tell this to. "Well, thing is, I always imagined the unseen as a place, a place I couldn't yet see, up ahead, where I'd be welcomed and accepted, just for who I am. And I still feel like it is a place, an imagined place, really, either here or somewhere else, that I'll get to someday. But first, you know, now I realize that there's work I need to do, too. I need to know—to really know—who I am, and accept who I am, deal with some of my own issues. That's got to come first, before I can expect other people to accept me. The good thing, though, is that it seems like I'm just now coming into focus to myself—you know, beginning to see myself more clearly."

Clarence looks at him tenderly, wanting, it seems, to second Cedric's insight. "The unseen may be a place in your heart," he says cheerily. "Well, God bless." They hug again, promise to write, and soon the Cutlass is on its way to Boston and Cedric is strolling buoyantly back toward the dorm. He discards the Bible magazine on a stoop on Brown's main green—maybe someone else needs it—and looks up, thinking he smells a coming rain.

The party at Harambee House is just getting under way at 10:15 when they arrive: Cedric, Chiniqua, and her black girlfriends from nearby hallways, Julia and Jodie, whom Cedric has gotten to know a bit. Cedric's outfit is distinctive—gray sweat pants, black Nikes, a plain white T-shirt peeking from under his beige coat, collar up, topped with a leather cap he bought with his mom on parents weekend. With the coat and hat, his '70s look is wildly inappropriate, as Julia told him it would be. Having finally gotten him to Harambee, Chiniqua, meanwhile, wants to make the most of it, poking at him playfully on the walk over about how there won't be anywhere in the party room to sit and how he'll just have to stand against the wall, like a statue, if he doesn't want to dance like everyone else. She knows he doesn't dance, at least not in public, and it would be a stunning added triumph if she could get him onto the floor.

The party's cover is $3 if you have your Brown ID. Chiniqua, dressed in a white lacy top and tight white slacks, goes in first, followed by Julia, with Cedric lagging behind because all he has is a $5 bill. It's so early, the guy at the door has almost no singles, so he tells Cedric it'll cost him five, unless he wants to come back a little later. Grimacing, Cedric mills about the Harambee lobby for a moment, and then tries again, this time arguing passionately, in a completely uncool display, for his $2 until the guy gives up the change.

Inside, the music is blasting, but the room is almost empty. Cedric, surprised to spot a lone white couch in a corner near the door, moves swiftly for it and settles in, glad to find a refuge with a good view. Chiniqua and Julia start dancing on the empty floor, watched by a few people, guys mostly, lining the walls. Chiniqua throws a beckoning look over at Cedric as she spins. He looks away. Dancing is one thing, but being the only guy in the middle of a nearly empty dance floor? Is she kidding? In a moment, though, Cedric's throat catches as two guys break from the wall and start dancing around the pair, encircling them until the girls eventually turn their backs on each other to face the boys. Cedric feels overmatched. By now, the floor is filling, and after a moment, Chiniqua and Julia are barely visible from his couch-potato perch.

Cedric watches the party unfold, feeling the room's pounding energy flow through him, while he tries to reconcile himself with crushing ineptness. There's no way he can compete in this realm, he decides, arching his neck to glimpse Chiniqua in the middle of the floor. He might as well be playing basketball with these guys (another thing he doesn't do, maybe because, way back, it was expected of him, just like dancing—he gradually thrived by sticking to what was *not* expected of a poor, black, drug dealer's son). God knows he paid a price for cutting his own solitary path, one he's still paying. But there's hope. He knows he's as coordinated as the next guy, and God knows he's musical. It will come, in time.

Tonight, though, sitting frozen on the couch in his pimp jacket and leather hat, he resigns himself to just watching, finally getting to see the mating dance up close, the real deal. By 11:30, the room is dense with bodies. Alpha Phi Alpha, a black fraternity, inducted new members earlier tonight, and the freshly minted brothers, most of them shirtless, charge the room with a raw physicality. Some other boys take off their shirts, too. There's no alcohol, but there doesn't need to be. Everyone seems intoxicated with the thumping music and muscle and clean sweat and girls in tight outfits—Cedric can't stop looking at some of them— touching and being touched as they spin on the packed floorboards.

He's finally able to watch it all, kids from nice homes and probably two-parent families wearing some of the same stuff he saw Head wearing three years ago, mugging styles and postures that spring from a bleak place none of them would ever dare visit. He starts to see some things more clearly. Like the suburban white kids who could afford to party and experiment in their safe realms, similar privileges were extended to these mostly middle-class blacks, who now can cherry pick some raucous ingredients from the black urban buffet to fire the mix.

What frightened Cedric about this place, what kept him away all year, went beyond a lifetime of admonitions from Bishop Long about black people ruinously giving in to temptation or Barbara's zero tolerance for alcohol and sexual indiscretion. Those dire warnings don't really seem to fit here, not with this crowd. No, it was intimidation— these kids intimidated the hell out of him! Even at a distance, even in theory, he was unnerved by the brew of black coolness and youthful achievement, a casual blend that almost mocks the brutal adolescent trade-offs he had to make to get here. He dealt with this crowd somewhat at MIT, black kids who say they're from New York though they live in Westchester County, black kids with bright futures who are as anxious to co-opt inner-city coolness as the white kids in the unit. The difference is that the black middle-class kids can really pull it off. He feared that, if he got close to Harambee, the undertow would be irresistible and his oaths about integration, about taking the toughest path, mixing with kids from all races and creeds, would give way to a separatist compromise. At Brown, that's the path of least resistance almost everyone takes. And where would that end? Cedric Jennings as a middle-class wanna-be, a poor imitation, trying to keep up with doctors' kids from good high schools who also happen to be black.

As midnight approaches, Chiniqua is gone, having vanished hours ago somewhere in the crowd. A smell of reefer drifts across the room. Cedric shakes his head, remembering the smell from Ballou's halls, from lost kids who seemed to rely on their pot for basic sustenance and sanity. He surveys the room, looking at the boys jiving in their Hilfiger shirts, all of them playing, dancing forward with an admirable light-footedness. But not him. Maybe someday, he muses, he'll have a son who will be like that. But, no, not him. Like going to the Underground with the white kids a few days ago, he finds that being here doesn't alter who he is, that he's becoming sure enough of himself that he can get right up close, feel the pulse, smell the air, see what there is to see, and not lose himself. He can stay or leave. He can decide, because now he knows what's here. The choices are all his.

A moment later he slips away from the din and out into the midnight air. A light drizzle is falling, and he feels settled and ready to sleep. There's so much to try but also plenty of time to move forward slowly and deliberately, to taste life judiciously, to savor it. He passes a beach party at one fraternity where they're playing "Can't Hurry Love" by the Supremes and a semiformal affair at another, where he glimpses couples dancing to "Copacabana" in a bluish light. From somewhere, probably an open dorm window, he hears salsa music and then walks by a silver van, called the Silver Truck, from which a long line of hungry kids, each having emerged from a different flavored party on the main quad, waits patiently, brought together by the universal craving for a late-night cheese-steak sub.

What a world, he laughs. What a world. And he removes his leather cap so he can feel the rain.

14

MEETING
the MAN

The final fitful month of the school year is an entropic period, when the usual glow from dorm lounges, late-night pizza parlors, and fraternity keg rooms steadily ionizes into free-floating panic and rushed preparations for final testing and departure. Very soon, the energy will escape completely, leaving Brown University empty, save for echoes, as the heat of summer arrives.

While upperclassmen understand all this, freshmen simply feel themselves dissolving, day to day, as they sprint, term paper in hand, by azaleas blooming on the main green or struggle to acquire a taste for coffee. The necessity, by April's end, is to have plotted a strategy for sophomore housing, and little cliques of two or three are now all set for off-campus apartments, multiroom Brown suites, or single rooms in the same dorm. Many of them will keep in touch with dormmates. Any upperclassman can tell you that. They'll bump into each other on the main green, maybe share a few meals in the cafeteria or grab neighboring desks on the opening day of a class next September. But by then everyone will have learned their introductory, adult lessons about how friends can return to being near strangers, how intimacy alone doesn't necessarily harden into a compound that lasts.

As the last month unfolds, the thirty-three students in Unit 15 root around for appropriate feelings and proper responses to onrushing events, starting with the final blowout weekend on April 19 and 20. While parties across campus jam to twice their usual size—accommodating interlopers from near and far—the kids of East Andrews, realizing suddenly how their days are numbered, try to recapture some of the rosy-cheeked spontaneity of last fall. They rove about in bands of fifteen or so—just like in September—gaping at the crowds and working hard to get drunk or high or both.

Cedric Jennings shows up for several parties and doesn't imbibe. Then he joins with nearly everyone in his unit for the weekend's high moment: a concert by the Fugees, a trio of middle-class black kids whose R&B/hip-hop/rock/reggae confection crossed from black to white audiences sometime back in February, pushing them toward the top of the charts.

It's the last of Cedric's memorable firsts (he's never been to a pop concert before) and a suitable capper to a springtime of exploration. He finally finds himself lost in a diverse crowd, swaying and singing in the front row next to Chiniqua. It's a moment without self-consciousness, where there are no distinctions, where what he loves is loved by everyone else, smart kids of all races from across the country. Swept up by the moment, Cedric falls in love with the Fugees' stunning lead singer, Lauryn Hill, an almond-eyed beauty who sings flawless reggae, jazzy hip-hop, and a lilting cover of Roberta Flack's "Killing Me Softly." She winks at this crowd; after all, she happens to be a sophomore at Columbia. Looking up at her on stage from the front row, feeling the audience tug and sway, Cedric realizes he hasn't felt so at home in a crowd since he was a kid at church.

All he has to do, ultimately, is join this crowd academically. It will take a strong finish. It will be a struggle. But he doesn't feel cowed by the challenge; he's ready to do whatever it takes, ready to clinch it with a show of force, feeling as though he's won a sort of conditional membership in the Brown community that he's desperate to make permanent.

He sits down one rainy Tuesday night in early May, the day before the beginning of reading period (a week when classes end or hold review sessions leading up to finals), mulling schedules and strategy. Spanish is cake; with a little studying, he'll easily pass the final and get a satisfactory for the course. With Cedric's calculus average in the high nineties, Berman told him a few weeks back that all he has to do to clinch an A is complete the project he'd forgone in March in favor of the midterm. Doesn't even have to take the final, but he will. He may well major in math and wants his average in the class to be conspicuously high.

Psychology, he knows, will be a battle, but at least he's made a passing grade a possibility. After scoring a 70 on his second midterm in early April, he went to Professor Wooten's office to plead for mercy. The professor, a distant character in the lecture, was warm and engaging up close. He invited Cedric in and gave him some valuable strategic tips, the sort of thing many other kids know walking in the door.

"Don't be a lecture-hall stenographer," he started. Instead, listen and take notes in outline form. The notes should be a guide to reading the thick textbook, highlighting only the sections with ideas mentioned in class. Once that's all done, carefully read each paragraph in those sections, listing the five key words in each paragraph on a separate study sheet. Use that last sheet for final cramming. Cedric nodded, grateful, and waited for something more. Wooten, like a lot of teachers of large, predominantly freshman, survey courses, is witness to heightened dropout rates for African American students.

Cedric knows such issues of racial attrition are subjects of debate on campus, and he looks intently at the professor, letting the silence hang, hoping for a break. Pass the final, Wooten finally says, and, based on "demonstrated progress," he'll pass Cedric in the course.

Running all that over in his head as he listens to the rain, Cedric thinks about how many paragraphs of his psych text he'll have to annotate and block out for cramming in the middle of next week. He marks it on his desktop calendar mat. He simply must pass.

Finally, there's the education fieldwork seminar—a ten-page term paper. His performance has been uneven: weak class participation with journal entries from Slater that were often disjointed, full of passionate rambling but little analysis, and the lukewarm B he received on the epic poem. That leaves him with a high C, thus far, a subpar grade for someone who's considering a double major in education. The final paper counts for 40 percent and could pull him up to a B.

He figures he might as well get started on the paper first and sprints across the campus, leaping puddles, to Rockefeller Library. He settles at a favorite carrel in the bowels of the huge building, an ancient wooden desk scrawled with clever graffiti, and spreads out three texts from the class alongside his Slater journal. Stacked near the cinder block wall are education texts and selections from library books on reserve.

He knows what he needs to do on this paper, which is supposed to connect the fieldwork with broader issues discussed in the class. He needs to get some distance from the subject, decide matters of context and theme, and then do it all justice with clean prose. He needs to make his points and then back it all up with something other than his personal perspective or experiences. He needs to be an intellectual rather than a preacher.

The library is warm and dry, an ideal place for retreat on a stormy night, and he smells the lemon wax floor polish, citrus clean, trapped in the airless subterrain of stale books and low-slung fluorescent lights. Other kids, all races and creeds, hunch forward in nearby cubbies, intently pressing down on notes and texts, anxious, for sure, but chipping away at their anxiety with steady exertion, just like he is. Cedric flips through a textbook filled with essays and studies about the collisions of race and equal education. Fiery issues he's lived through, he thinks, but, remember, he's only one person, one experience. He needs to look beyond himself.

After an hour of skimming and a few pages of notes, he hears a generator kick on somewhere inside the wall, and the passing sensation is like he's in a greenhouse, with all the potted students in this musty basement, groping just like he is, for the judicious heft of scholars.

He leans back in his chair and thinks back to one day last month, his last day at Slater. He said good-bye to Mr. Fleming, who turned out to be a pretty okay guy after all, and not a bad teacher, despite all the ugly things Cedric wrote in those early journal entries. It's a bad situation all around at Slater, and Fleming's gruffness, sometimes playful, sometimes serious, seems to get through to the kids. Cedric remembers he slipped out of the classroom and into the hallway, crowding up between periods as kids bustled toward the cafeteria. He lingered, moving slowly near the lockers so he could watch them all pass, and wondered whether he could pick a young Cedric Jennings out of this crowd. Could anyone? Fact is, there are probably lots of them—kids whose potential, whose spark, gets so dimmed by all the grime and despair that it's almost impossible to see. Just a few years, this and high school, when you can get to them, when you can nudge them onto a path that might well determine their course for the next fifty years. Near the exit, a Hispanic kid passed, sort of smiled at Cedric, then disappeared into the flow. No way of knowing, Cedric said to himself. No way of knowing.

He looks at the blank page and starts to write. "The first step is to agree that most people share the goal of true diversity, with many races competing freely and successfully. But everyone wanting the same thing doesn't tell us 'how'—how do we get there? How do we lift often poorly educated minorities to an equal footing in the classroom? How do we do this while respecting that being singled out for special attention—and often being 'tracked' into a lower educational rung—can result in crippling doubts about one's abilities?"

He appraises the paragraph and shrugs. Not all that bad. Not inspirational, but the goal here is not conversion. It's getting an A.

Rob Burton lies on the couch in the dorm lounge looking at his friend Caroline sprawled on a nearby chair. She's not his girlfriend. Just a friend who lives on a nearby hallway. She's petite, a brunette from Massachusetts, and smarter than shit. A girl he can really talk to.

"God, you look terrific, Rob," she says sarcastic but playful, looking into his bloodshot eyes. "So? Checking into the hospital after this?" He smiles ruefully. It's May 12, and his heavy schedule of taxing finals—mostly science classes—is almost over. They've been bears, biology in particular. His Dickens class turned out to be a bone cruncher as well, with a ten-page paper due yesterday. He'll be happy to come out with mostly B's, and at this point he feels like a somnambulist—barely conscious, shuffling across the finish line.

Caroline's eyes seem smoky, like she's thinking of something. "You know, Rob, if you and Cedric weren't roommates, I bet you'd have become friends," she says thoughtfully. "You're the kind of person that gets along with anybody."

He thinks on this a moment and sighs. "It's hard to think of any of that now," he says. "I'm leaving in two days. Whatever might have been, or might be next year, who knows? All I know is things have gotten pretty bad."

After a springtime of thaw, the last week with Cedric has turned ugly. Rob understands that it's an odd time as the unit dissolves, as people bump into each other with their glazed "outa here" looks and waxen smiles, and that Cedric, like everyone else, must be feeling a jumble of unruly emotions. But he didn't expect this—that he and Cedric, after bursts of headway, would slip back into deadlock and silence.

Not that he has time to focus on Cedric's behavior or much of anything short of that monster chemistry final tomorrow—his last. "Chemistry, my crucible," he murmurs, sitting up and bidding Caroline a brief adieu. He stops by his room to pick up books and notes for tonight's big push. The room, it turns out, is empty— Cedric's side, as usual, neat as a pin; his side, messier than it was a few weeks ago when he gave up efforts at spring cleaning. He throws his tastefully worn canvas bookbag on his unmade bed, checks for e-mail on his laptop, and then realizes he just passed by the sink without bothering to check its current condition.

The sink. It started with Rob shaving his beard last week and not cleaning up the little hairs. He was busy, exhausted. It happens. Cedric's response: mix in baby powder and Nivea. Rob, a few days later, added chocolate syrup. Cedric countered with hair shaved from his head and some kind of syrup. Each day one or the other adds a little personal marker.

Rob crosses the room and surveys the wreckage. The small, squarish basin might pass for abstract expressionism, Rob thinks, like Pollock or one of those guys, with the patterns of straight and curled hairs swirled under a chocolate glaze with threads of Nivea. It's a representative work, like he figures art should be, of two people who pass one another without words or eye contact but spend idle hours considering how to display their feelings with, say, a splash of condiment on white porcelain. God, he muses, they think about each other more when they're not talking than when they are. His mind wanders to ketchup. Yes, ketchup would be just right, he decides (makes a mental note to snag some little packets at his dinner break tonight), and then makes a beeline for a quiet corner of the library.

The next morning, Wednesday, he stops for a moment in the foyer of Metcalf Hall to catch his breath, letting the other kids pass him on their way into the auditorium, dense with tension about the chemistry final. He watches through the propped-open double door as the competition settles into the long wooden rows. It's not like he's even premed, like Chiniqua, whom he spots near the aisle, her birdlike arms akimbo, elbows out and pencil scribbling, with her face pressed close to the page. He wants to major in marine biology, something less frenetic and devouring than what his parents do. Not that any of it would excuse a middling score on this test. After all, he's Rob Burton, number two in his high school class, with a sister at Harvard and folks who excelled academically and always expected that he would, too. It was never a question. It was their presumption, in a way, but one he never needed to challenge because, deep down, it didn't really matter. If he failed, they'd still love him. He's sure of it, always has been. He takes a deep breath. Yes, of course, he'll do just fine. And no longer able to feel his heart thump, Rob casually walks the long aisle to get his test paper, his sandals clomping down the carpeted slope as he begins to feel loose all over.

That evening, halfway packed for his departure, he strolls down to Thayer Street to meet some friends for a beer at Cafe Paragon, feeling reflective and light-headed. Nursing a beer, unable to summon enough energy to get drunk, Rob finds himself recalling the year that has been "sort of surreal," a first year in this safe, Disneyland version of tolerance where he could stretch his perspectives and do a bit of experimenting.

Lifting the beer to his lips, he notices how good the dirt-brown bottle looks clasped under his electric-blue fingernails. A few kids on the hall did their nails earlier tonight, guys and girls both, after Sonya Garza found a bottle of this glittering stuff. A final, wild act. A little later, he sees a girl at a nearby table looking at his nails, and he smiles at her. He loves this, the reactions he's getting to his nails, how it makes people wonder, just a little, about ol' Rob Burton.

The next morning, he still has some packing to do when his father pulls up in the dusty blue Chevy Suburban 1500, one of the old ones, long as a hearse, built before they became the craze. Rob putters around, throwing things in hampers and boxes and casually saying farewells while Dr. Burton patiently mills about. Most people are leaving today—lots have left already—and a remaining cluster of Ira Volker, Florian Keil, and Billy Mosberg follow him here and there, like a Greek chorus. Rob is going to be a peer counselor in the freshman dorms next year, but he'll stay in touch with these guys. Standing in the hall with them, his dad checking his watch, Rob finds himself smiling dizzily. "I feel like Dorothy at the end of the *Wizard of Oz,*" he says finally, getting the laugh he needs to prompt a few closing hugs. He turns to his dad, who glances at Rob's nail polish—says nothing about it—and then slips outside to fire up the tightly packed Suburban. Rob says he'll be right out. He runs back into the room, thinking he may have left behind a fan but finds his side is barren—just a bare mattress, paper scraps, and dust balls. As he turns to leave, the sink glares at him one last time, and he pauses, remembering Cedric sitting on his bed earlier this morning while he awkwardly stood right about where he is now in the dead center of the room. He knew that his dad would pull up any minute and Cedric would soon be leaving for his calculus final. Rob cleared his throat, which made him feel stupid, and then waded in. "So, I guess this is it," he ventured tentatively, trying to affect a casual tone, like they'd last talked a moment before, rather than two long weeks. "You know, I'll be leaving and all this morning, so I may not see you." Cedric just looked down at his opened calculus book, not blinking. Rob remembers how, at that moment, his skin felt like it was on fire, how his mind grasped frantically for anything that would keep things from ending this way.

"Well, have good a summer, Cedric," he finally said, as though things were ending well, as they ought to. "Oh, and lots of luck on your calculus final. I'm sure you'll do great." And Rob Burton stood there for a hopeful moment, looking one last time at Cedric Jennings frozen on the bed, before he turned and walked out the door.

T hanks, Rob," Cedric had said softly as the heavy white oak slammed against its painted iron frame.

Did Rob hear him? Or did the words come too late and meet a shut door? Why had he sat there like a statue, while Rob made a final effort to reach out? Why couldn't he move?

Walking across campus late that afternoon, Rob now long gone, Cedric replays the scene over in his head for the umpteenth time, each replay ending with the "Thanks, Rob" and questions that he's sure will knot his gut over the summer.

It's not just the recollection of what Rob said and how Cedric failed to reciprocate that eats at him. There's also something his mother said. He finally called her three days ago, having not phoned for nearly a month. It was good to hear her voice, and they talked about his test schedule and when he'd be coming home before he got around to describing the strife with Rob. He could tell his mom was surprised. The last she'd heard over spring break was that they'd become friendly. As he rambled on about the sink and the silence, he could hear Barbara thinking across the phone line. At his first pause, she jumped in. "It's a test, Lavar, like I said a while back. But now I'm thinking that if you don't work this out with Rob, there will be another Rob right behind him. That's the way the Lord works. He keeps putting up the same test, until we get it right."

He mulls over Barbara's words for a moment, sitting in the late afternoon sunshine on the main green, drinking a ginger ale, and he finds his brow unknitting itself. Yes, she's right, and, yes, next fall, when they're no longer on top of each other, he'll make a point of reaching out to Rob. That woman's no fool, that's for sure.

When he gets back to his room, Zayd is at the door, looking hurried. It prompts a wide smile from Cedric.

"Cedric, I gotta go, my ride's here to the airport," Zayd presses in a loud whisper. He promises to call with his summer address as soon as he gets to Hollywood, where he's landed an internship at a film production company run by some friends of his parents. Cedric had thought he might have already left.

Zayd suddenly grins like a pirate and reaches out his long arms.

"Oh gaawd, no," Cedric wails as he tries to spin away.

"Come on, C, give me a hug," Zayd says, loving it, the cross-cultural frisson, throwing his arms around Cedric's shoulders.

"Damn, you white boys are so touchy," Cedric moans as Zayd squeezes harder and the two of them howl.

Zayd leaves, and Cedric smiles. A memory to hold on to. He putters around the empty room for a while, sees that the sun is still strong, and ambles back outside to lie on the clean lawn, blades of grass tickling his shaved head. He thinks about his calculus final this morning—leaving only that extra-credit project to finish before he leaves tomorrow—but it's only a moment's consideration as he drifts off, not caring a whit about who might see him sleeping out here.

Friday turns out to be a frantic day of packing. Twelve large boxes must be filled, taped, marked, and lugged over to the United Parcel Service office on campus. By the time he's done lifting the last box onto the counter scale, it's near dinnertime, only a few hours until the night sleeper departs for Washington.

Back at the dorm, it's eerily quiet, and he wanders through the humid hallway. At this point, the evening before the last day of finals, almost everyone is gone, and Cedric finds himself standing in front of his closed door, gazing at his memo pad. There's a message from Chiniqua, "I'll see YOU next year. Have a great summer," and, next to it, one from Molly Olsen, whose note beckons, "Hey, let's go dancing . . . Molly." Next year, he murmurs to himself, I'll dance.

Left with him are his beloved boom box (*that's* not going to UPS), a suitcase full of clothes, stuff that needs to be dry-cleaned, a plastic bag with some toiletries, and a new *Vibe* magazine for the train ride. With his white T-shirt and shorts soaked with sweat from lifting boxes on this warmish day, he showers and returns to the room in a towel, looking down at an outfit he'd set aside for the trip home. It's his last clean ensemble of garments, something he never wore at Brown: his Ballou High School Graduation T-shirt, with the blue and gold knight on the front and matching blue shorts. Maybe wore it once in nine months. He flips the shirt over and spreads it on the bed. On its back are three columns listing 220 seniors, just over half of whom actually graduated, in small type. He lets his mind wander across the names—Phillip Atkins, LaTisha Williams, James Davis, and then Cedric Jennings, a "professional name," he mulls, that he's growing into. He's finally close to feeling comfortable with that name, with himself and who he has become, and he feels a timely need to get back to Washington, to see what home looks like now that he can see so many things more clearly.

He slips on the shirt and shorts, calls a cab for the train station, and drags his stuff into the parking lot to wait, hoping, as he sits there on his suitcase, that the car doesn't come for a while, that this tingly, doubled-up sensation of both being and becoming might linger, that he could breathe this night's air forever.

It's already 82 degrees at ten o'clock on a Monday in mid-May, as Barbara Jennings settles into a fabric-covered office chair, her hands folded in her lap, inside the United Planning Organization office on Martin Luther King Avenue.

She was careful about her dress this morning. Not one of the new dresses she'd picked up this year, like the electric blue one she loves or that elegant black number with the hat that smoothes her figure and turns heads at church.

For this occasion, she opts for earnest sky blue, a simple one-piece with an ordinary rounded T-shirt collar. The shoes are low-heeled, black, and sensible.

She fidgets in the office's waiting area, rehearsing her lines. It's the type of place Barbara hates to picture herself in, a place for public assistance, for those who cannot conceal their need.

"We're very short on assistance money this month," says the smiling, businesslike woman at the UPO a few minutes later. "I can only offer you about $500."

Barbara nods, unable to speak. She was hoping for more, praying for more. The debt Barbara has been building since last December—groaning on a low shelf in her day-to-day thoughts for weeks—just collapsed onto her slouched shoulders. Obligations outstanding, including rent, court costs, and penalties: $2,790. It's not as though she hasn't been hustling to find a way to pay it. She has—making calls to aid agencies, thinking about what she can sell, checking if she can get some loans. This morning's meeting was a last chance.

"You can come by to pick up $491 tomorrow," the woman says, searching Barbara's face. "Is there something else?"

Barbara looks at her blankly. "No," she says in a faraway voice. "Nothing."

She leaves the office and takes a left onto V Street, pushing past a food stamp line that's beginning to wrap around the edge of a federal building's tinted windows. She begins counting her steps on the five-block walk to the apartment as a way to suppress panic.

When she arrives, panting and sweating from heat, she feels a tingling in her left side and slumps onto the white couch. The bathroom door is closed and the shower is on. Cedric has been home for three days, puttering around the apartment. His summer job doesn't start until next week. She can hear him singing "Killing Me Softly" over the drumming water. He seems so content, she thinks, oblivious to almost everything, even her.

Suddenly she shakes her head. What's she doing, sitting there. There's one more call she can make. She jumps up and dials a number for a Minister Borden, a Scripture Cathedral assistant pastor who does community work in this area. They talked a little last week—he didn't have any quick fixes—and Barbara kept it casual, saying she'll keep looking, wanting at that point to keep her troubles away from the church, a realm where her standing is so high.

She reaches him and goes through it all again. The direness of it all, with only two hours left, and the huge amount due. Borden is sympathetic but not particularly encouraging. "It's a lot of money, Barbara," he says, wondering if maybe he, himself, could borrow it from someone, sort of on her behalf. "I'll see what I can do," he tells her. "But, even if I can, I don't think there's enough time."

In a few minutes, creamed and brushed and slipping on a T-shirt, Cedric emerges from the bedroom.

"What are you doing home," he asks absently on his way to the refrigerator. "No work?"

She takes a deep breath. "I've failed you again," she says quietly.

"What?" he says, barely hearing, pouring some orange juice.

"I've let you down again, Lavar."

He puts down the glass. "What you saying?"

"We've got trouble. I fell behind, way behind and, umm. . . . You'll have to pack up your things. We're getting put out at one o'clock."

Everything halts. After a few seconds, he steps from the kitchen area into the well of the living room and glares at her. Barbara cannot meet his eye. Her own son, and she can't look at him. She looks down at her wrinkled hands.

"Put out?!" He seems disoriented, but a moment later he's clearly not. "So, how much?" Cedric says icily, in what sounds like someone else's voice. "How much is it . . . this time?"

"$2,790."

"Good God," he whispers. "How's that possible?" Barbara watches, standing there stunned. She gets up and calls Neddy at work. Neddy says she's calling the church, hangs up, and then calls back to tell Barbara that she'd just left a panicked message on the Scripture Cathedral answering machine.

"What happened, Ma?" Neddy starts in, and with each barbed question she unearths another corner of the debacle—the six months of back rent, the court hearing, the desperate attempts to cobble together a huge payment—as Cedric stomps in a circle nearby, picking up every syllable. Barbara finally tells Neddy about her conversation a few minutes ago with Minister Borden.

"He said he could do it all quietly. Thing is, I didn't want to call Bishop Long, call the church and have it all over church I was being put out," Barbara says, but now, with the hammer coming down in less than two hours, such concerns suddenly seem vain and foolish.

"Ma, me even calling the church now won't do no good. In any event, there's not enough time," Neddy says. She says she'll try to leave work. "I'll be over as soon as I can." Barbara hangs up, her hand shaking as she replaces the receiver.

"This is *really* the sin of pride," Cedric says, measuring each word.

"Too proud to tell you got a problem. Why didn't you tell anyone? I might have been able to help. Could have called Dr. Korb or something. Or taken from my $200 a month, or SOMETHIN'! Here I'm buying CDs and . . . oh my God, we are getting PUT OUT!"

"I didn't want to burden you with this," she says. "You had work to do."

"You don't tell me and Neddy nothing and then it blows up on ALL OF US!"

He sits on a dinette chair, head in his hands, and the yelling stops. As the minutes tick, both of them slip into hushed contemplation of their shared fate.

The silence is unbearable for Barbara, and she tries to reach out with something she wasn't going to tell him. "This has been terrible for me, Lavar, the stress," she says haltingly, and she describes how chest pains overcame her in the office last Thursday and half her body went numb. It's better that he knows. They sent her to the Agriculture Department medical office, where a doctor suggested she see a cardiologist. Cedric listens to this and nods, almost sorrowfully, then rises and slowly walks to his room. Barbara hears the lopsided double bed wheeze under his weight. Then she hears sniffling and wonders if she ever felt so low.

At 12:40 P.M., there's a knock on the door of Apartment 307. She answers it.

"Barbara Jennings?"

"Yes, that's me." A short, bald man with thick, freckled arms dangling from white cotton short sleeves is standing in the hallway. His tie knot is the size of a fist.

"Ma'am, my name is Steve Turner from the U.S. Marshall's Service and I'm here to evict you from these premises. You understand how this works?" He holds out a gold badge in a leather case, chest high, so she can't miss it.

Barbara swings herself back with the opening door as Turner leads in a procession of eight poorly dressed black men and a heavy woman about Barbara's age in an "I Love Coffee" T-shirt—the landlord's moving crew—all of whom pass inches from her without a glance. She feels outside of her body, underwater and moving in slow motion, but noticing every detail—the gun on Turner's hip, the cartoon of a steaming coffee cup on the woman's shirt, the dirty hands of the workmen, hands that are already being laid on all she owns.

"Let's get it out," the coffee woman yells as two grimy men hoist the white couch with the stitched irises. Barbara sits in a dinette chair and tries to get her bearings. She knows too well how the clock, which has been running for three months since the eviction order was first issued, continues to tick until all of the tenants' worldly goods are moved from the landlord's property to the closest public area, generally the nearest open spot of sidewalk. Once the removal is complete, the apartment door is locked, sealed—usually with heavy tape and various official, adhesive-backed notices—and the tenant, at that instant, no longer has a lease or any rights to live there. That's when the ticking stops.

But until that instant, the tenant can avert legal closure by coming up with whatever is owed. No guarantees, of course, that the stuff will be moved back in, but the lease remains in force.

Fifteen minutes pass. Barbara watches as one item after another is carried out the door. Finally, she looks over at Turner, just finishing a conversation with the work crew leader, and approaches him. "Excuse me, sir," she says meekly. "A minister from my church might be by with enough money to pay everything off."

He listens, asks her a few questions about who and what, then looks at his watch. "Okay guys, slow it down a little," he tells the crew as he turns his back on her and explains the scenario to a few guys just coming up the stairs. One of them rolls his eyes.

"It needs to be a cashier's check or cash, and be all there," says the coffee woman sharply. The movers slow, but not much. They want the dinette chair, so Barbara rises and begins to pace. A mover snatches the "Nothing Me and My God Can't Handle" sign as he passes out the door with a coffee table under his arm.

She feels hysteria rising and edges toward the large TV and stereo console cabinet near the hallway, leaning against it for balance.

"They say some minister may be coming with some money," one

workman says skeptically to another as he passes her and enters the short hallway toward Cedric's room. "Heard that one, plenty."

"There's no MAAAAYBE about it. He's coming!" Barbara turns. It's Cedric, emerging from his room and blocking the doorway. A wide-bodied workman in a torn black T-shirt steps up close to him. They're nose to nose.

"Reeeeeally now?"

"All I know is you're not coming in here," Cedric says, managing to keep his voice low and steady, his bony, wrecking-ball fist clenched. Cedric's frame, now six-foot-one and 190 pounds, proves to be a sufficient deterrent. "We'll be in there eventually," the mover sneers, turning away to roll up a carpet.

Barbara wanders out onto the patio. If Minister Borden comes, or if someone got Neddy's message at church, at least then she'll see him pull up. She holds the railing and looks down. On the sidewalk, the apartment's contents are piling like hourglass sand. A crowd is gathering. Everyone, soon, will feast on the misfortune. The Jennings family valuables will be carried off, nourishing other houses on the block with end tables and folding chairs, a VCR, a breakfront, her dishes. Turner's junior partner, a hulking redhead in a white marshall's uniform, stands by impassively. The grim protocol demands he guard the pile as it grows, so items aren't simply picked off as they hit the pavement, since Barbara and Cedric are still officially tenants. Once it's all outside, he and Turner will leave and the plundering will commence.

It's not that far to the pavement, and she can hear two dozen neighbors on V Street salivate over the inventory. A woman nudges close, looking at the throat of a shadeless lamp. "Hmmmmm," she says thoughtfully. "Is there a match to this?"

Turner comes out to check on matters. "No one touch or take *anything,* until the eviction is complete," he says, holding up his palms in a calming gesture. He looks hard at a cluster of hard-muscled young men assessing the weight of the white couch, and then he turns to his uniformed redhead. "They can run fast, but they can't outrun this," he quips, lovingly patting the 9-millimeter pistol on his hip.

Barbara looks away from the sickening scene, lifting her gaze to the lush maple that rises past her balcony. She thinks of the porch on 15th Street, where she stood so many days, hoping for more in this life, and she feels oddly still, past yearning, past giving and sacrifice and worry, like her life is passing through her.

She hears the door slam as Turner returns from the street. She wanders back inside to assure him, again, that the money's coming, but her heart's not really in it.

"All right, but even moving forward slowly, this is going to be over pretty soon," he says before borrowing her wall phone to call the U.S. Marshall's office and get his next address.

Three workmen are leaning their shoulders against the faux mahogany wall unit, slipping fingers underneath to lift, but someone is pushing through the apartment door.

"Am I in time?" blurts out a breathless man.

It's Minister Borden, panting, in a gray plaid suit, with a thumbnail-sized "I am a Positive Thinker" pin on his right lapel. "I got it right here." He thrusts forward a cashier's check for $2,750, and everyone instantly gathers in close, like they're huddling around a fire. It's made out to the U.S. Marshall's Service. No good, needs to be to Barac Realty, the coffee woman scolds. Borden says there's a bank around the corner, that he'll be right back, and he rushes for the door.

Barbara slumps against the wall, lets her head bang back against the painted plaster, and exhales through her closed eyes. Everything slips into reverse. Before racing off to redo the check, Borden talks to the coffee woman, saying he'll pay the work crew $80 if they move the stuff back in. Several movers snap out of their grim, steady movements and run downstairs to reclaim the furnishings.

Barbara hears shouting from outside and runs to the balcony. Down low, the crowd is crowing, seeing that today they'll be denied. "Hey, leave that shit," one man yells at two workmen lifting some chairs. "That ours."

Turner walks briskly to Cedric's room, Barbara close behind, asking him to go out and stand with the stuff. Barbara hears him say, "No, I'm not going out there. . . . I just can't." She's not about to force him, and she runs for the stairs, with Turner following her. Ascending rugs and strewn cushions pass by on her way down. Outside, Neddy arrives and hugs her mother. Barbara, having regained energy, grabs a chair to carry.

Minister Borden's gold Lincoln Town Car slaloms past two junked tow trucks and some strewn garbage to an open spot in front of the apartment's sloping front lawn. He has the reconfigured check. Turner looks at it, says, "Forty dollars short," and the minister ponies up a couple of twenties, sending the marshalls on their way.

But fifteen minutes later, as the last of the possessions are migrating upstairs, it becomes clear that those two twenties were intended for the workmen. Borden sheepishly offers $40—"I'm all tapped out"—and the head workman starts to yell.

"You motherfucker, I'll fuck you up," he says, grabbing a ballpeen hammer from the back of the work crew's Vista Cruiser and whacks a telephone pole near Borden's head. Neddy quickly offers up the $40, and, after more cursing, the work crew is gone.

The crowd has mostly dispersed. A lady asks Barbara for the cracked twenty-gallon fish tank. "Sure, whatever," she says. She picks up a pile of fashion magazines and a lone lamp and makes her way back up the crumbly concrete steps. Her apartment is in ruins, but it's still hers. Debts as big as ever, just that now she owes Minister Borden. Back inside, Neddy says she'll borrow $2,800 from her federal credit union to pay off the minister. "Together, Ma, you and I can pay off my loan a little at a time," Neddy says before she goes to talk to Cedric. He won't leave his room, and he won't talk to Barbara. He's frozen, mortified.

Barbara, standing in the hallway, not daring to follow Neddy into the bedroom, hears him say, "I don't belong here anymore, Neddy."

Barbara turns and walks out onto the balcony. Three floors below, the baking street looks wavy with heat. She remembers that some man in the mob of furniture rodents said it was the hottest May 20 in eighty-five years. Must be nearing 100, Barbara figures, feeling sweat run down her back. She thinks of the blistering words Cedric just spoke. Boy's right, of course. Then again, she doesn't belong here, either. Not that there's much chance of her ending up anywhere better. No, this is her spot, her street, and her role is to watch Lavar leave this place forever. It's what she worked so hard for, after all.

Down across the street, a burly fortyish man in an old-fashioned ribbed tank T-shirt emerges from a flat-faced brick apartment with a socket wrench and muscles open the hydrant. Two young boys, barely elementary schoolers, begin dancing in the knee-high cascade, one using his small Nike Air as a bucket, the other a Popeye's Fried Chicken cup from the gutter. She watches them playing for a moment. Over time, she thinks, they will be bruised, too, for having to pass their life here, seeing things, feeling things, worrying about things, that shouldn't be part of any kid's life. And Barbara watches the fresh water flow along V Street, cutting right at the corner toward Good Hope Road, getting hot and dirty.

Cedric stands in the entrance lobby of Lorton Correctional Institution, shoulders back, stretching the block letters of his Brown University T-shirt tight across his chest, and waits to be noticed.

The guard, a bull-necked Latino crew cut reading the *Washington Post* sports section in his lobby booth, spins the sign-in book on the Formica counter. "Sign," he says without looking up.

Five minutes later, after a pat-down frisk and four buzzing steel doors, Cedric lands on a green metal folding chair in a hallway. At Lorton, this is called a "special circumstance" visit, meaning a visit that's not during regular visiting hours. It's for lawyers mostly, who always book "specials," and family members of inmates who can manage to get someone in the warden's office on the phone and talk a good game, which is what Cedric did.

He looks around, pivoting this way and that. He seems to be in a honeycomb of offices and small visitation rooms. A woman appears in the hallway, murmurs something about the rooms being full, and directs Cedric to a folding chair in an empty office marked "Douglas Stimson, Warden."

"Where is he, the warden?" Cedric asks as she turns to leave. "Retired two weeks ago," she says from the side of her mouth, not turning. So, Cedric waits and tries to prepare himself. It's been three days since the near eviction, three days of jumbled emotions in which he hasn't spoken to his mother. Not a word. "We beefin'," he told Neddy yesterday on the phone. " 'Cause we ought to be beefin'."

He's not sure exactly why he's so angry at her, and he'd rather not think about it. All he knows is that Monday's trauma has left him feeling raw but cleansed, like he's shed a layer of skin. He's decided that, deep down, he had been feeling guilty for months now about not belonging in Southeast anymore, about leaving everyone behind. But watching through the venetian blinds as the mob picked over the couch he sat on and the table he ate on cured him of that. Burned that guilt right off. It made him angry, sure, but also clear that he needs to find his own way from here on.

The first big thing he decided was to come out here. He and his father haven't talked since last summer, and Cedric hasn't seen the old man in more than two years. It's something that has gnawed at him, that a whole side of his past is dark and indiscernible. Being nearly nineteen, maybe he ought to try to be more forgiving of the man's flaws, try to develop some sort of relationship. For so long, his father intimidated him. He seemed to toy with Cedric's exposed yearnings. A phone call or brief encounter would leave Cedric feeling wobbly and eruptive and kind of wild. But nothing seems to knock him reeling like that anymore. Now, it's different. Now he can finally get a few things off his chest, ask a few questions that have been bugging him, in some cases for years.

He gets up from the chair and noses around the barren office. He sees his reflection in a locked glass case with dusty trophies and starts doing jumping jacks to loosen up. Like he's preparing to engage an opponent.

When there's a knock on the white iron door frame, he turns, already standing. A black guard, wide as a Buick, pokes his head in. "Listen, you have twenty minutes with him," he says, and he steps back as Cedric Gilliam slips past him through the doorway.

Finally, it's just the two of them. "Well, well, Lavar," Cedric Sr. says with a head shuck and a "howdyado" wave. He angles across the room toward a smallish couch, avoiding a hug. "Damn, it's a surprise, you coming," he says, then sinks into a crease between brown vinyl cushions. "I didn't expect it. But, you know, it's real good to see you." Cedric, smiling broadly at his father, nods and returns to his folding chair.

"So, any girls up there at Brown yet?"

"Couple, maybe," Cedric says without skipping a beat. "Oh, I knew you'd ask that."

They both shake their heads and smirk. Gilliam, after all, has long demanded that manhood be proven through sexual conquest, and his son has always resisted, but the exchange, Cedric notices, carries no charge. He's starting to date now, he knows where he stands, and the challenge seems to bounce off him.

They chat amiably across a shin-high magazine table. His father's questions and comments carry more insight than he expected, well beyond the must-be-cold-up-there comments he gets from most family members.

"So, you know your grades yet?"

"No. Not yet. A few weeks still."

"How do you think you'll do? Good, I bet."

"Yeah, I think I might do all right this time."

"They got much grade inflation? I read about that somewhere, being a problem at colleges."

"Ummm, I guess. Haven't really thought about it, but, for my sake, I certainly hope so."

As they both laugh at this, Cedric studies his dad. He's certainly aged in the past two years. He's missing a few teeth, his hair is going a little gray. He seems shorter and heavier—got to be 220—and the blue two-piecer splits a little at his gut. He asks more about Cedric's classes, and then they talk about English and the humanities versus science and math. "That English training, you see, you can use in anything," Cedric Gilliam says, and goes on to explain how.

Cedric nods along to this, happy for a moment's cover in the conversation to collect his thoughts. This congenial tone bespeaks a change, no doubt about it. They're talking like peers, like man to man for the first time.

"Well then, there's something that I was wondering," Cedric

proceeds, betraying a little hesitancy. "Something I been wanting to ask you."

"Really? What."

"Yeah, ummm. Did you love my mother, or was it just a sex thing?"

His father shifts on the split of couch cushions. "Huh? What kind of question's that?"

"Something I figure I deserve to know. Well, did you? Did you love her?"

Cedric watches his father's left eye twitch and feels an unexpected surge—power or control, something—that he realizes he can sustain by not dropping his gaze, not looking away from hard things he must know.

"Ummm. Well, Lavar, you see I'm not much for talking about . . . for saying that sort of thing, using that word and all."

Cedric leans forward on his chair. "You mean *love*. The word *love*." With that, he pins the man to the couch.

There's silence. "That's right," Gilliam says, trying to muster some balance. "I'm just not the kind of man who can say those things."

"I suppose the key to being able to say it," Cedric presses, "is being able to feel it." He pauses and nods solemnly. "Just a sex thing, then. I guess I got my answer." Gilliam seems unable to find a place for his eyes and eventually gazes up at the white-cork drop ceiling.

Cedric, feeling smart and a little sad, mops up the mess. "Trouble saying it to me, too."

All Gilliam can muster is a shrug, still looking up at the white cork like someone underwater, searching for the surface. They sit for a while, not saying anything, while Cedric tries to decide where he'll fit pity into his mix of feelings about this aging, shrunken man.

After a bit, Gilliam perks up, like something's just come to him, like he's forgotten what they were just talking about. "I can't believe I didn't say nothing. I'm getting out tomorrow! I just got word last night."

Cedric smiles, happy for the silence to pass. "That's great," he says, and really means it. "Seems like about time you got out of here."

"I tell you Lavar, it's been a bad year—the worst. But they found me a spot in a real good drug treatment program." He talks on eagerly, reviewing how he was switched here to minimum security a few months ago from the miserable, dangerous Occuquan facility and how he's scheduled to live at least six months at the program's halfway house near Union Station.

The guard pokes his head back in. They both rise. He leads them through the labyrinth of buzzing doors toward the complex's entrance foyer and gives them some space for a last moment.

"Hey Lavar, thanks a lot for coming." His voice is raspy and grasping. Now, standing close, Gilliam looks Cedric up and down. "You got big, happened fast," his father mutters.

"Yeah, I guess," Cedric says, a little uncertain. "It's been good, I think, for us to talk, to, you know, really talk," he says, and it's unavoidably clear, there in the foyer's harsh light, that Cedric is now leading.

Gilliam glances over his shoulder at the guard, then back. "You know, I'll call you and all," he says, backpedaling inward and raising a farewell palm. "When I'm out, I'll call. If that's okay. I mean, I'd like to. We can get together."

Cedric, too, is treading backward, toward to the exit. "That'd be fine," he says, chuckling. "Yeah, whatever. See you whenever."

And with that he backs through the double glass doors, catching a final glimpse of his father disappearing into the gray steel.

A few steps onto the sun-sparkled blacktop, Cedric already feels himself trying to place some long volatile emotions, temporarily stabilized, in cold storage. Not such an awful guy, he thinks, turning his back on the prison. He squints at the bright green sweep of the Virginia hillside. "Not such an awful guy, really," he murmurs, and he's surprised at how good it feels to say it.

Cedric can't help but glance over at Barbara as he passes a few feet from the white couch. He detects that her eyes aren't making those little flecked, jerky movements that eyes do whenever someone's watching TV. She must be just staring at the screen to avoid looking at him.

He turns away quickly, before she changes her mind, grabs the *Billboard* from the chair, and takes it back to his room.

It has been more than two weeks since they've talked. And life has moved on. Besides visiting his father, Cedric started his summer job, an office gig with Fannie Mae, the federally backed mortgage banker, that's all ease and air-conditioning at $7.50 an hour. Not that the silence has been easy. He almost broke late last week after he got the envelope from Brown. Actually, she got it, with the rest of the mail, then left it—purposely, he's sure—on top of a pile on the dining room table and then went to her room. It was kind of late when he came out of his room to fix his dinner, from food he bought because they're each buying their own at this point. On the way back in, with a plate of day-old fried chicken balancing on top of a water glass, he saw the letter and snatched it with his free hand. How sweet it was to look at the unfolded, computerized grade sheet. An A in Calculus, B in Fieldwork and Seminar in High School Education, which means he must have gotten an A on the final paper. An S, for satisfactory, in Spanish and, praise God, an S in Psychology. Couldn't have passed that final exam by much, but a pass is a pass. Full membership in the Brown community, won fair and square.

Now, a week later, Cedric teepees the *Billboard* on his chest and looks up at the water-stained ceiling, hands behind his head. Keeping his grades from Barbara was hardest the night he got the letter, and it has gotten easier in the days since. Yes, she'd be happy to be told. And that's the point, he thinks. She can't live through him. She's got to start finding what makes her happy, to start living for herself. He's angry, and she damn well knows why. They've been through this before and now it's just tired. Her being the martyr. Her not taking care of herself. Her spending so much precious energy to hide her need. It's one thing to hide it from people at church, but from her own children? What, like we'd think less of her? Talk about not giving a person any credit!

So where does it end up? With a mother who's in debt up to her eyeballs, about to be put out, for God's sake. A woman, damn near fifty, who's under so much stress from not tending to herself and her own well-being that she's having chest pains. But has she seen a doctor like they told her to? 'Course not. Neddy told him last week that

Barbara said she has prayed over it and God will either take her or he won't. She loves saying that. Like he'll take her and put her out of her misery. And where, exactly, does that leave the rest of us?

He gets up, letting the magazine slide onto the parquet with a slap, and flips on the TV, searching for distraction. He'll watch it, he decides, until dawn if necessary, until every thought is cleaned from his head.

Nearly two weeks later, on a Thursday approaching mid-June, Cedric dresses early to go to church. He took the day off from work and bought some clothes, more office prudent than the flashy ones he bought last summer but still stylish, and he decides that they're right for today. Services don't start until 7:30, and he's scheduled a late afternoon meeting with Bishop Long. Cedric has been going to church irregularly and feels like he's there mostly out of obligation. Things have changed, and he needs to be straight with Bishop.

An hour later, he's sitting lightly on a red velour cushioned chair across a little round table from Long, getting past cordialities. They talk for a moment about Barbara. Word has gone around church about her woes. "I've had lot of experience with this sort of thing," Bishop Long says after a bit. "Some people get down and then they must rely on their faith to extricate them. And your mother is a woman of faith, pure faith, which means she'll eventually triumph over her difficulties."

Cedric, not sure of a response to such finality, talks for a bit about how ashamed he feels at church, worried that everyone knows, and Bishop Long offers a tsk-tsk smile. "Oh, come on now. You know plenty of people at Scripture have had troubles like your mom's having."

Long pauses.

"But, Cedric, I sense there's something else . . . ."

"You sure do know me by now," Cedric laughs, and then starts into a list of his doubts. "I still believe in God, that Jesus is my personal savior, and my friend, and my guide, but I just don't feel as tied to the church so much anymore. I like coming and all, but, at the same time, I feel like I'm ready to venture out." With each word, Cedric's ease seems to grow. These questions have been running through his head all year, he figures, and it feels good to finally let them out. He talks about how he's become more comfortable and confident at Brown, little by little, and how he's thinking lately about all the things he might try, all the avenues that suddenly seem to stretch before him. Bishop nods like he wants a for instance, and Cedric mentions how he's toyed with the idea of going into the music industry, "the real business side, sales, marketing, producing and whatever, to combine my math skills with my love of music."

Frustrated with his rambling about music and careers, Cedric feels an urge to be more clear, more succinct, to get to the underlying point. "The basic thing, Bishop Long, is that I feel I've outgrown the church."

Long sits forward, the shoulders of his pinstriped suit bunching up as he clasps his hands on the tabletop. He seems to be plotting out a response when something grabs him. "Most people don't ask my permission before they leave," he says with a husky laugh, and then settles into a whispery voice. "As long as you carry God with you, in your heart, you can go out into the world, Cedric, and you'll be fine. Just don't be too proud to let Him walk with you, to at least let Him be alongside you for those times when you will need Him."

Long looks at him hard, his one eye searching Cedric's face like he'll want to remember it later. "You'll always have a home here," he says, measuring the beat of his words. "And if you ever find yourself in need of love, you know you'll always be loved here. Loved for who you are rather than who people want you to be."

Cedric nods, surprised that hearing what he'd hoped to hear would feel like a kick in the chest. Long wants him to stay for the service, but Cedric—feeling like he wants to think over what the Bishop said—murmurs something noncommittal and then goes home.

On Sunday, he rises early and leaves the house. Barbara sleeps in, not going to Sunday worship—something she almost never misses. It's just as well, Cedric thinks. He feels a little uncomfortable about going to church, anyhow, and not having her with him makes it easier. He feels like he ought to show up to at least let Long know that he hasn't simply fled, that he'll be coming once in a while.

He gets to the church twenty minutes early. A few people are straggling in and offer their greetings as they make their way to the pews to chat quietly in clusters. Cedric, propping up a wall, sees one of his special people, Gloria Hobbs, the woman who first brought his mother to this church and one of Barbara's oldest friends. A moment later, they hug and slip into a long, empty row.

"I'm worried about my ma, that she's feeling bad and she just won't let anyone help her," Cedric says after a while.

"Oh, she's strong as she could be," Gloria replies. Cedric then mentions the chest pains and, to show just how worried he is, tells Gloria how he gets up every night to check if she's all right. He didn't want to mention that last part. "You won't tell her that I'm getting up or anything," he quickly adds, and Gloria, her features darkening with concern, assures him that she won't.

Early that morning, about three o'clock, he rises in the darkness and pads out to the living room. It's almost a full moon, and he easily sees Barbara's silhouette on the couch. Edging up close, he bends low and hears her soft breathing, making sure that it's regular and easy. Most nights, he gets quickly back to bed, but tonight he lingers, sitting cross-legged on the parquet floor. She looks fresh and young in the pale light, almost girlish, a soft-cheeked face that makes his anger feel misplaced. For so long, he thinks, he needed something to push against, to push himself forward. Except *she's* not something to rise above and leave behind. She's what got him this far. Give, give, give, her whole life, mostly to him, is part of what's left her hollowed out like this. But a person needs to learn how to receive once in a while. Yes, that's something she needs to learn. He silently uncoils to stand, reaches for the edge of her blanket, tangled near her waist, and pulls it gently to her shoulder.

A few evenings later, Cedric comes across his grade sheet sitting under a magazine on his night table and then roots around the apartment, looking for the pad on which he wrote down all the summer numbers from Brown. Maybe he'll call Zayd or maybe Chiniqua, just to talk. Sure, they'd talk about grades, but mostly he just wants to hear their voices. He's thought a lot about Brown lately and about his desire to get back to Providence. He figures that maybe next summer he'll just stay up there, get an apartment, a job, take some classes.

When he finally finds the pad, it's too late to call. He retires to his room, figuring he'll make calls tomorrow from the free phone at work. It's Thursday night, and he hears the door shut as Barbara comes back from prayer meeting. He doesn't hear anything for a moment but senses her presence in the hallway.

"Lavar? Are you ready to talk?" she says, standing in his doorway. Her voice is soft.

"I talked to Gloria tonight," she says, barely audible, as he pushes aside a magazine he was reading in bed and stands up. "You know, I don't want you to worry. I'm gonna be fine. I'm gonna take care of me now."

He steps a few feet toward her and sees that her eyes are moist. He wants to get the words out quickly, before he feels overwhelmed. He does, telling her, "You can't be the only one doing the caring. I'm strong enough to do some now, too."

It's the only thing he says before they embrace, all the tension of the past month, of not knowing how they ought to be with one another, spilling out in tears. His long arms squeeze tight around her, a big woman who doesn't need to be so damn big anymore.

EPILOGUE

In the fall of 1997, Cedric Jennings started his junior year at Brown University with a B average. He wasn't, quite yet, just another student passing through an Ivy League college. But, with each passing month, he grows closer to feeling inconspicuous at Brown and at once-foreign ports of American life.

Along the way, there have been a few stumbles on grades and episodes of social uncertainty, but they lack the intensity and confusion of the first year's treacherous encounters with the unfamiliar. Now in the winter of 1998, he is past that, and each time, it gets a little easier to hoist—or discard—baggage from his past and figure out a way to move forward.

It is a particularly long journey from one edge of America to the other these days, and a passage few can manage. For many of Cedric's peers at Ballou High School, there has been, sadly, little forward motion. Phillip Atkins still works in the mailroom of the newsletter company in Bethesda, Maryland, and doesn't think much about being a dancer or comic anymore. LaTisha Williams dropped out of UDC, bumped along through office support jobs, and joined a small, virulently fundamentalist church whose preacher sometimes screams on street corners. Recently, she said she discovered that "who I was before no longer exists," and quit her job to sell M&Ms on the sidewalk—50 cents a bag—to support her church. James Davis dropped out of Florida A&M at the end of his freshman year and was already on the streets of Southeast, dealing drugs, the following summer when another dealer robbed him and shot him in the leg. Despite police pressure, he refused to press charges against the shooter and, three months later, his brother, Jack, was arrested for murdering the rival in a hail of gunfire. In October 1997, Jack was found not guilty of the murder, a verdict that, among other things, rested on the confusion by various prosecution witnesses about which of the identical twins may have fired the shots. Cedric hears about such matters in passing, third hand. He rarely speaks to kids from Ballou.

Cedric Gilliam, in accordance with his parole, entered an intensive drug treatment program the day after he and his son met in prison. He stayed there for a year, living at a halfway house near the Capitol, getting therapy, and eventually working as a counselor to other drug addicts. It seems to have worked. By New Year's of 1998 he is still drug free, living with his mother, Maggie, in her house or with Sherene, who has stuck by him. He talks to his son from time to time, mostly over the phone, and both are attentive to avoid tearing a veneer of respectfulness that is allowing their relationship to evolve slowly. Not that it has been easy. As Cedric Sr. watches his son meet successive challenges, he plods along—unhirable after two decades of incarceration—cutting a head or two a day and rooting around for something to do.

Barbara Jennings, meanwhile, has managed to keep herself busy. Standing in the ruins of her near eviction, she said it was time to take care of herself, to do something other than martyr her life to Cedric's escape and success. It just took a while for her to back up those words. Ten months later, facing yawning debts that included Neddy's loan for the back rent, she was evicted. This time no one came. She quietly moved back to 15th Street, to an upstairs room in the old clapboard house, completing an odd life cycle that seemed to produce a fresh start. Living there almost free, she has since paid off nearly two-thirds of $11,000 in debts, including some old medical bills that have trailed her for years. Last summer, she began taking classes at Scripture Cathedral and attending meetings for single adults organized by Bishop Long. For her refuge and sustenance, Barbara still relies on the church, which continues to grow. (Bishop Long, meanwhile, continues to save souls and he recently upgraded to a Rolls Royce.) Even though they've walked several steps down diverging paths, Barbara and Cedric talk regularly. They often spend holidays and vacations together, and they have enjoyed each others' company by ignoring long-standing issues of obligation and sacrifice.

As for the students in Unit 15 at Brown University, the last year and a half has flowed downstream along the predictable, lazy current of college life. Rob Burton became a peer counselor, joined a fraternity, and is majoring in marine biology and English. Cedric and Rob did in fact become friends early in their sophomore year. They met and chatted and eventually were able to laugh about the Jackson Pollock sink and much of what was roiling them in room 216. Zayd Dohrn continued to thrive at Brown and went abroad to Oxford for his junior year, e-mailing his friend, Cedric, many times to fill him in on the latest chapter in his unfolding adventures.

Though he has white friends, Cedric has spent the past year and a half mostly socializing with black students at Brown. He regularly visits Harambee House, where Chiniqua lives, and sometimes hangs out with a few middle-class black guys he sees around the campus. In the spring of his sophomore year, he began dating Nicole Brown, a tall, lithe girl from northern Virginia, who is a forward on Brown's basketball team. They've continued to see each other since then.

The more things Cedric tries, the more things he is able to try. Certainly, he sometimes has to outwork the competition in his classes—play a little catch-up—but he's used to that. A building of skills in writing and clear thinking has allowed him to better handle work in education, history, philosophy, and African American studies classes. His major, meanwhile, is in applied math, a concentration that deals with the tangible applications of theorems, the type of high-utility area with which he has always been most comfortable.

Subtly, almost without notice, the passing days bring him self-knowledge, which is what all the lecturing, note-taking, testing, and endless intervening hours are really about anyway. He still hears the echo from rutted Southeast Washington and presses through gusts of thankfulness and survivor's guilt to figure out why he escaped when so many—who are so much like him—did not. As he searches and learns more in classes and discussions about the country's immigrant past, the phrase "a hope in the unseen" continues to resonate. That's the thing, he figures, that built the country, that drew often luckless people across oceans to a place they could barely imagine. He knows it is what propelled him from one country to another—even though he is anything but an immigrant, and even though these are anything but hopeful days for most African Americans. Nonetheless, the fact remains; he had hope in a better world he could not yet see that overwhelmed the cries of "you can't" or "you won't" or "why bother." More than anything else, mustering that faith, on cue, is what separated him from his peers, and distinguishes him from so many people in these literal, sophisticated times. It has made all the difference.

But such contemplations are, increasingly, just that: things he can mull over on rainy afternoons and then step away from to consider. Recently, on one such rainy afternoon, Cedric sat killing time at his clerical job in the Brown admissions office—one of several part-time jobs he's taken at Brown to supplement Donald Korb's $200 a month. Drumming the desktop with a pencil, he thought about his classes, girls, CDs he'd like to buy, and some modest plans for next semester. Things are so easy up here, he mused, looking out at the tended lawns and ancient trees on College Hill, so many avenues to choose from, every path cushioned. And that notion about ease swiftly drew its opposite, a passing recollection of his days worrying about gangs and guns, walking through garbage, keeping his head low. He snorted out a laugh. It's weird, he decided, but there is something about those days— the intensity of them, eyes watching him pass, always being alert or, to unearth an old phrase, having "something to push against"—that he misses. He nodded once and casually gathered up his things to go. An absence for sure, Cedric Jennings concluded, but one he can easily live with.

AUTHOR'S NOTE

While working as a *Wall Street Journal* reporter in 1994, I met a top student at a blighted Washington, D.C., high school who was "too proud" for his own good. That's what the school's principal told me. I decided to figure out precisely what he meant.

That was nearly four years ago. The student was a gangly sixteen-year-old named Cedric Jennings, and within a few months the *Journal* featured Cedric in a pair of long stories. During the last two and a half years, while reporting and writing this book, my aim has been to see America through Cedric's eyes.

At the outset, the project presented serious challenges. The notion of a white person trying to understand what a black person might see is increasingly considered a fool's errand. In the current parlance of racial coding and group identity, it's assumed there's simply no way a white guy can "get it."

I hope this book will go some distance toward refuting that. After years of effort, I know there are volumes of insight I will never approach about being black in America. Yet I have been fortunate. Because Cedric and his mother, Barbara, graciously opened their lives to my prodding and nagging questions—allowing me to witness their days unfolding, for better or for worse—they've allowed me to gain a genuine, heartfelt understanding of their lives. They are my friends, partners, and confidants in this project. Barbara says it was a "blessed day" that Cedric and I met at Ballou. I agree and tell her the Hebrew word is *mitzvah*. I will be forever grateful for their trust in me and in

the ideal that racial distinctions can be bridged by shared understanding.

I hope readers of this book will adopt that ideal as well. After the
stories about Cedric appeared in the *Journal* in 1994, I received calls
from several black newspaper reporters who, eventually, got around to
asking me their real question . . . "Are you black?" I considered the
query a sign that I had briefly crossed a divide. It is my hope that this
book will similarly confuse dug-in racial expectations and, in some
small way, help weave the black experience and white experience—so
commonly seen as parallel threads—into a shared national narrative.

It is an aim in which I've received immeasurable assistance and
support. This project was based on receiving the kind of access
reporters rarely receive. At the onset, the cooperation of administrators
and teachers at Frank W. Ballou Senior High School was invaluable—
especially that of Clarence Taylor, Cedric's Scripture-quoting mentor. I
strolled Ballou's halls, took notes in classrooms, and enjoyed free access
to the school for several years. Special thanks also goes to Ballou's
students, most notably Phillip Atkins and James Davis, who possess
potential that I hope they will one day realize. They, and many others,
eventually decided to teach me a few things about their lives. For such
acts of cultural outreach, I will be forever grateful.

Another realm into which I was welcomed was Scripture Cathedral
church, where Cedric and Barbara have spent so many years. Bishop
C. L. Long was gracious with his time and in allowing me access
to parishioners, even though the church is normally—and understandably—wary of outsiders. He offered guidance, tapes of sermons,
and insights into the peculiar dilemmas of being "one with God" while
doing what is necessary to build a congregation.

A special note of thanks is due to Donald Korb, Cedric's benefactor
and guide, who I've been in regular contact with for more than three
years. Though Donald was busy *doing* what many people say they'd like
to do (but never get around to), he still allowed himself and his family
to illustrate how fragile a dialogue of best intentions can be. That was
daring. Ultimately, I think, he shows how such acts of outreach,
though never simple, are cause for hope. Someone else crossing a

divide was Bill Ramsey, the black administrative director of the MIT MITES, who spent many hours educating me with his insights about race and achievement—only a few of which were included in the second of my 1994 *Journal* stories. Shortly after it's publication, Bill died. More of what he felt has been included in this book—though not my feelings that he was a wise, gentle man, who will long be missed.

The crucial moment in this project, however, was when Cedric's path curved into the freshman class at Brown University. A student like Cedric carries a heightened likelihood of failure at a place like Brown, and it would have been natural for Brown to have barred my access. It is a credit to a great and secure institution—to President Vartan Gregorian, to then-external affairs chief Robert Reichley, and to media spokesman Mark Nickel—that Brown, instead, provided me generous freedom. They also issued a limited description of my intentions—a judicious act that allowed Cedric to proceed unfettered, to succeed or fail, as would any other freshman. Professors Tom James and Larry Wakeford talked freely about their personal and professional lives, even though they, like other professors at Brown, didn't know which student, or students, I was following. It could have been a top student or one they were failing. Because so many people at Brown felt passionately about education and the search for truth, they took a risk that made this book possible.

Then there are the members of the freshman class's Unit 15, thirty-three students on two floors of a dorm. Early on, they understood that Cedric was a main character of the book, but they also knew that many of them might be portrayed in a narrative that would unfold—for better or worse—across the unknown arc of their first year of college. A freshman dorm is an emotional terrain, a place of search and stumble and fierce intimacies, but they allowed a thirtysomething to watch and listen. It was an act of trust that I will long appreciate. They were, however, just kids, and I was in their home—the dorm—so I agreed that they could assume aliases if they were significantly mentioned in the book in ways that made them uncomfortable. I am grateful that only a handful of students took aliases and most of those students were only mentioned briefly. The only significant student in this group is Rob Burton, Cedric's roommate, who requested that I give him a pseudonym. Like all the students who were granted aliases, Rob Burton's words, emotions, and details of his Brown experience have not in any way been altered.

Similarly, I felt it was proper to offer one alias in the book's first half. I invented the name LaTisha Williams to disguise a young lady who was going through a difficult period in her life and expressed confused feelings about having her name mentioned at the time of publication. But, again, only her name was changed. Everything else about her is an accurate rendition of this complex young woman.

The dozens of other characters in the book are represented accurately and, of course, by name. I am a newspaper reporter and used basic, block-and-tackle standards of fact gathering in this project. All the quotes in this book were either heard by me or recalled by various subjects and then checked with speaker or listener, and generally both. Most recollections were provided to me shortly after an event in question, a necessity since the book's narrative stretches across nearly three years and memories tend to bend over time.

In the book's portraits, there is a significant amount of what is sometimes called "internal voice," elucidating the thoughts and feelings of a character as he or she moves through visible actions or encounters in a day. Those "thoughts" are based—in almost every case—on a subject's immediate disclosure or fresh recollection of what he or she thought or felt at a particular moment. In a few cases, a subject described to me his or her thoughts or feelings about a situation or individual, and I've connected those thoughts to what I have witnessed—and then checked them with him or her later. In either case, all the internal voice passages, crucial to understanding various points of view, are drawn from literally dozens of interviews with each of a dozen main characters stretching over several years.

The combination of the quoted word, visible action, and interior thoughts creates the "points of view" of thirteen characters that comprise this book, edge to edge. In many cases, what subjects like Barbara Jennings, Cedric Gilliam, Bill Ramsey, Clarence Taylor, Phillip Atkins, Zayd Dohrn, Chiniqua Milligan, Bernadine Dohrn, Rob Burton, LaTisha Williams, Larry Wakeford, and Tom James are looking at is Cedric Jennings himself. Many of them have had sections from their points of view read back to them to test for accuracy. In sum, the views of all twelve of the supporting characters make up just over a third of the book.

I've told the rest of the tale, of course, from the point of view of Cedric Jennings. He and I have spent more hours together—on the phone and in person—than I could possibly count. I have interviewed him hundreds of times in the nearly four years we've known each other. We've talked through every issue, every emotion. As the book took shape, many scenes and quotes were read to him several times. Still, prior to publication, he was given the entire manuscript, along with a red pen, a three-pack of Post-its, and instructions to mark anything attributed to him that wasn't absolutely accurate. He read rigorously for several days, caught a few small errors, and penciled in supporting facts, especially about his evolved musical tastes. Although reading about oneself can be wrenching, Cedric told me he encountered nothing unexpected and, ultimately, confirmed that representations of his thinking, feelings, and actions are accurate.

But then again, he and I have spent a lot of life together. I've seen him grow from an uncertain sixteen-year-old ducking through a war zone to a young man of gravity and grace, now twenty and on his way to an Ivy League degree. Over those years, he has trusted me as a repository of his memories, fears, hopes, and most intimate feelings. It is that privilege—to be the trustee of someone's very self—that I've sought to measure up to with each page of this book.

While the author gets the credit—or, at least, his name on a book cover—the debt is more widely distributed. To start with, many people at the *Wall Street Journal,* my home for the past seven and a half years, are deserving of credit and thanks in this effort. The original stories in the *Journal,* which launched this book project, were made possible by the inspiration and guidance of John Brecher, the *Journal*'s singular page one editor and my longtime co-conspirator; the support and counsel of Alan Murray, the paper's Washington Bureau chief; and the artful editing of Joanne Lipman.

The *Journal*'s managing editor, Paul Steiger, whose integrity and wisdom have long guided me, offered rock-solid support through the two-plus years this book took to report and write. And John Brecher, always showing his creative constancy, assigned me an array of challenging tasks to keep me busy behind the scenes. To the both of them, especially, I am eternally grateful.

During twists and turns in this project, friends arrived with acts of generosity. The bulk of the reporting entailed spending much of the '95-'96 academic year in Providence, Rhode Island, a time when a new friend—the full-living Dr. Cornelius "Skip" Granai—came forward with an ideal pied-à-terre near the Brown campus. Months later, as I waded through writer's hell, close friends from D.C. arrived on cue. Robert Butler and Marcelle Dominguez provided their West Virginia cabin and, a bit later, Tom and Melissa Dann offered their splendid house on Maryland's eastern shore. Tony Horwitz, in frequent calls between our writers' garrets, provided his always adept commiseration, as did the always level-headed Joe White, regularly checking in from Detroit. Jill Abramson's wickedly wise counsel was, from the project's start, a godsend. Russ Allen, a lifelong buddy and accomplice, offered the sound advice of a born writer in numerous late-night calls. So many other friends have been gracious with their insights and confidences over the years—Larry Ingrassia, Ronde Baquíe, Nancy McMillian, Jack Hitt, Paul Hemp, Joe Rosenbloom, and the amazing Jorge Plutzky—that I regret there is only enough space to mention a few of them.

Not that I arrived at Broadway Books with much more than a muddled notion about how to write a book. Awaiting me, thankfully, was the skilled hand of John Sterling, Broadway's editor-in-chief. From the opening concept of looking for a shared American narrative in the biography of a young black male, to fits and starts in the writing, to a breakthrough moment in narrative style that he midwifed a year ago, to helping guide home the finished manuscript, John was my partner, always at my side, a dream editor. Others at Broadway rallied 'round with heartening enthusiasm and skill, especially Victoria Andros and Luke Dempsey. Eventually, Jenny Minton line edited the manuscript with astonishing artfulness and passion. To all of them, I am grateful and indebted.

I am, as well, eternally fortunate to have an agent and friend, Kris Dahl, whose flawless guidance was crucial to the launch and trajectory of this project.

In this exercise, I learned plenty, including much I will never be able to adequately express, about the constancy, faith, and support of my family. Beyond my brother, Len, the finest guy I know, and my mother, Shirley, a special mention is due to someone who is not here. Walter Suskind, a man of great wit and grace, who died when I was a boy, didn't get to try much in his life, and left me with the message to try some things in mine. He is a presence in this book, in everything I do. In some ways, looking back, he taught me to have a hope in the unseen.

A book like this is not a simple journey or one without costs in long absences and late nights that fall upon a family. Mine has made great sacrifices and still managed to buoy me. For that, and much more, I am inexpressibly thankful to my world-beating nine-year-old son, Walter, who, among his many contributions, did an artful job copy-editing chapter 7; and my six-year-old son, Owen, who joyfully works harder and accomplishes more on any given day than I have in this rigorous past year. And, finally, to my wife, Cornelia, who suggested some years back that I try writing and then proceeded—with her faith, wisdom, and unwavering support—to light my path.